NO MORE
BULLIES

NO MORE BULLIES

Frank Peretti

THOMAS NELSON
Since 1798

NASHVILLE   DALLAS   MEXICO CITY   RIO DE JANEIRO   BEIJING

Published in Nashville, Tennessee, by Thomas Nelson. Thomas Nelson is a registered
trademark of Thomas Nelson, Inc.

Thomas Nelson, Inc. titles may be purchased in bulk for educational, business, fund-raising, or
sales promotional use. For information, please e-mail SpecialMarkets@ThomasNelson.com.

The names of some individuals have been changed to protect their privacy. Some stories
represent composites.

Unless otherwise noted, Scripture quotations used in this book are from the New King
James Version, © 1979, 1980, 1982, Thomas Nelson, Inc., Publishers.

Scriptures marked NASB are from the New American Standard Bible, © 1960, 1977 by
the Lockman Foundation.

Library of Congress Cataloging-in-Publication Data

Peretti, Frank E.
    No more bullies / by Frank Peretti.
      p. cm.

    ISBN-13: 978-0-8499-4336-2
    1. Bullying. 2. Conduct of life. I. Title.
BF637.B85 P47 2000
302.3'4—dc21
                                             00-049975
                                              CIP

Printed in the United States of America

09 10 11 12 QW 12

To Mom and Dad, whose love and encouragement never wavered, and to John, who stood on the wall.

Contents

BOY'S
HELL

Chapter One

A separate room had been prepared for the boys. It was cold and impersonal, like a prison; the echoing, concrete walls had been painted dirty beige, then marred and chipped over the years, then painted again. The walls were bare except for posted rules, warnings, and advisories, and the only windows were high against the ceiling, caged behind iron grillwork thickly wrapped in paint, rust, and more paint. The air was dank, tainted with the odors of steam, sweat, and skin. Years of rust and sediment from the dripping showerheads and armies of bare, wet feet had marbled the floor with streaks and patches of reddish brown.

The authorities, clad in uniforms and carrying clipboards and whistles, marched the boys in, at least forty of them, all roughly the same age but many different sizes, strengths, and physical maturities. The dates of their births, the locations of their homes, and the simple luck of the draw had brought them here, and much like cattle earmarked for shipment, they had no voice in the matter. The paperwork was in. This room would be a part of their lives for the next four years.

He had never been in this place, or anywhere like this place, before. He had never imagined such a place could even exist. In here, kindness meant weakness, human warmth was a complication, and encouragement was unmanly. In here, harshness was the guiding virtue — harshness, cruelty, and the blunt, relentless confirmation of every doubt he'd ever carried about himself.

Mr. M, a fearsome authority figure with a permanent scowl and a voice that yelled — only yelled — ordered them to strip down. His assistants, clones of his cruelty, repeated the order, striding up and down the narrow aisles between the lockers.

The boy hesitated, looking furtively about. He'd never been naked in front of strangers before, but even worse, he'd never been naked in front of enemies. It took only one class hour for the others to select him, to label him, and to put him in his place. He was now officially the smallest one, the scared one, the weakling, the one with-out friends. That made him fair game.

And now he would be naked in front of them. Naked. His stomach wrung; his hands trembled. *Dear God, please get me out of here. Please don't let them do this to me.*

But every authority figure in his life said he had to be here. He had to go to school, do his chores, finish his home-work, keep his shoes tied, go to bed and get up at certain hours, eat his vegetables, and be here. End of discussion.

He removed his clothes.

Mr. M continued his yelling. "Come on, move it, move it, move it!"

The herd—pink, black, brown, and bronze—moved one direction, and all he could do was move with it, a frail, naked body among the forty, longing for a towel, any-thing to cover himself. Instinctively, he placed his hand over his private parts. Every other body was bigger and much stronger, and every other body had hair where the boy had none. He knew they would notice.

The showers were a long, high-ceilinged echo cham-ber, murky with steam, rattling with lewd, raucous joking and laughter. He didn't want to hear it.

After a big Hispanic kid finished his shower, the boy carefully took his place under the showerhead, afraid of slipping and even more afraid of grazing against anyone. Touching was dangerous; it could easily become a prelude to being hurt.

He let the water spray over him. He hurriedly lathered his body with some soap.

To his left, the talk started—about him. Then some laughing. The talk spread, the call went out—"Hey, get a load of this!"—and an audience gathered, a semicircle of naked, dripping bodies. The talk *about* him shifted to jeering *at* him. He tried to act as if he didn't hear them, but he could feel his face flushing. *Get through, get through, get out of here!*

He rinsed as well as he could, never turning away from the wall, then headed for the towel-off area, not meeting their eyes, trying to ignore their comments about his face, his body, his groin. But the arrows were landing with painful accuracy: *Ugly. Wimp. Gross. Little girl.*

He grabbed a towel off the cart and draped it around himself before he even started drying with it. Even that action brought lewd comments and another lesson: Once it begins, no action, no words, no change in behavior will turn it back. Once you're the target, *anything* you do will bring another arrow.

And so the arrows flew: two, then three, then more. Obscenities, insults, put-downs.

Along with his hurt, he felt a pitiful, helpless anger. He wanted to lash out, to tell them to stop, to defend himself, but he was all too aware of his body, just as they were. He could never match the strength of any one of them, much less the whole gang, and they were waiting, even wanting him to try.

Snap! Stinging, searing pain shot up from his groin like a jolt from an electric cattle prod.

"Oh," hollered a jock, "*good* one!"

Snap! He heard the sound again as a towel whipped past his backside, missing by a millimeter. A big lug with a hideous grin pulled his towel back for another try, then he jerked it toward the boy's body again, snapping it back hard, turning the moist end of the towel into a virtual whip. The edge of the towel struck between the boy's legs, stinging like a cat-o'-nine-tails.

He cried out in pain while they laughed. He raised a knee to protect his groin but lost his footing on the wet tile and tumbled to the floor, his hands skidding on the slimy, soapy residue. He struggled to his feet. A wet foot thumped into his back, and he careened toward a locker-room bench loaded with laughing naked bodies.

"Get off me, you fag!" Rough hands pushed him and he crunched into another body. "Get away, twerp!" They were angry with *him*. He was the Ping-Pong ball being batted about, and they were angry with *him!*

"Hey, squirt, you lookin' for trouble?"

"I think this kid wants a fight!"

He fled to the only square foot of floor that might be his own, the space in front of his locker. His body was throbbing, his bruises a combined chorus of pain.

And his soul . . . oh, his soul. He was choking back his tears, hurrying, fumbling to get his clothes from his locker, resolving to remain silent, desperately hoping no one would see him crying—but deep inside, his soul wailed in anguish, and there were no words or thoughts to heal it. Parental advice came to his mind, but it carried as much weight as a cookie fortune: "Just ignore them." Ignoring was only acting. It didn't stop the arrows from cutting through his heart. He even believed the taunts and stinging words. *Dear God, am I that ugly? Am I that weak and worthless?*

"Hey, nude boy! Hey, nature boy!" Now the teacher's assistant, just a few grades ahead of him, was getting in a few jabs. "Get the lead out. The bell's gonna ring in five minutes."

He got the lead out. Still wet, he threw on his clothes, missing one buttonhole in his shirt so that the shirt hung cockeyed on his back, but he didn't care. He grabbed his books out of the locker—

A hand slammed him against the locker, and his head bounced off the steel door. His books fell to the floor, the pages crinkling, his assignments spilling everywhere. He'd only begun the thought of picking them up when one of the jocks grabbed him around the neck, lifted him off the floor so his feet dangled, then dropped him on his books. He crumpled to the floor, gasping.

A whistle shrieked. It was Mr. M, angry as always. "Line up, line up!"

The T.A. yanked the boy to his feet. "C'mon, get in line!"

He gathered up his books, some of the pages wet, wrinkled, and grimy, and plugged an empty spot in the line.

One minute to go. He'd never felt such longing to be somewhere else. Somewhere in his memory—right now, a *dim* memory—was a kinder world than this, a place where he could find some measure of his lost dignity, the last broken tatters of his self-respect.

The bell rang. Could it be over? Could it finally be over?

Mr. M swung the door open. The lines started moving, a few boys at the front of the line darting off as though they were in a race for their lives.

"No running. WALK!" Mr. M growled.

The stream of bodies poured into the narrow hall, and

in a moment he was hurrying away from that place, taking several last looks over his shoulder, checking for danger, thankful he could still turn his neck.

In the main hall, he passed the trophy case, where the glories of his high school were on display. Here were the school colors, pictures of the school mascot, the trophies, the ribbons, the news clippings, the victories—everything a kid should be proud of. His eyes flooded with tears. When he first came to this school, he looked in that trophy case, and, yes, he was proud. He was filled with an exhilarating joy and a sense of belonging. School spirit, that's what it was. He couldn't wait to buy a pennant to hang on the wall of his room.

But now, all he could do was shed tears and wonder, *How could a school like this, my school, have a place like* that? *Does anyone care? Does anyone even know?*

In his next class, he sat at his desk, his clothes still damp, his body still aching, unable to keep his mind on the teacher's lecture or his eyes on the text. The mocking faces and the derisive, searing comments kept playing and replaying in his mind, overpowering anything and everything else.

And from the blood pooling on the floor of his soul, in the loneliness of his hurt and anger, in the escape of a neutral location, little thoughts were firing off in his mind like forbidden firecrackers: *Oh, right, Mr. T.A., sir, Mr. Big Tough Guy, Mr. M in miniature. You wouldn't be so tough if Mr. M weren't around. And as for you, Superjock and Dumb Thug and Towel Turkey, if I were bigger, if I were stronger, if I could . . . if I could . . . oh,* man, *if only I could . . .*

But he was a Christian. He wasn't supposed to think such things, so he tried not to.

And he said nothing, and he did nothing, and when the day for gym class came around again . . . he went back. After all, the authorities in his life had made clear certain axioms: He had to be there. There was no choice.

JANUARY
12-13, 1951

Chapter Two

Snow, and more snow. Howling wind that shrieked through the cracks. Darkness beyond the headlights of the old car, and in the headlights, white on white on white: frost and ice on the windshield, the snowstorm swirling in the lights like a universe of frantic white flies; and somewhere out there, only sometimes visible, the road, hidden under packed snow, fallen snow, blowing snow.

The windshield wipers were pushing aside ragged arcs of visibility, gathering and stacking the loose flakes but chattering ineffectively over the ice droplets encrusted on the glass. The windshield had the clarity of a shower door.

"Gene, we have to hurry," his pregnant wife urged, grasping her rotund belly as if holding it would lessen the pain. "They're getting close together." She stifled a whimper as another labor pain flashed through her body then said just audibly, "We're not going to make it."

"We're gonna make it, Joyce. We're gonna make it. Just hold on." With his sleeve he rubbed the condensation from the windshield of their eleven-year-old 1940 Ford. What was water came off. What was ice remained. What was breath became water that became ice just behind each sweep of his arm. *Grreshshunk. Grreshshunk. Grreshshunk*—the wipers kept working, but the blades were beating themselves to death on the ice. They wouldn't last the night. Gene's eyes on the road formed a direct link with his right foot on the accelerator, nursing as many miles per hour as the darkness, the snow, and the road would allow.

Gene was thankful they'd rehearsed this trip, due to a false alarm earlier in the week. Joyce had been sure she was going into labor, and they'd raced the thirty-five miles to Galt Hospital, in the town of Lethbridge, in Alberta, Canada. The contractions eased by the time they got there, and the doctor sent them home again. "It's not time yet," he'd said. "Soon, but not yet. We'll be waiting for you when the time comes."

The time came less than an hour ago. They'd gone to bed early, partially to get warm under the blankets since the outside temperature had plummeted to minus thirty degrees. Gene fell right to sleep, but Joyce could only fidget in the dark until, right around 11:00 P.M., familiar pains wrung her body, then subsided, then seized her again within the next ten minutes. She lay flat on her back on the bed, trying to relax, breathing deeply. Was it time? Should she wait to be sure?

She waited, wide awake, listening to Gene snore as the winter wind rattled the windows. The contractions didn't subside as an hour passed. Over the next hour they became more regular, the pain more pronounced. By 1:00 A.M., Joyce was sure. She reached over in the darkness and nudged Gene awake.

"Gene, it's time."

"Huh, wha . . . time for what? Time! You mean it's *that* time?"

"Yes, I think it is."

They didn't have a telephone, so they couldn't call ahead to let the doctor know they were coming. All they could do was go and hope someone at the hospital could contact the doctor once they arrived. Huddling together, they made a dash for the car, the vicious north winds pelting their faces with snow until they could climb in and slam the doors shut.

"Brrrr, turn the heater up high," Joyce begged as Gene turned the key, hoping the freezing winds hadn't caused the car's battery to go dead.

The engine groaned reluctantly. Gene turned the key again. *Errrrhhhrrrrr. Errr . . . Ummunnnhhh!* The car's engine roared to life.

He eased the car away from the parsonage of the quaint country church he pastored and headed across the rugged Canadian prairie, the snow-packed gravel roads vibrating Joyce's stomach as they traveled.

"Gene," she cried, "slow down or I'm going to have this baby right here in the car!"

"I thought you wanted to get there in a hurry."

"I do, but the pain is—OH! Hurry, hurry!"

Gene shook his head. Slow down, hurry up—what was he to do? He laid a hand on Joyce's stomach as he pressed the accelerator. "Lord, help us, please," he prayed quietly. Time was so precious, and there was so far to go. So far.

Their first stop was to drop off their little boy, a toddler, at the home of a minister friend. Then it was back into the car and back into the blizzard. Now the minutes seemed like hours, the arduous cadence of the windshield wipers incessantly reminding them of the ticking away of precious seconds, precious seconds, precious seconds. No other vehicles approached or followed them. They saw no lights from houses, stores, grain elevators, anything. A black, roiling nether world lay just beyond the window glass, and they dared not think about it. They dared not imagine how truly lonely, vast, and vicious the Canadian winter could be.

The road was full of potholes, and the car kept finding them, bouncing and bumping. Then came a jolt downward—Gene thought it was another pothole—but the front end of the car didn't bounce back up. Instead, the car lurched sideways and skidded. They could hear the shriek of metal grating against metal. Joyce screamed, bracing herself against the dashboard. Their bodies heaved forward and then violently backward as the Ford ground to a halt, the front end drooping.

"Are you okay?" Gene yelled loudly.

Joyce pushed herself back up in the seat. She put her hands under her bulging abdomen and pulled gently. "Yes, I think so." She straightened her rumpled, heavy coat covering the baby. "I don't think we hit the dashboard."

Gene let his head drop backward on the top of the seat as he exhaled a sigh of relief. "Thank You, Lord."

"What happened?"

Nothing came to mind. "I don't know, but I better find out."

"Yes, *please*." Joyce winced as she felt another contraction grip her body.

Gene reached for his wool cap. "Stay right here. I'll see what we're looking at." He put on the cap and grabbed his wool scarf. "Make sure the car keeps running so the heater will work; give it some gas once in a while so it doesn't stall."

"You be careful."

"I will. Don't worry." He wrapped his scarf tightly around his neck, put on his gloves, and opened the car door. The bitter cold air, filled with icy flakes, poured into the car as if into a vacuum. He quickly stepped out into the snow, slamming the door behind him.

The Ford's headlights lit the area in front of the car, but it was difficult to see into the front wheel well. As Gene's eyes adjusted to the dimness, he stooped down, felt for the tire—and felt nothing. No tire, no wheel. Only the lug nuts remained, still fastened to the brake drum. He squinted in the darkness, peering through the blowing snow, trying to trace any track the departing wheel might have left. It could have landed in a nearby ditch, but searching for it would be next to impossible.

The car had a spare, mounted on a wheel, of course, so that option made perfect sense. He could replace the lost wheel with the spare, just as if he were changing a flat tire.

Tomorrow in the daylight, after Joyce and their new baby were comfortable in the hospital, he could return and maybe find his other tire.

The trunk lid groaned and snapped away the ice in its seams as Gene opened it. He groped, found the spare, then loosened the clamp and pulled it out. He let it bounce on the ice—Good! It still has air in it!—then rolled it to the front of the car where he leaned it against the fender to keep it out of the snow. Now for the tire jack. He shuffled back through the snow to the trunk.

He quickly found a tire iron, but his groping hand couldn't encounter a jack no matter where he searched.

Then it hit him, like a sledgehammer in the stomach: *I left the tire jack in the school bus!*

He'd been driving the school bus to make some extra income—pastors of small, rural churches often did that sort of thing—and he'd needed the jack aboard the bus last week. That's where it was, right where he'd left it. He sagged against the rear of the car, filled with frustration for such an oversight. His wife was in labor, their car was slouched forward on three wheels, it was thirty-two below, it was dark, and he had to replace a tire without a jack!

What to do, what to do? *Think!* He looked through the car window. Joyce had leaned back on the front seat, her eyes closed, no doubt confident that her loving husband could rectify whatever the trouble was and they'd soon be on their way to the hospital. No use in frightening her. Let her rest.

What to do? He prayed, "Oh, Lord, help us. There's nobody around for miles, and we're about to have a baby in the freezing cold. What can I do?"

Looking around for an answer, any answer, his eyes fell on a road sign just within the car's headlights, a yellow diamond with a bent black arrow advising of a left turn ahead. It was bolted to a four-inch-by-four-inch post. A long post. Eight feet of it was above the ground, and there had to be at least another two feet under the ground.

A lever.

He needed a fulcrum. He peered into the dark trunk and spied his old, metal toolbox. It was only about eighteen inches long, ten inches wide, and about twelve inches deep, but it was rugged and strong. He pulled the box from the trunk and set it next to the bumper of the car, his gloves sticking to the metal in the cold.

Now to get that post out of the ground. The storm and the snowplows had piled the snow waist-deep around it. Gene pushed his way through, and then he dropped to his knees and dug the snow away with his gloved hands. The ground beneath was hard and crystalline with ice. He attacked it with the tire iron, gouging and chipping, scooping up the loose chunks with his hands. He dug and dug, the knees of his pants soaking through, his eyes watering, his nose running, the frost forming on his eyebrows, sweat pouring down his face despite the bitter cold. *How deep does the highway department put these poles, anyhow?* He stood up and wrestled with the post. It wiggled!

Gene dropped to his knees again, digging faster, gouging harder, his breath turning to ice in the car's headlights. He stood and slammed into the post with his shoulder, so focused on the task and so cold, he barely noticed the resulting bruise. He went to the other side and rammed it the other way. He slammed into it a few more times, back and forth. More digging and gouging, then some shaking, pulling, heaving one direction then the other. It had to come out. It couldn't be much deeper. Got to keep—

The sign tipped over.

With a desperate heave, Gene pulled the signpost off the ground and dragged it over the snow to the front left side of the car. His toolbox, his fulcrum, was ready. He pushed the part of the post that had been in the ground under the car's bumper and positioned the center of the post on top of the metal toolbox. The road sign at the other end lay flat, about fifteen inches off the ground. With the lever and fulcrum in place, he shoved the spare tire up against the wheel well. If he could raise the car just enough, long enough . . . if he could get the wheel on the lugs quickly enough. *If.* He might only get one chance at this.

He tried the makeshift lever. He could make the car rock upward, lifting the axle and brake drum off the ground, but he couldn't lift it far enough to get the wheel on. He needed more weight on the road sign. Gene looked around in the darkness, hoping that he might find a few rocks that he could pile on the sign, or maybe a heavy log. No such luck.

There was only one thing to do. He looked through the window at his young wife. Ordinarily, she was a small, petite woman, but with the extra weight she had been carrying through the pregnancy, she could barely waddle from place to place. Gene breathed a silent prayer of thanks for Joyce's extra pounds. Her weight, combined with his effort, might be their only hope.

Gene opened the car door. "Joyce! I need your help!"

The cold air shocked her awake. "What do you want me to do?"

"I need you to get out of the car. Wrap up warm. And

please don't make any sudden moves. Just very carefully slide out of the car. Here, take my hand. I'll help you."

Joyce reluctantly tightened her scarf around her neck, buttoned her coat, and put on her gloves. She moved her right leg toward the door, while Gene held both of her hands. Slowly, carefully, she slid her leg out and placed her foot awkwardly in the snow.

"You're doin' fine, Joyce. Just go slow. Take it easy. I've got a good hold on you, so don't worry; you won't fall."

Joyce struggled to pull herself toward the doorway, getting colder with every moment. Finally, her left foot pushed down into the snow, and she eased upward, Gene's strong hands and arms there to steady her. The moment she was standing, another contraction wracked her body, and she nearly tumbled over in pain. "Oh! Oh, Gene!"

Gene held her tightly until the spasm passed, and then he slowly released his grip. "You okay?"

"I'm fine." Joyce straightened as best she could. "What do you want me to do?"

"I want you to come over here and sit on this sign," Gene said, leading his pregnant wife by the hand toward the driver's side of the car. "Watch your step."

"Sit where? What are you talking about? Gene!"

"Right over here." Gene pointed to the road sign as he

helped Joyce through the snow. "Careful now. All you have to do is sit on the sign and try to put as much weight on it as you can. We don't have a jack, but if you can bounce on the sign a bit, I think the car will come off the ground enough that I can get the spare tire on."

Joyce recognized her husband's incredible presence of mind and ingenuity in rigging the lever and fulcrum from the post and toolbox in the freezing cold. She didn't even bother to question whether it was dangerous for her or the baby to be bouncing on a road sign. She carefully stepped up to the sign, turned, and planted herself on it. Then, by pushing against the ground with her feet, she raised her end of the signpost for the first bounce. She relaxed her legs and let the sign sink beneath her.

"Don't bounce too hard!" Gene called, kneeling in the snow next to the wheel well, waiting for the precise moment when the car raised enough to slide the tire on. "I don't want the post to snap." With a grunt, he shoved the tire closer.

The Ford inched off the ground, slightly at first, as the post caved in the top of the toolbox with a crunch. Another bounce, and the Ford creaked upward six more inches. They needed two more, if the lever could just hold long enough!

Gene worked feverishly, shoving the tire into the wheel

well. "Keep going! Sit as close to the end as you dare!" He put his shoulder under the wheel well, ready to push up with the next bounce. "One more bounce!" The signpost was bowing on the ends. It wouldn't last much longer. "Once more, now! Bounce on it, *now!*"

As Joyce bounced on the edge of the sign, the car eased upward just far enough. Gene slammed the wheel onto the lugs and held it while the car came back down on the tire.

"Hallelujah!" he shouted, scrambling quickly to retrieve the lug nuts with his bare fingers. The cold bit into his skin, but he couldn't care less. He had to get that tire secure. He twirled on one lug nut, then another, then another. His fingers felt like tree trunks as he reached for the tire iron to cinch down the nuts. The cold iron stuck to his hands but he kept working until—

"Okay!" The tire was on, fit and snug.

Joyce was still sitting on the road sign like a child on the low end of a teetertotter. Gene bounded through the snow to help her off the sign before she slipped into the snow.

"We did it!" he cried as he wrapped his arms around her and helped her to her feet. "Are you all right?"

"I'm okay. Just freezing!"

He got her back in the car, closed her in against the cold, then he returned to that blessed, hardworking,

God-sent road sign. Exhausted and nearly frozen, he mustered his strength, picked up the post, and lugged it back to where he'd found it, dropping it back in the hole. It was tilting a bit, but it was back on the job—not that many travelers might be along to see it anytime soon.

Gene hurried to the car and jumped in behind the steering wheel. He tried to squeeze his fingers around the wheel, but it took several minutes before the feeling returned to his fingers enough for him to drive. "Thank You, Lord," he said.

"Yes, indeed. Thank You, sweet Jesus," Joyce echoed. "And now, please help us get to the hospital."

Gene revved the engine that had continued running through the entire ordeal, and they were off again, Joyce's contractions growing more frequent and more intense with each mile. When they finally arrived at the hospital, it was approaching 3:00 A.M. on Saturday morning. Gene left the car in front of the emergency entrance and ran in to find a doctor, a nurse, anyone who could help him get Joyce into the delivery room. At that hour there was no doctor, but he found a few orderlies.

"Let's just get her inside to a delivery room," said one, "and then we'll proceed from there!"

"Here—please call our doctor." Gene handed a piece

of paper with the doctor's name and phone number on it to one of the orderlies as a woman in a blue uniform whisked Joyce down the hall on a gurney. In those days, fathers were not permitted in the birthing room, so Gene was directed to a room where he was instructed to wait.

Meanwhile, the intern took Joyce to an empty delivery room and helped her get situated. A nurse came in and told her, "We haven't been able to reach your doctor by phone, but we'll keep trying. Just try to relax, and don't worry. We'll be right down the hall in the nursery. Ring this buzzer if you need anything."

"But I'm—"

"The important thing is that we don't want the baby to come too soon. Don't force anything. Give yourself time. That way when the doctor gets here, you'll be ready."

"I don't think it's going to be that long."

The nurse scowled. "Try to wait until the doctor gets here," she said curtly. Then she walked out of the room, closing the door behind her.

Joyce lay flat on the gurney for what seemed like hours, enduring the contractions, counting the minutes between them. The contractions were coming very quickly now, and they were much stronger. The baby would be born soon. She reached for the buzzer and pressed the button.

She waited, trying to relax, gathering her strength for the impending delivery.

No nurse. She waited. And waited. She pressed the buzzer again. Still no nurse came through the door. The door was closed, and Joyce didn't dare try to get off the gurney to call for help. She squeezed the buzzer again—harder, holding it there. *Where are they?* She could feel the baby pressing against her. "Help!" she called out. "Somebody, please! Help me! The baby's coming!"

Joyce squeezed the buzzer again, alternately pressing and releasing it, pressing and releasing. Wherever the buzzer was ringing—if it was ringing—somebody was bound to notice. Finally, a nurse she'd never seen before—she turned out to be the head nurse from the floor *below*—came running into her room, took one look at her, and slapped an ether mask over Joyce's face. That was the last thing Joyce recalled. She still had not seen a doctor. She'd hardly even seen a nurse.

Sometime later—how much later, no one knows—the doctor finally arrived from his amblings somewhere out in the cosmos and got involved with the birth of the child. Because of the forced delay in delivery, the baby had shifted around to a near breech position.

"Forceps!" he called to the nurse. She slapped them into his hand, and he managed to clamp them around the baby's head. They had to reposition the baby to be born naturally. There was no time for a Cesarean section at this point. The baby needed to be born now . . . or never. They worked feverishly, pressing on the mother's abdomen, pulling on the forceps, repositioning, pressing, pulling. Finally, with one last yank, the baby was born.

But not without injury. At some point the forceps had slipped off the head and traumatized the right side of the neck just under the jaw. No matter. The little boy was badly bruised, but he was breathing and very much alive!

A short while later, the doctor stepped into the waiting room where Gene was pacing anxiously. "Congratulations, Mr. Peretti. It's a boy."

Gene made it to the recovery room only moments after Joyce woke up. In her arms lay a baby boy, his eyes closed, his tiny body bundled in blankets. "Oh, Joyce!" Gene gushed through tears of joy. "Thank You, God! Thank You for this new life." He kissed Joyce lightly on the forehead and gazed lovingly at their child. "So, I guess we're naming him Frank Edward."

Joyce smiled. "Mm-hm." They'd already discussed what they would name the child once they knew its gender. They would name a boy after Joyce's brother Franklin and give him Gene's middle name. "Frank Edward."

"Hello, Frank! Nice to have you with us." Curiosity,

and then concern, quelled his smile. He fingered the blanket away from the baby's neck. "What's this?"

"The doctor said it was nothing to worry about," Joyce replied, but her voice was troubled, unbelieving. She lifted the child and turned him gently. The baby's head just wouldn't lie naturally. The neck seemed strangely crooked. "Do you think something's wrong?"

Gene stroked the tiny head and said nothing.

"Gene?"

Their eyes met, and neither could hide what each was sure of.

Something was wrong with their child.

COMPLICATIONS

Chapter Three

t's called *cystic hygroma*, defined by the medical dictionary as "a lesion caused by a mass of dilated lymphatics, due to the failure of the embryonic lymphatics to connect with the venous system." It's a birth defect that usually develops on the side of the neck, so I suppose the role of the doctor's forceps in delivering me is debatable. Whatever the case, the folks at the hospital never got a clue—or never wanted one.

As was customary in 1951, Mom's doctor insisted that she stay in the hospital for several days before he would discharge her, and those days became a disconcerting la-la land of denial on the part of the medical staff. My head still rested awkwardly, I wasn't eating much, and what little nourishment I could handle didn't stay with me long. Whenever Mom expressed her concerns to the doctor and nurses, they all pooh-poohed the problem. "Don't you worry, Mrs. Peretti. You're gonna have a big, strong boy there. Just like his dad."

Mom also asked about the small lump on the side of my neck.

"Oh, it's nothing," Mom's nurse assured her. "The doctor used forceps to help draw the baby out during birth, so it's probably just a little bruise. It will clear up in a matter of days, and your baby will be fine."

Well, they *were* the medical experts, weren't they? Mom and Dad accepted the assessment and took me home, fully expecting the lump to dissolve within a few days.

It didn't.

Instead, it grew larger . . . and larger. Within a month, the lump on my neck had swollen to the size of a baseball. I could barely swallow.

As God's providence—oh, so mysterious and so painful at the time—would have it, Dad's ministry at the little church came to an end, and it was time to move on. Dad's folks, my grandparents, lived in Seattle, so we traveled there to live with them while Mom and Dad figured out the next direction for their life and family. Concerned that the lump on my throat was expanding, Mom took me to another doctor, to get a second opinion. This physician took one look at my neck and declared emphatically, "We need to get him to the hospital right away!"

My parents took me to Children's Orthopedic Hospital in Seattle, where the doctors quickly diagnosed my condition—and none too soon. Cystic hygroma can lead to obstruction of a person's breathing; it can cause nervous palsies, possible hemorrhaging, and infection, and I was showing signs of developing everything on the list. It was time to operate.

I was barely two months old when the doctors cut my neck open, trying to clean out a swollen mass that threatened to kill me!

They succeeded—mostly—and then kept me in the hospital for ten days to watch for possible complications. It must have been a long haul for a newborn. Mom recalls that when they finally placed me back in her arms to go home, I was a tiny "bag of bones," with a long scar and black sutures that made it appear as if my head had been nearly severed and then sewn back on.

"We've done all that we can," the doctors told my parents. "Just take him home and love him, and that will be the best medicine for him." Although the doctors informed Mom and Dad that a recurrence was possible and that cystic growth into surrounding tissues was unpredictable, they didn't expect any complications.

Mom and Dad got back to building their life. Dad went back to working at the luggage factory where he'd worked while attending Bible college, and we did all right. Thanks to the love of my folks and my older brother, Terry, I fattened up again just fine.

But then came complications the doctors didn't expect. As they'd said, cystic growth can be unpredictable, and the unpredictable happened. My tongue began to swell, and before long, it was hanging out of my mouth, oozing a fluid that turned to black scab when it contacted the air. I drooled constantly, leaving bloody, blackish residue around my mouth and chin, down the front of my clothes, and on my pillow. I was having trouble eating—imagine trying to swallow, even chew, without the help of your tongue!

I became a frequent and familiar patient at Children's Orthopedic Hospital. The doctors feared cancer, but one elderly surgeon had seen my symptoms previously in another patient, a little girl, whose precious face had been hideously distorted due to her condition. The doctor guessed that the swelling in my tongue was the result of my earlier operation, during which the tumor had been removed. Some lymph glands had also been removed, so now my lymphatic system was secreting infection into my tongue.

It was going to be a tough problem to fix. With the tongue so enlarged, there was no way to shrink it down again except to *carve* it down. In the first of many operations on my tongue and mouth, the doctors literally cut a wedge of flesh from my tongue in an effort to keep it in my mouth.

Next problem: With my tongue carved down to a stump, it couldn't do the usual tasks a tongue is supposed to do. I could barely move it. Eating was difficult, speaking even more so. The surgeons operated again . . . and again, removing flesh below my tongue to free it up, then performing plastic surgery on my face around my jaw and chin. By the time I was four years old, I had endured seven rounds of surgery. I vaguely remember some of the later operations; I can still recall how unpleasant it felt, being tied to a hospital bed, being fed through tubes shoved down my nose, and having wooden sleeves holding my arms straight so I couldn't touch my face. I missed my family, I wanted to go home, and I wanted to sleep in real pajamas, not those goofy hospital gowns that are wide open in the back.

When at last the doctors allowed me to go home, the journey wasn't over. My tongue was still big and unwieldy, protruding from my mouth, and by now I was learning to talk that way. My speech was slurred, like Sylvester the Cat, and my tongue was still oozing fluid that caked on my lips and chin like dark chocolate—and sometimes sprayed on others if I pronounced a really strong *s*. I drew stares wherever we went. Mom, Dad, and my brother, Terry, were protective, but they couldn't possibly shield me from the natural revulsion most people expressed, knowingly or not, once they noticed the raw flesh and brown gunk in my mouth.

"Ooh, what's wrong with him?" the children, and too often the adults, would say. "Ooh, *yuck!*"

Can you figure God out? My folks did a lot of praying for me, as did the members of our church and all the extended family, gathering around me, laying hands on me, and praying that God would heal me.

Even Oral Roberts prayed for me. When I was around three years of age, the famous healing evangelist came to Seattle to conduct a crusade in a huge tent. Mom and Dad felt it was worth a try—you never know what God might do—so they took me to the service.

The tent was packed with the faithful, the hopeful,

and the curious, and it was sweltering in there. Folks were fanning themselves with song sheets; you could hear the steady rustling, and the vast crowd looked like a forest of quaking aspens. But nobody left. They sat right where they were and listened in awe as Roberts preached an encouraging message about how Jesus healed everyone who came to Him and how we need to have faith.

Then came the climax, the moment the crowd anxiously anticipated: the prayer line. The evangelist invited those in the audience who needed a healing touch from God to move to the front of the tent so he could pray for each person specifically. Throngs of people went forward and formed the line along the front of the platform and around the side of the tent. This was it!

Mom and Dad pressed into the line, Dad carrying me in his arms, standing, then shuffling forward, then standing, then shuffling forward inch by inch while Reverend Roberts prayed for each person. Exciting things were happening up at the front of the line. Shouts of joy filled the air; some people were jumping, some cheering. The organ player was pounding out plenty of old-time praise songs for what God was doing. With each outburst, each victory, Mom and Dad's faith spiked upward.

Finally, it was our turn. While the organ played in the

background, the evangelist leaned over so he could hear Dad whisper in his ear what the need was. Reverend Roberts didn't need a lot of description; he could see the problem for himself, and he appeared genuinely concerned, even *stymied*, by the sight of my dangling tongue. "Hand the boy up to me."

My dad has never been much of a weeper, but tears filled his eyes as he lifted me up and presented me to the healing evangelist. It was a moment of desperate hope, of clinging faith, of deep, earnest longing that somehow, somewhere in His inscrutable, mysterious nature, God would see fit to hear this prayer where other prayers had failed.

Standing on the platform in front of the massive crowd, Oral Roberts held me up in his arms and confessed, "I've never seen anything quite like this problem before." He prayed, and the crowd of believers prayed with him, that God would heal me. The organ played, the saints believed, and the cry went up to heaven, while the little slobbering kid in the middle of it all had no clue what the hubbub was about.

When Reverend Roberts handed me back to my father, I grabbed hold of Dad tightly, just glad to be back in his arms. Mom took a cloth diaper from her coat pocket—my ever-present drool rag—and dabbed the ooze from my mouth and tongue. My tongue was still running, raw, and grotesque as ever. Nothing had changed.

There was nothing more to do but go home.

My folks were sorely disappointed that I had not been healed instantly. Why hadn't God answered the many prayers offered in faith, believing God for a miracle? It's tough enough trying to figure God out, but especially when, to fulfill His plans, God seems a bit deaf. Making matters worse, of course, we usually don't get an immediate explanation.

Mom had been beating herself up emotionally and spiritually ever since my birth. She'd seen me suffering and had kept asking herself, "What did I do wrong?" Satan was no help; he was always quick to tell her, "This is your fault." It was a lie and she knew it, but the thought stung her, clinging to her mind like a leech. At times, the punishing thoughts, the guilt, and the frustration hurt so badly she just wanted to take her baby and run away, to hide where nobody could find them and no eyes could stare at them anymore.

And now, it seemed that their last, best hope for my healing had proved disappointing. My disfigurement remained the same; the stares, snide comments, and Satan's devious accusations would all continue.

Dad kept a lot of his pain and frustration inside. That was just his way. But I still recall Mom telling me that the only time she'd ever seen him cry was when he was asking folks to pray for me.

Were the prayers doing any good?

Without a doubt! God has a knack for performing miracles that remain unseen only because of our short-sightedness. My folks knew that. Sure, it was painful and frustrating at the time, and the whole rotten mess could make them feel so helpless, but my folks knew that God heard their prayers, and applied every one of them to His divine purpose for Frank Peretti. *Of course* God heard the many prayers on my behalf . . . and He answered them in His time, and in His way. The resulting healing process is still at work in my life to this day.

So Mom and Dad persevered in faith, trusting that God would eventually heal me in whichever manner He wanted. The surgeries continued, along with repeated visits to the doctor. Everything seemed to go so *sloooowly*, but my parents never gave up hope. They continued to believe God, and they trusted Him, one day at a time.

And really, when I consider my condition at the beginning, the Lord was very gracious to me. For a while, the doctors were concerned that my face would be misshapen or that my teeth would come in crooked because of the constant pressing of my tongue, but amazingly, my face maintained its normal structure, and my teeth came in straight. I could have done a lot worse. In researching cystic hygroma, I've found that other kids with the defect have had to bear a much greater burden of disfigurement.

My burden was limited to my ugly tongue and one side effect: my small stature. Apparently, my body had been so preoccupied with fighting off infection that it had to postpone growing. The doctors assured my folks that I'd catch up eventually. We would just have to be patient.

We got on with our lives, and life at home was normal enough. Dad changed jobs again and began his thirty-year career at the Boeing Company, so we moved into a house in south Seattle, on a hill just above Boeing Field. That was during the heyday of the B-52, and I want to tell you, those big birds were *loud* when they took off!

Mom and Dad loved my brother, Terry, and me, and we played together and got into fights over toys and got in and out of trouble like any kids would do. Our younger brother, Paul, came along, and Terry and I got jealous because Paul got to have Ivory soap in his bath and we didn't. Life was normal.

I was small and I talked funny, but that didn't matter

at home. Mom and Dad always loved me and let me know that I was special, that I would grow up to be big and strong someday, and that the problem with my tongue would soon go away. I believed them, and, really, we did all right.

And then . . . I had to go to school.

MONSTERS
ON THE LOOSE

Chapter Four

"Come on, honey; it's time to go to school," I heard Mom's voice calling. "You are going to have so much fun. You'll get to color and play games and listen to stories. You'll love it!"

Mom checked my sweater to make sure I was dressed just right for my first day of kindergarten. My tongue still protruded from my mouth, and I had difficulty pronouncing many words, but I had developed my own way of saying words when my tongue refused to cooperate. For the most part, I could communicate fairly well.

Going to kindergarten was almost like being at home. The teacher was kind and loving, and she never said a word about my disfigurement. At first, most of the children were kind, too, or maybe they were just as awed by the school experience as I was, so I didn't receive many snide remarks. As the year went on, however, the teasing began.

Children can say the funniest things. They also can say some of the cruelest things imaginable. Even at that young age, the kids seemed compelled to remind me about the scab-covered tongue hanging from my mouth. By the end of my kindergarten year, I'd had quite enough of school and didn't want to return.

When Mom dropped me off at school to begin first grade, I decided not to stay. By now, I was extremely self-conscious about my size and disfigurement, so as soon as I saw our car disappear around the corner, I ran away from school and headed back home. I was like a human boomerang, returning to the person who sent me out. Sometimes, I got home before Mom parked the car in our garage!

"I don't wanna go to school!" I railed.

"Frank, honey, you have to go to school," Mom insisted.

"No, I'm not going!"

"Yes, you must."

I loved my mother dearly, and she loved me, even as she planted deeply in my mind the axioms of authority that would follow me for years: "You have to be there. You have no choice."

She herded me into the car and drove me back to school.

One morning, after I ran away from school again and Mom took me back, my teacher told her, "You just leave him to me. I'll handle him."

Mom peeked through the window of the door to the classroom while the teacher took me back inside and kindly but firmly sat me down at my desk. I burst out in tears and wailed wildly. The teacher remained nonplussed. She gave me some special assignments and told me, "Now, Frank, stop your crying. You're in school now. It's time to do your work like a big boy." The teacher arranged my work on the desk for me and gave me enough to keep me busy for a while. She checked on me regularly, and before long, I became interested in the work and forgot about the incessant teasing of the other children.

Until recess, when it started all over again.

The scenario was repeated throughout my elementary school years. On one occasion, Mom and Dad complained to the school principal about the teasing. The principal listened attentively and apparently passed the word on to some teachers, but no amount of adult supervision could prevent the arrows from piercing my heart on the playground, in physical education class, or in the school bathrooms, away from the watchful eyes of the teachers.

The only safe havens were at home and at church. The kids at church had known me most of my life and understood that something was wrong. They were good friends. They had heard some of the adults praying for my healing, and some of them had even prayed for me themselves.

One Sunday morning, when I was about seven years of age, I was sitting in church, trying to keep from squirming around as Dad led the song service. My tongue was throbbing. Intense pain began to flare around my throat. Before long, I felt as if a lump of meat was stuck in my throat and I could barely breathe.

We weren't supposed to talk in church. We weren't supposed to fidget or make noise. So, since I had to scream and cry, I did it while running out of the sanctuary.

Mom came running after me. "Frank! What's wrong?"

I clutched at my throat, choking, tears streaming from my eyes. The more I cried, the worse the pain got. Mom took one look at my neck and saw the swelling around my throat.

Mumps! A serious enough affliction for any child, but far worse for a child with cystic hygroma! Mom raced to a phone and called our doctor, who prescribed medication to reduce the fever and swelling.

The medication did the trick and I was able to breathe more easily, but getting any food past my doubly swollen tongue and badly constricted throat was another matter. Mom and Dad had to feed me through a straw for several weeks. My bout with the mumps served to notify them that I was probably going to need more surgery on my tongue and mouth.

And so it went. Life was painful at times because of sickness, the world was cruel at times because of taunts and teasing, and the laundry could get gruesome whenever my tongue decided to have another "eruption."

But I just have to brag about my mom and dad. Along with the Lord, they were the solid rock under my feet and never neglected any chance to encourage my creativity. I became interested in drawing and cartooning, so they supplied me with paper, pencils, and art books. I wanted to build a twenty-foot model of the *Titanic* in the backyard, so Dad let me use his tools and scrap lumber—provided I put everything away when I was done. My brothers and I set out to build some airplanes in the garage, so Dad moved the cars out and let us have at it. We were going to build a foot-powered paddleboat as well, and got as far as stacking some old oil drums—flotation—on the back patio for several months. I came up with an idea for a gas-powered, one-man blimp, but that never got off the ground.

Most of our big projects never floated or flew. Usually, we'd go nuts on one project for a few weeks, then we'd tear it all apart so we could use the lumber and nails to fulfill the next big vision. Mom and Dad just watched to make sure we didn't hurt ourselves, made sure we put things away and got our homework done, and went with the flow. Dad gave us advice, let us use his tools, and granted us room in the garage, on the patio, or in the basement, for as long as it took. Never once did he tell us it wasn't worth it or that we'd never succeed or that our ideas were dumb.

I *did* succeed with many smaller projects more within my reach, working wonders with the cardboard from empty cereal boxes. I built a spaceship, a three-story haunted house, a jet airliner, a whole fleet of Boeing 727s and KC-135s, the Space Needle, the Seattle Coliseum, and the Century 21 monorail out of cereal boxes and good old, dependable Elmer's glue—they were *toy* size, of course. I even got my picture in the paper, standing next to my cardboard Space Needle. Guess who made that happen?

One Christmas, Mom and Dad surprised me with a ventriloquist dummy named Jerry, and that little wooden-head became my alter ego, bringing out the ham in me.

We entertained our family members and put on shows, and Jerry even went to school with me a few times to perform for my class. Jerry and I became pretty close. He helped me come out of my shell, we won ourselves some new respect from my classmates, and he never had a problem with my looks or size.

I will have to say that, all things considered, kids having a loving mom and dad has always been a great idea.

But even Mom and Dad had to wonder about another buddy of mine who came later.

Zenarthex was my most memorable creation. He was more than eight feet tall, with a jaundiced complexion, blue and red blood vessels stark and visible under his parchment skin, and a long, flowing cape that blew in the wind. His arms needed a little work, and he had no hair on his head, but his jaw moved, and his eyes—big, round, and bloodshot—gave him a chilling gaze. We still had several parts of him lying around the lab, but Terry and I figured he was finished enough for a test run. We threw him together and told him to stand out on the corner near the Graham Street Grocery late at night.

The breeze that night kept his big cape moving, and the cold blue of the streetlight made him look downright eerie. I couldn't have been more pleased. We gave him a thumbs-up and a quick slap on the back, then we hid behind some parked cars to see what passing motorists might do.

For his first time out, Zenarthex handled the job quite well. He stood there boldly, as an approaching car's headlights illuminated his huge frame and hideous face, his expression never changing, his big eyes never blinking, his toothy grin always steady. Most of the cars just drove on by—after all, this was in the middle of Seattle where most folks had already seen everything—but one car slowed down, and another actually stopped for a second look before speeding away with a roar and a screech.

Cool!

After about a dozen cars, we were satisfied. Zenarthex had had a successful debut; he had even scared some people! What more could we ask for?

Besides, Zenie was getting nervous. "It's after curfew."

Mm, good point. Terry and I joined him on either side and helped him see his way home, taking him back to our lab in the basement of our house.

We had a great lab, full of jars, bottles (mostly empty canning jars and ketchup bottles with dyed water inside), and cool mad scientist gadgetry (a dead television, the insides from an old Philco tube radio, the chopper from a broken cider press). We'd crayoned a brick pattern on the concrete walls, hung some of Mom's nylon stockings from the ceiling to simulate stalactites, and provided Zenarthex with his own slab (a door lying on orange crates) and a super electrical heart zapper (an empty can of talcum powder fastened to a length of gooseneck conduit with duct tape). We thought it might have been cool to get a red light bulb for the ceiling or maybe one of those Christmas tree floodlights with a rotating, colored disk to add some mood to the place, but this was a low-budget operation.

Zenarthex was too tall to fit under the basement ceiling, so we had to take him apart and carry him inside in pieces. Our lanky, six-foot friend Glen was glad enough to get the stick and cloth framework off his shoulders. I'd used a lot of plaster in making Zenie's head, and Terry had used a lot of hardware to get his mouth to work, so Zenarthex was heavy. He looked great, though, lying on his slab, all put together again, staring at the ceiling with those big, Ping-Pong-ball eyes. A few more dollars from returned pop bottles, and we might just make that monster movie for which we'd built all this stuff.

Ah, monsters. My friends. My associates. My obsession. By now, I was just on the brink of thirteen. John F. Kennedy was dead, the Beatles had just invaded, skirts were short, and pants were tight. My younger brother, Paul, and I had expanded our territories to the point of war in our old room, so now he had his own room, and I had mine.

But I was not alone in my room, no sir. The Frankenstein monster was there, both as a wall poster and as a plastic model on my desk. I had other plastic models, as well, each meticulously assembled and painted: Dracula, gesturing hypnotically; the Creature from the Black Lagoon, poised to scratch someone's face off; the Mummy, all wrapped up and rotten; the Phantom of the Opera, singing an aria with his mask in his hand; the Hunchback of Notre Dame, bleeding from a whipping; the Witch, stirring up a potion in her pot. I had posters of monsters, monster masks (Terry looked better than I did in the Frankenstein mask; he was taller), monster magazines, and monster comic books. I wrote stories and drew comics about monsters and mad scientists; I told the neighbor kids stories about dead bodies and spooks, and I made audio dramas on my folks' old reel-to-reel tape recorder about devious, monster-stitching, body-snatching scientists with silly foreign accents.

I never missed Saturday afternoons on Channel 11 or *Nightmare Theater* on Channel 7, unique cultural opportunities to view some of the worst sci-fi and horror flicks ever made, all sponsored by our local honest and upstand-ing used-car dealer who would never lie to us.

I got to know by name the finest Japanese monsters ever to don a fake rubber suit and destroy toy cities in slow motion.

I marveled at the possibility of things coming from else-where: Martians all slimy and slithery; Venusians with tiny bodies and big brains; and hovering, whammy-eyed Brains with no bodies at all from some planet that starts with a Z.

I saw just about every plot idea that can be milked from atomic radiation gone amuck:

Things made *big* by atomic radiation: giant ants, giant grasshoppers, giant lizards, a giant praying mantis, an amazing, colossal man, a fifty-foot woman . . .

Things made *small* by atomic radiation, like the incredible shrinking man . . .

Things made *weird* by atomic radiation: three-eyed, four-armed atomic mutants, one-eyed cave dwellers, goofy underwater monsters that swam like people . . .

Things made *invisible* by atomic radiation, *invincible* by atomic radiation, *wicked* and *depraved* by atomic radiation.

I saw atomic radiation depopulate the world—except for the leading man and leading lady, who survived to start the human race all over again—several times.

My world was filled with scientists fooling around with things best left alone while a younger, wiser scientist tries to warn them not to, as the pretty girl — always in love with the younger, wiser guy — gets carried off by the monster while the scientists are busy arguing.

But through it all, my keenest interest was in the monsters, those ugly, misunderstood, abused, captive monsters who escaped from their cages, traps, and laboratories; scared people; broke things; and got back at the unfeeling people who abused them. The three-eyed, four-armed atomic mutants may have been victims, but they turned around and *made* victims.

The Frankenstein monster was tormented relentlessly by Igor, Dr. Frankenstein's humpbacked assistant, but the monster got even. The Creature from the Black Lagoon was captured and imprisoned in a huge aquarium, but he finally clawed his way out of there and got some respect. King Kong was captured and put on display, but he snapped his chains, escaped, grabbed the girl, and had a real heyday in New York City, at least for a while. The Mummy got a raw deal in his time, but eventually, he got a chance to even things up in ours. Dracula could give his victims the Eye and cut right to the chase. Both the Phantom of the Opera and the Hunchback of Notre Dame were scarred, ugly, and misunderstood, but at least for one poignant, wishful, intense moment, they had the appreciation of the girl.

No wonder I kept those guys around. Somewhere in my head, planted there repeatedly over the years, was the notion that I was one of them—ugly, rejected, picked on, and somehow less worthy of membership in the world of normal kids. I was entering adolescence, that weird age when the size, shape, and appearance of your body mean everything, and everyone seemed to be growing except me. On the right side of my neck, a visible scar and a depression could be seen where once there had been a tumor. Because of the problem with my tongue, I spoke with an obvious lisp and often mangled words when my mind darted faster than my mouth could follow. I wore glasses and one of two favorite vests every day, and let's face it, if I wasn't a bona fide nerd, I sure came close. Girls? Hey, I couldn't have been better protected from temptation. Once I lamented to my mom, "I'm so ugly, nobody would ever want to marry me!"

So it was predictable that some of my classmates— all of them bigger and proud of it—would take special pleasure in making my life miserable. I was pushed, shoved, thrown, hit, insulted, badgered, manhandled, teased, and harassed, and just as any monster must get tired of everyone screaming at the first sight of him (Why can't they just skip that part for once and say hello?), I was tired of kids asking, "Ooh, what's wrong with your tongue?" before they'd even ask me my name. Increasingly, through the eyes of others, I saw myself as a monster.

But my monster friends had one significant advantage I admired and wished I had: Yes, they were trapped and mistreated, just like me, but they found a way out. They were scarred and ugly, just like me, but if anybody ever knocked their books out of their arms, shoved them in the halls, drew insulting pictures of them, or called them put-down names, you can bet ol' Frankenstein or Phantom or Hunchback could do something about it. They had power over their situation. They had control. People were afraid of them and not the other way around.

Maybe you can relate. Ever been there? Maybe you're there right now, in a situation in which someone is constantly stabbing you with words, kicking you with cruel acts, hurting you, and taking away your dignity. You wish you could do something about it, get out of that situation, but all around you are those invisible walls, those axioms of authority that hold you in: "Well, you have to be there. You have no choice. You have to go. You have to be in that situation. We can't change anything."

You have to go to that school, sit in that classroom, eat in that lunchroom, work at that particular job, endure the taunts of that particular group, or put up with that boss, supervisor, or coworker.

Maybe you're the one who lies awake at night dreading every morning because of the people waiting for you at school or work. They have a name for you — it's not your real name; it's the one they gave you, something that labels you as inferior, ugly, or stupid. And there are others whom you don't even know, who don't know you, who call you by that name because it's fun for them. They have never bothered to ask you what your real name is. It's their mission to take away your dignity. They spit on you, trip you, knock the books out of your arms, and stomp on your ankles from behind. It doesn't matter what you wear, they laugh at it. If you own something new, they steal it, spill on it, tear it, and destroy it.

There is no particular reason for the torment. Any reason that can possibly be found or contrived will do. They pick on you because you're smaller, because you have a rare blood type, because you pick apples on your way home, you sing a particular song, you wear a particular sweater, you can't throw or catch a ball, you can't run fast, you don't have the right clothes, or simply because you're different.

And in physical education class, your oppressors have the perfect opportunity to harass you, because they're in close proximity, and all the activity is physical. It's a convenient time to take physical advantage of you because you're small or weak or maybe not so great an athlete. So they push you and shove you, throw you, kick you, and trip you.

And there's nothing you like better than taking a shower with that bunch, being naked before your enemies, laid bare for them to spot your most intimate physical secrets so they can laugh at you, spread the word about you, torment you. Strangely, it's similar to a child being molested by a family member in authority. Parents and teachers—just like the stepfather, the father, the older brother, the uncle, or the live-in boyfriend—insist it's okay. They make you do certain evil things, simply because they said so; they tell you there's nothing wrong with it, but all through the obeying and the yielding, something deep inside you is crying out, "This is wrong! This shouldn't be happening to me!"

Those to whom you look for love, shelter, and protection tell you to ignore your tormentors, just to stay away from them, but the authorities do nothing to stop those who are verbally, physically, or emotionally abusing you. What's a person to do?

Ignore them? Let's be honest: Ignoring is *acting,* and

nothing more—acting as though the words or actions of your oppressors don't hurt. You hear the words, you feel the insults, and you bear the blows. You can act deaf and impervious to pain, but the stabs and the arrows pierce you anyway.

Just stay away from them? Don't you wish that you had a choice? Can you choose which lunchroom to sit in, which squad to line up in, which desk to sit at, which bus to ride home, or which direction to walk home?

Remember? In P.E., "everyone is required to take a shower!"

If you say anything about the bullying you endure, you're a snitch or a wimp, and you only compound the problem. At least, that seems to be the universal, unwritten code of conduct.

If you had a choice, you wouldn't be there, but you don't have a choice. You are hemmed in by the rules and requirements of the adult world, the expectations placed upon you from birth. Of course, you obey, of course, you do what you're told, of course, you submit to authority and authority's axioms, and, yes, in many cases, that is as it should be.

When an authority tells you, "You have to go to school," you go. You get dressed, grab your books and your lunch, and go. When an authority reminds you that your boss has a right to badger you at work because he signs your paycheck, you swallow hard and, with a sense of resignation, go about your work as though the belittling behavior by the boss never occurred.

By their indifference to abuse, bullying, and harassment, parents, teachers, and employers send additional, subtle messages often written between the lines: You must also endure whatever comes with the package. It happens. Life is tough. Kids will be kids. We all went through it. It's part of growing up. It's a rite of passage. Get over it. It'll make you stronger. Suck it up, kid. Hey, you wanna work here, you don't make waves.

Hemmed in, and with few options, you go every day, and you get stabbed every day, and you bleed every day.

But wounds can fester. They can become infected, and then they can infect others.

And they can *change* you because you haven't merely cut your finger or bruised your knee. You've been wounded in your spirit, and that wound pierces deeply, painfully, sometimes even permanently. As Proverbs 18:14 says, "The spirit of a man will sustain him in sickness, but who can bear a broken spirit?" When tough times or injuries come, we must be able to draw upon a reservoir of hope, faith, and self-confidence that God has stored up inside us through the love and encouragement of friends and family. If enemies, through cunning and cruelty, have plundered that reservoir, what will sustain us then?

Won't God sustain us? Won't He give us the grace we need? Don't we find our hope and strength in Him? Won't He get us through?

Absolutely. I wouldn't be here today if God's presence and grace were not true and ultimately provable.

But that's the rub: To prove anything *ultimately* takes time and experience. You have to live it out for a while, sometimes a *long* while. A process is involved. Even now, in so many of our lives, there are issues to be resolved and wounds that have to be faced squarely, forgiven, and healed. Many of us adults have been carrying unhealed wounds since we were children.

At the time of this writing, I'm close to fifty years of age, but I still remember the names and can see the faces of those individuals who made my life a living hell, day after day after day, during my childhood. I remember their words, their taunts, their blows, their spittle, and their humiliations. As I review my life, I think of all the decisions I shied from, all the risks I dared not take, all the questions I never asked, all the relationships I didn't pursue, simply because I didn't want to be hurt again.

Moreover, I am haunted by the tragedy of Littleton, Colorado, on April 20, 1999. We've heard the many theories and pontifications on why two students, Eric Harris and Dylan Klebold, strode into Columbine High School and massacred their schoolmates and a teacher. I'm sure the theories about violence on television and movies, violent video and computer games, the availability of guns, and the unavailability of parents all have their legitimate place in the discussion. I don't pretend to know with certainty what was happening in the hearts and minds of those young killers, and yet . . .

I remember the thoughts I had, sitting alone in the school library after D. H. picked me up by my neck or sitting alone on the street curb, eyes watering, after P. B. sprayed deodorant in my face. I remember what I wished I could do if only I had the strength, the skill in martial arts, or the advantage that a baseball bat might give me over the bullies who bludgeoned and batted me around verbally and physically.

Of course, my parents taught me never to fight. I was a Christian; I had a loving God to turn to when times got tough, and I had a biblical code of conduct that required a nonviolent solution. I knew the Savior, who taught us to turn the other cheek and forgive. So, instead of retaliation or confrontation, I sloughed off the wounds inflicted by my abusers and retreated to the solitude and safety of my room, where I identified with monsters and tried to get by.

But immersing oneself in make-believe stories about monsters isn't the only way to deal with the pain and humiliation of being devalued by other people.

Nowadays, kids are devising all sorts of ways to identify with those who feel trapped and put upon, and this new breed of monster will do almost anything for the power to change his situation and get even.

Instead of getting into monsters, a modern-day victim of abuse can gravitate to violent video games, in which he can vent his pain and anger by blasting his enemies into atoms.

He can watch movies—so many movies!—in which the hero solves his situation by shooting everybody and blowing everything up.

He can live in a fantasy world, in which he's the guy with all the power and all the guns.

He and his cohort can make a video for a class project, in which they dress in dark trench coats, carry guns, and blow away all the jocks.

He can customize the bloody "shoot-'em-up" game "DOOM," creating two shooters instead of one, giving them extra weapons and unlimited ammunition, and programming the game so the people he encounters can't fight back.

He might identify with a historical monster: Adolf Hitler, a tyrant who had total life-or-death control over millions, who could scare and terrorize people, and who could solve all his problems with guns and bombs.

He can fill his mind with Nazi mythology, wear a black shirt with a swastika, speak German in the halls and on his Web pages, and talk about whom he hates and whom he'd like to kill.

He can vent his rage with threats and obscenities on the Internet. The rantings of the Columbine killers are terrifying:

> . . . for those of you who happen to know me and know that I respect you, may peace be with you and don't be in my line of fire. For the rest of you, you all better hide in your houses because I'm coming for everyone soon, and I WILL be armed to the teeth and I WILL shoot to kill and I WILL KILL EVERYTHING!
>
> . . . Dead people can't do many things, like argue, whine, . . . complain, narc, rat out, criticize, or even talk. So that's the only way to solve arguments with all you out

there, I just kill. God, I can't wait till I can kill you people. I'll just go to some downtown area in some big city and blow up and shoot everything I can. Feel no remorse, no sense of shame. I will rig up explosives all over a town and detonate each one of them at will after I mow down a whole area full of you snotty, rich, high-strung, godlike-attitude-having worthless pieces of ____. I don't care if I live or die in the shoot-out. All I want to do is kill and injure as many of you as I can. . . .[1]

He can give in to the hate that grows out of his wounds and talk about a plan to attack his school so much, and for so long, that eventually, as James 1:14–15 warns, the thought becomes an act, and the act brings forth death.

Finally, on April 20, 1999, Hitler's 110th birthday, he can carry out his most gruesome fantasy. And what better place than the school, where everyone, from the parents and teachers on down, has all the power, and he doesn't? What better place than in the high-school cafeteria, where students once surrounded Eric and Dylan and squirted ketchup packets all over them, laughing at them and calling them faggots while teachers watched and did nothing?[2]

And he can leave behind an e-mailed suicide note to the police (allegedly written by Eric Harris):

. . . Your children, who have ridiculed me, who have chosen not to accept me, who have treated me like I am not worth their time, are dead. THEY ARE _____ DEAD. Surely you will try to blame it on the clothes I wear, the music I listen to, or the way I choose to present myself— but no. Do not hide behind my choices. You need to face the fact that this comes as a result of YOUR CHOICES. Parents and Teachers, YOU [fouled] UP. You have taught these kids to be gears and sheep. To think and act like those who came before them, to not accept what is different. YOU ARE IN THE WRONG. I may have taken their lives and my own—but it was your doing. Teachers, Parents, LET THIS MASSACRE BE ON YOUR SHOULDERS UNTIL THE DAY YOU DIE. . . .[3]

Everyone has his or her own theory. Here is mine: Simply put, I believe that what happened at Columbine was the result of *a wounded spirit.*

Although the authorship of the above suicide note is in question, as are many details surrounding that day, to me, in the overarching scheme of things, it doesn't really matter. Whoever wrote it pegged the problem. We now have in our society myriad young people and adults who have been deeply wounded by the demeaning words or actions of authority figures or peers.

It is no secret that kids on the fringes of the cool crowd of Columbine endured their share of taunts and abuse. They were called faggots, were bashed into lockers, and had rocks thrown at them. They were shoved, pelted with pop cans or cups of sticky soda, splattered with mashed potatoes and ketchup, even sideswiped by cars while they rode their bikes to or from school.

One anonymous teen spoke of waking on school days with a knot in his stomach and the dread of having to face more humiliation at school. He would avoid certain hallways and even make his way to classes outside the school building to escape being ridiculed or bashed against lockers.[4] He knew Harris and Klebold were being tormented as well, and he said, "I'm not saying what they did was OK, but I know what it's like to be cornered, pushed day after day. Tell people that we were harassed and that sometimes it was impossible to take. Tell people that . . . eventually, someone was going to snap."[5]

I know how that feels. Maybe you do too.

Why is it so important that we address the problem of bullying and other demeaning attitudes and behaviors in our society? Because one in four bullies will end up in the criminal correction system.[6] Because those who have been wounded often become those who *wound* others. Because we could be allowing the creation of more monsters—the kind you never see, never expect, until they snap and take desperate, violent measures. And all of us—those who have been wounded as well as those who wound others—need healing, forgiveness, and a new heart attitude toward our fellow human beings.

No longer can we hide our heads in the sand and pretend that atrocities such as Columbine don't happen in our backyard. No longer can we live in denial, pretending that abuse does not occur in our family, church, or workplace.

It's time for change.

FINDING A VOICE

Chapter Five

Long before I became a published author, I was a public speaker. I spoke at youth rallies, retreats, Bible camps, church banquets, you name it. I did Bible studies, lectured on Christian world-view, preached the gospel, told wacky stories, delivered sermons, and covered all manner of subjects—all, that is, except the subject of this book.

I guess it seemed just a little too esoteric, too narrow in scope. After all, to my knowledge, I had never heard anyone stand before an audience and address the matter of boys, girls, men, and women demeaning each other, picking on other people needlessly, and treating each other with abject disrespect. Nobody talked about it in a public forum—not parents, teachers, preachers, or college professors.

Sure, we've all heard the subject of bullying mentioned once in a while, usually treated as an unpleasant nuisance, a rite of passage that happens to everyone, no big deal. But I'd never heard anyone actually *preach* on it. I'd never heard anyone come out and say that bullying is *wrong*. I had to wonder, *If no one else considers it important enough to talk about, how can I be sure any audience will think it important enough to hear about?* Though it was a significant burden I had harbored secretly for most of my life, I never seemed to find the right reason, place, and time to talk about it.

But then came the Life on the Edge conference for youth and their parents in Ontario, California, on Saturday afternoon, May 22, 1999. Focus on the Family sponsored the event, and I was scheduled to be one of the speakers during that weekend. I'd done LOTE conferences before and had some prepared messages in my files already, but things changed after the killings at Littleton. The more I read and heard about that whole tragedy, the more I felt a quaking and stirring in my spirit, as if God were saying, *Frank, here is your reason and your place, and yes, it's time to talk about it.*

You may have heard the talk broadcast on the *Focus on the Family* radio program. When I first delivered it in

Ontario, I was almost afraid I'd flopped, that I had failed to get my message across to the audience. As I presented the speech, I was way outside my comfort zone and choked with emotion half the time, being completely vulnerable about my experience. I told no jokes. I did no humorous routines as I normally do. I simply stood on the platform and shared from my heart. Nervous, and with little confidence in my memory, I leaned over my notes, even reading aloud from them at times. I rarely strayed from the podium, gesturing and moving around as little as possible while I spoke. I agonized through every word of the talk.

The audience of fifty-five hundred teens and their parents were respectful and receptive; they even applauded at times, but, for the most part, they remained still, subdued, and strangely quiet during my presentation.

Afterward, I came to understand why. This wasn't a talk an audience could enjoy, applaud, and then yak about as they left the auditorium. This was a deep digger, a grave opener that scraped off layers of dirt revealing issues that had been buried long ago but were not really dead. For many in the room, my message was a painful reminder of past hurts and a call for reflection. For others, it was the emotional equivalent of a dentist drilling through a live nerve.

It's not a light and simple matter to open up and admit you're still harboring wounds from your childhood or to admit that, when you were a kid, you were bullied or abused or that you were the bully in someone else's life, the *cause* of the hurt. It's difficult to admit that you are being bullied or that you *are* the bully right *now*.

Heavy stuff. No wonder the audience responded in self-conscious silence.

Following my speech, the first feedback I received was from the sound technicians backstage. Of all people! These guys were adults, professionals, employees of Focus on the Family. They appeared to have perfectly normal, grown-up exteriors, all decked out with their Life on the Edge T-shirts and walkie-talkies. Nobody would have guessed that they had lived for years with a wounded spirit, with memories of sorrow, abuse, and loneliness, of being pariahs at their schools, on the job, or in their families. But they hadn't forgotten what those wounds felt like, and now, having heard me broach the subject and admit that the faces of my oppressors still haunted my memories, these adults felt free to talk about the ghosts from their pasts.

Later, I sat down with a charming couple, a drama duo who presented some remarkable parables and skits during the conference. They too had a story to tell about demeaning experiences in their pasts, and the similarities were disturbing and comforting; disturbing because the problem is so universal, but comforting because we could share so freely from a common experience.

After I got back home, I heard from the organizers of the event. No, I hadn't flopped as I had feared. Actually, I'd hit a nerve.

Dr. James Dobson heard a tape of my talk while exercising on the treadmill one morning, and it touched him so deeply he took his wife, Shirley, out for a drive that evening, and they listened to the tape again in the car. They agreed they had to share it with the *Focus on the Family* radio audience.

The opening words of the broadcast are worth recounting. First came the telephone voice of an anonymous woman: "I was one of those kids who at one time in my life was mean to everybody else. I'm sorry . . . I'm sorry from the bottom of my heart. Please forgive me and forgive everybody else, because nobody deserves all that."

Then Mike Trout, Dr. Dobson's radio cohost, gave a warm and evocative introduction: "Did you ever pick on someone? Tease him or her for whatever reason? Well, of course, you did. Unfortunately, it's an event that happens far too often, and I'd go as far as to say you remember at least one occasion when you were made fun of too. Those memories are etched in our brains, and each occasion, each offense is an ingredient in the recipe that has come together over the years to create who we are today."

The recording of my talk followed, and I don't know what sort of response Focus on the Family anticipated, but *I* had no idea how vast an audience would identify with those words. After the talk was broadcast in October 1999, Focus on the Family received 3,375 telephone calls. When the same program was rebroadcast in December 1999, Focus received 1,264 calls. At least 316 callers requested tapes after the first broadcast and 1,117 callers requested tapes following the rebroadcast. The folks at Focus informed my publisher that these numbers are much higher than the usual response to a broadcast. Ordinarily, a response by one thousand callers is considered good; two thousand callers is beyond the best expectations. When *three thousand* calls come in, they know they've touched a nerve.

Now, I'm a writer with a name and an audience, so I wrote this book, but I realize that my story is nothing exceptional, that the wounds inflicted on me are marginal compared to those who have suffered severe child abuse, spousal abuse, verbal, sexual, or emotional abuse. My pain pales in comparison to that endured by the brave men and women who survived Hitler's concentration camps. When I think about the victims and families involved in the senseless murders of those who died in Littleton, Colorado, or the students who were shot to death in Paducah, Kentucky, or the tortures that many people have overcome in their personal lives, I'm embarrassed even to mention the bullying I experienced.

But we do have an issue here, don't we? I'm only one small voice in a sea of voices, and our issue is more than just a simple case of teasing. While we can all accept that bullying and abuse betray a lack or loss of respect for other human beings, there is a deeper issue: the devaluing of human life; and that in turn indicates a lack or loss of respect for the Giver of human life and dignity, God Himself. The message a bully sends is a mockery of God's handiwork, a lie that slanders God's nature and negates His love for us.

This could be important, don't you think?

Consider, for example, how such behavior can distort our view of God. In their book *The Sacred Romance*, authors Brent Curtis and John Eldredge describe the awful feelings of doubt and despair following the piercing of our heart by an offender's "arrow":

The terror we enter and the seeming lack of rescue from it leave us with a deeply imprinted question about God that we hide in our heart, sometimes not allowing the light of day to touch it for years, even deep into our spiritual journey. We cover the question with rationalizations that let him off the hook and allow us to still believe, but our beliefs rest on foundations that move and quake under us. It is easy to reason that Jimmy and those sixth graders were just bad; you know, "not raised in very good homes." And of course, our rationalizations do bear a modicum of truth that keeps us from dealing with the question lodged deep in our heart, hidden from our conscious mind: "Do you care for me, God?"[1]

Curtis and Eldredge go on to trace some of our misgivings about God to our childhood experiences, including the infliction of wounds by others. See if you can relate to any of these: "Parents who were emotionally absent; bedtimes without words or hugs; ears that were too big and noses that were too small; others chosen for playground games while we were not; and prayers about all these things seemingly met with silence."[2]

Ever been there? I'm beginning to find out that many people can strongly relate to these issues, more than we've ever imagined. It brings an interesting, television-like image to my mind: I see myself walking along in the center of a vast room, sort of like those all-white, cornerless sound stages you see in a television studio. For a moment, I think I'm the only one with a story to tell about childhood wounds that still hurt, but then, from one side, a sound technician comes along, an amicable guy wearing a Life on the Edge T-shirt, carrying a walkie-talkie. He was the pariah of his class. He knows what I'm talking about. So we walk together.

Then comes a stage technician for Life on the Edge. And then the drama team that performed, and then a lady, a friend and listener of *Focus on the Family* who could hardly listen to the broadcast because it reminded her of the deeply buried pain from her past.

Then more people walk in from the sides and seemingly pop up out of nowhere, all shapes, all sizes, and all walks of life:

I see a columnist for a major Midwestern newspaper who once interviewed me. He's in his sixties now, and he has polio, so he walks with the aid of crutches. He's needed the crutches most of his life, but he's used to that. What really pains him are the wounds he can still feel, delivered by the kids who taunted him when he was a child.

Ah, here's the middle-aged woman who refuses to sing, even though she has a perfectly good voice and plenty of latent talent. She can remember the very day, during music appreciation class in the sixth grade, when she stopped singing. The other kids laughed at her and told her she sounded like a bird. Humiliated, she closed her mouth and has never opened it again to sing.

Here comes a beautiful, well-known screen actress. Nobody would guess that she had to wear a body cast for four years during her childhood. She was treated so cruelly by her classmates that she dropped out of school in the tenth grade and spent her teenage years as a loner, often hiding away in her bedroom with the door shut. Years later, after she had established a relationship with Jesus Christ, she was finally able to accept herself and to forgive those who had hurt her.

Please don't stare at that young man who is so excited about counting, "One . . . two, three . . . four, five, six, seven, eh-aa . . . eight . . . nine, TEN!" For him, this simple act is a major accomplishment, the opening of an immense door in his life. His father always told him he was so stupid he'd never be able to count to ten.

And along comes Shawn, the boy with the stutter and the harelip. He gave up learning to read because his schoolmates laughed and mimicked his attempts. He's thirty-seven now, and he still can't read.

"Hi, Joseph! Good to see you." Joseph has one leg that is shorter than the other, severely impairing his ability to run. He might have done well at any sport that didn't require him to run fast, but his gym teacher never told him that; the drill-sergeant-style teacher simply knocked points off Joseph's grade and mocked him, calling him "Slow Susie." Joseph didn't bother with any kind of physical fitness until well into his forties.

Meet Linda. She was excited about attending college until the very first day of classes, when a couple of senior girls insulted and belittled her for no reason other than the fact that she was a freshman. The upperclassmen didn't know her; they didn't even ask her name. Linda had been stung and hurt enough, all through junior and senior high school. She was not about to subject herself to that sort of treatment all over again. She walked off the campus and never returned, and, to this day, she's never obtained the college education she once dreamed of.

I look around at the growing crowd. Some people in our group are overweight. Some are small and weak. Some have physical deformities, cerebral palsy, or Down syndrome, or scars from burns. Others are Asian, African,

Native American, racially mixed. It's not too hard to guess what their stories might be.

Others are more of a mystery. They look so normal, so "together," so everyday: One's a landscaper, another is an electrician, and over there is a mailman, and now I see a wife and mother, and next to her, a minister. You can't guess their stories. You're even surprised to learn they're carrying the same sort of wounds as you.

There's an important lesson in that: The wounded spirit is borne by many, yet it often can't be seen. It can be a burden heavy enough to bend and warp the course of our lives, but it's buried deeply, hidden in a secret place, and we've been afraid to talk about it.

Until now. I never thought I'd be some kind of Pied Piper, but suddenly, all these people who recognize the validity of what I'm saying are coming out of the wood-work. Some are still carrying deep wounds from long ago; some are enduring fresh wounds each day. As in the case of other secret scars, those individuals who have suffered a wounded spirit often suffer in silence, unwilling to talk about it.

But maybe it's getting to be *that time*.

Our society, and especially the Christian community, has been slow to discuss many sensitive subjects. Not too many years ago, domestic violence was something we only whispered about across the back fence: "Have you seen Lois this morning? She's all black and blue. Guess he's beating her again, poor thing." We gossiped about it, but beyond that, we felt it was none of our business. After all, those things didn't happen in our families, and certainly not in our church!

Similarly, just a few years ago, child abuse was something we suspected (and sometimes we were dead certain of it), but we hesitated to say anything. We weren't sure what to do. Besides, surely Christians would never be guilty of such a heinous crime. Sadly, we now know better, that such offenses happen in Christian homes almost in the exact same percentages as those of nonbelievers.

During my childhood in the 1950s and 1960s, the black man in some parts of the country was expected to "know his place," and we were comfortable with that. We were extremely uncomfortable talking about racism or attempting to change it. "Let them have their own baseball teams. Let them worship in their own churches. Not in my backyard."

So what about *this* problem? We call it by many names: Abuse. Teasing. Taunting. Harassment. Bullying. Until now, we've been strangely quiet about it. It happens, we say. We all go through it. All the kids do it. It's part of life. It's no big deal. It happened when we were kids.

Is it wrong?

Let me ask again, *Is it wrong?*

Consider your answer carefully. If the answer is yes, that immediately raises another question: Then why do we allow it? Why do parents, teachers, teacher's assistants, fellow students, friends at school and church, coworkers, extended family members, and others see it happening, hear it happening, and know it's happening but fail to take it seriously? If devaluing human life—and thereby mocking God's creation—is wrong, why do so many do so little to stop it? Worse yet, why do so many participate as part of the problem?

Surely Mr. M was aware of what his students—and his teacher's assistants—were doing to that poor little kid in the shower. Surely the teachers and staff at Columbine—or any school for that matter—could hear the sounds of bodies hitting lockers, can see the ketchup stains all over some students' clothing, can hear the laughter of the bullies and the cries of the victims. Surely the bus drivers know when a gang of losers descends on one helpless kid, knocking his books all over the street at the bus stop. Surely the teachers notice when a child comes into class with his shirt torn, his shoes missing, and his clothing soiled. Most certainly, the kids know what's happening; they're a part of it. They face the bullying, badgering, and other such treatment almost every day in school; they're immersed in it. Why don't they attempt to put a stop to it, to refrain from such behavior themselves, and to confront it in their friends?

What about the parents of children who are being bullied? Do they have no options? Do they have no voice? Must they sit by in silence when they know their child is near vomiting from stress before leaving for school each morning? Or are they even aware of the problem?

But we're not just talking about school.

Even grownups have to put up with it. Sometimes it creeps into a marriage or into other family relationships. We might experience it at the hands of an overbearing minister, board member, policeman, or coach. Many people endure it in the workplace, sometimes even in businesses ostensibly run according to Christian principles and values.

Do we address it as something wrong that should not be done, or do we just go on pretending we don't hear it, don't see it?

What about you? Are you being wounded senselessly, mercilessly, needlessly, by someone stronger than you, more powerful than you, someone who has leverage over you in some inexplicable, yet very real way?

Or are you the person who is perpetrating such despicable acts, either overtly or secretly?

It's time to talk about it, friend. It's time for a change.

Let me restate what I said earlier: The message a bully sends is a mockery of God's handiwork, a lie that slanders God's nature and negates His love for us.

Or do we really care about God?

As you can well expect, I will argue that a right attitude toward God will bring a right attitude toward our fellow-man. As we have all seen clearly demonstrated, when God is removed from our thoughts, our lives, our schools, our society, any evil is possible, for we have no ultimate argument against it. Whether on an international scale, in your own neighborhood, or in your own family, the results are the same: People are no longer intrinsically precious, so it's easy to find petty reasons to mistreat the weak, the less intelligent, the less affluent, the physically disfigured, or those who, for whatever arbitrary reason, don't measure up.

In the next chapter, I'll share a parable with you that illustrates the absolute necessity for the inclusion of God in our thinking, our families, our world. If we really want to bring about change, this is where the change must begin.

THE PLAYGROUND PARABLE

Chapter Six

I t was the daddy of all playgrounds, stretching out acre upon acre and filled with laughing, ebullient, playing children. Boys and girls were running, chasing, and screaming playfully. Jump ropes were spinning as little girls chanted rhythmical rhymes; baseballs arced through the air, glove to hand, hand to glove, ball to glove, glove to ground. From the paved basketball and Four Squares area came the constant *boing, boing, boing* of big red, inflated playground balls bouncing from one child to another.

This was a happy place—usually. The kids played well together and followed the playground rules—most of the time. Sometimes a quarrel broke out, occasionally even an actual fight, but these skirmishes were quickly resolved. All in all, the playground was a wonderful, fun-filled, safe environment for kids to enjoy.

The playground rules, clearly posted on a big wooden sign beside the entrance, helped to provide every recess with the desired peace, order, and domestic tranquillity. The rules were clear enough for any eight- or nine-year-old to understand:

> NO HITTING.
> NO PUSHING OR SHOVING.
> NO FIGHTING.
> SHARE THE EQUIPMENT.
> TAKE TURNS.
> NO SPITTING ON THE GIRLS.
> NO CHASING THE BOYS.

The playground rules were sacred, omnipresent, and inscribed on every heart and mind; there was hardly a child there who hadn't had cause to appeal to those standards at one time or another.

For instance, when Jordan Smith first arrived on the playground, he brought with him the assumption that once the baseball was in his hand, he had sovereign control over it in perpetuity. His would-be teammates tried to explain to him that unless he relinquished possession of the baseball from time to time, there would be no baseball game. Reason alone would not change his mind. Appealing to the playground rules finally did.

Clyde Saunders always seemed to have extra saliva in his mouth and apparently felt compelled to put it somewhere else. Rachel Parks was the nearest available depository, and he was happy to share with her out of his abundance, until she appealed to the playground rules, and he was required to swallow.

Ah, the playground rules—steadfast and sure, a shelter for the oppressed, the defender of the weak, the guarantor of social stability.

Of course, we cannot overlook the importance of Mrs. Kravitz, the teacher on playground duty. Mrs. Kravitz represented the authority that put up those rules in the first place. Without her presence, the playground rules would have been nothing more than words painted on a board. She was sharp-eyed and elephant-eared, always ready to help in time of trouble but also ready to deal with troublemakers. She had a stern expression for that purpose, as well as a whistle, a clipboard, and a stack of pink slips that could mean a visit to the vice principal.

Some of the kids appreciated her presence on the

playground, and, naturally, some of the kids preferred she not be there. The former felt secure; the latter felt imposed upon. But like it or not, the playground was reasonably safe and orderly, because Mrs. Kravitz and the playground rules kept it that way.

Then one day, something was different on the playground. It took a while for the kids to notice, but eventually they realized that Mrs. Kravitz was nowhere to be found. Some were glad, of course. "Good riddance!" they said. But some were concerned and asked the other teachers where Mrs. Kravitz had gone.

"Well," said the teachers, "we've decided there is no authority, and you kids are inherently good and able to decide for yourselves the right thing to do. You have the capacity within yourselves to solve all your own problems and make this a better playground. You don't need Mrs. Kravitz."

"But what about the playground rules?" they asked.

"You can decide for yourselves if the playground rules are right for you. It's really not our place to say that any one set of rules is better than another."

And so the kids were left to their own wills and feelings and the whims of their own hearts.

For a time, the playground rules still held sway in their

minds. The rules worked well enough in the past; they continued to bring stability in the days that followed.

But then, one day, Clyde Saunders stopped to consider the excess saliva in his mouth and whether or not he should swallow. "It's my mouth and my spit," he reasoned to himself. "I don't see what business anyone else has telling me how to get rid of it." Whereupon, he fired off a huge, viscid, undulating glob that hit Rachel Parks right in the eye.

Rachel was beside herself. She felt violated, betrayed, insulted, and infringed upon—not to mention wet and gross. "Clyde! You aren't supposed to do that!"

"Oh, yeah?" he responded. "Who says?"

She promptly took him over to the old sign displaying the playground rules.

"See here?" she said, pointing. "The rules say, 'No spitting on the girls.'"

"Well, I can choose to live by those rules or not."

"But you *hurt* me and you *know* it!"

"That depends on your definition of *hurt* and your definition of *knowledge*."

Not long after this, the baseball game came to a screeching halt when Jordan Smith caught a pop-up fly and abruptly walked off with the baseball.

"Hey," the others shouted, running after him, "that's our ball!"

"It's mine now," he replied.

"But you have to share!"

"Oh, yeah? Who says?"

They pointed to the rules. "It says, 'Share the equipment.'"

Jordan was unmoved. "You really *believe* that old sign? Come on, we don't need those rules. We have Reason to show us the way."

So they tried reasoning with him. After all, in the absence of authority, Mrs. Kravitz, and the playground rules, Reason alone should suffice.

"Well," he responded, "A: I want the ball; B: I don't want you to have it; and, therefore, C: You aren't going to get it!"

The other boys were stymied—except for those who weren't afraid of a little roughness. The rules didn't apply anymore, and Reason wasn't giving them justice, so . . . they ganged up on Jordan, knocked him to the ground, and got the baseball back.

Following Jordan's line of reasoning, Sally and Jennifer promptly took possession of a jump rope. The girls from whom they'd taken it tried to be open-minded and tolerant, but they still couldn't help feeling cheated somehow. "We think you should share," they said.

Sally rolled her eyes as Jennifer responded, "We think you should stop trying to impose your narrow-minded, middle-class morality on us."

"But remember the rules?"

Sally and Jennifer laughed mockingly in the other girls' faces. "We've evolved beyond the rules and attained a higher perception: We think the jump rope is ours. We think we're entitled to it. Therefore, the jump rope is ours."

This new way of thinking caught on. The children had no need of authority or Mrs. Kravitz anymore. Each child was his or her own authority. As for the rules, although the standards on the old sign beside the playground never changed, the rules became increasingly offensive. The children finally tore down the sign and threatened to kick and punch any kid who tried to put it back up.

So the playground was all theirs, and all the kids lived and behaved according to what felt right to them.

When the first real fight broke out and Tracy Sorenson beat the living tar out of Stevie Boland, the kids watched and debated what may have caused such a fight, but none of them could say it was anybody's fault. Nor did anyone say that it was wrong.

Since nothing was wrong or anybody's fault, every kid soon felt entitled to have or do anything, by any means. Since there were no rules and reasoning was inconvenient, the kids resorted to hitting, shoving, fighting, spitting, and chasing. The jump ropes, balls, bats, and other playground equipment became plunder to be captured, always going to the strongest kid or the biggest gang. Sharing came only with a price, and as for taking turns, the next turn always went to the toughest kid.

The playground fell into chaos. The big rubber balls didn't go *boing, boing, boing* anymore, and there were no more baseball games—no one wanted to play by the rules, and most denied there were any rules at all, so no one played.

A few, unwritten rules did crop up eventually, dictated by the toughest, meanest, strongest kids and very easy to demonstrate: Might Makes Right. Survival of the Fittest. Natural Selection.

Jordan Smith liked those rules because he was tough.

Unfortunately for Jordan, Tracy Sorenson was tougher. He beat the living tar out of Jordan Smith and established his reputation as the toughest, meanest, strongest kid on the playground.

Now it was forbidden to speak of the old authority the children had once known, and the memory of Mrs. Kravitz quickly faded. The playground rules were gone, not only from the old wooden sign, but also from the minds and hearts of the children.

Tracy's will was now law. He controlled all the bats, balls, and jump ropes, and he decided who could play with them and when. He had a gang of tough boys and girls around him who enforced his will upon all the others through sheer brutality. There were no rules except his.

There was no longer any fun either.

The playground parable illustrates a familiar, historical pattern that is really no more complicated than the downward spiral we just traced on the playground. When we consider Stalin's Russia, Hitler's Germany, or the killing fields of Cambodia under Pol Pot, we see clear examples of what happens when man cuts away his moorings in God. At first, he thinks he is free, but then he realizes he is actually adrift, without a moral compass, in dangerous waters, where only the big fish win.

And the big fish can be horrendously mean to all the little fish when they have no absolute authority to whom they are accountable.

The Scripture records numerous times in the history of God's people when the majority of the population rejected God's revealed Word to them, and hence, God's authority. In describing one such period, one of the saddest, most poignant refrains in the Bible states flatly, "In those days there was no king in Israel; everyone did what was right in his own eyes" (Judg. 21:25 NASB). While at first glance that seems to imply that the Hebrew people enjoyed enormous freedom and autonomy, the exact opposite was true. The Book of Judges records a time of rampant immorality and chaos, with horrendous crimes against humanity. Predictably, the people fell into bondage to one tyrant after another, and God had to raise up a series of judges to deliver them.

In America, we haven't fallen under the heel of a ruthless dictator—at least, not yet. But we might ask ourselves: What point in the playground parable describes where we are today as a society? Here's a sobering hint, excerpted from the Eric Harris autopsy report:

> HISTORY: This is the case of an 18-year-old, white male who was the alleged victim of a self-inflicted gunshot wound to the head that occurred in the Columbine High School library on 04/20/99. No other history is available at the time of autopsy.

> EXTERNAL EXAMINATION: The body is clothed in a bloodstained white T-shirt with the inscription "Natural Selection" on the front. . . .

On his Web page, Eric Harris listed many things he hated, but Darwin's theory of evolution, particularly his suggestion of natural selection, stood in stark contrast. Harris's words are the haunting result of a playground in chaos:

YOU KNOW WHAT I LOVE???
Natural SELECTION! . . . it's the best thing that ever happened to the Earth. Getting rid of all the stupid and weak organisms . . . but it's all natural! YES![1]

When we pause to ponder what Eric Harris was wearing on the day he helped shoot to death thirteen people, we are well on our way to explaining why it happened.

Highly respected author and theologian Ravi Zacharias offered a profound insight in the days following the Littleton tragedy:

When we have told our young people today that Naturalism is true—we have evolved from nothing more than some primordial slime; when we have told them objective moral values do not exist—you decide what is right and wrong for you; when we have told our young people that there is no ultimate designer; when we have told our young people that there is no ultimate destiny;

when we have told them that man is the measure of all things, that there is no transcendent basis on which to find out what life is about and what life's goal is, why then are we surprised when we see the hell that is unleashed by that kind of philosophy?[2]

Ravi is right! I wish every teacher who indoctrinates his or her students with Darwinian evolution, pawning off unproven theories as fact, could be shown Eric's blood-stained T-shirt. Remember the old movie *Inherit the Wind*, in which Christians were portrayed as bigoted nin-compoops for opposing the theories of evolution? I won-der if the makers of that movie (and a host of films similar to it) might change their minds if they were called upon to clean up the bloody mess in the Columbine High School library. Oh, we've inherited the wind, all right— and a lot more.

It's all perfectly logical: If evolution is true, then there is no God. If there is no God, then there is no fixed, exter-nal source of truth and morality. If there is no fixed, exter-nal source of truth and morality, then truth and morality are left up to the individual. If the individual judges that killing all the "stupid and weak organisms" in his life is justified and right, then by what basis can we question his judgment? He's only following the moral compass evolution provides.

If all this sounds a bit boring, too pedantic, or too philosophical for you, keep in mind that the end result is extremely personal and practical. It touches nearly every part of your life, from what is being taught in your high-school and college classrooms, to what you hear in pop music, to what you see on television and in the movies, to what is being espoused by supporters of homosexual lifestyles, abortion, euthanasia, and assisted suicide, to radical, anti-Christian political movements, to neo-Nazi skinheads, and more.

Why? Because Mrs. Kravitz is barred from the playground. The rules have been abandoned and, in too many cases, jettisoned from the public square completely. In their absence, we are left to the dictates of our own hearts, and as Jeremiah 17:9 warns us and history has proved, "The heart is deceitful above all things, and desperately wicked."

Given all this, the question is not, Why did the tragedy at Columbine happen? but rather, Why *shouldn't* it have happened?

Why shouldn't kids taunt, tease, and torment each other? Why shouldn't bosses make unreasonable demands of their employees and then publicly berate them when the goals are not met? Why shouldn't a husband blacken his wife's eye as a reminder that he is the one in control? Why shouldn't the strong, the rich, the powerful, or the cool people prey upon the weak and the outcast? And why shouldn't the wounded retaliate with guns if they so choose? After all, if we as human beings are nothing more than grown-up goo, what does it matter? Animals will be animals.

It's not my purpose to debate the fallacies of evolution (at least, not in this book). For those who are intellectually honest and want to know the truth about this ideology, the information is widely and easily available. I am simply pointing out that the ultimate issue for the evolutionist is not bones, fossils, and strata—it's *God*. Rejection of God and our accountability to Him is foundational to evolutionist thinking. The rejection of God comes first, and *then* comes the interpretation of the data.

But with God rejected, morality becomes arbitrary. The rights and dignity of others become secondary. Unbridled violence by a Hitler or a Harris, to get what he wants, to guard what is his, or to seek revenge, becomes a perfectly logical alternative.

If a personal, loving Creator God does exist and rule

this universe, then we have in Him a transcendent source for meaning, value, sanctity, and dignity, not to mention a fixed and objective point of reference for determining right and wrong—God's Word, the Bible. But if we attempt to remove God from our culture, from our value system, and from our thinking, then we have none of these things, and neither do our children.

My hat is off to authors John H. Hoover and Ronald Oliver, who recognize the relationship between abusive behavior and the absence of spiritual values. In *The Bullying Prevention Handbook,* Hoover and Oliver astutely point out:

> In the end, bullying is related to our ultimate beliefs about the worth of individuals and the way they should be treated. The topics of morality, moral education, ethical reasoning, and spirituality lie at the core of society's problems, including child-on-child aggression. As practitioners think about bullying in the future, it would be beneficial to examine the role that moral development plays in learning to care about one another. Educational leaders may look to the world's religions for answers to the problems of how we interrelate. For example, the Judeo-Christian-Islamic view that man is created in the image of God has enormous

moral implications for how the weakest among us are treated. In the Christian tradition, Jesus stated that whatever was done to the weakest was done to him.[3]

Imagine that! The antidote to our "playground poison" can be found in religious faith and values.

Of course, there are those who would fight this notion tooth and nail, but no matter. We humans can't help proving our need for God most every day, whether we believe in Him or not.

Consider the extremely moving memorial service held in Littleton following the Columbine tragedy. Seventy thousand people attended. The vice president and the governor of Colorado were there, along with other senators, representatives, and dignitaries. Millions more watched on television as Christian artists ministered through music and Franklin Graham delivered a stirring message. Thirteen white doves were released—one for each of the victims. Silver and blue balloons—the Columbine school colors—filled the sky.

With no intention whatsoever of diminishing the solemnity and beauty of that gathering, let me point out something that is going to seem obvious at first: I think it's safe to say that everyone in attendance was in agreement that something horrendously wrong had happened at Columbine High. During the memorial service, people were mourning, crying, lamenting, and sharing a common grief that literally spanned the globe.

But that raises a sticky question: Among the millions of folks who were grieving and agreeing that something wrong had happened, how many, in their normal, everyday lives, believed, talked, taught, and lived by the misguided notion that truth is relative, that there are no moral absolutes, that everyone should decide for him- or herself what is right and wrong? Were there any atheists, evolutionists, or relativists in the crowd?

If the "let's-tear-down-the-rules" crowd is right, and there are no absolutes, no ultimate right and wrong, no transcendent scheme of justice in this universe, then what were those people crying about? According to their world-view, nothing *wrong* happened at Columbine. What happened just *happened*, that's all. Lions eat gazelles, bats eat bugs, and kids shoot kids. What's the big deal?

The truth is, of course, that we all *know* something horrible happened at Columbine. Interesting, isn't it? No matter how adamantly men and women attempt to deny God, we still hint at His existence every time we "get moral" about something.

As Ravi Zacharias explains it (and I'm paraphrasing): In order to say that something is good or evil, you have to have some overall moral scheme, a moral law, by which to figure out what things are good and what things are evil. In order to have a moral law, you have to have a moral law Giver. If there is no moral law Giver, there can be no moral law, and what is, is. You can't make any judgment about it.

And yet we make judgments all the time based on a morality that is, I suggest, beyond ourselves.

Some people may argue that morality is merely a function of culture, that any particular culture develops a morality for the purpose of survival, and that no culture's morality is any better than another's. Then, in almost the same breath, they'll decry Nazi Germany's slaughter of the Jews, the white Europeans' slaughter of the Native Americans, and the burning of widows in some parts of India.

Others might say that our morality has evolved from worse to better: After all, we once had slavery, and now we don't; once women couldn't vote, and now they can; once we trashed the environment, but now we're cleaning it up. But didn't they just say that no particular morality is better than another? By what basis do they fault any agreed-upon morality we may have had in the past? What is, is. What was, was—unless something (or Someone) from somewhere has planted in their hearts a sense of what a better morality would be.

I got a kick out of watching the movie *Contact*, based on the novel by atheist astronomer Carl Sagan. The story deals with the search for intelligent life elsewhere in the universe, and it brings up provocative spiritual and moral issues, sometimes intentionally, and sometimes—I think—by accident. One example is the main character's rationalization for believing that extraterrestrials must be out there someplace: It's such a huge universe that if there's nobody else out there, it would be a terrible waste of space.

If you think about that statement, you quickly realize that it's a moral judgment. It's a good thing to occupy and utilize space; it would be a bad thing to waste all that space. But wait a minute! A moral judgment in an accidental, random, impersonal universe? A waste of space? Who says so? By whose moral standard do we decide what is and isn't a waste of space?

The lead character in *Contact*, played by Jodie Foster, is unfairly bumped from the opportunity to travel to meet the extraterrestrials. It seems her egotistic and ambitious superior has reserved that role for himself. Now we have a moral dilemma because someone has been treated unfairly. But wouldn't it be more consistent with Sagan's atheism to say that the fittest have survived? Funny, isn't it? Avowed atheists and relativists who ardently declare that we should not be encumbered by moral laws still recognize when they have been wronged, and they protest.

We see this same truth wherever two people engage in everyday squabbles and quarrels. Each is convinced of how right he or she is and how wrong the other person is. Imagine a married couple having a fight: Somebody feels he or she has been used, abused, or treated unfairly and the other person had better straighten up. The element of fairness always comes into it.

But who decides what is fair? And where did they ever get the idea that there is such a thing as fairness? Who taught them that?

Even little children know about fairness, and most of them have never taken a philosophy class or majored in theology:

"Johnny, put that cookie away; you'll spoil your supper."

"Well, Susie gets to have one!"

Or . . .

"Sam, it's time for bed."

"But Jimmy gets to stay up!"

Even kids who have not been raised and schooled in theism still know when they're being ripped off. I suggest that every human being is born with a sense of transcendent justice because every human being, whether they acknowledge it or not, is made in the image of God. God is a moral God, a moral law Giver, and He has written His moral law upon the heart of every human being.

When people try to get around this, it makes for a wacky world. They'll often smack into themselves coming the other way in the same sentence:

"It's wrong to impose your morals on others!"

Uh . . . pardon me, but when you tell me it's wrong to do something, aren't you imposing your morals on me?

"There are no absolutes."

That in itself is an absolute statement.

"No one's moral opinion is valid because we all speak from how we've been indoctrinated."

Well, I guess that would apply to you as well, which means what you've just said isn't valid either.

"Everyone should be able to believe whatever they want!"

Then why are you arguing with me?

"Life is meaningless!"

Would you consider that a meaningful statement?

"You can't know anything for sure."

You seem rather sure about that.

"Students, no view of reality is superior to any other."

Then why are you grading our papers?

"You have no right to say truth is external! We all create our own reality!"

Then I'm *your* fault.

"Oh, here we go again, another right-wing fundamentalist making bold assertions of fact!"

Pardon me, but didn't you just make a bold assertion of fact?

"There is no right; there is no wrong."

Is that statement right or wrong?

"You can't tell anybody they're wrong."

Am I wrong in doing so?

See what I mean? A lot of this stuff can get pretty silly, especially for those of us who ascribe to a biblical code of ethics. The simple truth is, because objective, external truth and morality exist, we cannot build an argument against objective, external truth and morality without falling back on objective, external truth and morality!

This is why some folks will pontificate about tolerance and open-mindedness and deny absolute truth or morality—until someone crowds in front of them in the grocery checkout line. They will scoff at such antiquated ideas as honor, virtue, and integrity—until their spouse cheats on them or a burglar ransacks their home. Then, suddenly, they will appeal to transcendent absolutes: "That's not fair! I've been cheated, robbed, violated!"

Oh, yeah? Who says?

God says.

God, the external, objective Giver of truth and morality, says that some things are right and some things are wrong. Furthermore, if you examine His Word, you will find that He can be quite specific about what matters to Him. The prophet Micah reminds us, "He has shown you, O man, what is good; and what does the LORD require of you but to do justly, to love mercy, and to walk humbly with your God?" (Mic. 6:8).

God has created us in His image and put each of us here on earth for specific purposes. That means every human being has intrinsic value, preciousness, meaning, and dignity. Why? Because we matter to Almighty God! Moreover, not only is it wrong for me to devalue another person, to belittle, to bully, or to abuse another person created in God's image, I must do what I can to defend those who cannot defend themselves from such abuse. We really are "family," whether or not we choose to admit it.

The Scripture says, "And He has made from one blood

every nation of men to dwell on all the face of the earth, and has determined their preappointed times and the boundaries of their dwellings, so that they should seek the Lord, in the hope that they might grope for Him and find Him, though He is not far from each one of us; for in Him we live and move and have our being" (Acts 17:26–28).

God says that it is right to respect my fellowman, to love him, to care for him, and to protect him. It is wrong to abuse, tease, taunt, intimidate, hurt, harass, or violate anyone. Taking it a step further, to demean another person is sin. When we indulge in such practices, we are doing so in direct disobedience to our Lord Jesus Christ. Quoting Old Testament passages found in Deuteronomy and Leviticus, Jesus said, "'You shall love the LORD your God with all your heart, with all your soul, with all your strength, and with all your mind,' and your neighbor as yourself" (Luke 10:27). Don't miss that last part. Another time, Jesus stated it plainly: "Whatever you want men to do to you, do also to them, for this is the Law and the Prophets" (Matt. 7:12).

That's not a bad code to live by.

HELP FOR THE WOUNDED

Chapter Seven

Up to this point in the book I've spoken from my own experience, bringing to light a problem many of us share but have seldom talked about. I've suggested that it's a significant problem that should be talked about and dealt with. I've presented one concise argument—there are plenty of others—that we do have a moral foundation from which we can address the problem.[1]

Just to let you know, this and the following chapters are going to have a common thread you'll see cropping up continually: the whole matter of attitude. If we're going to deal with this problem, it's going to require a change in attitude, not just on the part of the bullies, but also the victims, the schools, society, the powers-that-be, you name it.

We've had the wrong attitude about this for too long, and it's time to change it.

Although I'll often be addressing the plight of the young, these chapters aren't just for kids. A wounded spirit has no regard for time or age. Wounded kids grow up to be wounded adults, and wounded adults were most likely wounded kids. Nobody likes being picked on now, nobody liked being picked on as a child, and I've found in my experience and research that *everybody* remembers the hurt and pain associated with being bullied and abused.

When it comes to wounded spirits, three categories of people can relate: those who are wounded, those who wound or have wounded others, and those who fall into both categories—they've been wounded themselves, and they also wound others. This chapter is addressed primarily to the wounded.

When I told a friend of mine that I was writing a book about teasing and peer abuse, he quipped, "Oh, so you're writing a book about *life!*" He had a point there. Quite simply, garbage does happen, and we've all been touched by it in some form at one time or another.

But the questions now are, How do I get over the pain? How do I deal with the wounds inside me? What can I do about the hurtful situation I'm in right now?

Well, let me share some helpful observations and pearls of wisdom with you.

First of all, *if you're wounded, you're not alone.*

Hang on. Before you shrug this little truism off as just another trite phrase or cutesy emotional Band-Aid, please consider how *normal* it makes you.

People come in all shapes and sizes, with all kinds of different abilities *and* disabilities—some are slim, some are fat; others are handsome, ugly, inferior, strong, weak, dorky, or nerdy—but God made us all, so that makes every one of us special, despite our shortcomings. *All* of us have something, or lack something, that potentially can make us a target for abuse.

But that doesn't mean there's something "wrong" with you. Everybody has something they wish they could change about themselves. If you have discovered some "defect" in yourself, welcome to the human race. Regardless of your failures, foibles, or defeats, you're just as human (and just as precious) as anybody else. You're a member.

Think you're ugly? You're a member.

Do you have cystic hygroma, cerebral palsy, muscular dystrophy, or polio? You're a member.

Do you have freckles? Are you too tall, too skinny, too much . . . *anything?* You're a member.

Do you feel left out simply because you're smart? You're a member.

Do you feel left out because you're mentally or physically challenged? You're a member.

Have you ever been raped? Molested? You're still a member.

All of us, with all our wrinkles, shortcomings, bumblings, and imperfections, are God's creation. We're all precious in His sight and should be precious to one another—and don't let anyone tell you otherwise, not even you.

And how about this startling revelation: *It wasn't (isn't) your fault.*

One of the most common mistakes made by victims of abuse is to think that for some reason the abuse was justified, that they actually deserved it. Nothing could be farther from the truth!

This came as a real lightning bolt for me while I was working on this book. As I reluctantly trudged back through my dark, difficult memories and encountered the faces and voices of my abusers once again, I finally saw them for what they were: bullies, not to be feared, but to be pitied. Suddenly it dawned on me: *It wasn't my fault!* What those kids did to me had nothing to do with me. There was never anything so terribly wrong with me that other people had no choice but to be irresistibly, uncontrollably compelled to abuse me. Yes, I was a sinner who needed to be saved by God's grace, but I was not some freak of nature who merited the disdain with which I was treated. It wasn't my problem; it was theirs!

I guess it's just one of those quirky, human tendencies: We tend to believe what others say about us and to view ourselves through their eyes. The moment we get around other people, we start wondering, *Am I okay? Are they going to like me? Will they accept me?* If we manage to make a good impression and everybody seems to like us, we usually go home feeling pretty good about ourselves.

On the other hand, if we stumble or make a blunder, if somebody in the room brands us as the fool or the whole gang of them ignores us entirely, it's quite easy to go home believing we are what they have made us out to be.

When I was in junior high, I was very small for my age. That shouldn't have been a problem, but of course there were those in my class who made it a problem, as if there were something wrong with *me* for being small. Well, I believed it. After all, it was *my* smallness. *I* was the one who brought it to school with me. If I was being heckled, bullied, and thrown around, it was because I deserved it. If I'd just had the common sense to be bigger before coming to school, the other kids would have had no choice but to accept me. No one has the right to be small. I should have known that.

Weird, isn't it? For some reason we focus on ourselves as the cause of the abuse, as if our tormentors have no choice (or responsibility) in the matter, and we buy into their program of lies and humiliation. Before long, we begin thinking, *I'm no good. I'm dumb. I'm a fool. I'm a shrimp. I'm a klutz. That's what the bullies say, so it has to be true!*

Tragically, we can go through the rest of our lives believing those lies. Even as adults, we shy from new relationships, we're afraid of taking risks or being wrong, we get hurt easily, we fumble in conversations, we huddle in a corner at gatherings, and we keep kicking ourselves over every little mistake, because we've been conditioned to believe that *we, of all people, don't have the right to be imperfect.*

Face it. You're not perfect, and that's okay! It's *okay!* Nobody's perfect, and if anybody ever made an issue of it, *they* were the ones in the wrong, not you.

To put it simply, what happened to you shouldn't have happened. What was said about you shouldn't have been said, and what was done to you shouldn't have been done. Nobody deserves to be abused.

So please don't blame yourself.

Now, here's where a change of attitude comes into play, because the third important observation is, *you don't have to put up with it.* You really don't.

And as for whoever is in charge of the school environment, the workplace, the home, or the street, *they shouldn't expect you to.*

Looking back, one of the greatest mysteries of my life is why I did put up with it for so long. I can only explain it this way: I thought I had to. Most of the abuse I endured happened at school. There was no way I could avoid it. After all, it was *school*. While transferring to another school district, attending private school, or homeschooling may be viable options for some families today, these were not options for my family. I was stuck in that one school. My parents made me go. The teachers made me sit at my desk. I was a good kid trying to be obedient. No one ever told me, "Frank, you're in school to learn, not to be picked on and tormented. Teasing and abuse are not part of the package, and we won't allow it. We care about you, so if anyone causes you trouble, let us know."

Here comes that word again: *attitude.* In my case, parents and teachers simply weren't dealing with abuse—if they *were*, it sure wasn't on *my* planet. As far as I, the timid, obedient, little kid, could see or understand, my parents said I had to be there, the teachers implied through inaction that it was okay for me to be tormented, and the unwritten, anti-snitching law among the kids warned me that I dare not tell anybody. I resigned myself to enduring the abusive behavior of the bullies in my life for most of my junior-high and high-school education.

Attitude, attitude, ATTITUDE! We must change our attitudes regarding this sort of behavior. Those in authority need to care, and you should expect them to care. It matters to you, and it should matter to them. Forget about that foolish, childhood code of silence: Speak up. Let someone know what's going on, and ask them—yes, *expect* them—to do something about it. If you're a kid under someone's legal authority, you still have rights as a human being. You deserve to be regarded as God's unique, special creation—because you are!

The same holds true for bullying on the job. If you are being physically, verbally, or emotionally abused at work, speak to your supervisor, and if I may suggest it, make it a matter of productivity and money. If fellow workers are bullying you, help the supervisor to understand that it's keeping you from doing your job effectively, and, therefore, it's affecting the smooth operation of the department. Furthermore, it's going to affect the bottom line. The supervisor isn't going to make his numbers because the crew isn't working well as a team, and it's going to be his rear end in the ringer. Any boss, from supervisor to CEO, wants the business to run smoothly and therefore shouldn't stand for such disruptions.

Speak up. You really don't have to tolerate the abuse any longer.

So by now you should be ready to *do something!*

Yes, it's going to take the right attitude on the part of the boss, the teacher, the parent, the principal, or whoever is responsible for the school or work environment. They have to care. They have to be approachable. But you may have to take the first step, at least be ready to respond when you see an opportunity to bring the abuse to the attention of the proper authorities.

For example . . .

It occurred to me the other day that most gym teachers are athletes or former athletes. They were athletes in high school and in college, they naturally hang around other athletes, and now they're at the center of the athletic program at the school. Consequently, some of these men and women haven't a clue what it's like to be a nonathlete, and their physical education program reflects that: The winners get the points, and the losers fall through the cracks; the athletes enjoy the game, and the nonathletes just want to get out of there.

Despite my small stature as a boy, I always enjoyed physical activity and physical challenges. To this day, I exercise, I work out, I enjoy physical labor, and I relish a brisk walk on the logging trails that run through the mountains around our home. I run around and enjoy life outdoors as much as anybody. I'm just not an athlete. I happen to think that tending a garden for all to enjoy, fixing a machine that performs useful labor, and writing books that minister to millions carry more importance for me than putting on little shorts and passing a bouncing, spherical object through a metal hoop more often than the other guy.

For a nonathletic kid, who is already at the bottom of the food chain at most schools, a big, muscular, gruff-voiced, suck-it-up gym teacher with a tight T-shirt and a whistle around his thick neck is the last person on earth he's going to approach about a bullying problem. At the same time, does the gym teacher really know how it feels to be in a world where he has never, and will never, really fit? How are the two going to relate?

I guess that's why I never expected much compassion or mercy from my gym teachers. Most of my P.E.

teachers didn't seem to care how I felt; they just yelled at me and blew their whistles. But all that changed when one man, a gym teacher, took the time—a brief moment, actually—to care.

Bullying is a remarkable phenomenon, the way it follows you. In junior high school, I attracted specific people who became my self-appointed tormentors, and that went on for the full three years. When I started high school, I was with a whole new crowd of classmates, and yet the bullying picked up right where it left off. It didn't miss a beat. You'd think the junior-high bullies had held a tie-in meeting with the high-school bullies: "Okay, be looking for Peretti. This is what we've done to him so far . . ."

Remember the young boy in chapter 1? That kind of stuff happened to me all through junior high and all through my sophomore year in high school until suddenly, even astonishingly, everything changed. I don't remember the exact times and dates, but I do remember the chain of events. It started one day when I was running an errand for my mom.

The Graham Street Grocery was a little neighborhood grocery store less than a block from our house. We had an account there, and Mom often sent me to pick up small items: a loaf of bread, milk, ice cream, whatever. A young man from my high school got an after-school job there, and though I'd never done him wrong and he hardly knew me, he became my enemy. I guess, to him, it was the cool thing to do.

On this particular day, I was minding my own business, just going up and down those short little aisles and picking up items on my grocery list, when my nemesis met me toward the back of the store, out of his boss's earshot.

"Whatcha doin', Peretti?"

"Oh, just buying some stuff."

"What do you need?"

I looked at my list. "I need to get some deodorant."

"Which kind?"

You know deodorants. There are so many different brands, they can fill a whole shelf. "Well, we usually use this one. . . ."

He grabbed a can off the shelf. "This one?"

I thought he was going to hand it to me. "Yeah."

Suddenly, without provocation, he popped the cap off and sprayed the deodorant directly in my face! I forget what he said as he did it, but it wasn't kind.

That stuff stings! My eyes were watering, and tears streamed down my face. I was shocked and incredulous. I just couldn't believe a guy waiting on me in a grocery store would do that to me! I quickly made my way to the checkout counter, rubbing my eyes and wiping my nose. I could hardly see as I signed our tab and made a hasty exit from the store.

You may well ask why I didn't report the incident to Vern, the man who owned the store. Looking back, I can only wonder the same. It must have had something to do with the devious power of that old maxim that has protected bullies for generations: You don't snitch.

I stumbled out of the store and around the corner, my grocery bag in my arm, and then . . . it's hard to describe . . . I was like a hunted animal who has been shot but still runs several yards before collapsing from loss of blood. I made it around the corner, but that's as far as I could go before something just broke inside me. I dropped to the curb, weeping, devastated, despondent. I'd come to the end.

"Oh, dear Lord," I prayed, still wiping the sting out of my eyes. "Please . . . I just can't take it anymore." It felt just a little strange to be praying such a thing because, in my mind, I still linked God with all the other authorities in my life. They were all making me go through this, and so was He. As I prayed, I was actually pleading for mercy. "Please, God; please don't do this to me anymore. Don't make me go back there. Have mercy, dear Lord. I haven't fought back; I haven't snitched; I've turned the other cheek. Haven't I suffered enough?"

I'm reminded of God's response to Moses: "Surely I have heard the cry of My people in Egypt." They'd been crying to Him for the better part of four hundred years! But, at last, it was God's time to answer.

And, after so, so, long, God answered me.

A few days later, I faithfully and obediently stepped through the big, ominous door for another hour of Boy's Hell. My despair must have been showing. One of the teachers paused—he actually took just a moment—and spoke quietly to me. "How you doing? You feeling okay?"

I looked back at him in disbelief. Somebody in authority was actually asking about me, and he seemed genuinely concerned! He wasn't even *my* teacher. He had other classes, other coaching duties, but he was there, and he had noticed that I was looking ill. This was so unexpected, so unusual, I didn't know what to say, or whether I should say anything at all. I was afraid of those gruff P.E. teachers. Not one of them had ever, *ever* before asked me how I felt.

I muttered some look-down-at-the-floor answer, just as an insecure boy my age might do, and he went on about his business.

But the gentle tone of his voice did something to me: It gave me just the tiniest, years-in-coming ray of hope, something I'd never felt before. Somebody really wanted to know how I was doing? Somebody might really listen? I grabbed onto that hope for all I was worth, and then, suddenly, an idea came to me. I didn't think I could express myself orally to a teacher who still intimidated me, but by now, I knew I could write. I decided to write my gym teacher a letter. I would tell him everything. Maybe things *could* change.

The first chance I got—study hall, I think it was—I started drafting a letter. I can vividly remember sitting in the quiet of the library on the third floor of Cleveland High School in Seattle, addressing a letter to Mr. Sampson, my P.E. teacher. First of all, I let him know that it was the kind inquiry of his colleague that prompted my letter, and then I began. I wrote that whole period. I wrote during lunch. I wrote during any opportunity I could find the rest of the day. I chronicled everything I could remember: all the insults, the abuse, the assaults, the humiliations, everything over the past several years. The letter filled several pages, handwritten in blue ink, single-spaced, both sides of the paper. That afternoon, before leaving for home, I went into the school office and slipped it into Mr. Sampson's mailbox.

Gym class was every other day, so he had a day to read my letter before I had to face him again. By the time I came through that door the next time, Mr. Sampson was looking for me. "Peretti. Hold up a second," he called from inside his locker-room office.

Well, Mr. Sampson had obviously read my letter. Now what? He didn't seem very angry. Who else had seen that letter? What if he wanted to read the letter in front of the other guys in the locker room? *Oh, Lord, this is it. Please don't let me down.*

I stood there against the wall, nervous, schoolbooks in my hand, a stream of boys passing before me on their way to the locker room. From my vantage point, I could see through the office door. Mr. Sampson was talking on the phone, and I just barely made out the words, "You want to see him now?"

See who? Me? Who wanted to see me?

He hung up the phone, filled out a hall pass, and sent me to the school office to see the counselor, Mr. Eisenbrey. I'd always been afraid of Mr. Sampson, and I'd always been afraid of Mr. Eisenbrey, but that day changed everything. Those guys had compassion on me; they really did care.

Mr. Eisenbrey had reviewed my letter and was actually

warm and cheerful as he helped me rework my class schedule, excusing me from P.E. for the remainder of the school year. "We'll just call it a medical excuse," he said, scribbling some notes on a piece of paper. He signed me off and sent me back to Mr. Sampson so he could sign the forms too.

Mr. Sampson didn't say anything as he filled out the form on his ever-present clipboard. He just smiled at me.

When he handed me my class transfer, my *parole*, I told him, "If you were a girl, I'd kiss you!"

"You're welcome," was all he said.

I went out that door and never saw the inside of that locker room again.

I can't overstate the pivotal nature of that day in my life. From that moment onward, everything was so different. I could enjoy school. I could get excited about being a Cleveland Eagle. I bought a red-and-white pennant and put it on my bedroom wall. I donned my red-and-white Cleveland beanie, went to the football games, and felt great about my school. I got involved in school drama productions—where I could actually use some of the gifts God had given me—and I *burst* out of my shell, making lots of new friends, and just going nuts being creative. For the first time in my life, I began to enjoy being *me!*

So, I said all that to say this: I hope someone in your

school, or workplace, or *wherever*—maybe someone you don't even suspect would be kind—will be kind to you. I hope they will have the caring, compassionate attitude that is necessary to bring about a change. I hope you will speak to that person, or do as I did and write a letter. Talk about it. I understand that the custom, the expectation, the legacy of our culture up to this point has been to keep it to yourself. Listen, if you think you need some kind of permission to bring up the subject and deal with it, *I give you that permission*. You needn't hide behind the facade of having it all together any longer. Get help! Talk to someone who cares—and don't go another day carrying the burden alone.

If possible, *become a one-to-one peacemaker*.

Granted, some bullies are not the reasonable type. They pick on you because they are warped and maladjusted. For any number of reasons—a dysfunctional family, low self-esteem, low achievement, too much lead in their drinking water, or some other malady, real or imagined—they think they have to push their weight around in order to feel better about themselves. Unless they have a major turnaround in their lives, they'll either wind up in prison or become DMV license examiners.

But for the most part, bullies are human beings just like

you and me, and sometimes they can be reached with a little bit of honesty and friendship—if you can talk with them one-on-one. I've known a few bullies who were actually very intelligent A students, who went on to be successful adults. Oftentimes, the reason they allowed themselves to become cruel and insensitive was because of the crowd; it was the "cool" thing to do.

Consider going to that person and having a private discussion with him, away from his friends. Be sincere, kind, and honest, and lay the issues on the table: You would rather be friends than enemies, and what he is doing is hurtful to you. If you have done something to offend him, apologize and make it right. If you've done nothing to offend him, ask him why he wants to hurt you.

Attempt to get to know the person who has been bullying you. In nine cases out of ten, the bully doesn't even know the person he's picking on. If he really knew the victim as a person instead of as a punching bag, he might ease up. And who knows? You could end up being friends.

Perhaps you and the bully have a mutual friend or acquaintance to whom you could appeal for help. I remember sitting at lunch with a friend named Paul in junior high school, and I started sharing my problems with him.

"Who's picking on you?" he asked.

I didn't have any trouble thinking of a name. I could even point the guy out, sitting across the lunchroom. "He's really mean. He just won't leave me alone."

Paul was astonished. *"Neil? Are you sure?"*

I told Paul what Neil had been doing to me in the locker room during gym class, and Paul shook his head, perplexed. He was genuinely surprised and dismayed to hear about the way Neil had been treating me. "But Neil's a nice guy."

"Well, he sure isn't nice to me."

The next time I encountered Neil in the locker room, he was friendly. He complimented the sweater I was wearing. He never badgered, bullied, or bothered me again.

It's easy to figure out what happened behind the scenes. Paul went to Neil and told him, "Hey, Frank's a decent guy. He's a friend of mine. You don't want to pick on him."

Attitude. Sometimes a bully is a "nice guy," too, who just needs to be awakened to the fact that his victim is a person, maybe even a likable person. Once confronted, if he has the moral fiber and some common decency, he'll change his behavior.

Certainly, one of the most important steps toward healing of a wounded spirit is to *forgive*. It can be tough to do, but if you don't forgive those individuals who have hurt you in the past, bitterness will eat you alive and rob you of a peaceful future. You'll be granting the bullies the power to take away your happiness and to make you feel rotten when *they aren't even there!* Let it go. God will give you the grace you need, if you will make the conscious choice to forgive. Throw off those chains of bitterness and resentment that have been constraining you for so long, and get on with your life.

Finally, take heart: A *wounded spirit need not be permanent.* Please understand: It's never too late to start doing the right thing; it's never too late to change for the better. Especially if you're young, life as you know it right now is not fixed in cement. As we grow, we change, our circumstances change, and we find ourselves in different places and situations. Through it all, God has a purpose and a plan for your life. He made you the way you are for a reason, and don't worry, you are going to find out what it is. You're going to be okay.

When I was a kid, I felt terrible about myself. My self-image was in the toilet because I couldn't throw or catch a football, I couldn't run very fast, and I was considered small and frail for my age. Today, I'm an adult; I'm an author and a public speaker, I play in a talented acoustic band, I fly my own plane, I have a lovely wife, and a comfortable home tucked in the woods on the side of a mountain, and frankly, I don't cry too much about the fact that I still can't throw or catch a football.

Every once in a while, as I sit back in our living room, looking out the large picture windows and admiring the majestic grandeur and beauty of the snowcapped mountains, I wonder how many of those big, brutal jocks I once knew are now limping from old sports injuries. I can't help but smile as I picture some of those big lugs reporting to a smaller-framed boss who has a better-developed brain and a much bigger office! As Bill Gates has said, "Don't pick on the nerds. You'll probably end up working for one."

God does have a way of evening things out.

Just follow His way. Live your life well, according to His principles. He'll take care of the rest.

FOR THOSE
WHO WOUND

Chapter Eight

Okay, it's time to confess; I need to come clean on some things. Up until now, I've been writing mostly from the perspective of the victim, which puts me in a safe place. I can be the sweet, innocent hero of the story, while all the other characters are the bad guys. Well, it was nice while it lasted, but in real life there is always another side to the story. Whether we regard ourselves as bully or victim, the Bible is quite correct when it tells us that "all have sinned and fall short of the glory of God" (Rom. 3:23). Truth be told, bully or victim, we're all made of the same stuff. We're all capable of the same things.

Have I ever wounded anyone? Yes, I'm sorry to say that I have. I never considered myself the bullying type—with the small-framed body I had, badgering or pushing other people around physically wasn't much of an option for me—but there were times when I could say mean things. I could spread malicious gossip, cut people down with insults, or go along with the crowd by ostracizing someone. It's so easy to do, and it amazes me how a victim, who knows how it feels, can still be insensitive to the feelings of others. Know what I'm talking about?

So . . . ouch! This could get uncomfortable, but let's be honest with ourselves and allow God to change us as we work through this chapter together. Most of us have been wounded by other people, some of us have *wounded* others, and some of us have not only been wounded, but for whatever reason, don't get a clue, and go on to wound others!

As with most other aspects of sin, wounding other people comes naturally. We don't feel the pain as we dish it out, so—here it comes again—we go along with the attitude that says, "It's no big deal. All my friends are picking on so-and-so, and I want to be accepted as one of the group. I want them to like me, and I want to be like them. Everybody does it. It's the thing to do."

We know better, yet somehow this type of abusive behavior falls outside our definition of *sin*.

So let's rethink that definition. Based on what the Bible, or even your God-given conscience, tells you, wouldn't you say it's wrong to hurt, injure, or abuse another human being? Is it wrong to mock, tease, or bully people, hurting them, violating their personhood, and destroying their dignity?

Need I say more?

But even Christians wound.

For example, let's talk about all those squeaky clean, born-again students attending Christian colleges. Hey, they know their Bibles. They worship and pray at all the chapel services. They're out to spread the good news of Jesus Christ and change their world for the glory of God.

And yet, when you get a chance to observe the social fabric on campus, it's sad to discover things haven't changed much since junior and senior high school. The upperclassmen—yes, those fine men and women who claim to be followers of Christ—find it easy to put the underclassmen in their place. The jocks laugh and needle the nonathletes; the girls establish their social cliques and close the door to outsiders. Derogatory names and rumors float around freely. The very mention of certain names produces snickers among the elite in the student lounge.

On any college campus, it's normal to find a particular

type of young male who takes great pride in his physical prowess and virility but seems stunted when it comes to character. He shoots baskets to show the world he can toss a ball through a hoop but doesn't help the kid who would like to learn; he presses iron to show the world how much weight he can lift but never thinks of coaching anyone else; he flexes his muscles to show the world he has bulging biceps and disrespects anyone who doesn't.

I encountered a young man of this description some time ago, and he was the quintessential bullying jock. I'd never before seen someone purposely wearing a tight muscle shirt and flexing his muscles at everybody. I thought only professional wrestlers on television did that! This guy could even make his neck bigger than his head, and he was really proud of that.

Unfortunately, along with all those muscles came an attitude. This fellow had the idea that his finely chiseled, powerful physique entitled him to be the king in any group, and he was more than willing to use his brawn to get that point across. I saw him grab a smaller guy, lift him off his feet, and pin him against the wall, purely to intimidate him. Now mind you, these were not children in junior high or youths in high school; this incident took place among young men at a Christian college! I must have been naive at the time, because it shocked me so severely that I didn't say a word.

In retrospect, I think about the film A *Few Good Men,* featuring Tom Cruise, Demi Moore, and Kevin Pollak. Jack Nicholson plays Colonel Jessup, the bad guy. Don't take your kids to see it — the language gets a little salty — but that movie has powerful moral lessons that apply here. The story involves two marines, stationed at the Guantanamo military base in Cuba, who are ordered by their superior officer to carry out a "code red" on a fellow marine. A "code red" is an unofficial, even illegal form of discipline that can take the form of a beating, hazing, head shaving, or any other humiliation, and the purpose is to "encourage" a foul-up to get his act together. The foul-up in this case is a weakling named Willie who, for undetected but legitimate medical reasons, is having trouble running, breathing, and keeping up with the other soldiers in the stifling Cuban heat. Unfortunately, as Willie's "encouragers" try to beat him into shape, Willie's medical condition brings about his death, and the two marines are put on trial for murder.

Thus arise some great moral issues and some great quotes.

The defendants' lawyers, played by Tom Cruise, Demi Moore, and Kevin Pollak, work together as a team even though they are divided regarding the marines' innocence. Tom Cruise thinks the two marines are innocent because they were following orders, but Kevin Pollak feels that is no excuse: "I believe every word of their story—and I think they ought to go to jail for the rest of their lives."

It is no secret that Pollak's character has no sympathy for two tough marines who, even though following orders, killed a fellow marine. When Moore's character asks him, "Why do you hate them so much?" Pollak responds, "They beat up on a weakling! That's all they did, all right? The rest of this is just smoke-filled, coffeehouse crap! They tortured and tormented a weaker kid! They didn't like him, so they killed him, and why? 'Cause he couldn't run very fast!"

The issue leaps out from the movie screen: the strong preying upon the weak.

But then, within seconds, the other side of the issue, the *answer* to the issue, also leaps from the screen when Pollak asks Moore, "Why do you *like* them so much?" and she responds, "Because they stand on the wall, and they say, 'Nothing's going to hurt you tonight, not on my watch.'"

The strong *protecting* the weak. Yes!

As the trial ends, the marines are acquitted of murder, but they are convicted of conduct unbecoming a marine and are sentenced to be dishonorably discharged from the

Marine Corps. The younger marine protests, "I don't understand. Colonel Jessup said he ordered the code red. What did we do wrong? We did nothing wrong!"

But the older, wiser marine responds, "Yeah, we did. We were supposed to fight for people who couldn't fight for themselves. We were supposed to fight for Willie."

By this point in the movie, I get tearful. Yes. This is the answer. This is what it's all about. The filmmakers have addressed something that we who spend most of our lives in safe Christian confines rarely confront: Namely, the depth of a person's character is not measured by his or her physical strength, but by the depth of his or her nobility. How do we treat those who are weaker?

Have you ever replayed an incident in your mind the way you'd like it to have happened? Here's my replay of that scene with Mr. Muscles and his victim on the Christian college campus:

I'd step up to that big lug, look him right in the eyes (when you're a white-bearded wise guy pushing fifty years of age, you can do stuff like that), and I'd ask him, "Just what in the world do you think you're doing? You unhand him immediately!"

And then I'd grab a telephone—in my mental replay, a phone is always handy—and tell that musclehead, "See this phone in my hand? Young man, you have a choice. Either you sit down and listen to a lecture, or I dial the police and file a criminal complaint against you for assault. Which will it be?"

He agrees to the lecture, so there *are* some brains buried under there somewhere. Having his undivided attention, I tell him, "It's time you seriously considered why God gave you all that strength and physical superiority. It wasn't so you could abuse, oppress, and violate those who aren't as strong as you are. He gave you that strength so you could *defend and protect* those who are weaker, fight for those who can't fight for themselves, and stand between the defenseless and anyone or anything that might harm them. Remember the biblical cities with the wall around them, and how guardians would stand on that wall to protect the people inside the city? That's what God has called you to do.

"*Any* gift you receive from God is not for yourself, but for others. The strong are strong to protect the weak; those with abundance are blessed so they can help the needy; the smart and the wise are gifted to help the befuddled and foolish.

"The measure of a man is not his strength; it is the depth of his nobility. The measure of any person is how he or she treats those who are less gifted, less intelligent, and less able. The measure of a Christian is how willing he or she is to reach down and help those who are less fortunate—to take the strength and advantage they have to help those who have not.

"God has gifted you with strength. You should thank Him for that privilege by standing on that wall and telling others, 'Don't worry. Nobody's gonna hurt you, not on my watch.'"

In my best replays, the now former bully and his victim become best friends and both go out to change the world for Christ . . . hey, it could happen!

On a recent book tour, I stopped in at a major Chicago newspaper to be interviewed by their religion editor, a pleasant gentleman with whom I immediately felt comfortable. We discussed my book *The Visitation* for a while, going through the obligatory questions and answers, and then, perhaps because he walked with the aid of crutches, we got on the subject of abuse, teasing, and harassment. He shared with me how, when he was growing up, the other kids gave him no end of teasing and harassment because of his polio.

"You still feel it, don't you?" I asked him.

He nodded. "Oh, yes." He was in his sixties.

I was even more impressed with the reporter when he

told me about his two sons. Both of them are big, strong fellows, and throughout their childhood, he taught them to put their strength to use in standing up for the weak and defending those who cannot defend themselves. Because of their father's experience with polio, they grew up with a unique sensitivity regarding their own gifts and the needs of others. The reporter raised his sons to be protectors, rather than bullies. Now that's the way things ought to be.

I told you that I never forgot the names and the faces of those who hurt me. There's one other name and one other face I will remember all my life, but for the opposite reason. I won't give you his full name, but his first name was John. It was a classic situation, commonplace and sadly predictable: I was a pitiful creature in my gym class, and some character with a truckload of dysfunction in his life came after me. Well, John happened to be there, and he stepped in. He had a size advantage, he was strong, and he was quite persuasive. With an assertive presence and a calm voice, he convinced Mr. Dysfunction that there were better things to do and better places to be, and Mr. D bought his argument. I don't recall that Mr. D ever bothered me again.

More than thirty years later, I still remember John, and

I pray for him whenever I think of that moment. He came between me and harm. He stood on that wall. I think he's the only one who ever did.

We need more people like John in this world, and you may be that kind of person, or at least somebody who can become one. Perhaps, up to this point, you've been a teaser, a source of pain rather than a source of comfort. You can change all that. All it takes is a decision, a pivotal moment when you decide you will put a stop to the bullying and abuse and begin treating everyone who passes your way as a priceless, precious, miraculous creation of God, a person for whom Jesus Christ bled and died, a person who matters to God just as much as you do.

The first step is to wake up to what you've done and what you may still be doing. Admit your sins honestly before God, ask Him for forgiveness, and then declare that from this day forward, with God's help, your bullying and malicious teasing days are over. You will begin to treat every person as valuable, even sacred.

Grownup, do you remember being a teaser and abuser when you were in school? As you entered adult life, did you ever stop? Have you ever apologized to those people you hurt? Have you ever let go of those childish ways, or have you merely found new faces and bodies to demean?

Now is the time to break with the past and start afresh. Right now, right where you are, can you remember the people you've tormented?

I can tell you with great certainty that *they* remember *you*. It's a sobering thought. I know how abuse in my youth hurt me deeply and still affects me today, and I've met several folks who can relate to my experience because they've suffered similarly.

But now flip it around: How many folks out there in the world, most of them my age, are still living with the effects of the teasing *I* dished out at *them?* How many people are still wounded because of what you or I did to them?

I can see the faces of some of the people I hurt. How about you? How many faces can *you* count?

Young person, are you inflicting wounds on others? What kind of memories do you want to live with? Will you really be proud of yourself for teasing that person who is weaker than you are in some way? Is your self-esteem so low that you must step on somebody else to feel good about yourself? How do you want people to remember you—as a lowlife bully who wallowed in self-delusion, or as a courageous friend who stood nobly on the wall, who stood up for what was right, and who defended those who could not defend themselves? These tough questions need honest answers.

Second, you need to go to God for cleansing. If we confess our sins—sure, you know the rest—He'll forgive us and cleanse us from all unrighteousness (see 1 John 1:9). But we need to take it a step further. Here's what I've done: I've gone to the Lord in prayer and asked Him to bring to my mind the folks I've hurt. Then I've apologized to the Lord, in prayer, and I've apologized to them, asking God to grant each person the grace to forgive me and to help them find healing in their lives.

Third, just as I have done, ask God to change your heart and make you like Jesus. Consider how Scripture describes Him in Matthew 12:20: "A battered reed He will not break off, and a smoldering wick He will not put out" (NASB). Jesus never took cruel advantage of anyone's disadvantage. The bruised, He helped. The weak and dying, He renewed. That's what I want to do; that's how I want to be.

Fourth, you might consider a new way of thanking God for whatever advantages He has given you: your physical strength, your intelligence, your sense of humor, your reputation, that position on the cheerleading squad or the football team, or the opened doors of opportunity at your job.

You can thank Him by putting your gift into service on behalf of others. You can become, in your own way, the guardian who stands on the wall and says to those who are weaker, smaller, and less advantaged, "Don't you worry. Nobody's going to hurt you, not on my watch."

To borrow from Shakespeare, it's time to "grace this latter age with noble deeds." Rather than flaunting our gifts, our success, our popularity, our privilege, we should realize that it's time to be noble and consider those gifts for what they are: our means, our resources by which we are to help others.

Now it's my turn.

Wounding can be so easy, and the line between playful teasing and thoughtless tormenting can become dangerously blurred. I could try to rationalize that my teasing was the playful variety, but as I look back on it, I have to admit that some of the kids I teased were not laughing along.

It's so easy not to think about what you're doing as you join with others in selecting that one person who doesn't quite fit. It's so easy to join in the mockery and the gossip rather than come to that person's defense.

I can still see the faces and remember the names of those who tormented me. But I can also remember some of the names and faces of young men and women toward whom I was less than a friend. I have to wonder how they feel about what I and others said about them and how that may have affected the course of their lives.

May I go on record?

Friend, if you remember Frank Peretti teasing you or hurting you in any way, I want to say I'm sorry. Sure, I've thought about it at other times, but the writing of this book has brought me face to face with my own culpability, and I repent and apologize. There were words that came from my mouth that I wish I could recapture and banish forever. There were moments when I wasn't there for you and should have been. There were times I sided against you, when I knew that side was in the wrong.

Friend, you didn't deserve it. Please forgive me, and may God grant you grace to forgive any others who have hurt you as I did. May you find freedom from pain and bitterness and healing as we grow together in God's unconditional love.

THINGS COULD
BE DIFFERENT

Chapter Nine

A separate room had been prepared for the boys. It was cold and impersonal, like a prison; the echoing, concrete walls had been painted dirty beige, then marred and chipped over the years, then painted again. The walls were bare except for posted rules, warnings, and advisories, and the only windows were high against the ceiling, caged behind iron grillwork thickly wrapped in paint, rust, and more paint. The air was dank, tainted with the odors of steam, sweat, and skin. Years of rust and sediment from the dripping showerheads and armies of bare, wet feet had marbled the floor with streaks and patches of reddish brown.

The boy was nervous and afraid on his first day through

that big door. He was small, nonathletic, and timid. He'd never been in this place, or anywhere like this place, before. Though he excelled in academics and felt comfortable in most any classroom, to him this was a different, threatening world, a world of muscles, workouts, sports, and sweat. As he lined up along the lockers with the other boys his age, he could see some of them sizing him up. "Hi, wimp," one of them said, a sneer curling his lip.

"Hey!" It was the teacher's assistant, a few grades older, overseeing the lineup. He went over to the kid who'd spoken and got right in his face. "You don't do that in here."

The name-caller was about to come back with something, but a shrill whistle made him jump.

It was the gym teacher, Mr. Akers, entering the locker room like an officer coming on deck. "All right, silence! Everybody, eyes forward, straight and at attention!"

He got immediate compliance, and with good enough reason. This guy was built like a tank, and his expression made it clear he was not to be trifled with. He carried a clipboard. He had a whistle around his neck. He wore a tight T-shirt. He carried a baseball bat planed flat, the perfect implement for administering swats.

"Mr. Lane will take the roll."

The teacher's assistant, Bruce Lane, called out the names

of the students and checked them off as they answered, "Here." All through the roll call, Mr. Akers stood there with his clipboard and his swatter, studying every face.

When the roll call ended, he said, "At ease. Have a seat on the benches, fellows. Make room over there. Let's go."

They sat down facing him. He leaned against the wall, one foot flat on the wall behind him so that his knee extended, forming a desk for his clipboard. "Gentlemen, welcome to my class. On your class schedule you see this hour designated as '*Physical* Education,' but let me assure you, this class will involve more than just your bodies. Any education worthy of the name doesn't just build the body or the mind; it also builds character. So you'll need more than a strong body and athletic skill to excel in this class— sorry to disappoint some of you. You'll need to apply your minds and your spirits as well.

"It is our hope that you'll leave here healthier and more physically fit than when you first came in. But it is also our hope that you'll leave here having improved the personal qualities you'll need in every other area of your lives: discipline, perseverance, the ability and willingness to work as a team, and a sportsmanlike attitude.

"If you enjoy competition, I encourage you to turn out for the basketball, baseball, football, tennis, or soccer teams.

I assure you, in those programs you will have every opportunity to one-up the guy on the opposing team and show everybody what a great athlete you are. In this class, the only person you'll be competing against is yourself. We're going to help you set reasonable goals for improving your fitness, strength, and stamina, and then we're going to do all we can to help you achieve those goals.

"Now as you look around the room, you'll notice that human beings come in all sizes and shapes, all different levels of strength and ability. I want to emphasize that none of that matters here. Regardless of your size or physical maturity, each and every one of you deserves the chance to feel proud of what you can accomplish. That's why we're going to be a team. We're going to think as a team, act as a team, and learn as a team. We expect you to help each other out, to cheer for each other, to do all you can to help your teammates rise to the top of their potential."

Mr. Akers toyed with the ominous, flattened baseball bat as he looked every boy in the eye. "That's why we do not tolerate bullies in this class. We do not allow teasing, harassment, put-downs, one-upmanship, or the mistreatment of any teammate by another." He paused to let that sink in, and then added, "You will maintain sportsmanlike conduct at all times, showing courtesy and respect for your teammates."

The boy had come into this class feeling timid and afraid, but by the time Mr. Akers had finished his orientation remarks, he could see he had an advocate if he ever needed one. He was starting to feel safe.

In the weeks that followed, Mr. Akers and his assistants worked with each class member, planning out a physical fitness program appropriate to each boy's capability. Because of his small stature and clumsiness, the boy had always been intimidated by any sport that threw him among bodies bigger than he was. The workout room with its treadmill, stair stepper, and weight machine appealed to him, because he could work on his own, without embarrassment.

"Just remember," Mr. Akers told him, "you're not here to be like somebody else. You're here to improve yourself and to help the others do the same."

With encouragement from Mr. Akers, the young man set reasonable goals for himself. With encouragement from his classmates, he exceeded those goals. On the last day of the semester, he cheered for his classmates, and they cheered for him.

He didn't think he'd ever look forward to gym class, but by semester's end, he decided he could enjoy P.E. class. He even liked Mr. Akers.

Well, we all like happy endings, but is this one realistic? I believe it can be. All it takes is a change in attitude on the part of parents, principals, teachers, and others in positions of authority. We teach our children to say please and thank you, not to burp at the table, to share, to clean up their rooms; we try to educate them to stay off drugs and to abstain from sex outside of marriage. Why do we not teach them, from the very beginning, the sanctity of human life, the dignity of the individual, the responsibility we have to respect and safeguard our fellowman? Why aren't such ideals made perfectly clear to the students in the halls of our schools?

From the outset, on the very first day of school, the principal should address the entire student body and let them know that teasing, harassment, bullying, and abuse absolutely will not be tolerated—and yes, that would include upperclassmen picking on underclassmen. A senior razzing a freshman may seem cute and traditional, but all it really does is divide two human beings who could have been friends and helped each other. It also sets a "tradition" that opens wide the doors of cruelty, that tells the students it's fun and okay to make someone's life miserable.

Whatever attitude the school leadership displays will

trickle down through the student body. If teasing a younger kid is okay, then having no regard for the feelings of others is okay. If the principal and teachers remain aloof and indifferent toward bullying, the kids will remain indifferent and simply watch as it goes on all around them. If the gym teacher is cruel, brutal, and unapproachable, the boys in his gym class will be the same way toward each other, equating brutality with manliness and depriving our world of that many more *true* men.

Imagine a school that openly, directly enforces a zero-tolerance, anti-bullying policy, instructing and encouraging kids to call witnesses and to back each other up when a bullying incident occurs. Imagine students being instructed that they are responsible for their fellow human beings and that it is right and noble to get involved when someone is being hurt. Imagine a student being able to attend school knowing that his or her classmates, whether friend or stranger, are there for them if the need should ever arise.

If the school leadership, from the outset, establishes a policy of mutual respect at all levels and backs it up with rules, instruction, procedures, and *example*, we just might have a safer, more ennobling school environment and a few more compassionate human beings walking our streets after graduation.

Who knows? Such a refreshing attitude might just spill over into our families, into the workplace, our churches, and civic groups, making it a better "playground" for all of us.

Please take this matter of bullying seriously. You were a kid once. Would you want your child to suffer the taunts you had to suffer? Have you really forgotten how it felt?

Imagine this situation: A loving husband approaches his wife from behind her back, puts his arms around her, and calls her a particular nickname just to be funny. Suddenly, she turns on him, lashes him up one side and down the other, and breaks into tears. When the smoke and shrapnel finally settle and he has prepared an ice pack to put over his black eye, she informs him that she was always called that name in grade school and she hated it, hated it, hated it!

Well, okay, he won't call her that name again, but even so, the incident has smacked them both in the head with one realization: That stuff comes back. When we've been hurt, tormented, abused, or teased as children, we still have raw spots that remain into our adulthood. We remember how it feels, and we don't like it when people in the grown-up world—a friend, a spouse, a traffic cop, a crabby clerk— treat us the way we were treated years ago. Ever have a friend, spouse, or associate throw a little stinger your way? Perhaps they called you a name similar to the one you hated in grade school. Perhaps they called attention to a physical characteristic for which you paid dearly when you were young. Maybe they made a snide comment about the clothes you were wearing or the way you combed your hair. Part of you feels as if you're right back on that grade school playground or in that junior-high hallway all over again. That wounded child is still inside you.

So think twice, parents, before you shrug off your child's suffering as something he or she will just have to go through and outgrow. Did you ever, *really* outgrow it?

A close friend of mine who never cared to go to men's retreats finally gave in and attended one not too long ago. He came back deeply affected by what he saw and heard.

All the men, about a hundred in number, were given an assignment for the weekend: to write a poem about something that affected them deeply and emotionally. Through this exercise, each man was able to share his vulnerable side with sympathetic peers. The poems spoke of precious things as well as painful: the birth of the first child and the death of a child, the finding of true love and the loss of a spouse, a special praise from a parent and a crushing disappointment in a parent.

With a hundred men contributing, the group saw a kaleidoscope of life, and they realized how life can, at times, be so kind and so cruel.

During the last evening of the weekend retreat, a successful businessman in his forties stood to address the group. As he began to read his poem, he broke down weeping. He'd never talked to anyone about it before, but for him, one of the most painful experiences of his life was being overweight as a kid and being mocked and ridiculed about it in school. The teasing was merciless and it never let up, year after year. It framed his entire concept of himself, a concept he carried well into adulthood, and it was only now, when he felt safe among the other guys, that he could face it.

He sat down, and a brief, awkward silence enveloped the room, as if the men were wondering, *What can we do for this guy? What can we say? After all, it all happened so long ago.*

The next man stepped to the front to share his poem, but he was weeping before he could even unfold the poem to read it. He looked at the forty-year-old businessman and confessed, "Brother, when I was a kid, I was one of those who picked on kids like you. I thought it was fun. I guess it made me feel cool, like I was somebody. But I want to tell you, it was wrong, and until right now I've never faced up to it. Brother, I need to ask your forgiveness. I'm sorry. Please forgive me."

He embraced the businessman, and the room fell silent once again. Some other men started crying. In a coincidence so remarkable that it had to be a "divine appointment," two kids from different backgrounds and different schoolyards, the wounder and the wounded, had found each other and were making things right. The room was shaken.

See? We remember.

So parents and teachers, please talk about it. Bring up the subject yourself if your kids don't. Let your children know that they don't have to put up with bullying and abusive treatment and that there are steps they can take to prevent it. My parents didn't know the full extent of what I was suffering because I never said anything. I never said anything because it would be snitching, and, for all I knew, nothing could be done about it anyway. I never heard any teacher, counselor, or principal at my schools say that teasing and abuse were wrong. Not one teacher ever stepped in to prevent it. I even heard one teacher ask a friend of mine, "What's the matter—those guys picking on you?" The teacher then laughed about it, walked away, and did nothing. But he sent his message: "You're on your own, bub. You won't get any help from me."

In the aftermath of Littleton, we heard so much talk and fretting about "looking for the signs" that might lead kids to resort to violence. How can we know? What should we look for?

To this I say, *Wake up to wounded spirits!* A bruise or a cut is visible, but a wounded spirit can remain buried deep inside a person unless you provide the environment that will bring it out and heal it. The letter I wrote to Mr. Sampson was my final act of desperation. Thankfully, the pen was mightier than the gun, but I've often wondered what might have happened, had not that one special teacher paused to ask me how I was doing. Believe me, there are kids in your school, and maybe right in your home, who have a story to tell.

And yes, you as an adult may also have a story to tell, and it may not be a tale about the bullies of your youth. It may involve the bullies you have to put up with in the adult world. As research has found, bullies in school often go on to be bullies at home and at work (see the resource list in the back of this book for research supporting this fact). Have you ever had a boss—even a *Christian* boss— who doesn't mind belittling his or her employees in front of coworkers, spouting obscenities at them, and demanding unreasonable sacrifices? How about that DMV license examiner who thinks his uniform authorizes him to be rude and to make you feel like a criminal just because you're there to comply with the law? Ever met a minister who thinks God has appointed him to cuttingly critique the lifestyles of the members of the congregation, right down to the choice of socks, slacks, shirt, or tie someone wears? Do you derive a certain wicked pleasure from humiliating your spouse by telling your friends, in your spouse's presence, about the embarrassing mistakes he or she has made?

This list could be endless. It would have been nice if we'd all learned at an early age that there are better ways to resolve our inner problems and that there is a better path for human beings to follow. Well, it's never too late to start doing what is right.

It's never too late to change things.

A FRESH START

Chapter Ten

I t's been quite a journey, a stretch of fifty years, from helping Mom raise up the car on that deadly winter night, all the way to the writing of this chapter. Now that I can look back from this vantage point, the hard knocks of my childhood are starting to fit into a much broader context. They haven't shrunk in significance, but they have found their place as one of many seasons in my life. The bad things really happened, but they aren't the *only* things that happened. They aren't even the *main* things that happened. God's plan for each of our lives covers a lot more ground, a lot more time than just that one, difficult season. The journey continues. His grace and mercies are new every morning and sufficient for each day.

But we have to wonder, Just what was that "one, difficult season" all about? What was the point? Well, speaking as a typical, nearsighted mortal, I can offer a few guesses.

Because I went through it, I can encourage and minister to others who have been there or who are there right now; and, as I've discovered, there are plenty of people who have abusive experiences that continue to dog them. God will use what you and I have gone through to help others find healing and deliverance from the wounds that still bring pain to their souls. Indeed, it may well be our wounds that provide the common ground on which other people can relate to us and we to them. As Brennan Manning writes in *Abba's Child*, "Grace and healing are communicated through the vulnerability of men and women who have been fractured and heartbroken by life."[1] Quoting Thornton Wilder's one-act play *The Angel That Troubled the Water,* based on John 5:1–4, Manning reminds us that in a strange sense, our woundedness qualifies us to point others to the Healer. "In Love's service, only wounded soldiers can serve."[2]

Since first giving my talk on the subject of wounded spirits, and as I've worked on this book, I've found it comforting to think that after thirty or forty years, the Lord and I can finally make some good use of all that trouble I went through. God does not waste an ounce of our pain or a drop of our tears; suffering doesn't come our way for no reason, and He seems especially efficient at using what we endure to mold our character. If we are malleable, He takes our bumps and bruises and shapes them into something beautiful. Maybe, because of what you and I have experienced, we can inspire a few changes in the way people think about and treat each other in this world.

I can see how God has worked through my wounds. Being a man of flesh, I could have turned out more careless and cruel in my conversation if I hadn't suffered some pain myself. Having been hurt by words, I have a better appreciation for what words can do. Wanting to be like Jesus, I try to watch my mouth; rather than lacing my conversation with sarcasm—an arrow with the tip only slightly dulled—I attempt to speak words of encouragement, and I try to uplift people I meet.

Similarly, having suffered at the hands of bullies, I've wanted very much not to be one. It's important to remember that many bullies who abuse others have been abused themselves. As Suellen and Paula Fried point out in *Bullies and Victims*, "They were not born bullies; they became bullies through their life experience."[3] Some were physically or verbally abused as children; many witnessed violence in the lives of their parents or other family members; most bullies have parents who have been or are too busy to give them the attention they need. Or perhaps they have been ignored by parents who are unaware of what is really going on in their children's lives. Sometimes even well-meaning parents are hard-pressed to spend the needed amount of quality time with their child, leaving the child with a sense of being unloved.

Often bullies have received inconsistent messages regarding discipline and boundaries. Bullies see threats where none exist; they see their anger as justified.[4] Because of these and other serious problems, bullies often end up as losers in life.

We don't rejoice in their hardship, nor do we condone their response to it, but if we develop an awareness that most bullies themselves are suffering wounded spirits, we will understand more about their inner pain, and we will have more compassion for the abusive person. We will recognize that often, just below the harsh exterior, there is a wounded child crying out to be noticed, and yes, to be loved.

So, I can see a lesson in the unhappy life of a bully: There is definitely a better life to be had by living life correctly, God's way, and there is a certain enabling grace

God provides to help us do so. Consequently, I've sought God's wisdom and tried not to let this lesson pass me by.

On a practical level, having experienced how sour this world can be, I've tried to spread around as much sugar as I can. If I encounter a waitress having a bad day, I try to be as nice to her as I can be, and I usually leave a generous tip. It's a tangible way of saying, "You're doing a good job, and I appreciate you." Have you ever worked at a fast-food restaurant? If so, you probably have a greater appreciation for that young man or woman behind the counter who is trying to juggle several orders while customers wait impatiently. No doubt some irate customer has already yelled at my waitress for spilling something or counting the change wrong. I'd like to be the *nice* customer she has that day, the customer who gives *her* a break.

I try to use humor and display goodwill toward everyone with whom I do business, from bank clerks to telephone operators to FedEx delivery truck drivers. People appreciate kindness, and although virtue is its own reward, the Bible does promise that I will reap what I sow. Pass some sugar around, and Jesus will throw some sugar back to you, even more than you gave in the first place. It is, after all, the Lord Jesus whom we represent. As Saint Francis of Assisi put it, "Preach Christ . . . and if you must, use words."

Comforting others puts our pain into perspective. Having encountered others who have suffered multiple rapes, domestic violence, permanent disfigurement from disease or birth defect, molestation, and violent crime, I can tell myself, "Okay. You had some tough times, but be thankful. Compared to many people in this world, you had it easy."

I'm convinced that cruelty in and of itself is not fruitful, and to the fullest extent of my power, I won't allow it. Yes, God can make it all work together for good, but that's His miraculous way of redeeming a rotten situation, not His will for our behavior. I'm not impressed by the old argument that cruelty toughens us up for life. That's tantamount to saying it's right. Life is cruel enough by itself, thank you, with endless opportunities to suffer. Given that, one kind word or one encouraging touch teaches more lessons than one hundred cruelties.

We all have our "difficult seasons." Some of us are in the middle of one right now. We don't like them, of course, but they do have a way of finding their place in the overall scheme of our lives, welcome or not. There will be pain, and years afterward, there will still be questions. The sweet part of this is, as long as the Lord God is guiding your life, more years and more wisdom will bring a better perspective of what those tough times were all about. So trust God. He'll make things clear eventually.

I do see better days ahead. I intended this book to be a wake-up call, the cry of a lonely prophet, so to speak, but happily, I'm not the first one to raise this issue. As you'll see from the reading list in the back of this book, there are folks out there concerned with the problem of bullying and abuse, who want to advise and assist us in doing something about it. Check it out if you want to examine things further, and don't forget the Internet: Search the word *bully*, *bullies*, or *bullying*, and you'll be surprised how much material is available. You'll also be pleased, as I was, to find that much of the material is by or for those in education, meaning that our teachers and school administrators have plenty of practical resources from which to draw and no excuses for ignoring this matter ever again.

Maybe we're entering a new era in which bullying and the intimidation of other people are at last consigned to their rightful place alongside racism, hatemongering, drunk driving, littering, spitting in public, and passing gas at parties.

People are slowly waking up to the prolonged impact of the problem—that bullies in school often grow up to be bullies in the home, abusing their spouses and children and perpetuating the downward spiral. Bullies in the home leave the house and go to work, where they continue to abuse employees and coworkers. The cycle can only be stopped by a change of the heart, and that is precisely the place where God's power is more than sufficient to give people a fresh start. With other options exhausted, many people are finally beginning to give the spiritual solution some serious thought. Let's encourage more of that, and while we're at it, let's search our own hearts and instruct our children regarding what it means to be noble, to protect and help the weak, to love our neighbors—even the smaller, clumsy ones—as ourselves.

Most of all, we are called to be Jesus to the world around us, to demonstrate in word and deed, not simply in slogan, "What would Jesus do?" As we follow Christ and strive to be more like Him, may we also encourage people and share His love with each person we meet along the way. He is our Savior and Lord; He is the Answer for every broken heart, the one Answer we cannot live without—He is the Healer of the wounded spirit.

Endnotes

Chapter 4: Monsters on the Loose

1. Gavin DeBecker, "What the Columbine Report Didn't Tell You," APBnews.com, 19 May, 2000.

2. From Alan Prendergast, "The Missing Motive," from westword.com, originally published by *Westword*, 13 July 2000, copyright 2000 New Times, Inc. All rights reserved.

3. Gavin DeBecker, "What the Columbine Report Didn't Tell You."

4. Susan Greene, "Teen describes school life filled with taunts, abuse," DenverPost.com, 24 April 1999.

5. Ibid.

6. Suellen Fried and Paula Fried, *Bullies and Victims* (New York: M. Evans and Company, 1996), 87.

Chapter 5: Finding a Voice

1. Brent Curtis and John Eldredge, *The Sacred Romance* (Nashville: Thomas Nelson, 1997), 49.

2. Ibid.

Chapter 6: The Playground Parable

1. Gavin DeBecker, "What the Columbine Report Didn't Tell You," APBnews.com, 19 May, 2000.

2. From the tape series One Week in October, copyright 1999 by Ravi Zacharias, Ravi Zacharias International Ministries, 4725 Peachtree Corners Circle, Suite 250, Norcross, Georgia 30092.

3. John H. Hoover and Ronald Oliver, *The Bullying Prevention Handbook: A Guide for Principals, Teachers, and Counselors* (Bloomington, Ind.: National Educational Service, 1996), 96–97.

Chapter 7: Help for the Wounded

1. For more detailed reading on the subject of Christian morals and world-view, I heartily recommend the works of Ravi Zacharias, Francis Schaeffer, Josh McDowell, and C. S. Lewis.

Chapter 10: A Fresh Start

1. Brennan Manning, *Abba's Child* (Colorado Springs: NavPress, 1994), 26.

2. Ibid.

3. Suellen and Paula Fried, *Bullies and Victims*, 89.

4. Adapted from *Bullies and Victims*, 89–90.

Resources

Where You Can Find Help

The following list of resources is not exhaustive, nor is it necessarily a personal endorsement of the organizations listed, but it is a good place to start when you need help in dealing with bullying, abuse, intimidation, or the effects of other compulsive or addictive behaviors. It's normal to be nervous when reaching out for help, but don't let that hold you back. Be bold and courageous; contact someone on this list to help you. Begin today to do something that will bring about positive, Christ-centered change in your life, and in the lives of the people you love.

AMERICAN ASSOCIATION OF PASTORAL COUNSELORS
    9504 A Lee Highway
    Fairfax, VA 22031
    phone: 703-385-6967

CANAAN LAND CHRISTIAN CENTER FOR WOMEN
    2377 County Road 65
    Marburg, AL 36051
    phone: 334-365-9086
    www.wrldnet.net

CANAAN LAND MINISTRIES
P.O. Box 310
Autaugaville, AL 36003-0310
phone: 334-365-2200
canaanland@bellsouth.net
Ministry to men.

CELEBRATION MINISTRIES
Al Denson
222 West Las Colinas Boulevard
Suite 1750
Irving, TX 75034
phone: 972-501-1456
aldenson.com

Christian musician, author, and minister offers Bible studies, public school programs, and an on-line prayer request ministry.

CENTER FOR THE PREVENTION OF SEXUAL AND DOMESTIC VIOLENCE
1914 N. 34th Street
Seattle, WA 98103
phone: 206-634-1903
Emergency: 800-562-6025

CHRISTIAN GROWTH CENTERS
P.O. Box 40
Hillsboro, NH 03244
phone: 603-464-5555

Specializes in helping young people who have been battered and fragmented through broken homes, drugs, alcohol, etc.

DORCAS HOUSE
phone: 501-274-4022

Specializes in helping women and children who are victims of domestic violence.

EXODUS INTERNATIONAL
P.O. Box 77652
Seattle, WA 98177
phone: 206-784-7799
fax: 206-784-7872
www.exodusintl.com

Equipping and uniting organizations to communicate freedom from homosexuality.

FAMILIES IN CRISIS, INC.
7320 Ohms Lane
Edina, MN 55435
phone: 612-893-1883

HOLY HIGHWAY
phone: 903-866-3300

Recommended for families with rebellious teenage girls.

LORD'S RANCH
Box 700
Warm Springs, AR 72478
phone: 870-647-2541
fax: 870-647-2337

LOST AND FOUND
phone: 303-697-5049

Help for those involved in drugs, alcohol, and sexual abuse.

MERCY MINISTRIES OF AMERICA
P.O. Box 111060
Nashville, TN 37222-1060
phone: 615-831-6987
fax: 615-315-9749
mercyministries.org

Mercy Ministries of America is a residential facility, provided free of charge, for troubled young women and unwed mothers between the ages of thirteen and twenty-eight, who are willing to commit six months to deal with life-controlling issues such as: pregnancy, drug and alcohol abuse, eating disorders, etc.

NATIONAL SCHOOL SAFETY CENTER
Pepperdine University
Malibu, CA 90263
phone: 805-373-9977

NEW CREATIONS
phone: 765-965-0099

Help for families with rebellious youth.

NEW HORIZONS MINISTRIES
1002 South 350 East
Marion, IN 46953-9502

Family and Christian character training.

NEW LIFE
phone: 800-NEW-LIFE

Counseling center and telephone crisis lines.

PARENTS ANONYMOUS
Contact:
Child Help USA
P.O. Box 630
Hollywood, CA 90028

A program for parents who already have or are afraid they might abuse their children.

RAPHA
4351 Shackleford Road
Norcross, GA 30093
phone: 800-383-HOPE
fax: 770-806-7641
www.raphacare.com

Rapha features Christ-centered, professional counseling for emotional and substance abuse, anxiety attacks, stress, unhealthy relationships, eating disorders, depression, drugs, alcohol, suicidal tendencies, etc.

REMUDA RANCH CENTER
One East Apache Street
Wickenburg, AZ 85390
phone: 800-445-1900

SHELTERWOOD
12550 Zuni Street
Westminster, CO 80234
phone: 800-584-5005
shelterwood.org

"Restoring families through Christian relationships."

TEEN CHALLENGE INTERNATIONAL
P.O. Box 1015
Springfield, MO 65801
phone: 800-814-5728
http://www.teenchallenge.com

Specializes in seeking spiritual solutions to addictive behavior patterns.

WALTER HOVING HOME
P.O. Box 194
Garrison, NY 10525
phone: 914-424-3674

"Rebuilding lives shattered by drugs and alcohol, and other life-controlling problems."

Web Sites

(Please note: This is not necessarily an endorsement of these sites, or the information included on them; however, this brief list will give you a place to start in searching for other resources.)

http://www.successunlimited.co.uk
   (Dealing primarily with bullying in the United Kingdom, this site also includes a section on bullying in the United States.)

http://www.mobbing-usa.com
   (The terms "mobbing" and "bullying" are often used interchangeably in the U. S.)

http://www.bullybusters.org
   (This site charges for their services. The other listings provide free information.)

http:// stopbullying.com
   (A one-stop resource on dealing with childhood bullying and teasing.)

Recommended Reading List

1. Bernall, Misty. *She Said Yes: The Unlikely Martydom of Cassie Bernall.* Farmington, N.Y.; Nashville: Copublishers, Plough and Word, 1999.

2. Curtis, Brent, and John Eldredge. *The Sacred Romance.* Nashville: Thomas Nelson, 1997.

3. Fried, Suellen, and Paula Fried. *Bullies and Victims.* New York: M. Evans and Company, 1996.

4. Gaddis, Patricia Riddle. *Battered But Not Broken.* Valley Forge, Pa.: Judson Press, 1996.

5. Kroeger, Catherine Clark, and James R. Beck. *Women, Abuse, and the Bible.* Grand Rapids: Baker, 1996.

6. Manning, Brennan. *Abba's Child.* Colorado Springs: NavPress, 1994.

7. McDowell, Josh, and Bob Hostetler. *Right From Wrong.* Dallas: Word, 1994.

8. Zacharias, Ravi. *A Shattered Visage: The Real Face of Atheism.* Grand Rapids: Baker, 1993.

9. Zacharias, Ravi. *Can Man Live Without God.* Nashville: W Publishing Group, 1994.

10. Zacharias, Ravi. *Deliver Us from Evil.* Nashville: W Publishing Group, 1996.

The Oath

Master of supernatural thrillers Frank Peretti brings us *The Oath*, a chilling novel of murder and mystery. A 110-year-old town has fallen prey to an unexplainable predator and no one wants to talk about it. Layer upon layer, this serpentine plot peels away at the ramifications of an ancient oath.

The Visitation

Sightings of angels, messianic images, a weeping crucifix with the power to heal, and a self-proclaimed prophet bring the national media and droves of curious people to this small Northwestern town. The startling secret behind this visitation pushes one man into a supernatural confrontation that will forever change the lives of everyone involved.

Also in *The Wounded Spirit* Product Line Available February 2001

- The *Wounded Spirit* Workbook
- The *Wounded Spirit* Leader's Guide
- The *Wounded Spirit* Curriculum (includes one workbook, one leader's guide, and one 45-minute video)

THOMAS NELSON
Since 1798

Also Available from Frank Peretti

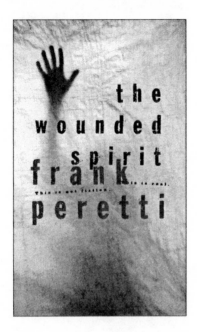

THE WOUNDED SPIRIT VIDEO

The message of *No More Bullies* brought to life as Frank Peretti discusses with schools across the country the powerful effect of harmful words and actions. And how this affects people for the rest of their lives. The message has connected with thousands and has become a national movement. To assist youth and community leaders in communicating this powerful message, Thomas Nelson has developed this single video with workbook included.

PRAISE FOR *Imperfect Birds*

"[A] powerful and painfully honest novel . . . Lamott's observations are pitch-perfect—likably, even brutally unsentimental, not just about parental hopes and anxieties but about the particular and touching fragility of simply being a teenager. Laughter redeems this book, and so does the fact that it's ultimately not just a novel about deception and drugs but about the great big bloody battle of love and sorrow that is parenthood."   —*The New York Times Book Review*

"It won't surprise fans of Lamott's work to hear that in this book, as in so many of her others, her fine-tuned ear for dialogue and her flawless eye for the perfect, telling detail are in high gear. It is compelling to see characters engaged not only in the familiar struggle of parenting as perfectly as they can amid their own imperfections but also with the complicating demon of drug and alcohol addiction. Many readers will recognize the problems faced if not by themselves then by friends or family in the world of *Imperfect Birds*. . . . [A] richly populated world of believable, understandable people, places and situations."   —*Los Angeles Times*

"Not only is it a moving and perceptive portrayal of raising a substance-abusing teenager, but it implicitly offers the kind of advice that many parents need to hear. That's the tension that powers this story, the parental schizophrenia that Lamott describes with such sympathy and tenderness: feeling disgusted by your child's behavior and living in terror of losing her. It's a startlingly honest depiction of middle-class teenage life in all its baffling contradictions. This is a mature, thoughtful novel about an all-too-common family crisis, and in typical Lamott fashion, it doesn't ignore the pain or exalt in despair. The salvation she offers in these pages is hard-won."   —*The Washington Post*

"A stark illustration of deception, denial, and parents' desperate desire to stay loved." —*Time*

"The psychological acuity Lamott demonstrates for all her characters is the biggest payoff in this novel, giving the narrative a startling 3-D roundness of vision . . . It is easy to think of the Fergusons and their extended family of friends as living people, just as infuriating and ridiculous and lovable as all we fleshly humans eking out our tender ways through the world." —*San Francisco Chronicle*

"Fans of Anne Lamott—and they are legion—will be delighted to hear a favorite author's voice in her latest novel, *Imperfect Birds*." —*The Christian Science Monitor*

"Heartbreaking and delightful, moving and hopeful, *Imperfect Birds* reminds us how our children are connected to and independent of us, and that no matter how difficult our struggle is with them, love underlies it all and saves us. This novel captures the deepest, purest, most terrifying experience of parents fearing for their children. With great insight and humor, Anne Lamott shows us what it means these dangerous days to be a parent, what it means to be a child, and what it means to be a family." —David Sheff, author of *Beautiful Boy*

"*Imperfect Birds* details with frightening accuracy the ease with which teenagers can be derailed and how quickly adults believe the lies of the children they love." —*The Miami Herald*

"This is brilliantly witty, powerfully emotional fiction that has the power to change how readers think. In my book, that's the highest compliment a writer can earn." —*The Dallas Morning News*

"[A] page-turner . . . This novel explores all the heartbreak and hazards of being a mom." —*Redbook*

"Engrossing . . . a poignant family story, at times heartbreaking, but ultimately uplifting . . . Lamott gives readers a fascinating peek into the inner contradictions driving the teenager's outwardly baffling behavior—the anger, vulnerabilities, and desires warring against a sincere wish to do the right thing."   —*BookPage*

"Straddling a line between heartwarming and heartbreaking, this novel is Lamott at her most witty, observant, and psychologically astute."   —*Publishers Weekly* (starred review)

"Wonderfully rich . . . fans of Anne Lamott's work will find everything they love in *Imperfect Birds*."   —*Pittsburgh Post-Gazette*

"Her most stylistically mature and thematically circumspect novel to date."   —*Booklist*

"Compelling, full of the sucker-punches teenagers routinely deliver to their parents. *Imperfect Birds* is a psychologically astute, scary, throat-tugging novel about parents who wake up and rescue their teen from the frying pan just before she hits the fire."

—*The Kansas City Star*

"This is a deft, moving look at an extremely fragile and codependent mother-daughter relationship and how an out-of-control teenager affects a life, a friendship, and a marriage. Lamott is consistently wonderful with this type of novel, and once again she does not disappoint."   —*Library Journal* (starred review)

"Whether Lamott's narrative terrain is fiction or nonfiction, the temporal or the divine, critics and readers alike relish her ability to make sense of an absurd world. . . . Thank goodness Lamott is here to help us find our way through the morass."

—*The San Diego Union-Tribune*

"Narrated by mother and daughter, this novel is a real look into the dynamics of a family struggling to overcome betrayals and become whole again."   —*Glamour*

"This is a hell of a book, tough and wonderful. A heartbreaker and a heart-mender."

    —Martin Cruz Smith, author of *Gorky Park* and *The Golden Mile*

"Anne Lamott writes . . . with the trenchant wit that has won her legions of fans . . . refreshingly open-minded and irreverent even in her reverence."   —National Public Radio

"Lamott's writing is evocative, as she skillfully navigates the emotional landscapes of the worlds of parents and teenagers. *Imperfect Birds* is a finely wrought story of parental love, the self-loathing and narcissism of youth, and the light at the end of the tunnel."   —*Bust*

"Anne Lamott's seventh novel features alcoholism, drug addiction, and family dysfunction. This will not surprise Lamott's fans. Her characters . . . are always 'imperfect birds', and some are clearly on the endangered list. Most are also sensitive, funny, intelligent, and frightened by the messes they keep getting themselves into. That's why we love them, and their author, so much."   —*Christianity Today*

"*Imperfect Birds* is not a tragedy, but it explores the possibility of tragedy and lays out with convincing authority some of the terrible temptations to which American teenagers are subject. Lamott writes with conviction and a strong sense of place. She is funny, witty, and wise."   —*Oregon Live*

"Lamott is doing what she does so well, teaching us about survival and charting the very rough road to redemption."   —*The Seattle Times*

"Lots of people love Anne Lamott, because she's funny and she tells the truth, and truth and laughter are two things we need more of."
—*The New York Times Book Review*

"For readers trying to live a kind of faith that's centered on social justice, who are saddened at the state of our nation and feel mired in a world gone mad with war and greed, Lamott and her quirky, funny perspective are nothing short of a salve for tired souls."
—*Los Angeles Times Book Review*

"Anne Lamott is a cause for celebration. [Her] real genius lies in capturing the ineffable, describing not perfect moments, but imperfect ones . . . perfectly. She is nothing short of miraculous."
—*The New Yorker*

"Anne Lamott is walking proof that a person can be both reverent and irreverent in the same lifetime. Sometimes even in the same breath."
—*San Francisco Chronicle*

"Lamott writes about subjects that begin with capital letters [Alcoholism, Motherhood, Jesus]. But armed with self-effacing humor and ruthless honesty—call it a lowercase approach to life's Big Questions—she converts potential op-ed boilerplates into enchantment."
—*Newsweek*

Imperfect Birds

◘

ANNE LAMOTT

RIVERHEAD BOOKS

New York

RIVERHEAD BOOKS
Published by the Penguin Group
Penguin Group (USA) Inc.
375 Hudson Street, New York, New York 10014, USA
Penguin Group (Canada), 90 Eglinton Avenue East, Suite 700, Toronto, Ontario M4P 2Y3, Canada
(a division of Pearson Penguin Canada Inc.)
Penguin Books Ltd., 80 Strand, London WC2R 0RL, England
Penguin Group Ireland, 25 St. Stephen's Green, Dublin 2, Ireland (a division of Penguin Books Ltd.)
Penguin Group (Australia), 250 Camberwell Road, Camberwell, Victoria 3124, Australia
(a division of Pearson Australia Group Pty. Ltd.)
Penguin Books India Pvt. Ltd., 11 Community Centre, Panchsheel Park, New Delhi—110 017, India
Penguin Group (NZ), 67 Apollo Drive, Rosedale, North Shore 0632, New Zealand
(a division of Pearson New Zealand Ltd.)
Penguin Books (South Africa) (Pty.) Ltd., 24 Sturdee Avenue, Rosebank, Johannesburg 2196,
South Africa

Penguin Books Ltd., Registered Offices: 80 Strand, London WC2R 0RL, England

Grateful acknowledgment is made to reprint the following:

James Wright, "A Blessing," from *Collected Poems* © 1962 James Wright.
Reprinted by permission of Wesleyan University Press

Excerpts from *The Odyssey: A Modern Sequel* by Nikos Kazantzakis. Verse translation by Kimon Friar. English translation copyright © 1958 by Simon & Shuster, Inc. Copyright renewed © 1986 by Simon & Shuster, Inc. Reprinted with the permission of Simon & Shuster, Inc., and the Estate of Nikos Kazantzakis.

First Riverhead hardcover edition: April 2010
First Riverhead trade paperback edition: April 2011
Riverhead trade paperback ISBN: 978-1-59448-504-6

The Library of Congress has catalogued the Riverhead hardcover edition as follows:

Lamott, Anne.
　　Imperfect birds : a novel / Anne Lamott.
　　　　p.　　　　cm.
　　ISBN 978-1-59448-751-4
　　1. Drug addicts—Fiction.　2. Parents of drug addicts—Fiction.　3. Psychological fiction.
4. Domestic fiction.　I. Title.
PS3562.A4645I67　　2010　　　　　　2009036107
813'.54—dc22

PRINTED IN THE UNITED STATES OF AMERICA

10　9　8　7　6　5　4　3

For Bonnie Allen and Jax Lamott

*For Doug Foster and Neshama Franklin and the people of
St. Andrew Presbyterian Church*

Thanks beyond words.

Just off the highway to Rochester, Minnesota,
Twilight bounds softly forth on the grass.
And the eyes of those two Indian ponies
Darken with kindness.
They have come gladly out of the willows
To welcome my friend and me.
We step over the barbed wire into the pasture
Where they have been grazing all day, alone.
They ripple tensely, they can hardly contain their happiness
That we have come.
They bow shyly as wet swans. They love each other.
There is no loneliness like theirs.
At home once more,
They begin munching the young tufts of spring in the darkness.
I would like to hold the slenderer one in my arms,
For she has walked over to me
And nuzzled my left hand.
She is black and white,
Her mane falls wild on her forehead,
And the light breeze moves me to caress her long ear
That is delicate as the skin over a girl's wrist.
Suddenly I realize
That if I stepped out of my body I would break
Into blossom.

—JAMES WRIGHT, "A Blessing"

ONE

The Parkade

◘

There are so many evils that pull on our children. Even in the mellow town of Landsdale, where it is easy to see only beauty and decency, a teenager died nearly every year after a party and kids routinely went from high school to psych wards, halfway houses, or jail. Once a year a child from the county of Marin jumped off the Golden Gate Bridge.

Elizabeth Ferguson looked around at the Saturday-morning comings and goings of townspeople, and saw parents who had lost or were losing their kids, kids who had lost or were losing their minds. She and James sat with their coffees and newspaper on the wide steps of the Parkade, which was what everyone in town called the parking bay in the center of town, making it seem a lot more festive than it was. It was a big parking lot that abutted the boulevard that ran from San Quentin, to the east, all the way out to Olema, on the Pacific coast, but several feet higher than the town's original crossroads, so that you had to climb up steps to reach it, and drive slightly downhill to exit. A bean-shaped lot for eighty cars, it was ringed in skinny trees and foliage, lavender rhododendrons whose blooms wouldn't last much longer as spring faded, and geraniums. There was a bus kiosk on the north side, and two weathered sets of concrete steps, the one where Elizabeth and her husband sat reading, another at the far end, across from the movie theater.

She and James were waiting for her daughter, whom they were going to take shopping in town if she ever arrived. Rosie needed notebooks and some summer tops for her last weeks as a junior at the local high school, and shops fanned out below the Parkade, stretching almost to the northern face of Mount Tamalpais. But Rosie was nowhere in sight.

Elizabeth felt large and worried. Even sitting down, she was taller than her husband (and her otherwise dark thick hair was slightly more gray-streaked). But Rosie was taller than either, almost five-eleven, black-haired, strapping and fabulous, except when they wanted to disown her, like now.

James read the paper in vexed silence and Elizabeth sipped her coffee and watched people go about their business. A tidal feeling ebbed and flowed around them, of people on foot, shopping or going back to their cars. You never knew for sure who would be there, someone you'd been missing or were trying to avoid. Two teenage boys took their spots on the bottom steps. Their pose was a flop that said, *I've arrived and I'm not moving.* Others stepped past them to get to their cars or up to the boulevard. Over by the bus kiosk there was a sense of marketplace transactions among the high school kids—punk, funk, hippie, straight—of intrigue, nonchalance, commerce, boredom, opportunity. On the main street people dropped off DVDs and videos, stopped to chat, ducked into the liquor store, flirted, picked up after their dogs or not, riffled through dresses hanging outside on racks. Elizabeth read the paper over James's shoulder.

"How long are we going to wait?" he asked. "It's been twenty minutes."

"Five more?"

"It's like waiting for goddamn Godot."

Some of the young men converging at the kiosk had cultivated the look of homelessness, but without the inconvenience and hardship: car keys dangled from their belts as they drank four-dollar lattes. Some looked like star athletes, because they were or had been. But you saw a feral, dark energy in some of the young here, of despair, blankness, failure and indirect gazes, ill health, or sometimes, a dangerous raw male potency. The grunge, the piercings, the clothes that deliberately didn't fit, that said, *I am the best, I am the worst,* the tattoos psychic Band-Aids to cover the wounds.

They were home here, and only here. You could tell by the loose-legged swagger, instead of the back-alley prowl they used at their parents' houses.

Some of these guys had been to Elizabeth's home in the year since she and Rosie and James had moved here from Bayview. Two were Rosie's friends from school, and one had briefly had benefits, which meant she had given him oral, as they called it, which Elizabeth had learned by reading Rosie's journal. She had had to do Lamaze after reading the entry about Rosie's giving Jason Brewer head. Rosie had lambasted Elizabeth after guilt forced her to admit having read the journal, and so she rarely admitted to Rosie that she dipped into the journal from time to time. Also, Rosie began hiding it better, but Elizabeth could always find it eventually, hidden in tennis racket covers, hollowed-out books, behind the headboard, under the dresser and night table.

Elizabeth rationalized it as recon, and found herself reading the journal on a regular basis. When she got new intel that she did not tell Rosie she knew, she obsessed about the dreadful news— for example, that Rosie had tried cocaine a few times last summer, and smoked cigarettes every so often. And when Elizabeth did admit to snooping—for instance, when she'd discovered that Rosie was not a virgin—Rosie rightfully went crazy and didn't speak to her for days. When Elizabeth tried to break the habit and go without any new information, she fixated on the grisly teenage possibilities. So it was torture in any case, as Elizabeth had to try to keep the files straight in her head: what she knew and had admitted to, what she knew but must keep a secret, and what were only her dark imaginings.

So Rosie had given guys head, gotten laid, and done cocaine a few times: for God's sake, what did Elizabeth expect? It was not ideal, but Rosie was seventeen and gorgeous and had been on the pill, for an overly heavy monthly flow and acne, since she turned fifteen. Her skin was under control now, with only small clusters of pimples, and she got much less crazy every month. The mention of cocaine upset Elizabeth, but it was apparently in the past, having not been mentioned again in the journal.

Rosie's guys had smelled of marijuana the times Elizabeth had been close enough to sniff, and she had found a pack of rolling papers while snooping in Rosie's purse a few months ago, but she rarely smelled weed on Rosie. They had apparently dodged a bullet when it came to drugs, knock wood. *Kinna hurra, kinna hurra,* as Jewish friends exclaimed, laughing while knocking wood or their own heads: no evil eye.

James glanced up from his paper again. He sighed heavily but got into people-watching with Elizabeth: yoga ladies with their baseball caps and rolled-up mats leaving the yoga studio; people in groups and couples and alone, shopping at the health food store or at Landsdale Hardware and Lumber, at the foot of where the mountain would usually be. It was missing today, but the fog was supposed to burn away by noon. She looked at James surreptitiously, with a sad and mooning face; she loved him so much. He was not the tall, handsome man her first husband had been, elegant and calm and amused. But he was her perfect companion much of the time, and she loved his looks: his crazy frizzy hair had been cropped and styled now. He had told his hairstylist to make him look like the gay scion to a great fortune, and she had. He'd also had his front teeth capped, so while he was never going to star in toothpaste commercials, he had the sweet pleasing smile of someone with a lifelong shyness about his teeth.

As they sat on the steps, James pointed out a tiny Ralph Steadman dog on a red leash. "It looks like an ink-blot test," he whispered. "Like a little chemo dog."

"It's a soap-on-a-rope dog," she replied. She laid her head against his shoulder while he scribbled this down in his notebook. He was the smartest person she had ever known, on literature, politics, psychology, and yet he could also be so dorky, with the silly Monty Python walks and weird voices that still made Rosie laugh, most of the time. On the wrong day, however, she might announce snidely that this or that behavior was the main reason she wanted to move out. For the ten-plus years since he'd entered their lives, James had been making the same dumb jokes. But people always laughed, which encouraged him. Passing diners at outdoor tables or in the park, he'd peer at their food and ask eagerly, "Are you going to finish that?" and everyone laughed. It had begun to embarrass Rosie a few years ago, but she always forgave him for being so corny. "Don't pet the sweaty stuff," he'd tell her friends when they seemed upset, a line he'd gotten from one of the many doctors he and Elizabeth now needed to tend to their deteriorating body parts.

They had problems now in areas where they hardly used to have areas. They both wore glasses. James had had two skin cancers removed from his widening bald spot. Elizabeth had a hammertoe and ensuing gigantic corns, which always grew back after removal. James's best friend, Lank, had a bad rotator cuff. Rae, his wife and Elizabeth's best friend, was getting carpal tunnel syndrome from the years at her loom, and wore a wrist brace. Both women leaked urine if they laughed or coughed too hard. Elizabeth had to wear napkins all the time now, and was not even fifty.

Everyone's back ached except Rosie's. But Rosie had a visible glob on one eye from sun damage, seven years on tennis courts for ten hours a day. Also, Lank had such terrible vision now that no one would drive with him at night, even though he wore glasses, which magnified his already big brown eyes to the size of a rainforest mammal's. He had lost a lot of his hair except for a light red fringe that he kept short. Rae often stroked his head and cooed like a lap dancer about how soft and sexy it was. He had had a melanoma removed from his upper arm, probably the result of all the years he and James had backpacked together. They had met Rae and Elizabeth on a trip to Yosemite, coming up on eleven years ago, but they rarely camped anymore, because of bad backs, aching feet, and skin cancers.

But by their age, so many wonderful people in their lives had died or were going to die soon; and besides, they were all in relatively good health. So when the sun came up, you felt around for glasses, got out of bed, limped about on stiff feet, and slathered on sunscreen, grateful for the poignancy of daybreak.

James, who was usually so mellow, could be stern and pissed off at Rosie. She could make him lose his mind, especially when she was cruel to her mother. He periodically grounded her and took away her allowance, something Elizabeth did not always agree with, as she felt that Rosie, a year away from graduation, was too old to treat like a child. James, on the other hand, felt that if you didn't use parental muscle and control, the homework didn't get done, classes got skipped, grades would fall off, and Rosie would have to go to a junior college, and they'd be stuck living with her defensive moods and contempt for another year or two. He had become the primary disciplinarian around the time Rosie turned sixteen, when she began to plead for more and more independence, because unlike Elizabeth, he did not fear Rosie's wrath or worry about being seen as the bad guy, all that stood between her and eternal joyful congress with her friends. In fact, he seemed to enjoy the role of enforcer.

On good days, when everyone got along, Elizabeth believed she'd die when Rosie left, keen forever like an Irish fisherman's widow. On bad days, she felt like a prisoner at the Level 1 Reception Area in Pelican Bay, marking off days on the prison wall until Rosie's graduation.

James had first called Rosie the angry clubfoot in the early weeks of his romance with Elizabeth, as they drunkenly listened to her clomp around upstairs in a bad mood, resentful that James was stealing away her mother. And she still fit the bill on a regular basis, although to judge from anecdotal evidence that Elizabeth culled from other mothers, Rosie was not nearly as awful as many of the town's teenage girls, not by a long shot. She did not scream, hit, run away, or throw things. She had not gotten pregnant—Elizabeth knew of at least four girls who'd gotten abortions. Still, life with most teenagers was like having a low-grade bladder infection. It hurt, but you had to tough it out.

Lank, who taught high school in Petaluma, had responded to Elizabeth's periodic misery by inventing a church just for her, called Seeing the Light Ministries. Not long ago, during an awful patch between Elizabeth and Rosie, Lank had, in his capacity as pastor, reminded Elizabeth of the doctrine against raising your kids as if they were precious equals. This seemed to be the current national parenting trend, but it was utterly misguided.

"You are the sun," he told Elizabeth over the phone. "The child is merely a moon. A moon. She has no light of her own, no income, no car. She is a satellite. Her judgment is frequently poor, and she is mean. She is South Africa before the revolution, cruel and crazy. Divest! Divest!"

Elizabeth knew this was the path toward freedom, away from the tweaking and gnashing of teeth, but it was so hard not to hook into Rosie's teenage bullshit; hard not to react when Rosie was arrogant or cutting or blinked at her like a lizard and walked away while Elizabeth was in mid-sentence. Lank provided Elizabeth with Seeing the Light responses to everyday demands, such as "Rosie? The instructions are inside the lid of the washer." He had an all-purpose response to any teenager trying to provoke a fight: the silent chanting of a mantra, which was WAIT, for "Why am I talking?" Parental non-engagement drove Rosie crazy and out of the room.

Elizabeth adored Lank: the two of them were the quieter ones in their marriages; James and Rae were the great conversationalists, the raconteurs, the stars. But when Lank couldn't gently help Elizabeth with the pain of having such a mouthy and spoiled child, he'd turn the phone over to Rae.

Rae preferred the spiritual approach, which could either exasper-
ate Elizabeth with its kindness and optimism or get her breathing
again. "The love you have for Rosie is absolute, right?" Rae, Rosie's
chosen auntie, had asked a month ago, neutral as Switzerland.

"Not really, not anymore. I don't actually like her half the time."
This was one of Elizabeth's two darkest secrets, how many times
over the years she had felt a sense of hopeless disgust at Rosie's values and behavior. The other secret was how constantly, since Rosie's
birth, Elizabeth had lived in terror of losing her, from crib death, or
a rogue wave, kidnapping, cancer, and now, teenage car accidents. It
hadn't helped when two kids in last year's senior class had died in a
post-party accident, or that one of Rosie's friends had ended up in
the emergency room getting her stomach pumped after overdosing
on alcohol. One of Elizabeth's antidepressants was for the obsession
and anxiety that Rosie would die. The other helped control her rage.

"Would you love her less if she killed or molested someone?"
Rae asked.

"Of course not."

"Then by definition your love is absolute. Stand in that. The
rest'll pass."

Elizabeth took long, deep breaths. "Why does she have to be so
mean?"

"It's the nature of teenagers. They're like that. We probably
were, too."

"It's true. I was mean to my mother. I mean evil mean."

"So was I. So was Desmond Tutu, probably. And Dinah Shore.
Remember in high school, when your teacher reads you a scathing
diatribe on teenagers, and you think it's Spiro Agnew? But it turns
out to be Socrates?"

Still, there were times when nothing helped, and Elizabeth

imagined digging into her daughter's contemptuous face with her badly bitten nails. James was more patient than Elizabeth, until he snapped, after which he was more apt to ground Rosie or take away her allowance. A beam of good nature shone through him most of the time, through the crucible of adolescent explosion and experiments with drugs, and Rosie's transformation into a tall and voluptuous beauty, and the subsequent parade of young men; and through Elizabeth's menopause, depressions, and slips she had had around alcohol, the last only two years behind them. He loved them both like a good dog, a rescue dog, which is how he sometimes felt. At times he'd study them over a pleasant meal, and enthuse, almost in tears, "It doesn't get much better than this." He helped Rosie with her homework and picked up around the house without being asked. And the two best things: he loved to gossip, anybody doing anything with anyone else, anywhere, in the family or out in the world; and he loved to lie in bed or on the couch or beach or anywhere, and read.

But Rosie could push him over the edge into heavy peevishness, as now, by being late. He growled: "What time'd she say she'd meet us?"

"Noon."

"If she's not here in three minutes, we're going."

"When did you get to be so bossy?" But she knew the answer. He had become more anxious and vigilant in the last few years, since Elizabeth's little breakdown on the trampoline, as they still referred to it. Three years ago, while bouncing with Rosie on a neighbor's trampoline in Bayview, something had jiggled itself loose, all the suppressed loss and devastation she'd kept to herself after Andrew's death, and it poured forth without ceasing. She had spent a month dazed or crying in bed, on new medication, seeing her psychiatrist every two days. Then, two years ago, she'd had that brief AA slip, which is to say she had started drinking again after many years clean and sober. James hadn't a clue she'd been nipping at the bottle late at night for a week, until he'd found her that morning at dawn on the bathroom floor. She held up a bottle of prescription pain pills for his sciatica. "My back hurts," she said, which it did, as she had slept crumpled up on the cold tiles after falling sometime during the night. She didn't recall much of the previous evening, except that it had involved the last of the sake that James's Japanese publisher had sent him three years before, when he got his book published in Japan. They'd kept the sake for the sheer beauty of the painting of rice fields at sunset on the white ceramic bottle.

His depression showed up as unpleasantness, grumbling self-pity, and running complaints about life. Normally this was their main amusement, good-natured comments about how ridiculous and hopeless everything was. Sometimes Elizabeth had to cross her legs to keep from peeing at his observations and outlandish lies. He'd say anything to make them both laugh and to lift his own spirits. Just the other day, he had told people in line at Macy's that Elizabeth was a falconer. Another time, he had told people at a protest rally that she had won a silver medal in the Munich Olympics—in dressage, of all things. She had just nodded upon hearing this and tried to look more horsey.

But while his depressions were infrequent, hers were chronic, lifelong and deep. They required extensive medication and periodic therapy to keep at bay the thoughts of killing herself or starting to drink again or both.

"Oh, who doesn't?" Rae had exclaimed when Elizabeth shared this with her recently. "Life on earth is a head-scratcher for any-one who's paying attention. This place has been a bad match for me since I was four."

"Really? But you're so kind and positive."

"Nah," she said, pooh-poohing it. "I'm just happy around you."

"So what are we supposed to do again, when we hate everything?"

"You stop pretending life is such fun or makes sense. It's often messy and cruel and dull, and we do the best we can. It's unfair, and jerks seem to win. But you fall in love with a few people. Like I love you, Elizabeth. You're the angel God sent me."

Rae said this fairly frequently. It was ludicrous; there was no one less angelic. Rae would tell this to perfect strangers at the movies or the health food store, pointing to Elizabeth. She used to protest. "But I'm so erratic and depressed!"

"Hey, I like that in a girl. Look, if you don't have a bad attitude and lots of things wrong with you, no serious person is going to be interested. If you feel scared, outraged, confused most of the time, come on over. Have a seat."

That people like Rae and James and Lank adored and needed her, three people of the highest possible quality, who could have anyone they wanted, was all Elizabeth had to go on most days, and unless she was in a depression, it was enough.

She looked over at James sitting beside her on the steps of the Parkade. Any woman in her right mind would love to be married to such a kind and hilarious man, but he had chosen her, and then stayed. It kind of boggled the mind.

He started to stand but abruptly reached for the notebook in his back pocket, sat down, and began scribbling.

Surprised by the stay of execution, Elizabeth looked even harder for Rosie. They had been in Landsdale a year, after selling Andrew's house in Bayview and buying a much cheaper one here, where the zip code was not as desirable. It was a pretty, almost rural town of three thousand generally ordinary, educated, outdoorsy Bay Area citizens, but with more than its share of tie-dye and vegans. Bumper stickers proclaimed it Mayberry on acid. The women here owned more horses and had had much less cosmetic surgery than women in the wealthier parts of Marin, and many let their hair go slowly gray, as Elizabeth had begun to do a few years ago. (Still, she got her hair cut at a slightly upscale salon in Sausalito, pricey for their budget, but necessary—she insisted—for her emotional well-being.) She and James had made a profit on the sale of the Bayview house, even after capital gains, which they would use to live on—James had not broken out as a writer and had gotten only a small advance for his second book, which had taken him two and a half years to write so far. Rosie would be going to college in a year, and while there was some money socked away from Andrew's trust fund, they had dipped into it over time for urgent home repairs and for psychiatric expenses after Elizabeth's various crises. It had been necessary and helpful for her finally to deal with the catastrophe of Andrew's death, but it had cost them financial security. They had mediocre health insurance, and she needed expensive antidepressants, and nonaddictive antianxiety meds that did not threaten her sobriety. She sometimes wanted to get a job in a bookstore or a gallery, but there was so much to do around the house, keeping their lives and schedules in some semblance of order, that she had never seriously pursued it. She planned to, though, after Rosie left for school.

◻

Leaving Bayview had meant moving ten miles from Rae, who still lived in her great studio with the massive loom in its center, and it meant Rosie's leaving behind her old friends and going to a new school for her last four semesters of high school. But it also meant they could make ends meet if they were careful.

Elizabeth had started going to AA meetings in Landsdale after they moved. The alkies at the meetings in Bayview had helped her get well after her little breakdown on the trampoline and her slip, even though she had not let anyone there know her well. And while she did not agree with Rae that a pulsing seed of God was inside each person waiting to bloom, she had stopped seeing the people in recovery as a bunch of fundamentalist bowling-alley types. She practiced the slogan "Live and let live" as well as she could, even when it came to their higher powers, which seemed to range from celestial butlers to schizophrenic voices to her personal favorite, that of a New Age mother who described God as a giant beanbag chair into which she could sink and whose loving arms wrapped around her in comfort as she rested.

Elizabeth saw that James had stopped scribbling, and she looked around the Parkade for something to distract him and buy more time. "Oh my God," she said. "Look at Lisa Morton." James nodded at the emaciated woman with the yoga mat coming out of the general store, who had a son in Rosie's math class. Once, when James had become convinced she was dying of cancer, he had asked her if she was okay, and she'd replied, smugly, "Yoga."

"Look—that will be us someday," Elizabeth continued, pointing at an old couple coming out of the health food store. She recognized them from the few times she had attended Rae's church, which was nearby. They were raising their grandchild, who was one of Rae's church-school kids. The child's mother lived on the streets in San Rafael, between stints in county rehab. The grandmother sported what looked like goggles you'd wear on glaciers, through which she kept looking around like a little bird. Maybe you didn't see well anymore, Elizabeth thought, but you wanted to see as much as you possibly could for as long as you could, and you wanted to be seen. The couple were dressed in flowing linen pants and shirts, down vests, and thin bright knit caps with ear flaps, like off-duty Sherpas.

"Go give them a hand," said Elizabeth. The grandfather's canvas bag was heavy with food, pulling his right shoulder several inches lower than the left. James got to his feet and walked toward them. Rae's church was called Sixth Day Prez, although it was not Presbyterian. It was not anything in particular. Rae and the founding minister, the formerly Very Reverend Anthony Small, had liked the sound of it when they first considered the idea of breaking away from the old church, after he had had an awful rift with the governing board over, of all things, God's omniscience. Anthony had begun to waffle on the precept after his scholarly young son was shot in a drive-by on New Year's morning in San Francisco two years before. He was nineteen, no longer on Anthony's family medical plan, and his care at County Hospital in Oakland had been barely passable, so that when he recovered, he had a severe limp and hearing loss.

The theme of the old church was that God had a perfect plan for everyone, but Anthony had come to believe that God was nowhere near done with the job of creation: this was why everything seemed so tragic and inadequate. He or She and we were still all on the sixth day, together. You weren't going to understand much while on earth, except that God was present with us in the whole catastrophe. Anthony had not formulated this belief; it had been part of an ongoing rabbinical conversation for centuries. But he had added his own progressive convictions—that those who could must help take care of those flattened by the wheel of the System. The thing was, the church responded, this didn't really work for them anymore.

Rae, on the other hand, old Berkeley activist that she was, heard the words "the System" and signed on as part-time office manager and lay minister at the cabin in a redwood grove that Anthony rented in the town next to Landsdale. She loved it, and the small salary and good benefits helped during lean times for her as a weaver.

The formerly Very Reverend Small was light brown, half Haitian, tall with funky teeth and a hat rack that he festooned with African caps and scarves, which he wore instead of ties. Rosie had gone to hear him preach several times, and while she did not exactly believe in God, she loved the scarves, the caps, and the fact that he did not make you call him Reverend Anthony. "Anthony" was fine, although Rosie called him Anferny, after a character in her favorite teenage movie. He told her she resembled his Black Irish mother, with her long black curls and cerulean eyes. She had worked beside him and Elizabeth to set up an organic community garden in the poorest part of San Rafael, and had gone with him and the four kids in the Sixth Day Prez youth group to help clean up after oil spills in San Francisco Bay, and after floods from the late-winter rains.

Rae was Rosie's authority on all things spiritual, because her beliefs were so simple and kind. You were loved because God loves, period. God loved you, and everyone, not because you believed certain things, but because you were a mess, and lonely, and His or Her child. God loved you no matter how crazy you felt on the inside, no matter what a fake you were; always, even in your current condition, even before coffee. God loves you crazily, like I love you, Rae said, like a slightly overweight auntie, who sees only your marvelousness and need.

◘

Elizabeth turned to look over her shoulders at a commotion across the Parkade by the bus kiosk. A group of young people had gathered, passing a joint and sniggering, shoving, sharing: it was ridiculous, like a last-chance preschool. Some were older kids who had already graduated from high school but stayed around,

who had dropped out of college or been kicked out, or who had forgotten to move out of their parents' houses. There were men in their
mid-twenties, too. A couple of them were known to be dealers. You
didn't ever see them dealing, but you did see them with sexy stoned
adoring girls.

She glanced around for Rosie. James had gone off with the old
couple, but he should be back in a few minutes. There would be no
more stalling in the hopes that Rosie would appear. Cars drove in at
the western edge of the Parkade, and exited to the east, across from
the movie theater, near the other set of stairs. People were parking
and getting out of cars, or walking to check out library books, or buy
hardware, or order muffins at the KerryDas Café. They bumped
into one another, checked in briefly, and Elizabeth eavesdropped:

"Where's Chelsea for the summer?"

"Habitat for Humanity, in Georgia." That might be a good plan
for Rosie next summer, come to think of it.

"Hi, April—long time! Did you get your tomatoes in yet?"

"How about those Giants? Look to you like the fire sale's about
to begin?"

"Hey, Smitty—why weren't you at soccer Saturday morning?"

"Special Olympics, remember?"

"Oh, yeah. Did Hannah have a good time?"

"Yes, but this year she got stuck next to the pincher." Elizabeth
smiled and made a note to tell James. They went to the Special
Olympics every couple of years, and knew the pincher.

James came into sight, on his return from helping out the old
folks. She hung her head. The jig was up and she walked toward
him. Someone had put new geraniums in the flower boxes that lined
the steps. Bees and white butterflies flew above the pink flowers. She
reflexively nipped off the dead heads.

"I'm going to go put this in the recycling," he called to her, hold-ing up his paper and changing course. She watched him pass a group of teenagers, lowering his eyes like a spy, then glancing back over his shoulder. He constantly pumped Rosie for details of the lives of the people who hung around at the Parkade, for the novel he was working on. One of them in particular interested him: a hand-some surfer type in his mid-twenties named Fenn, who wore wire-rimmed glasses and always seemed to have a young beauty in tow. James had pointed him out to Rosie. "There's a guy in my book like him. The same great looks and flat confidence. As if he has an internal story he doesn't have to explain to anyone. Or maybe a kind of predatory patience."

Rosie had rolled her eyes. "Oh, for God's sake, James, it's all in your head. Remember how panicky you guys were over Luther?" Luther was the old wino who'd started watching Rosie play tennis the year she turned fourteen, her last year on the courts. The year she and her partner Simone were ranked number one in the state for fourteen-and-under doubles. The year Simone got pregnant and moved to Ukiah. When Rosie was still fretful and shy and skinny, before the breasts and contempt. Luther, darker than shadows, ter-rorized the parents of girls on the tennis circuit, who thought he was a pedophile. "And remember what dastardly deed he ended up doing to me?" Rosie glared. "He helped me with my *serve*, for God's sake."

This was her new phrase, said with clipped disbelief at your stupidity—*for God's sake*. And, This is the reason I want to move out. And, You are so lame.

Still, she provided James with great stuff for his writing. She told him about teenage chatter and slang, the dope, and the kids who had been in rehab. She described how they all clustered together to make themselves a village in which a few rare people seemed to have knowledge and power.

"Oh, baby," James told her, "it's always been the same." His novel took place in the years when Reagan was governor, when his generation was still walking around the Haight with girlfriends and boyfriends, accepting what came along, giving away what they had to share whether it was a burrito, a bouquet, drugs, a dollar—it had all felt so heady, delicious, and right. Then as now, young people liked spectacle, especially musical, but also watching the random bust, as long as it was people you didn't like. Then as now in the Parkade, talismanic amulets hung from their necks, strange caps kept them warm and said how different they were, especially when it was a hundred degrees out. And how, at the same time, all that mattered was fitting in. There was fitting in, somehow, anywhere, and there was the Abyss.

The last time Elizabeth and Rosie had gone on a hike together, Elizabeth had brought up the friends-with-benefits business, not for the first time. "Tell me again—help me understand—what's in it for the girls?"

At first Rosie said, "I told you. It is so exaggerated, just something the moms are obsessed with. And there's nothing I can say to help you understand." Then she allowed that maybe some skeevy girls did it too much, like without even having affection for the guy. Or guys. But mostly, it was just . . . friendly. And it meant that you were desirable.

"Plus," Rosie said, "the guys are so grateful."

"Well, yeah, I *guess*," said Elizabeth. "But do the guys ever go down on the girls?"

"Mom! Stop."

"But what's in it for the girl? It's like the women's movement never happened."

"It's nice for the girl. It's like kissing. It makes you feel really close to the guy. I mean, you know, for that night. And it makes the girls feel powerful."

Just then a Steller's jay had squawked rustily from a manzanita branch, bright blue against the maroon wood, and Rosie had cried out in imitation, "Oil can! Oil can!" They both laughed in the sun and let the conversation slide. Elizabeth pointed out a red-tailed hawk on solemn patrol overhead against the blue May sky. There were cactus impersonators on the trail beside them—spiky-looking flowers that were soft and fuzzy if you stopped to touch them, which they did. Rosie cried, "Ouch," as if the fluffy flowers had thorns, and gripped her fingers in pain, to make her mother laugh. Oh, Rosie. The sun beat down and the air smelled like toast. The rattle-snake grass that covered the hills was dark gold, the color you spray-painted pine cones at Christmas.

"I'm leaving," James announced as he caught up to Elizabeth at the foot of the steps. "I want a divorce. You can keep the children. I don't know how long I am going to live, but I do not choose to spend whatever remains with your passive-aggressive daughter. It's not like we're dragging her off to the dentist. We want to spend money on her, and still she blows us off. We have to leave now, Elizabeth, trust me. If we stay, it injures her character. You must not reward brattiness or flake."

Elizabeth knew he was right. You want so desperately for your child to be a great kid, just like you, mature, conscious, and cool—you in another body. At the very least, you want your child to have good manners. Maybe that was considered reactionary now, but this was how she had raised Rosie. The worst humans on earth kept you waiting. And James had been in such a good mood when they woke: he had gotten laid, there was toasted brioche for breakfast, roses from the garden on the table. Now he was shoving his notebook into the back pocket of his khakis, fuming. Elizabeth exhaled loudly and held her head as if it ached. Just yesterday, he had been singing Rosie's praises, about a journal entry she'd written and shown him. It was about her two best friends, Jody and Alice:

"You don't always like the same guys or movies or books, but you share the knowledge that most of 'life' is just people faking it, trying to stay busy so they feel important and not afraid of their shadows. But my friends and I know that this busyness is like collecting Franklin Mint plates and you have to fight for meaning in your life, for truth and goodness and authenticity."

James had been astonished. "Can I have this?" he asked her, handing back the journal, and she laughed. "Oh, for God's sake, James."

At one point during the recent walk with Rosie, the day of the rattlesnake grass, they'd been catching their breath at the clearing on the trail where you could see Alcatraz, Angel Island, the Berkeley hills, and the Bay Bridge. They stood beside a posted sign of a mountain lion that looked just like an animal cracker. They could see the entire East Bay, on which the morning sun usually slanted in fingers or in dappled splatters of white on the mirror of water. But this time, a solidly frothy tunnel of light transected the whole bay from Alcatraz to Richmond in the east. They stared as if at an ancient churchyard.

"How would you describe that?" Elizabeth asked Rosie when they started walking again.

After a moment: "I'd say it was a surfer's perfect tube of foamy light."

"Can I have that for James?" Elizabeth asked, to make her daughter laugh. Rosie smiled. She had a pretty smile, with one funny snaggly tooth to the side, definitely not the shining straight white teeth that seemed the norm among teenagers now, at least the ones whose parents could afford braces.

Elizabeth slipped her arm through James's and they headed toward the car, but just then she heard, from across the street, "Mama, Mama! James!"

There she was, smiling, waving, walking toward them, tall and broad-shouldered after a childhood of being so thin, her black hair piled on her head, the way Rae wore hers, too, like hippie girls, secured with pencils, silver clasps, porcelain chopsticks. Her breasts were nearly as big as Elizabeth's now. Everyone, men and women alike, checked them out; even children checked them out, with memory and fear and desperation. She wore short shredded cut-offs and a white gypsy shirt over the spandex tank top that contained the sprawl, dangling earrings she'd borrowed from Elizabeth, red Converse All Stars. She and Alice and Jody bought most of their clothes at secondhand stores, except for shoes and their hundred-dollar jeans. Elizabeth made eye contact with James, to convey solidarity, her refusal to forgive fully, but a moment later, she stepped into Rosie's hug, relieved and happy as a devotee or a golden retriever. Rosie smelled of the vanilla extract she wore as perfume, with the faint smoky odor of incense and campfires and the rare cigarette, and the foundation with which she, like Alice and Jody, was spackled.

Elizabeth stepped back and touched Rosie's smooth fair skin with the backs of her fingers, avoiding the scattered pimples. You could hardly notice them except right before her periods, and of course, unless you were Rosie, to whom they might as well have been carbuncles. She had not picked them today. Elizabeth pushed a tendril of hair out of Rosie's deep blue eyes, noting as she did so the pterygium on her left eye, the raised and wedge-shaped growth of sun damage from all those years of light reflecting off tennis courts. She had not picked up a racket in more than two years, but it had not gone away. James called it her terrigenous pterygium: it looked like a blob of underwater sediment trying to sneak across her cornea. It did not affect her sight, and she could have it surgically removed someday if she chose.

Rosie peered at James, as if looking around a corner. He scrutinized his watch. "I'm sorry, James. I swear I'll make it up to you."

"I hate waiting!"

"Well then, next time, just leave."

"I'm going to."

"Why aren't you wearing sunglasses?" Elizabeth interrupted. Rosie shrugged, but Elizabeth persisted. "This is important—it's your only real protection from more damage." And was that concealer under her eyes? "Did you get a good sleep?" she continued, worried, studying the faint blue crescents she now saw under Rosie's eyes. "I didn't hear you come in last night. Have you eaten? Did you at least eat some fruit before you came? Let's get you a muffin before we go shopping."

"God, Mama!" Rosie said. "Stop! I'm not a child."

James started to say something, but Rosie made a face of exasperation, and reached forward with a burlesque flourish to choke him, and in spite of himself, he smiled. Then he ambushed her with a wrestling move, his famous ninja tango hammerlock. She easily slid out of his grasp: each of them knew all the other one's moves.

"God," she said, "you are so loked."

It rhymed with "stoked" and meant crazy, out of control, about to beat somebody up. James leered at her as lokily as he could, and she countered with a karate chop to the neck. He took three steps back and went into the one yoga pose he knew, Downward Facing Dog.

Elizabeth and Rosie exchanged a look—he was such an idiot. When he got up, the three of them set off together down the street.

TWO

Memorial Day

◘

At sunset a few days later, a parade of small clouds lined up low over the westernmost hills of Landsdale, perfectly spaced and aligned. James and Elizabeth sat in a rasping wicker porch swing that the sellers had left behind in the trashed garden of the rickety and voracious house, overpriced until you factored in the sunset. The sky was soft pink; the night was cool. When the clouds crashed and stumbled forward one into another, James gathered up the tea tray and they went inside.

Rosie had not eaten with them that evening, as she was heading out soon to a party with Jody and Alice in Stinson Beach, forty-five minutes away. She was in her bathroom, reapplying foundation. She was actually going to two parties, although her parents knew only about the first.

Rosie had told them about the one at Jody's aunt Vivian's house.

She said they were spending the night there, which was true if you substituted "evening" for "night." But none of the girls knew yet where they would sleep. After the party, a bunch of kids from Landsdale, Bolinas, and Stinson were meeting on the beach. The girls would figure out where to crash later, depending on who else showed up, who was holding, and how things in general shook down.

Aunt Vivian's party was to celebrate Jody's return from three months at a rehab in the mountains of Santa Cruz. She had been home a month already, but this was the first Saturday that worked for everyone in the family. Her parents had sent her off because she did too much alcohol and cocaine—she had ended up at the ER one night around Christmas, having overdosed on both, and Alice and Rosie were relieved that her parents had stepped in, although having her kidnapped at three a.m. by morbidly obese Samoans seemed a little extreme. What sucked, though, was that she was now expected to stay off marijuana, too—as if that had been part of the problem. At the rehab, she had received enough credits in independent study to finish out the current semester, plus had earned a whole semester's worth of credit toward her senior year. So she had only one more semester to go before graduation. She had stayed clean nearly a week after her return, and was still off alcohol, coke, and weed. The other stuff, which she used mostly on weekends, was legal, like Alice's Adderall for ADD, her parents' sedatives, the family cough syrup, and salvia, which you could buy in variable strengths at any head shop. Nothing that would show up in the urine tests or on a Breathalyzer. So if Rosie wanted to do Ecstasy, say, or mushrooms, she and Alice did them when Jody wasn't around.

James and Elizabeth greeted them after they barged in. They wore camisoles over tank tops, and jeans. Alice, who had already been assured by the dean of the San Francisco Fashion Institute of Design that she would be accepted next year, wore a silver sweater that seemed to be made of spiderweb and bugle beads, cropped at the armpits, and a pale orange silk scarf.

"Oh my God," said Elizabeth. "You'll freeze to death."

Rosie appeared in the hallway. "Mom, please don't mom everyone to death and wreck this for us."

"It's okay, Elizabeth," Alice said. "We have down jackets in the car."

James advanced in his most menacing way toward the girls. "Look me in the eye, Jody." He seemed ridiculous: she towered over him, like a tree, taller even than Elizabeth. He wagged a finger in her face.

"You are totally loked," Jody said, and smiled. Rosie felt half in love with Jody, because she was so smart and cool and beautiful, even with that straggly hair that required expensive cuts to look barely okay, after a great deal of mousse and fussing. Tonight she had punked it out with plastic barrettes gathering up the thin sheaves. Jody thought of herself as a freak, a giraffe, but Rosie found her exquisite. She had written a poem about her in English class, about her soft brown eyes, and about how in her company you felt that there was a shimmery barrier around her, or a channel to a higher realm, of spring weather, the clouds and breezes, the shifts in the air. Maybe Elizabeth had given off that same sense once when she was younger, of being a conduit—tall, slightly alien, stately, reserved, and lovely, hard as this was to believe.

Like, would it kill her mother to dye the gray streaks in her hair?

James shook his fist at Jody like an old man angry with the weather: "You don't drink anymore, right, Jody? Still off the sauce, Jody? That's all behind us now, right, Jody? *Right, Jody?*" he shouted.

"Right, Jody," Jody said. They gave each other a smile, and touched fists in a gang handshake James had invented, roe-shambeau, that segued into gobbledygook sign language.

"Okay, then, sweetheart," James asked, "how is your writing coming along?" Jody gave him two thumbs up. Rosie had shown him some of Jody's stories and poems, and he'd told everyone that she had a gift, like duh, hello, she'd only been winning prizes since third grade. A number of times, he had edited her stories while she paced like an expectant father in Rosie's room, and he lent her books that she had to read if she wanted to be a writer: lending meant a future discussion. It was great to have a stepfather who could genuinely help your friends.

"And you, Alice," he now said. Rosie watched him turn to threaten Alice. "Are you an alcoholic, Alice? *Huh, Alice?*" She gave James a look of wounded and amused scorn, and Rosie smiled. Alice drank, but preferred weed and mushrooms. Moony, dewy Alice, with long reddish-blond hair and pale blue eyes, looked so innocent, her face an angelic foil to the tight camisoles and baby-doll tops she favored. She was the most sexually active of the three girls, and had been since she was thirteen. She usually wore jean skirts no longer than Rosie's tennis dresses, torn tights, rakish caps, scarves, and always perfect earrings. "Cool duds, dude," Alice told James. "Very Mr. Rogers." Rosie smiled as Alice looked him over, holding her palms out in wordless appreciation of the magnificence of his madras shorts. He polished his nails on his gray cardigan.

"Have you decided whether or not to apply to Parsons, Alice?"

James asked. Rosie loved this about him, the way he remembered details from your life, like names, or what you were reading. Alice shook her head. James offered her his fist for the special handshake.

Rosie would not have admitted to anyone that she loved Jody more than Alice. Alice had come with Jody; they were a set when Rosie started school here last year. There were lots of girls like Alice at school, sexy and fun, giddy, the life of the party. James said that having her to dinner was like inviting a bubble bath to join you. And Rosie loved her, but she'd never met anyone quite like Jody, who had some sort of quiet power. Jody looked like she'd stepped out of the first Mozart opera Rosie had seen—very restrained, but like she might flick her crop and all the horses would rush right at you.

"I'll need you all to do a Breathalyzer when you get back," James continued, and everyone knew he was teasing. He shook his finger at them. "Urine tests, lie detector, stool samples . . ."

Elizabeth swatted at him. She and Rosie exchanged put-upon glances, but in fact, Rosie's parents had never tested her for drugs or alcohol. She had successfully weaned herself off cocaine without Elizabeth's having known that she'd even tried it, let alone done it every weekend for months. Let alone stolen twenties from Elizabeth's purse, and from the family emergency fund, which she hated about herself. But her parents were so fixated on Elizabeth's reclaimed sobriety that they did not particularly worry about whether Rosie was drinking or not. She was discreet about it. If she smoked dope or drank, she had a tiny kit in her purse, with Visine, breath mints, and towelettes with a strong scent.

They were so clueless about Rosie's private life that the first time James had confided in her about Elizabeth's slip, two years ago, Rosie was coming down off Ecstasy, trying not to grind her teeth into paste as she listened. He wanted to share his belief that in the long run, the slip had been a blessing in disguise. Rosie nodded, paying extra attention so James wouldn't notice how tweaked she was: Okay, blessing in disguise, what ev, as Alice said. He wanted her to go to his Al-Anon meetings now, for the families of alcoholics, or Alateen, but so far she had evaded him. He told her stuff about the meetings, hoping she would glean kernels of understanding or amusement the way he did, such as that people there said that AA was for problem drinkers, and Al-Anon for problem thinkers, spouses and parents of alcoholics, who hid out in their rooms, secretly thinking alone, having good ideas on how to rescue and fix the drinker. She pretended to listen. He always came back in a better mood after meetings.

He had made Rosie go to a psychologist with him after Elizabeth's slip. They were still in the old house and Rosie was finishing her freshman year. The therapist had said a few very cool things that Rosie remembered, like that they had not caused Elizabeth to start drinking again, which was good, and that they couldn't keep her from drinking if she decided to, which was bad. Rosie had not understood why they couldn't keep her mother from drinking, and James had tried to explain that addiction was like dancing with an eight-hundred-pound gorilla: you were done dancing when the gorilla was done. Wow, the drinker thinks at first, the music is great, and what a wonderful dancer! But then when you get tired and want to sit, the gorilla wants to do the merengue, and you have to keep going. You feel sick, you hate yourself, you want to stop, but now the gorilla wants to waltz.

"So what do we do?" Rosie asked when James told her all this.

"You stay out of the gorilla cage. You don't even go in to clean it."

"What about when it needs it? Like when she gets very down?"

"You don't clean it, just for today. Because after you freshened it up, if she was still sad, you'd think it made sense to get between her and the gorilla."

"But what's the worse that could happen?"

"Well. It could tear your arms off."

"Sometimes I want to push her down the stairs for starting to drink again," Rosie admitted.

"Just for today, you don't push anyone down the stairs. Okay? Maybe tomorrow."

The next morning when Rosie woke, she found a sign James had taped by her desk that said, "Tomorrow." Elizabeth saw this, loved it, made her own sign, and taped it to her mirror. She shared it with Rae, and now there was a sign in Rae's house, too, taped to a kitchen cabinet, "Tomorrow." And Elizabeth had not had a drink since.

But in Jody's aging Camry, a campaign button on the dashboard insisted on the opposite—"¡Ahora!" Now! It was from a recent rally for immigrant rights in San Francisco that she, Rosie, and Alice had gone to with Rae and Elizabeth. There were feathers stuck into the stereo speaker on the dashboard, and a small plastic Mary standing on top, although Jody did not believe in God. Rosie believed in something, some sort of energy field or force, like a cross between the oceans and their cat, Rascal. More on the Rascal side. No, more on the ocean side—force, beauty, vastness, sheer rhythmic being: her physics teacher, Mr. Tobias, was helping her with a paper for her college applications that said you could prove this with quantum theory.

The girls drove along the windy road in the dark, past all their favorite places: low hills, talkative creeks, redwood groves. Björk sang from the speakers in the car, all weird emotional beauty and snowy purity, and Alice passed out Adderall to help them stay awake for the long night ahead.

* * *

J ames and Elizabeth sprawled in the living room all night and
read with Beethoven on the stereo. They were not celebrating
Memorial Day, although Rae and Lank had invited them to a jazz
concert in Napa. Every so often Elizabeth looked up and asked
whether James thought Rosie was dead in a fiery car crash, and
James said jeez, he hoped not.

They gave Rosie a lot of independence, partly because she
seemed to have such a good head on her shoulders, had never gotten
into any real trouble, but mostly because she did so well at school:
the three girls had gotten almost all A's, even when Jody was going
down the tubes, even in honors classes, and for Rosie even in physics. She was a good writer, but not like Jody, and arty, but not like
Alice, who was like a hip-hop Coco Chanel. Alice was the one who
would put Landsdale on the map, with awards in fashion design.
It was the physics that made Rosie unusual among Landsdale students. Andrew had had a gift for physics and math, and had almost
gone into engineering, and he always insisted that Rosie had inherited the genes: before she could walk, she'd begun tinkering with
strollers, her own and those parked nearby. She would crawl underneath to have a look. Once, at two years old, before she was talking, she had started Andrew's car. It seemed a philosophical thing,
or instinctive hardwiring, that she could see relationships between
things, a scientific version of what James had—the noticing genes
necessary to be a good writer. Rosie's mind liked to do things with
its hands. She liked to imagine things that you could not see, like
black holes and the far side of a pyramid. She was at home in the
abstract realm of witnessing and synthesizing.

Elizabeth watched James read. Looking up at him from the window seat, she remembered the first years after Andrew's death, drinking so hard, flailing, all those sexual encounters one shouldn't have had. It was unbearable that he was gone, gone-gone, as if a Hoover had vacuumed him up.

"James?"

He put his book down, looked over the top of his glasses. "Do you think we should worry more about Rosie? The odds of her being an alcoholic are way better than average. And her two best friends, Jody with her history of abuse, and Alice such a party girl, even though she's so accomplished—"

James interrupted her. "We know she's gotten drunk a few times with them. And we know they smoke a little pot. But first of all, you can't worry yourself into serenity. We keep our eyes open. And secondly, Rosie is her own person now." Though he said it in the spirit of reassurance, this insight had the opposite effect. Elizabeth clutched at her throat and breathed like a dying asthmatic to make him laugh, but then panic and sadness rose inside her like a swamp monster, and tried to pull her down.

◘

Rosie stayed on the outskirts of the party, feeling like her usual loser self, shadowy as a frond. There were greetings and friendly confusion around her, Jody's relatives pouring in from all over Northern California. Rosie knew some pretty squalid details of the family—alcoholism, infidelity, and even incest, although the incest guy in the family was not here, and two of the alcoholism people held cans of Diet Coke. Jody's oldest uncle had come down from Santa Rosa, looking unchanged since Rosie had last seen him, while his wife looked older; all the wives here looked like their husbands' big sisters, watching out for baby brother. This completely freaked her out.

Jody's mother, Sarah, was medium tall, with frosted hair, a perfect nose, and a nice sense of humor. She worked as a copywriter for an advertising firm in San Francisco and had a no-nonsense way about her. Rosie liked her for her strength—she seemed like the kind of mother who never panicked, who stayed calm by drawing on reserves of inner strength; the sort of mother who would be able to lift a car off her child, unlike Elizabeth. Alice liked her for her normalcy and casseroles, as her own mother ate mostly raw food and some sort of vegan seed disks, like you'd attach inside a bird's cage for it to peck at. Jody's mother dressed like a relaxed woman with style and money, lots of fitted fancy third-world blouses. Alice's mother was only thirty-six, and a Sufi teacher. She thought of Alice as her roommate or little sister, and rarely came home before midnight. Alice had met her father only a few times over the years, which was fine. He was sixty-five and had many young children with many young women.

Jody's grandmother Marion sat in a safari chair with a cup holder. She was ninety, weighed about forty pounds, and looked like polished bone. Rosie had met her a few times with Jody, and a couple of times at Rae's church. She was across the patio, under the trees, and Rosie signaled to her that she would join her in a minute. She always tried to hang out with the oldest people because otherwise they got ignored. Old people seemed to like her. Also, she was good with kids. Great: old people and kids; why couldn't she be good with guys?

Alice came over to show Rosie the bottle of wine she had just stolen from the pantry, and tucked it into her backpack to share on the beach later. They hung out for a while: Alice kept looping her fingers through Rosie's hair, combing it, and gathering hanks of it, to coil around her hand.

Jody really couldn't hang out with the two of them, she had to schmooze with the relatives, so when Alice wandered off, Rosie went over to talk to Jody's grandmother.

Grandma Marion grasped Rosie's hands with her papery moth fingers like something from the grave, and begged to hear about James; women of all ages loved James. That's one thing Rosie appreciated about her mother—that she'd gotten a guy all the other women in town wanted, even though he was short. And that her mother had managed to get him to stay, and to adore her.

Rosie shook her head at Marion with hopelessness—where did you even start? James was a treasure trove of silly behavior. Like he might point to a tall middle-aged black man and say in a hushed tone, "Oh my God, is that O. J. Simpson?" Once he'd stopped in his tracks and gasped at a scrawny old gypsy woman, and said, "Is that Keith Richards?" But she didn't know whether this was Grandma Marion's kind of humor.

So she told her about how he'd stumble across a funny line and then run it into the ground, and for some reason, it just kept making you laugh. Not that long ago, he'd discovered Old Bay seasoning, and he'd say it like Walter Brennan, he'd go, "I'm going to add me a shake of Ollld Bay." Then he'd find a way to work it into every other sentence, about anything. He'd say, "When summer approaches, there's nothing better than the lingering taste of Ollld Bay."

Marion clapped and laughed, so Rosie continued. "Then there was the old-Indian-saying stage, where you could be talking about anything, and he would get a far-off look on his face and say solemnly, 'That reminds me of an old Indian saying,' and he would say, 'What goes around comes around,' or once, 'With time, even a bear can learn to dance,' which was *Yiddish*, for God's sake. And the Indian-name stage, where he would announce that his Indian name was Bucky, or Lemonhead." Marion laughed like a whale clearing its throat, a clicking whistly moan.

When she ran out of James stories, Rosie asked Marion about when she was young, until Marion needed to get up to use the bathroom. It took a while to get her to her feet—you'd think you could lift her up easily like a feather, but because of her arthritis, even though Rosie tried to lift her as carefully as possible so nothing got yanked, she kept folding up like a card table. Rosie thought of Amish people lifting the wall of a barn they had finished but that had started to come apart. Finally Jody's father noticed what was happening, and arrived at his mother's side. Together they got Marion up and in balance, and she walked off on his arm like a marionette.

Rosie went upstairs to the aunt's bathroom for a little recon. There was a half-full prescription bottle of Valium, and she shook a bunch into her hand, a few for tonight, a few just to have. If you washed one down with wine or whatever, along with an Adderall, you were pretty animated, but calmer than you would have been. She tucked them into the watch pocket of her jeans for later.

She liked being a fly on the wall here. She felt welcome and trusted. She could tell that Jody's parents liked her. Rosie thought it was because she was kind, excelled in school, and had been a tennis champion: if any of the three girls seemed a bad influence, it was Alice, who dressed wild and had been sexually active for so long, and whose mother was home so rarely. And Rosie liked watching Jody's family because you could see that they cared about one another.

They had pulled together for Jody, like a web around her. She felt a pang of jealousy, because she had such a tiny pathetic family herself, but she was relieved that the parents had stepped in. The relatives kept sneaking peeks at Jody, holding their breath with worry, but also trying to give her as much room and slack as possible. Jody had been on perilous ground before, doing so much cocaine, blowing guys to get some of their stash, and she could have died one night in a car crash that killed the girl in the front seat. So now she was back and people wanted her to be safe and well, and maybe they felt like if they were toxic and fake around her, she would get sick again. So they reflected their very best at her and she was reflecting it back.

There was not a single guy at the party to flirt with, let alone hook up with later, except for one cute football player Alice sort of had dibs on. None of them were virgins anymore, Jody and Alice not by a long shot. Rosie had had sex three times, but not yet with anyone she loved. She obsessed about it all the time, about how next time she wanted it to be romantic and meaningful, so you could cuddle, instead of just having to get it over with or get back into the cocaine. Romantic meant you had been gazing into each other's eyes for at least a couple of weeks, and the first, slow kiss with him was not the night you went all the way; more like in a beautiful romantic movie. The first time was very nice, actually, at some older girl's apartment on Blithedale who didn't even go to junior college yet, who would probably not even ever leave town. Rosie and a senior had gotten to use the girl's bedroom, and the senior was actually the perfect person to lose her virginity to, and afterward, for a few days, every bump in the road that she drove over triggered her, reawakened the erotic feelings she had had. Everything did, as if a lava lamp of being fully alive and soft would bloom in her crotch and rise up through her. Then the next two times, once with the senior at his house, and once with another guy in his car, she'd hated it.

She went to find Alice. The food on the grill smelled like it was ready, and Rosie wanted to leave as soon as they ate. Jody would have to stay until the party was over, but she and Alice could go early to the beach. Alice was totally male bait, and you could usually get something going with a guy if you were with her at a party, and in the mood. A lot of guys had used their hands on Rosie when they hooked up and she gave them all oral, but only a couple of the boys she'd been with, friends with privileges, had ever gone down on her. It was great and she had come, but maybe because it was so rare it was almost too intense, so crossing an inside line.

The smell of barbecue mingled with the scent of the pumpkin spice candles on tables under the plum and apple trees, and blended with the smell of charred ribs and salmon, plus people's various body products, and the smell was too strong, like the Old Testament, like meat at the altar, like people being grilled. It made her think of cannibals. She considered taking a Valium. She used to have nightmares of being boiled in a cannibal stockpot. Cannibals, quicksand, dinosaurs, and murderers, those were her hugest childhood fears, but more than anything she'd been afraid of her mother dying.

She still had an obsessive fear of Elizabeth's dying, which was weird because she hated her half the time. Her mother could be so lovely and regal, but also self-centered and self-destructive. It made Rosie sick. Now her mom was so intent on keeping everyone around her calm, so desperate for everyone to love and forgive her and be happy and trust her that sometimes she vibrated with it, like brass wires.

Rosie hated herself for being so afraid. That's why she made herself do so many things that scared her. She couldn't decide on her looks, whether she was pretty or hideous. Or plain. The last time she took acid, with Alice at a rave in Richmond, she had already taken a couple of tabs of Ecstasy, because she could no longer get off on just one. The acid was an afterthought—it was supposed to be very mild, this cute purple candy dot—but she'd sort of lost it. She'd had to go into the bathroom to pull herself together, things had gone from shimmer and rainbow to stark, the sky from kaleidoscope to shifting electromagnetic sand beneath her, expanding out to the bad kind of infinity. Her face in the mirror looked like a sweaty terri-fied old woman's, with wrinkles from too much sun, and the ugly globby pterygium on her iris like her eye was rotting from the inside out. She looked and felt insane, like some schizo you'd see at the bus stop at the Parkade at two in the morning, catching the last bus to San Francisco. Quavering, she whisper-sang all the words to "Let It Be," and after a while started tripping out on the sweater she was holding, pretending for a few seconds that Rascal was in her arms, hiding his big orange head between her chin and chest like he always did, and this calmed her. She washed her hands and sat on the floor, and the smell of the Ivory soap also calmed her; it smelled like Rae's neck.

She couldn't help noticing that the men at Jody's party were sneaking glances at her breasts. All men did, and all boys, even little guys. She didn't mind. She was glad tits had come along later in life, instead of earlier; there had been an older girl named Jeannette who was one of the great singles players at twelve but at thirteen had had

to adjust her backhand so that her backswing went high enough up
to avoid the voluminous breasts that had sprung up. And that was it
for old Jeannette. At least Rosie had gone out on a high note, ranked
number one in fourteen-and-under doubles with Simone.

Rosie found Alice out on the front porch with one of Jody's older
cousins.

"Dude!" Alice exulted when Rosie stepped into view. Rosie
ducked her head shyly like a mother bird, exactly like her mother
did, and she hated this but couldn't help herself. The cousin
looked like Jody, only smaller, pretty but too thin, in a skanked-
out way. The way her bones jutted out gave Rosie the creeps, like
those cornucopia paintings with fruit, candles, flowers, all kinds of
beautiful things, and amid it all, a skull. Terror rippled through
her. She was afraid of getting old. She took the Valium out of her
pocket, and displayed the pills in her hand. Alice studied them
before selecting one, as if Rosie were offering a variety of choco-
lates. All three girls washed down a Valium with Alice's Sprite, but
because she could not have Alice to herself, Rosie felt very alone.
She craved a moment with her mother, on the couch at home,
doing nothing together, letting her mom comb her hair with those
mothering fingers.

◘

T he sky on the beach was huger than all creation, and the sand
so reflective. She hadn't noticed the full moon until she'd gotten stoned on the beach. Here the moonlight played on the surface
of the sand. It was so incredible, not like the sun, which you couldn't
even look at.

She and Alice staggered around with rubber legs. They hung

out with some friends at the campfire, and then by themselves at the surf line for a while. Alice thought she saw a shooting star, and they talked about this for quite a while, and about songs they loved that were about stars. Rosie had to keep closing her eyes here with Alice because everything was so beautiful. She wasn't very stoned, they'd had only a couple of hits of weed so far. Everyone was waiting for a bunch of kids to arrive who had been to the Parkade and connected with Fenn or Michael Marks, who always had totally bubonic weed. She felt like her old self again, and had an idea for a poem, about how the sun was so male, how it came up glaring and went across the sky and dropped down out of sight abruptly, but the moon was like her and her friends, introspective and stunning and changeable, taking its female time.

She wondered whether anyone had ever used the words "The moon weeps long soft tears of light." Probably. Everything was pretty much used up by now; even the *earth*. The planet was pretty much shot. She turned to study the dunes behind them. They were so womanly, too, like the moon, voluptuous, like women's hips, reclining. She had been here a thousand times with her mother and Rae and James when she was young, sitting in the sand, watching people cross the channel to Stinson Beach at low tide. She remembered standing here once in wild surf, letting it smash against her, and then it swept her off her feet into the channel, where she tumbled like clothes in a dryer and James had to fish her out. Her father had fished her out of the Russian River when she was four. Her mother had told this story lots of times, maybe because they had a limited number of memories of him. "Blue by the time he finally got to her," her mother always said, emphasis on "blue," instead of "finally," like what kind of incompetent parents would take their eyes off a toddler in the river long enough for her to turn blue?

A figure appeared in the sand, walking toward them, and someone dropped the joint into the surf to be extinguished, and Ethan, the only smoker, whipped his cigarette behind his back, so Rosie turned, thinking it must be the police, but it was her physics teacher, holding a child by the hand. Robert Tobias, her favorite teacher, here, in real life, on the beach.

"It's okay, Ethan," he said, smiling. Maybe the cigarette smoke covered the pot. He had another child in a backpack, who was wearing a knit cap with stars all over it. Both children had gigantic martian eyes. Robert was pretty handsome for his age, probably mid-thirties. Feeling shy, she ducked her head, but he said her name. "Rosie! You get your grades yet?" She shook her head.

"No one has. They're late this year. Did I . . . ?" she began. He shrugged, and held out his hands in a gesture of *Who knows?* But she knew it meant she had aced the class. God! She was so pumped. It was weird to be so good at this one thing, this and writing. She was pretty sure she was one of his favorite students; someone had called her the teacher's pet once. He ran his fingers through his cropped sworly brown hair, and said hello to the crowd as a whole. "Hi, Mr. Tobias," they replied in unison. His eyes were big, like his children's, and ringed with thick, dark lashes. Amazingly, he had five-o'clock shadow; he must not have been shaving on summer vacation. Rosie wondered whether his wife liked it rough and stubbly like that. She would run it by Alice and Jody. This was one of their big topics, the teachers, what their wives and husbands were like, and what they were all like in bed—who gave head, who didn't, who came fast, who could last. Rosie imagined reaching forward to touch his stubble, and how it would prick her hands.

* * *

James and Elizabeth crawled into bed around ten. You could still hear voices and laughter from backyard barbecues. Their domestic machine involved early nights, even on holidays, although Elizabeth often stayed up for hours reading. She loved being in bed. She could spend her whole life in the cave of her bed, empty until her person climbed in beside her and pulled up the covers, Andrew, then Rosie, now James. It was so much lovelier than being in all that light and exposure, and warmer because you were skin to skin. There was a lot more holding these days, in their middle-aged years, less sex, and James often fell asleep in her arms.

She loved to listen to him sleep, unless she was pissed off. She knew every single personal noise—how he groaned when he repositioned, or got up, the weird throat-clearing that lasted forever first thing in the morning, although also sometimes he did it while he slept. There were random peeps, grunts when a little cramp got relieved, quiet farts, a lovely faint snore. He had described her equivalent sounds as concerto for woman and wind instruments, and used the phrase in the novel he was working on.

They still had sex once a week or so. She didn't have much drive, partly from the new medication she'd been taking since her last slip, but she had always come easily with him, and it reinforced the idea that they were normal and sexy. It was workmanlike but comforting, their legs wrapped together like clasped fingers, making one person out of two. She had always dreamed of this, of the Other, maybe everyone did. It was so lonely on the inside all those years. After she lost Andrew, she had lost half of herself, the most trusting and the sexiest parts, and when James miraculously appeared at the campsite in the mountains all those years ago, there was not one full woman to meet him. There were parts of her, the rest made up of Andrew being gone. Parts of her had never come back, and so it was amazing, really almost a miracle, if she had believed in that sort of thing, that she could get so close to another person, who breathed when she did, turned when she turned. It was not always the sexy closeness she had signed up for—they had gotten older and tired much faster than she had expected—but it was a closeness that worked.

The breathing was a mutual pact. You tuned your breath to your person because then the little cave vibrated differently, in harmony: no longer two anguished individuals. It was like when her mother lay beside her when she was very little, when a person's skin was one whole piece of beauty, like something Rae had woven out of silk, and your mother had access to your skin, and you got to be part of a breathing, touching organism that might ease into sleep.

◙

Rosie's friends said good-bye to Robert Tobias, and drifted away, but she hung back to talk. She tried to think of something to say. Did he like to talk about physics on his days off? She remembered the first progress report she'd gotten last fall, when he'd written to her parents that she had an amazing mind for physics, answering on one day alone three increasingly difficult questions. She could remember the first one now, how she thought he was joking that day in class because the answer came so easily to her. What was $e = mc^2$? Duh! The world was made up of energy that was frozen into matter. If you took matter and speeded it up, it was energy, like light, or radio waves. If you divided up energy, and slowed it down, it was matter. People, wood, raspberries—everything was slowed down energy.

"Rosie!" he said to her, and she realized she had been spacing out. Could he tell she was stoned? She peered into his face. "I was asking you if you'd like to make some money this summer, and give me tennis lessons."

"Oh my God," she said. "I'll do it for free. It would be fun for me."

"I won't let you. I'll pay you twenty an hour, once or twice a week. We can play at Pali Park. How does that sound?"

"I haven't played in a few years," she said. Twenty bucks!

"I haven't played since college, and besides, I wasn't very good."

They made plans to meet at the park one day that week at two; his wife got home from teaching summer school at one, and could take the kids.

After he left, euphoria caught her up like the wave that had sent her tumbling that time; she wanted to run like a child, but she made herself walk slowly, elegant, head held tall, like her mother, like this sort of thing happened to her all the time, a teacher seeking her out socially. By the campfire, she could see Alice taking a sip from a bottle, maybe the wine she had stolen from the party. Not watching her feet in the sand, Rosie felt something thick and rubbery against her ankles, and saw that she was standing in a pile of dark green seaweed. She remembered all the snakes of seaweed they'd played with as children, she and Beatrice Thackery, she and Simone, the boa constrictors they'd wrap around their necks. Burying beach balls in deep holes so the wind wouldn't blow them away, digging deeper, stopping from time to time to try out the ball and the hole for size.

She started walking again. She could see bird tracks by the moonlight, jeep tracks, footprints, all sizes, hers. It had been a long time since she'd thought of Beatrice Thackery and her pervert dad.

She meant to stay in touch with Simone, who had sent a framed picture of her three-year-old son, which Rosie kept on her dresser, next to all those trophies they had won over time. It was so long ago, tennis, Simone, Mr. Thackery.

She quietly sang a stanza from a Prince song to knock the memory of him out of her thoughts. She had started wondering at thirteen whether she'd be able to enjoy being with boys after seeing Thackery's woody when she was eight, but it turned out she liked it fine, about a third of the time so far, which was pretty much par for the course for girls.

The wind picked up, but over in the dunes they would be protected. Out in the open, the sandy air was hard on your skin and eyes, not like the feathery dust that coated you out on the trails when the wind kicked in. She went to stand by the fire. A boy she didn't know teased her about having a crush on Mr. Tobias, and she sort of liked this. The smoke took a convoluted and circular path up from the fire, rising on currents of air.

She remembered when she and Simone were ten or so. They'd won a local tennis championship and there was a closing party out here that the tournament committee put on. They were the youngest kids, along with two dweeby boys they ditched right away. The adults were grilling hot dogs and hamburgers. It was unbelievably hot, but only she and Simone went into the water. They did it because the older boys hooted with appreciation; the Pacific was almost as cold as Lake Tahoe, which was snowmelt. She remembered Simone already had breast buds and wore a light blue gingham two-piece, and Rosie still had her horrible bleached-out Speedo with the flannel fish sewn badly by her mother in the bottom corner so she could swim in the deep end at the rec center; she was able to tread water for three minutes and save herself if the adults weren't watching her closely enough. Unlike certain mothers she could name. After they'd gotten out of the water, she and Simone built monuments, castles of sand, with feathers and rocks and glass, and talked about the babies they would have one day, girl babies because they hated boys, although maybe Simone hated them a little bit less since the breast situation began. The beach that night was as big and white as a glacier field. Simone went off to use the smelly public bathroom, and turned to wave to Rosie like Marilyn Monroe. She was wearing seaweed draped around her neck, like a beautiful green scarf, like one Rae might have woven, with her usual secret tucked inside.

Once, when Rosie was in sixth grade, at the closing party of another tournament, she hadn't been asked to dance. She watched as Simone danced with her boyfriend, slowly, barely moving. Afterward Rosie was in a deep, weepy funk; she wouldn't go outside, eat, or talk to her mother for days.

Rae had whipped up a loose, airy mohair scarf to cheer Rosie, pale pink with a green secret inside.

Rosie kept asking Rae, through tears, just to please tell her this one time what the secret was. She had never felt lower, skinnier, uglier, more deservedly alone.

"Okay, okay," said Rae. "Here it is." She wrapped the scarf around Rosie's shoulders, then leaned over to whisper in her ear: "You are preapproved." A calm sense of relief had filled Rosie's chest, like stepping out of the cold into a warm car.

She remembered the night of Simone and the seaweed scarf as a line of demarcation, the last time she still had a naive power, right before they became obsessed with boys and what they looked like; when she and Simone were inseparable, the only person the other one needed; when she had been number one for someone. She remembered looking up when a man called from the grill that dinner was ready, and how all the older boys leapt to their feet and raced over like dogs, while the older girls looked at each other and got up languidly; and that Simone was staggering across the dunes to get back to Rosie across the fathomless wasteland of sand that in her memory now looked like the moon.

THREE

Fenn and Robert

◘

Elizabeth saw Fenn Cross up close for the first time at the farmers' market on a Wednesday night right after school let out for the year. She was waiting for Rae in the southeast corner of the Parkade, across the street from the movie theater. Its parking lot was useless for theater parking, with only eighteen designated spaces, but it held thirty booths of organic produce perfectly.

James was in for the night, working on a short essay for a producer at National Public Radio, who had loved James's novel. He was being auditioned for a weekly three-minute gig, great exposure if it worked out, and two hundred dollars a week—eight hundred extra a month. But he had been stuck on this three-page piece for days, was not even close to letting Elizabeth read it, but she knew he would pull it off. "Focus," she'd said with mock menace when she'd left the house that night. "Trusting you."

She'd heard it said at meetings that a functional alcoholic was someone with a spouse who had a good job.

Rae had warned her that she might be late that night, caught up in the final planning stages for the first annual Sixth Day Prez Vacation Bible School. Elizabeth was waiting in the shade under the movie theater awning when she saw him.

Ten feet away from her, a fine-looking young man stood reading the posters in the glass display case. He was sturdy and tan, looked older than Rosie by a few years, with shoulder-length sun-streaked hair, and wire-rimmed glasses that added an air of studious ballast. He acknowledged her with a faint Buddhist bow and turned back to the posters. He smelled of salt and sea and sun, of sweat and muscles and lovely skin. It was sort of sickening. What did she exude? Atrophy and skin flakes.

Rosie had first pointed him out not long after they moved to Landsdale. He was seated at a table on the sidewalk outside the coffee roastery, and Elizabeth had seen him there many times since, reading, or bent over a notebook, or holding court, or canoodling, as her father used to say, with some young hippie goddess or another.

She glanced at her watch—Rae was twenty minutes late now—and when she turned to search the streets for her, Fenn was gone.

She went back to studying movie posters. The theater played old art movies during the week, and first-run shows on weekends. She'd seen the current film with Andrew when she was very pregnant with Rosie, Truffaut's *Small Change*. People always remarked on its charm, but she had been scared to death in the theater and forever after of all the ways children could and did die, how a pulse of danger bounced like sound waves against the most innocent, everywhere, every day. Andrew had gasped when the two-year-old fell out of the ten-story window—the child then bounced on the ground and clapped with joy—while she had sat there dark and nauseated with the general hopelessness of life. She had wanted to be a mellow and trusting parent, but had gone on to be the most terrified mother of all, rising like a shroud through Rosie's life at every open window, every big wave that came near, every lone man and every gang, every swollen lymph node and lingering bruise, always vigilant, except for that one time when Rosie was four, at the Russian River.

Elizabeth left the theater and walked onto the blacktop of the market. She bought a bottle of icy water from the man who'd been selling his flavored honey straws when Elizabeth and Andrew first stopped by, a hundred years ago, when they had to drive twenty minutes from Bayview to get here. Rosie had been four when they had discovered the weekly market. Most of the plastic straws' worth of honey would end up on her clothes or in her hair, and all over Elizabeth, too, blueberry honey in dark navy straws, root beer float, orange cream, lime.

Now when Rosie and her friends ate here, it was figs, mild California pistachios, cheeses wrapped in stinging nettle leaves.

Elizabeth realized she would not be able to stay here—there were too many people and way too many smells: barbecued chicken wings, soy-and-tomatillo tamales, bouquets of local flowers, ripe strawberries, a hippie B.O. cloud of patchouli, weed, the brine of feta from Olema, and the sweet glue of honeycomb and sticky children. She turned to walk home, frustrated with Rae and herself and even with the poor innocent farmers' market. There was something self-congratulatory about the whole thing, and a Loehmann's quality, everyone so intent on getting huge amounts of the choice produce. Elizabeth never needed things in quantity, but on weeks when she didn't buy a lot of stuff, she felt like a piker, wondering to herself why she was not overloaded with joy like everyone else.

She hurried across the street to the steps of the Parkade, where a few teenage and slightly older males blocked her entrance to the ancient concrete steps. They were smoking, bored, sullen, superior, and like most teenagers everywhere, since all eternity, waiting for something to happen. One young man already had the aggressively tattooed neck you saw on middle-aged junkies in AA. She wanted to shake him—"What the *fuck* are you thinking? Is anyone ever going to hire a guy who has Jesus and a rattlesnake duking it out in front of a wrinkled sunrise?"

Just then, Rae called out her name. She turned to glower at her friend, who stood across the street in front of the theater, but caught a rangy peripheral blur, more familiar to her than the various old women she saw in mirrors: brown limbs and long black curls. Holding up a finger to Rae, she called out, "Rosie!"

Rosie was coming out of the bus kiosk, two hundred feet away, toward the group of boys sprawled on the steps now behind Elizabeth. "Rosie!" Elizabeth called again, as if it had been weeks since they'd last spoken, and they walked toward each other. Rosie took a few steps to the right, so that she could gesture to the teenagers on the steps, a gesture of exasperated, masculine apology—I'll be right there, guys, the little lady needs me first.

Rosie lowered her gaze to size up Elizabeth's outfit, khaki shorts that were now perhaps a size too small, and a frayed floral blouse with an admittedly funny collar, with such shock and hurt that a stranger might have thought that Elizabeth stood there in snorkel flippers and a thong.

"Mommy," Rosie admonished. "I thought we had talked about that shirt. It really just will not do."

"But the color is good for me, right?" Cream, with soft orange flowers and pale olive leaves. Rosie rolled her eyes, and stepped into her mother's arms for a quick hug. "May I please have some money? Like ten or so, for tamales?"

Money was the way to Rosie's heart, a five here, a ten there, a shopping spree every so often. Rosie and Elizabeth got high on shopping sprees like stylish crackheads, and the high could last the night. Otherwise, Rosie's most frequent addictive need was to get out of the house and hang out with her friends, Elizabeth's to see that Rosie was happy—both experienced the anxiety of withdrawal when these needs could not be met. Tonight Elizabeth bargained with her: she got to smell Rosie's neck for a moment, and then she'd give her dinner money. Rosie paid stoically, standing straight and long-suffering, like someone at the tailor's, while her mother burrowed under Rosie's chin.

"Narm, narm, narm," Rosie joked now, the sound she had made up as a child to imitate a giant gnawing on a leg of lamb. "Don't eat me! I'm young and have my whole life ahead of me!" Elizabeth laughed gently and fished a ten-dollar bill out of the pocket of her shorts.

Rosie grabbed the bill from Elizabeth's hand, cried out, "Thank you, I love you," and without a backward glance raced off to the stairs.

Elizabeth watched her go. It had been lovely to have a moment of public affection instead of the minimal grunt. Full-frontal time with Rosie was getting rare. Her energy at home was either complete exhaustion or racing to leave, muffled galumph or black-hole silence. She always seemed to be either on her last legs or just passing through on her way to real life, fueling up, needing money, always in hustle or flop. Leaning against the rail, towering above the tattooed boys, Rosie looked like an orchid. Elizabeth's heart skittered at her youth and beauty; the devil is drawn to the light, being an angel himself. *Get away from her,* Elizabeth commanded him, although she did not believe in the devil, or angels, or for that matter, God. Yet an old saying fluttered like a ribbon in the catacombs of her mind, *There is no devil, there is no hell, he assures them as he lulls them down his path.*

◘

R ae was no longer standing outside the theater, but Elizabeth soon found her among the market booths, sitting on a wooden table made of a cable spool, watching the old lady who played the saw set up her boom box. Elizabeth glared at her watch.

"I'm so sorry, baby. Something came up. Are you mad?" Rae asked.

"No. I hate you, though, and you're not my friend anymore. Plus I'm starving, and my hip hurts like an old dog, and I have to pee."

"So go pee at the theater. I'll spring for tamales when you get back."

By the time Elizabeth returned, Rae had persuaded the old lady who played the saw to attend Vacation Bible School, and was drawing her a map to the church.

"I thought you said you'd get Rosie some work there," Elizabeth reproached.

"I did and I can. It doesn't start for four more days. Plus, we need a special-events coordinator for the summer, one night a week, at fifteen dollars an hour."

"Oh my God, that's great. Does she have to do toilets or floors?"

"We have a janitor for that. So you forgive me?" Rae handed her a plate of tamales in red sauce, and Elizabeth nodded.

The old lady plugged her boom box into the power strip that ran into the theater, and sat down on another cable spool. White fluffy hair, craggy face with a sweet, shy smile, she rosined her cello bow, arranged the saw between her legs, pushed a button on the boom box, and waited.

An instrumental version of "Edelweiss" began to play, and she bent forward lovingly, eyes closed, a faint smile, Yo-Yo Ma on the saw. A crowd quickly gathered. It was so damn strange, like getting radio transmissions through your fillings. "Somewhere over the Rainbow" followed, then "San Antonio Rose." Rae and Elizabeth stayed for the whole set. The notes were not going through your ears, but through the holes in you, the cavities. Chinese opera affected her in the same way, beautiful yet so improbable, exultant in the off-pitch. The tone was awful, horrible, and yet breathtakingly beautiful, almost more than Elizabeth could bear, and she could not figure out why she was so vulnerable to it, as the old lady worked away, creating vibrations that took you to places you hadn't planned or agreed to go, an artist stripping away the jolly tune so you could see anguish, yearning, elation. The tone of the saw was so awful, and yet this woman was playing and loving it, and everyone loved it together, in actual wonder, with no bones to pick, no grades or cars or problems to compare, people so excited that an old lady in the age of synthesizers could get into all the old empty rumpled places in their bodies, where perfect pitch couldn't take them.

◘

From her first morning at Vacation Bible School, Rosie loved working with Rae. Rae always brought her baked treats, or dollar bracelets from Cost Plus, and before class they'd cuddle on the extra-wide easy chair in the space Rae used for an office. They'd share stories about James and Lank, and how hilarious the two men were, or how something one of them had said was just so great or infuriating. On Rosie's first day there, Rae told her a story she'd never forget, about a girl who was very close to her grandmother. Once a week, the girl and her grandmother walked from their house to the beach, where a lot of starfish would always wash up onshore. The grandmother had taught the girl that if a starfish was flexible, it was alive, and so you should throw it back into the ocean. If it was stiff, you could take it home.

The day after the grandmother died, the girl was in such deep grief that she could not bear hanging out with her relatives at the grandmother's house, crying, reminiscing, eating, offering up prayers. So she walked down the road to the ocean by herself, and started lifting starfish off the sand, to see if they were alive. She was still crying, but she felt better. Then someone in her family came to find her, and said, "Honey, you need to be with your relatives now. We have to stick together. What you're doing here is just not really significant."

And the girl replied, "It's significant to the starfish."

Rae said the whole Vacation Bible School was about this theme: that you were tended to, by tending to.

Rosie thought for a moment. "The girl was the starfish she was throwing back," she said. Rae nodded.

They went to welcome the kids for their first lesson. Grown-ups would be meeting with Anthony in his office, for Bible study, faith walks, sacred Taizé chanting, prayer-shawl knitting, and voter registration in town.

Children had always flocked to Rosie; for some reason, they could sense she had a knack for silly patience with kids, and this group was no different. They clung to her like she was a rock star, wanting to be lifted, noticed, and she saw how helpless and vulnerable they were. Rae had told her that some of their parents were really sick—part of the church's outpatient ministry to drug addicts. One six-year-old didn't have any parents, just a guardian named Sue; her single mother had died of AIDS, and she had a little sister who was only three and in with the nursery kids. A couple of little kids were shy as turtles, and you had to coax and trick them into trying out your games or snacks. The thing they loved best was when she threw a few of them at a time into a big plastic bucket with rope handles, which must have been used as a toy box, and dragged them all over the church grounds, up and down steps, over rocks, as they screamed with laughter.

She called the whole gang of them her bucket kids; she also did arts and crafts with them, and read them stories. She held them on her lap when they fell or got their feelings hurt, and she made sure always to pay the same amount of attention to each child, even though she liked two of them the most. And the money was so great, fifteen dollars an hour, four hours at a time.

Sometimes she and Alice lifted a pair of jeans or a camisole from shops in Sausalito or the Haight, and now she could tell her mother she'd spent her own hard-earned money.

Jody didn't go to the city with them very often, because they always ended up doing stuff that she couldn't risk getting caught doing. Like the last time Rosie and Alice had been in Golden Gate Park, freezing to death in a sea of fog, they had ended up smoking dope under a tree with some homeless guy. It turned out not to have been a good idea, there was something besides weed in the joint and Rosie was tripping mildly and having scary thoughts, especially one where she saw herself trap a couple of the bucket kids underneath the dome of plastic, to scare them, and to have power over them; she saw herself pound on the sides of the bucket and not answer when they called her name. What was so awful was that she kept having these thoughts well after that day in the park; maybe she'd had it before, too, this bad mind. It just came into her head from time to time, to trap and scare the kids so that they would know how she felt a lot of the time, since you couldn't very well trap adults under buckets.

◨

Her early days of summer were more full than she had meant them to be, with VBS every morning, and tennis lessons with Mr. Tobias.

But she loved the lessons, too, and was good at both. By the end of just one lesson, she had managed to untangle his forehand, at least when she hit him balls from her bucket at the net, but when she tried to incorporate what he had learned, by rallying, he regressed to his former duffer ways, hitting with his weight on the back foot, swinging late, slashing at the ball like a swords-man with arthritis. His serve was like nothing Rosie had ever seen, with a leap straight into the air at the point of contact, a pirouette without the courage of its convictions. But the ball usually went in. The first time Rosie tried to straighten things out for him, to get his body weight forward, he ended up smashing himself in the shin with his racket head, which was how they ended up sitting together in the grass.

He held a cool can of Coke to the mass below his knee while they sat on the knoll beside the public court, talking about his lesson. She could smell his sweat and soap-clean skin so strongly that she had to wrap her arms around her shoulders and look away.

"You don't have to pay me for today."

"Of course I'm going to pay you. It was my fault. Besides, I'm not done. I've still got a little left in me. But do I really have to change my serve? It successfully throws *every*body off. No way even Agassi could touch it."

Rosie did not know how to say delicately that he risked serious bodily harm if he continued to serve using only the strength in his arm, without getting his whole body behind it. "I've just known some . . . older people who've gotten shoulder injuries from serving wrong. Tennis elbow—bursitis."

"Older people?"

"I didn't mean that." She flushed.

"I'm barely thirty!" He held up his racket, as if he might smack her, and she ducked, feeling flirty and forgiven.

"Why take lessons if you don't want to do it properly?"

He did not hurt himself playing after that, although she could not figure out a way to correct the way he moved on the court, lacking any shred of elegance or athleticism, herky-jerky rat-dashes that made him run too close to the ball, and compensate with wild side steps and spin. Two lessons a week, which was forty dollars for her. He always brought two icy cans of Coke, and gave one to her. He couldn't practice between lessons, though, because he had three kids, the two she had seen on the beach, and a baby, named Morgan. His wife must be the luckiest person on earth. He reminded Rosie of James, but handsome; all the kids at school loved him, and she felt privileged to spend time with him.

She got to have fifteen minutes in the grass with him after the second lesson, drinking water and watching the very good players on another court.

She'd thought of stuff she could casually bring up with him that he'd like to discuss. Like today, she'd begun the lesson at the net, where she had said, "So the universe is three spatial dimensions, right, moving through time, the fourth dimension, at the speed of light, right?"

She had practiced it with her mother, dropping it into the breakfast conversation.

Elizabeth had said, "Jeez—no wonder I'm so tired all the time." Then James said, "In practical terms, this is why, after we dry our laundry, we fold it before all the creative motion and heat slow to a seeming halt—and inertia sets in and manifests as wrinkles."

But Mr.Tobias had nodded respectfully at the net, and went on to explain an early experiment that proved this. It was great when someone took you seriously.

She continued, "The reason I mentioned it was, don't you see how incredible it is that on top of it all, you are semi-successfully hitting a moving ball while running around the court? That everything is in motion, including the ball, our arms, our legs, the court, the earth, and yet every so often we hit a perfect backhand?"

He looked utterly charmed for a moment. "Well, you do," he said.

"Oh, you're doing just great. You've come so far, so fast, Mr. Tobias."

"Robert," he said. "And that is very sweet of you to say." She could feel her cheeks redden again, and she jerked her thumb back to his baseline, as in, "Go."

"Ready position," she barked a minute later, and hit him a hard low forehand that she knew would give him a chance at a hard low return.

Later he asked her what her mother did for a living. "She doesn't really do anything," Rosie said. "She stays at home, and takes care of James and me, picks up the house, pays the bills. James vacuums, she makes dinner most of the time. Also, if one of us needs a bag lunch, like if James takes off to do research or tape something in the city. She does the shopping, makes appointments. The garden is her big thing. Nothing in terms of real work. She's like a subsistence farmer."

◉

I'm going out tonight," Rosie announced at dinner.

"I want you home early, though, Rosie. You get up so early for VBS."

"I don't remember asking for you to be my employment agency, Mom. You've got me working twenty hours a week. I don't have any time to be a kid having a summer vacation."

"Oh, Rosie," said Elizabeth, passing her a bowl of butternut squash. "It's a great job, and you get to see Rae every day. And you need the dough for your clothes in the fall."

"Yeah, but you did it behind my back. I'm just asking for some consideration."

"What about thanking your mother for brokering this?" James snapped.

"God!"

"Stop, Rosie. Everyone stop and breathe."

James stabbed a cube of tofu, slick with peanut sauce, flecked with Thai chili and basil. Rosie drew her knife across the pile of silver noodles. "I'd had a great story I was going to tell you, but now I'm not going to, because it would be wasted on you." James looked at Elizabeth and shook his head. "You're such an asshole, James."

"Rosie, go to your room," her mother said calmly.

"I'm going out," Rosie said, getting up and flouncing off.

"You're not going anywhere tonight, Rosie," James said. "Plus, you just lost the car for a week, for breaking Rule One: Don't be an asshole." Elizabeth glanced up at the refrigerator, where James had posted his Updated Family Rules a year ago: *1. Don't be an asshole. 2. Wait a few moments before entering a crosswalk. 3. When all else fails, follow instructions.*

"Yeah? Then how do I get to the child labor job you trapped me into?"

"You can use the car for work."

Rosie stalked toward her room.

"And I want your laundry done tonight, too," James added.

Rosie screamed.

Elizabeth smiled at James. "It's so hopeless, darling."

"It really is," he said. "Maybe we'll kill ourselves tomorrow, okay?"

"We can't. Rae and Lank are coming for dinner."

◘

They were doing the dishes together when they heard Rosie stomp around in the hallway, open, and then, after a few moments, slam the door to the garage, where the washer and dryer were.

"I can't find my best jeans," Rosie yelled. "Where did you put them, Mom? They were right here." Elizabeth rolled her eyes. Half of Rosie's sentences now began with "The reason I want to move out is," and in a moment, Rosie delivered. "The reason I want to move out is that you are constantly messing with my stuff. . . ."

"I didn't touch your pants," Elizabeth yelled back. "Keep looking."

"I can't find them anywhere. Why do you always do this to me? I hate living here. I am going to go crazy if I don't get out soon."

James handed Elizabeth a plate to dry, and kissed her. The silence in the house was pristine. "I love you," she whispered.

"Mom," Rosie shouted. "Will you grant me emancipated-minor status?"

◧

James went to bed early to read, as usual, while Elizabeth stayed up and puttered, stacking mail she wanted to get to tomorrow, fluffing the couch pillows. She sank onto the cushions. Rascal leapt up beside her, rubbed his head against her shoulder. One of his eyes was runny. "What are we going to do, Rascal?" Elizabeth whispered. He climbed into her lap, clawed in a push-push motion on her thighs, butted her face with his great tabby head, and finally curled into an improbably small ball and nestled in her crotch, like a bird sitting on its egg. Rae had once made a room-sized weaving for Audubon's Bolinas Lagoon Preserve, of egrets and herons nesting in redwood trees, and Elizabeth remembered now the secret ribbon woven into one branch, which bore the words of Rumi: "Each has to enter the nest made by the other imperfect bird." It was a beautiful line but a lousy system if true, as it offered only the most meager support. And what did it really mean? That you encounter the divine in only the most humble, improbable places? Or that the solace and support the world has to offer are through your tiny tribe's inner, patient hospitality, its willingness to accept your impossible lacking self. Could this be enough? And whose imperfect nest could she enter? James's, Rae's, Lank's. But not Rosie's these days. Teenagers offered their nests only to one another, far from their parents' attention. Elizabeth closed her eyes. Rascal purred from her lap like a leaf blower. The house creaked. A siren went off in the distance, and instantly she thought of Rosie in the back of an ambulance, Rosie in a burning house—but Rosie was right down the hall, wasn't she? Her stomach tightened. Elizabeth tried to calm herself by stroking Rascal, but his claws dug into her, and she imagined Rosie shooting dope. Climbing out her bedroom window after their fight, heading to the Parkade. Elizabeth knew it was crazy, but she got up anyway and padded toward Rosie's room to check.

Rosie was at her computer. She quickly closed up the site she'd been studying, got up and went to the door, where Elizabeth stood. "I'm sorry we had a fight, Mommy. But I never found my best jeans. And I paid for them myself." She held the door like a shopkeeper trying to close up, with one last customer lingering in the doorway.

Elizabeth reached out and touched her daughter's cheek with her fingertips, and they looked quietly into each other's eyes, like friends.

◘

Rosie tried to get out of dinner with Lank and Rae the next night. Elizabeth was arranging flowers from her garden in a heavy glass vase, yellow roses of three shades, light pink tea roses, purple Mexican sage.

"Oh my God, I see her almost every damn day!" Rosie said.

"You see Alice and Jody, too," James pointed out. "You don't see so much of Lank. He's my best friend. You're having dinner with us. End of story."

"Mom!"

"Stay for the first course, darling. Okay? It's something you like. Those big lemony seared scallops. And I need you to set the table."

Rosie looked at her, doubtful and pessimistic. "Yeah, but realistically, how many will each person get? Two or three, right?"

Elizabeth wanted to throw the vase at her head, but it was one of the few left of her mother's. She looked at the flowers lying on her cutting board, and then cut them slowly with the bread knife, with menacing pleasure, like Sweeney Todd. James smiled.

"God, don't mock me!" Rosie whined. "That's all I get from you these days."

"Don't come," said Elizabeth. "It's fine. We'll divvy up your one microscopic scallop."

"No, Elizabeth—I already told her she's staying. And that's final." Rosie made a clicking sound of derision and Elizabeth started to protest, as she no longer wanted Rosie to join them, but James held up one finger. "Stop," he told Elizabeth. "Don't do that. We agreed." Then he left.

Rosie clicked with disdain on her way to the silverware drawer.

◙

She stayed for the first course, questioning Lank about summer school, teasing Rae, flirting with them both, more or less ignoring her parents. She and James were both wearing tight Grateful Dead shirts, his stretched taut over his chubby belly, hers cropped above her navel. She cut up the two big scallops on her saucer, and savored each lemony, buttery bite, but Elizabeth believed she was doing this as an act of aggression.

She picked up her plate when she was done, got up from the table, nibbled on Rae's temple, kissed Lank's soft, fuzzy bald spot, and saluted her parents good-bye. Elizabeth looked around at the company at her table. No one spoke.

"It's so wonderful to have you all here," she said finally. "To be with people who aren't mean to me. Who don't make clicking noises at me."

"Is she being awful?" Rae asked.

"She's a pill. I spoiled her."

"We're thinking of letting her go," said James. "Do you want her?"

"Hell, no," said Lank. "I'm a high school teacher. I get that all day. If it's any consolation, Elizabeth, this is what they're all like with their parents. They can be perfectly lovely with other adults. It's par for the course. In fact, you've gotten off easy. I've got kids in my class right now who've already done time in rehab and juvie. I have parents sobbing in my office, scared to fucking death. She's really a beautiful person—with everyone but you."

Elizabeth shook her head. "It's as if she can seal herself off from me, like in a zip-lock bag."

Rae reached over to stroke Lank's pale cheeks. Looking into his face, she said, "Those are such lucky kids, though, to have you. Think of having had teachers like you."

"I did have teachers like me. That's why I wanted to become one myself. And what has it gotten me? Hair loss, weight gain. No savings. And instead of having an inner child, like other people, I have an inner little old man. All teachers do."

James concurred. "I have an inner old man, too, now that I think about it. Tired a lot, quietly appalled every time he goes out in public."

"Exactly. The incompetence is killing him, and the rudeness. He tries to be a good sport, but I think he sort of misses Eisenhower." James nodded and reached for the salad. It looked unadorned and boring, but there were surprises in every bite—crunchy jicama, candied nuts, peppery sprouts.

"Lank," Elizabeth said. "Knowing what you do about teenagers, what would you do if you were Rosie's parents?"

"Consequences, consequences, consequences! Pay attention. Snoop around. Take in what is what, no matter how it scares you. You know when you were a kid, and you had to pretend not to see what was going on right beneath your nose? Because if you did, you would see that your parents were crazy as rats, right— and that no one was in charge? So you unconsciously agreed not to notice, in order to survive? Well, that was then. Notice now. Notice good."

◘

Elizabeth had one of those nights of shining metallic insomnia that she used to have every other night, before she started taking sleep medication. She had taken a pill at midnight—James had already been asleep beside her for an hour—but was still awake at one. She had had to put down her book because her eyes were so dry and sandy with wakefulness, and let herself rest with her eyes closed. Sometimes she would doze, but was up every forty-five minutes with a new bad dream: Rosie dead or dying, in all of her nightmares' greatest hits—car crashes, leukemia—James with his other wife, whom Elizabeth was supposed to be a good sport about, and his little towheaded toddlers on swings, instead of the brooding and angry clubfoot of a teenager he was helping her raise. These were the hours of the black dogs, and she saw them watching her like jackals, cool and patient from the dark corner. At four she got up to pee again, out of wired boredom and exhaustion, and sat on the toilet, hanging her head like someone in a confessional. Then she went to snuggle beside Rosie.

Even with Rosie beside her, she felt utterly alone in the dark, the space in her head stretched as tight as the silence between the notes of the old lady's saw. Then Rosie flopped over loudly and nestled her butt against Elizabeth's, and after a while Elizabeth fell asleep. It was five-thirty by Rosie's bedside clock when Elizabeth woke. She padded down the hall and crawled in beside her quietly snoring husband and cat, and eventually fell back to sleep.

❑

She woke in the morning filled with details of everything wrong with her, a deconstruction of her life since the high-water mark of college, her fraudulence, her long-term lack of employment—a life wasted in a ping-pong game of narcissism versus self-loathing, punctuated by sloth and depression. Otherwise, the night had gone swimmingly. Besides, what were you going to do? She went back to sleep.

❑

James brought her coffee, juice, a toasted bagel, and *The New York Times* on a tray, and after she ate, hungover with lack of sleep, she closed her eyes again and slept until noon. She walked down the hall to James's office, and poked her head in to say good morning. He told her he'd come find her as soon as he was done. She stopped at Rosie's room, on the other side of the office, but Rosie was gone. Her bed was made, and there was a note in the kitchen that she was at Sixth Day Prez. James took a break from his work, sat with her near the new roses, made sympathetic noises, and helped her plan a day that would wear out the clock with a minimum of misery. The garden could use a hand, and he would load the van with boxes of clothes they'd saved for Goodwill.

* * *

Elizabeth's first thought when she found Rosie's lost jeans jammed under the front seat of the beat-up old van they shared was how happy this would make Rosie, and what a hero she herself would be for at least a few hours when Rosie got home from VBS. Sand fell like tinsel from the pockets. Elizabeth stood outside the van and held them upside down, while sand spilled out. What, had she been planning to build a sand castle in her bedroom when she got home? And when had she even been to the beach? The party for Jody had been weeks ago. Elizabeth shook her head to clear it. Rosie had a secret life now, was putting together her own tribe, finding her identity there, and it was great to see, and it hurt like hell. She walked toward the garage to throw the jeans in the washer. She would surprise Rosie by having them clean and folded on her bed when she got home. Maybe she would enclose them in a band like the ones James's dry-cleaned shirts came wrapped in. Hers would say "Pulling Out All the Stops for Our Cherished Customers." She reached into the watch pocket, checking for coins. Her finger hit against something that was soft and hard at the same time. There were a few of them, and she rolled them out. Blue; light blue pills, Valium, with rounded V's punched out at the centers, to emulate tiny hearts, like the yellow ones she had taken for a few days after the breakdown.

Her stomach dropped as if she had just driven over a hill in the city. The yellow ones had been very strong, five milligrams each, all but knocking her out, and hard to get off. But the blue ones were the strongest, ten milligrams. She had had to be weaned off the fives slowly, over two weeks, by her psychiatrist, to the white ones, which were only two milligrams. She felt around the watch pocket until four pills sat in the palm of her hand, like breath mints. She thought of throwing them down the hatch all at once with one fell swoop. James was in the city recording an essay at KQED. Rae was at VBS. So she put the pills in her own watch pocket, put Rosie's jeans and some towels in the washer, and started the load. She had no idea what to do next. She made herself take deep breaths. Maybe there was a reasonable explanation, she told herself, but something deep inside flickered.

◻

Oh, God," Rosie said with amusement and contempt when Elizabeth showed her the pills. "They are not even mine! They're Alice's, she takes them sometimes for migraine. Remember? God, I'm sorry you got so worried, but Mommy, you actually knew this. You're having a senior moment."

And even though Elizabeth didn't remember this, she was flooded with the narcotic of relief. "I thought they were yours," she said in a little voice. But after thinking it over, she squinted one eye and asked, "Then why doesn't her shrink give her five-milligram ones?"

"He does. But she ran out on a Friday, the night we went to the party at Jody's aunt's, and Alice got a total migraine, and Jody's aunt gave her some of these, but they're ten milligrams, so she told her to split them in half."

"But why did she give her so many?"

"Because the pharmacy was closed for the three-day weekend, remember? It was Memorial Day."

Elizabeth thought this over. "You swear?" Rosie nodded. "You're not in any trouble with drugs?"

"I told you, I have smoked dope. But it is totally no big deal to me. I got all A's last term. I'm holding down two jobs. I'm a good kid, Mom."

Elizabeth stepped back, amazed to feel her old self again.

Rosie's face was soft and magnanimous. "Poor Mommy. Call Jody's aunt if you need to double-check. I'd understand. I won't be mad. I won't think it means you're spying."

Elizabeth shook her head emphatically, as if this was the most ridiculous thing she'd heard all day. She took her daughter's hand, and brushed the back of it with her lips, gallantly, like a knight.

Rosie took Elizabeth's hand, turned it over like a palm reader, studied the network of creases, wrinkles, and age spots, then raised it forward to kiss with slightly chapped and very gentle lips.

FOUR

The Heat

◻

By the time *The Seventh Seal* came to town, the summer's heat bore down like a fever. It was hard to be arrogant these days when you felt like a panting dog in a steam bath, but you could still be cranky. Hardly anyone was happy about the weather, except for the little kids splashing in the creek at the park, and Rosie's bucket kids, whom she spritzed with water during lessons, and the teenagers horsing around at the picnic tables under the shade of the redwoods. Rosie was jealous because Jody had fallen in love—with a soldier, for God's sake, who was five years older than she. Alice was unhappy because her boyfriend, Ryan, was turning out to be a dick. Rosie's parents were unhappy, because James's job at KQED meant he spent less time at home. Robert was unhappy because something had come up at home and he could take only one tennis lesson most weeks now, and Rosie was unhappy about losing that extra money and that lovely time alone with him.

Yet everyone's solution seemed to include making plans to see *The Seventh Seal*. It was like the circus had come to town, the Death 'n' Decay Cabaret: Alice's mother had gone opening night, Jody's grandmother Marion was going tonight with a grandson. Rosie and her parents were going tomorrow, Rae and Lank were going the day after. It was ludicrous. Adults didn't have the sense of the little kids splashing around in the creek in their Batman underpants. There were many things that made it hard to respect them. A, they had destroyed the planet. And B, it was so easy to pull the wool over their eyes. All Rosie had to do to put her parents' minds at ease was to say she was giving a tennis lesson that afternoon after VBS and she didn't have to check back in with them for hours. Then she would call and breathlessly recount how far Robert had come this summer. Then she could say she and Alice were stopping by the Sustainability Center to see if the people there needed help. She would feed them details to make it sound more authentic, like tonight, for instance. She'd told them that now there was a sign out in front of the building that said, "If you are here and we aren't, we'd love you to come inside and take this shift." James had laughed over the phone and said to be home by curfew, midnight during the summer. She and Alice had only passed the sign on their way to the Parkade. They had bought Quaaludes from a guy who'd just been to Florida, ten dollars a tab, which was a rip, but she'd make twenty during her lesson with Robert the next day, so she treated Alice. Someone on the street had given them each a lager, and the 'ludes started coming on fast, so she called to say they had passed out leaflets on the street for the Sustainability Center and she was going to stay at Alice's.

Her mother asked if she could volunteer, too, someday, and Rosie said, oh, sure, the center needed all the help it could get. Not that she and Alice had ever actually gone inside.

They had a great night, perfectly stoned with a bunch of other teenagers on the open-air expanse of grass at Pali Park, surrounded by redwoods. Older people came by and played guitar, and they sang and floated and flirted and drank only a few sips of strawberry wine that a cute hippie mother offered them. Then they went to Alice's and listened to rap because her mother still wasn't home, and they tried on combinations of textured scarves and filmy tops to wear over their camisoles and cut-offs—wild color combinations, lots of orange. Alice said, "Everything goes with orange," and she had impeccable taste. Apricot, coral, persimmon, and tenne, which was tawny orange-brown tinged with gold.

She felt groggy the next morning at VBS, even though she'd stopped for a double latte on her way from Alice's to the church. It didn't matter, though, Rae was unusually distracted, and the kids were easy and funny. Rosie read them the story of Moses in the bulrushes, and when their attention flagged, she spritzed them with the misting sprayer people used for houseplants. But when she tried to review what she had read to them, not one of the kids remembered a thing about Moses. "What's with you guys today?" she asked, although it was she who was not with it. "Just tell me about baby Moses." The kids could see that she was discouraged, and one boy finally raised his hand. "Okay," he said, with a look of grim concentration, "wasn't he the little guy with the monkey?"

She still felt strange and trippy in the afternoon on the tennis court, and when Robert asked if she felt okay, she said she hadn't slept well. His strokes had improved greatly, although when he served he still looked like someone fending off a cloud of bats.

Even through the foggy Quaalude hangover, she took pride in his improvement, in what they had managed together, and when they sat down with Cokes in the grass after the lesson, she felt a real closeness with him.

They were a foot apart, but their arms, resting on bent knees, were nearer, and she could feel a vibration between the dark hair on her long arms and the golden hair on his. The closer they got without actually touching, the more she could feel it, hear it, like a tuning fork, or some phantom instrument you'd play to make spirit music at a séance.

"'Love is life,'" he said all of a sudden. Oh my God: they'd been discussing his serve. "'All, everything that I understand, I understand only because I love. Everything is, everything exists, only because I love. Everything is united by it alone. Love is God, and to die means that I, a particle of love, shall return to the general and eternal source.'" Oh my God—was he proclaiming his love for her? She couldn't think of what on earth to do in response, so she squinted at him skeptically.

"Leo Tolstoy," he said.

She smiled. "Will you write that down for me?"

"Beside it being all we need to know most of the time, it is *not* incompatible with quantum physics—especially the field theory. Only mistake he made is that he is not a particle, he's a wave."

Rosie nodded. He fished around in the cover of his tennis racket until he found a pen and a scrap of paper, and began writing. She was going to memorize it, recite it to her parents that night, and the part about Tolstoy being a wave. But not say that he had told her. Just while passing the salad, whip it out.

He was studying her with a slightly worried look.

"What?" she demanded.

"You okay?" he asked. "Should I be worried about you?"

"Yeah," she said. He looked at her sideways, amused. She yawned expansively and got to her feet. "The heat is really getting to me. I'm going home to take a nap."

"See that you do," he said. He worried about his students. Last year a girl in honors physics had slit her wrists on her bedroom floor and died, was dead in there all night because her parents didn't find her until their alarm rang, and the van from Aftermath Crime Cleaners came to remove the rug, and paint over the blood splatters on the walls, and somehow get rid of the smell. Other gifted students of his were big stoners by senior year, failing and even sometimes dropping out. She was his star, though. She gave him nothing to worry about. Just heat prostration.

Robert smiled at her and said good-bye, and the funny thing was, she actually did go home, although she'd told Jody she'd go to her house after tennis and meet her soldier, Claude. She called instead and said she didn't feel well. Jody was hurt that Alice and Rosie had done Quaaludes without her, since those didn't show up in urine tests, plus now they'd both blown off meeting Claude.

Rosie felt queasy driving home. She found her mother weeding in the garden, and said she felt funny. It must have been the sun, she said. She was going to lie down for a while. When she got up, her parents had already had dinner, but her mother heated up some pumpkin ravioli with pesto, and served her in the living room. James had made a salad from the garden, and was playing Bach concertos. The three of them ended up in the living room, reading, listening to Bach, and it was not awful. Rosie felt that disembodied séance feeling again a few times, but it passed; it was sort of nice, once you stopped fighting it and no one noticed.

* * *

She met up with Alice, Jody, and Claude in Alice's bedroom the next afternoon. Alice's room was so great. There was not one inch of empty wall space or ceiling. Her mother was cool and had even let Alice shellac the posters, photos, artwork, mementos, so that they didn't fade and shred like some of Rosie's best pieces. James's rules amounted to censorship. Your room was supposed to be your own goddamn world.

The layering and hodgepodge of Alice's room was a cozy thrill. Alice, Jody, and Claude were lying on Alice's bed when Rosie arrived, so she sat at the desk and tried not to stare at Claude. He was older than they were by several years but he seemed much older, and there was something about him with his buzz cut, long-lashed eyes, and big nose. He was handsomer the moment he spoke with his faint southern accent. Alice was telling them about their Quaalude night. Claude had to pass urine tests, too, at the Presidio, where he was stationed for the time being, so he couldn't even smoke weed. "But I can drank," he drawled, and pulled out a half-pint of Southern Comfort. Rosie had never had this before; he took a pull and handed it to her, and it went down both hot and smooth, like whiskey cough syrup.

Jody wasn't drinking, but Alice took a swallow and handed it back. They peppered Claude with questions. He had already done basic training in North Carolina and was going away to an American base in Germany after a brief stint in San Diego. Then he was going somewhere secret, to fight in a peacekeeping mission.

"Isn't that an oxymoron?" Rosie asked.

"Yeah, you want to know what oxymorons are?" he retorted. "Oxymorons are a couple of teenage gals who take drugs someone says are Quaaludes, which they don't even make anymore. That could be full of lye, or GHB."

Rosie sneaked a look at Alice. Her face was flirty and indignant.

"They make them in Africa," she scolded. He rolled his eyes. "I saw it on the Internet."

"Well, thanks for that, sugar. So you buy what someone tells you is a Quaalude from Africa, which could mean any old crazy chemical combo, even lye, that they use for crank. What if you girls accidentally took date-rape drugs? Huh?" He said it like a brother might. Jody looked both relaxed and royal in his arms, shimmery with love, longer and leaner than Claude—she had to bend her knees to intertwine her feet and legs with his—and more grown-up, even though her dark, wispy hair was garnished like a child's with cranberry-colored clips.

Rosie approved. He even left them the rest of the bottle when he had to get back to base. Jody went with him, after hugging Rosie and Alice. The two of them lay on the bed like puppies, and every time Rosie started to drop off, Alice woke her with some fearful thought about what Claude had said. "I'm so tired I feel like I have leukemia," she said. "Do you think there was African voodoo lye in the pills?"

"Nah," Rosie told her. "They just make you tired the next day. Price of admission. What ev."

"Maybe we should just sleep it off."

Rosie threw her hands up. "Every time I drift off, you wake me to ask if we've been poisoned." Alice laughed and promised not to talk. They lay back to back in the hot room. Their favorite hip-hop and rap stars were on the wall and the CD player, like people of their daydreams, tromping through their very own lives. There were mementos from when Alice was younger, like ribbons and backstage passes, from when stuff had been easier, and you weren't pressured to death every living second. Everything was inside out and upside down in Alice's bedroom, like she'd gotten to shake up a glorious container of all her favorite images, and spill it out onto the ceiling and walls. It was like a kaleidoscope.

This time Rosie was wide awake, while Alice snored softly beside her. Rae came into her mind, and Rosie breathed deeply, the way Rae had taught her. She let her eyes roam around the room. Half of this stuff was code—you knew what it signified, but a grown-up would think it was gibberish, like they used to think about the songs of humpback whales, that they didn't mean anything, just because scientists couldn't interpret them. There were pictures of whales and otters all over Alice's walls. They used to thrive in San Francisco Bay, till the traders killed them all.

Rosie had to keep her room neat enough so James would not freak out, but not so neat that they could figure it all out, break the code, of who you truly were, what you were up to, your values, your truest parts. The code was all that you were made up of—the whole, not a neat little version for your parents to admire and trot out for their friends—you were layer upon layer of ideas and erasures and new ideas and soul and images.

She looked at the pictures, most of which Alice had downloaded from her computer—foreign cities, female hip-hop stars, oceans and sunsets and tide pools, rivers and creeks, and all the animals that swam and flew and clung to the seaweed, like the otters that the adults had killed off. Rosie was particularly troubled by what people had done to the otters. And to polar bears. It just freaked her out. She started to doze, and when she woke up, three hours had passed, and Alice was still asleep. Rosie shook her roughly. "It's six!" she said.

"So what?" Alice asked groggily, sitting up, rubbing her eyes. "Do we have something we have to do?"

Elizabeth was in the middle of making dinner when Rosie called, but luckily it was two things Rosie hated—split pea soup and swordfish—and it was easy to ask if she could stay for dinner at Alice's. "Her mother's making paella," Rosie announced, which made Alice clap in silent appreciation. "Oh, Mommy, I'm sorry, I forgot—can't we go to the movie some other time? . . . Okay, then, I promise. It would be great if you could let me off the hook tonight . . . Yay. Thank you."

She hung up the phone and raised her fists. "What movie are you going to see?" Alice asked.

"*Seventh Seal*. We were supposed to go tonight. It's not a big deal, only now James can't go with us. What should we do tonight?"

"I wonder if we could get more 'ludes." Alice's face was pensive, but Rosie didn't respond, in case Alice was joking. "I'd do it again, would you?"

Rosie shrugged, noncommittally. The good parts had been great. The séance feeling afterward, the drugged exhaustion—not so great. Alice's mother wasn't home, so they left her a note saying that they would be eating at Rosie's. They each took two of Alice's Adderall, being so groggy and all, then headed to the Parkade to check out what was happening.

◘

The next morning, Elizabeth and Rae walked up a trail halfway between their homes. The fog layer below was so thick it looked like you could walk to Japan on it. Even in the heat, which here managed to be dusty and steamy at the same time, this was a place of spectral beauty, white flashes blinking on and off in the sunlit bay, hills flocked with Renaissance golds and greens.

"How is my Rosie?"

"Doing fine. She's having a great summer, working with you and Anthony, teaching tennis, hanging with her buds."

"Not getting into trouble?"

Elizabeth shrugged. They walked along the dry brown trail.

"It's always so beautiful up here. Even now, my least favorite time of year."

"I know—it's still so pretty in this horrible, dusty scorched heat. It's like saying how beautiful a woman is when she's in labor—just wait. Just wait until fall and winter." Elizabeth nodded, and they walked along in silence.

"Rae, you know, I haven't felt tempted to drink in a long time, but sometimes these days I would kill for a cigarette," Elizabeth said after a while. "Just to take the edge off."

"No, no," Rae begged. "Smoking is disgusting, and kills innocent bystanders. But darling, how about chewing tobacco?" This made Elizabeth smile. "No, seriously—you could carry a lovely light blue glass cup as a container for spit." Elizabeth jabbed her lightly with an elbow. "Is there something in particular that's getting to you?"

"I have a bad feeling lately. Sometimes with Rosie I'm not sure she's telling me the whole truth. She's very up-front about smoking marijuana from time to time, and she's told me the few times she was drinking at parties. But I get a grippy feeling in my guts sometimes, when other kids get busted or sent away, because their parents usually didn't have a clue how deeply their kids were into drugs and secrecy. I think Jody is clean, but Alice seems like a player, like someone who'll do anything for—and around—guys. Plus her mother isn't home much. I don't know, Rosie loves her so much. And she gets A's. You see Rosie every day—do you think she's okay?"

Rae nodded. "With me, she's great. She's the picture of health, tan, strong. The children adore her. She's like a movie star to them. And she's so patient, so empathetic."

"Maybe it's me I'm worried about, then. All my decisions are so tentative—it's hard for me to say no to her if she wants to go out. I'm so afraid of her wrath that I cave. I've also been getting that grippy feeling with James lately. Not that I think he'd ever have an affair, but I've sort of lost him to the bitch seductress NPR. He's gone much more, off to the city to record, or meet with his producer, or off on adventures that might lead to a radio piece. It's like living with an addict—he gets high when he turns in a piece that they love, or when he goes in to record, and crazy high when they air it, and then he crashes, and needs me to pet him back to life. We don't make love very often. I don't know. He gets home late from the studio, after spur-of-the-moment dinners with the producers and other radioheads. He gets up at dawn. He's never been happier."

"Oh, baby."

"I dreamed the other night that he was having an affair. It was hell. He'd given a woman a huge diamond ring, like those lollipop rings but real."

"When I've had an upcoming show, and Lank is preparing for a new semester or grading finals or term papers, we get funky, too. The braid starts to unravel."

"It's just miserable. What makes it all sort of work again?"

Rae pursed her lips, mulling this over, pushing her way through a misty curtain of spiderwebs. Elizabeth followed. "Nothing magical. Hooking back into ordinary rhythms—getting up at the same time, letting down together at the end of the day, offerings of food."

"Sitting together and reading at night, talking back and forth about what we're reading. Talking about the people we know. Now I remember, and that's what I crave."

It wasn't supposed to have turned out this way, that when a dream came true for James—a weekly gig on NPR—their marriage took a hit. Before, they'd been a couple in which the husband was a brilliant writer and the wife was his muse, his most astute reader and advisor. Their house had been organized around the novel he was working on, which she loved so much: he needed to be left alone and quiet, or needed to pump her for details, imagery, compliments; he needed her total invisible immersion in his work. They were outside the stream of time: artists. Now everything in their lives was either grist for the mill or of no interest. It was emotionally exhausting for both of them, the ups and downs, his stock in himself rising and falling according to external stimuli. A failure, a hero, a star, a goat, all within a couple of days, or even hours.

"What can we do about it, Rae?"

"In my experience, there's not much you can do about it from the outside. You just live with the bad patches, with the held breath and held body, clamming up, withholding the twigs of connection, and then something comes along, maybe a coincidence, or something bizarre, or he'll say something that's both surprising and familiar, and you'll say to yourself, Oh, my person is not gone."

"But you have so much faith, and I have so little."

"So fake it. Act as if you believe that this is all being sorted out for you, by God as Kelly girl or caseworker."

* * *

That night, Elizabeth and James stopped off at Safeway on the way home from the library for milk, muesli, and tinfoil. They went to stand in the express line. There were three people ahead of them, and four in the next line over. James noticed with a groan that the red-haired matron at the front of their line had a full shopping cart of items, which she had begun placing on the conveyor belt. He growled quietly to Elizabeth, who patted him.

"Excuse me," he asked the checkout clerk, "isn't this the express line?" Elizabeth shot him a look, but he ignored her. "Wait, maybe we got in the wrong line."

"This *is* an express line." The clerk pointed up to the sign, "Twelve Items or Less." Now the matronly woman groaned and turned to glare at James. Then she started returning items to her shopping cart.

The checker waved her arm to stop the woman from putting things away. "It's fine," she said.

James stared blankly at the packed cart. But right then, the young woman behind James reached around Elizabeth and said, "I recognize your voice! You're James Atterbury, aren't you, from KQED?" James smiled and nodded quickly, turning back toward the register, clearly not wanting to start a dialogue. "I love your stuff, Mr. Atterbury—your stories, essays, whatever they are. We all do."

He nodded his thanks again and smiled tightly, and Elizabeth noticed several people in their line and the next paying attention to him now. She heard the checker's chirpy voice reassuring the matron, "Really! It's fine. I'll do you really fast." The redheaded woman laid some items back on the conveyor belt, and turned to smile with great satisfaction at the people in line, like a triumphant child.

But then she leered at James. "Well," she said smugly, "I've been told by management that I can *stay* in this line, even though I guess you're a famous movie star." James visibly recoiled. The woman was staring at him like prey as she now blindly placed more and more things on the belt. She raised her white eyebrows with amusement, bovine, unblinking, like an aggressive Swiss cow. James actually shrank back from her.

"Please don't talk to me," he said.

The woman turned to mug for the people in the line. "I guess we're lucky to have a celebrity with us tonight—even one in such a hurry . . ."

"Please don't talk to me or look at me," James said.

"Lady, *stop*," said James's admirer. "Lighten the fuck up." James shot her a grateful look.

"You don't get to tell me what to do," the red-haired woman said happily, and smirked.

James flung his items onto the conveyor belt, grabbed Elizabeth's hand, and dragged her past the matron.

"Come on, lighten up, buddy," said the woman next in line, and people murmured their agreement. The redhead looked as if she'd just stepped into her own surprise party.

Elizabeth dragged a stunned James out the door, hot fluorescents lighting their way outside. Inside, people were explaining their positions—the clerk, the admirer, the other customers—while the red-haired lady spoke baby talk.

"God almighty," James thundered, sweating in the passenger seat of the car, wiping at his brow. "I just got abused! And I didn't even get my milk. What did I do wrong? I try to be a person of goodwill, and reason, and modesty—and I was just standing there!"

"She was batshit, hon. Let it go."

"I hate that place. I'm never going back. It's like some faceless Soviet system."

"Is it possible you're mad about something else? Like, say, hypothetically, Rosie?"

"No. We were getting honest food, and something to keep it fresh. We weren't buying caustic substances that eat the earth." They sat in silence. He looked up. "Do you think I need to go in and apologize? Or am I just nuts?"

"Maybe both," she said. James sighed, thought for a moment, and got out. She shook her head with affection, watching him go. She couldn't wait for him to come back. All these years together, and she still felt like a lovingly anxious dog around him, thrusting its nose into its person's thigh.

He was hanging his head sheepishly when he returned ten minutes later, holding a shopping bag and a gallon of milk. "I apologized to the checker," he said, getting into the car. "Now she's my new best friend." He put the grocery bag on the floor, shimmied into the driver's seat, snapped on the seat belt. "I am not a psychiatrist, but that woman was a sadomasochistic death-dog. I say that without judgment. But I overreacted because she made me feel the way Rosie does—abused and totally powerless. I want to say out loud that you were right, I am furious at Rosie, for her snottiness, her lies, the way she sneaks around and plays us, her bland derision towards us, the way she talks to you sometimes. The bullshit about those pills you found in her jeans, and the whole contemptuous lie machine of Rosie. Okay? There. I've said it."

She patted him. His outburst calmed her, made her feel useful and sort of elegant: it was nice not to be the crazy one all the time. James started up the car, put it in gear, and together they headed home.

◘

I t took James all day to write a three-page story of the treachery of everyday life. It was called "Ducks in a Row." Elizabeth thought up the title. It was amazing what a smart, charming piece he had made from the insanity. He had turned it into an allegory about how when you think you've finally got your ducks lined up, they turn and peck you to death. How life and time were a conveyor belt moving you along, and blessing came when you realized it wasn't your conveyor belt. And that no matter how protected and noble you felt, how much in control, we were all being conveyed, all the time, borne astride the Möbius strip of time.

"You're a genius," she told him, handing back the essay with a few typos circled. She stood behind him at his computer and pointed out last-minute typos, which he corrected.

"You helped me so much with it. You're my Alice B. Toklas, my muse, and my beloved."

Their rift was healed, not by the ordeal, stupid and exquisite, nor by the alchemy that gave him this essay, but by what was revealed: the depth of their fearful stress, the gag snake coiled inside the peanut brittle can, and how much they needed each other.

He went into the city on Thursday night to record it, after making Rae and Lank listen over the phone. Lank said, "You're a better man than I. I would have gotten in my car and driven through the front windows of the store."

Rae said, "What an experience. You got humility out of it, James. And you got to experience your self-repair mechanism."

"Humility is so overrated, if you ask me," said Lank.

"I agree," said Rae. "But it's like a stone in the gizzard that helps us digest the indigestible stuff of our lives."

"Whoa, Rae, that is so incredible," said Lank. "Can James use that?"

◻

There was no way out of seeing *The Seventh Seal* with her mother. She'd promised to be there on time. Rosie met Alice at Pali Park after Bible school, and they'd eaten some dope banana bread someone was passing out, hiked around Bon Tempe Lake in the heat, gone for a swim, although that was illegal, because Bon Tempe was part of the watershed, fallen asleep in the shade of a laurel grove, gone back to Pali Park and nibbled at banana bread crumbs. They tripped out under the redwoods, let their friends spritz them with spray bottles, used Visine, and then walked arm and arm into town.

They made plans to meet later. Sighing wearily, Rosie stepped inside the theater and found her mother in the lobby, waiting in line for popcorn. Almost everyone there was old—Elizabeth's age or older. They said hello to each other in a sort of hushed way, like they were at church or in the presence of a baby. Two people said how much they loved James's work on NPR. She and her mother got popcorn, Diet Pepsis, peanut M&M's to share.

Rosie felt loopy, mildly disoriented, probably not the perfect space in which to see *The Seventh Seal*. She started eating M&M's to stabilize herself, then caught her mother shoveling popcorn in like one of the Coneheads eating mass quantities. It made her lose her appetite.

The movie started. A seriously bummed knight and his squire

were sitting on the rocks at the beach. Mist and smoke—so far so good. But then Death arrives on the beach. Death, for God's sake. This was going to be a long movie. Even the squirrel on the fallen log looked like the end was near. The knight challenges Death to a game of chess, and says he wants to meet the Devil, because the Devil knows God. The squire was all yawns and belches, and then terrible ugly drinking songs.

Rosie watched as well as she could, closing her eyes whenever she needed to escape. She imagined Robert beside her, the hair on their arms glowing like it had in the sun. She saw herself trace the outside of his lips with her fingertips.

"Pretty amazing, right?" Elizabeth whispered, and Rosie wanted to cry out, "You dragged me from Bon Tempe for this? For corpses and filth, plagues and bugs?" She held her tongue, but, in her mind started telling Alice how smack this movie was, how out there—and she realized that telling it as a story made the bad stuff watchable. As soon as she turned it into a story to tell Alice and Jo, or Robert, she got her humor back.

So she paid attention, and started telling Robert what she saw: "So let's see, it gets festive all of a sudden, because Death decides to mingle more—he pays a visit to a woman who's dying of plague, in a rotting house. But he's a *bad* houseguest. . . ." Finally the dope started wearing down a little, thank God. "Oh, now what's this?" Rosie told Robert in silence. "Here's a sweet little family, all spirit and light and bounce. The dad is a happy-go-lucky entertainer. Boy, is he in the wrong movie. But I don't have a good feeling about this. Why would you make a movie like this?" Why, on the other hand, would she and Alice take the poisoned Quaaludes a second time? Go figure. "Oh, darn," she said to Robert: "The nice family is gone, and now the guy who talked the knight into joining the Crusades is stealing a bracelet off a plague corpse. Don't you hate it when people do stuff like that?"

Talk about a buzz-kill. This movie was the exact opposite of everything she loved about life. Like a great rave, for instance, the highest thing on earth. All the great energy, the scene, decorated to glow and inspire under black light. The Hard Candy one in Oakland was great, with cut-outs of lollipops covering the walls, and during Easter vacation, the Trip and Dicular one, which Rosie never quite got the concept of, but which was so totally incredible, lots of people wearing white, which was totally the most beautiful look under black light. It was totally PLUR—peace, love, unity, respect. Like the complete total opposite of this movie. Except for their fashion thing was kind of hooker *Seventh Seal*: Rosie and Alice both wore corsets, torn black fishnet stockings they'd bought at a lingerie store in the Haight, with money Alice got from selling her ADD meds, plus a tiny theft she had done with Ryan, a fancy set of harmonicas. Rosie always stashed her rave clothes at Alice's; her mother did not obsess about Alice's private life.

Rosie looked around in the dark at all the attentive old people in the theater. She closed her eyes and tried to doze to the fluty Swedish voices as a backdrop. She was definitely coming down now, and it must not be too much longer. She ate a handful of M&M's.

Back on the Swedish beach, the light was all wrong and the silence was way too silent. Even the nice old moon was bad, like a vapor lock into another world. Then, in a church, the knight confesses to Death accidentally and gives away his strategy. The place where the knight is supposed to come clean and have prayer turns out to be the place of betrayal. Oops.

Then the family appears again, on a beautiful hillside, like

Landsdale in the spring, and the earth is providing for them and their little guy, their little bucket kid: the sweetness of strawberries, the milk, like the earth is giving them communion after all this flesh and blood. She wished like mad that the movie would end this way. Would that have killed the guy who made it? Because for a few minutes there it was actually like the energy at a rave, all love and kindhearted community, all the good parts—obviously not when the thugs showed up and hung out in their red bandanas, staring down hot girls, selling whatever they had that night, probably E, or GHB, or Valium to come down with. That was the only bad part; that, and the whole day after, when you pretty much wanted to kill yourself.

But things in the movie were okay; the knight seems to be with his wife. He has come home. He gets to see her again before he dies. And he is okay in a certain way, in a plaguey dying kind of tragic way, because there's light in his face. She's feeding the fire, and is not startled to see him. She says to him, lovingly as can be, "I see the boy you were before you left," and that pleases him. Who would have thought he could ever feel this again? So that is kind of a trip.

Then the movie cuts to the glade where the family is waking up, and Jof, the dad, is having one of his visions that makes his wife think he is nuts, he's seeing the dance on the hillside at dawn, Death leading the way, and the Fool at the end. And then it's all over; thank you, Jesus. Rosie and Elizabeth sat there together in the dark for a very long time. It was the most terrifying, terrible movie Rosie had ever seen, but people were going, "Oh my God, so great, so great," and blah blah, and Rosie felt like she should never smoke dope again, in case she got trapped in memories of the people with boils and thirst and plague, and Death's face.

"Talk to me, Mommy," Rosie said like a little child.

"Let's go get cocoa at the Roastery," her mother said, and they got up in the dark. Rosie wanted to take her hand but couldn't risk any of her friends' seeing her outside the theater. There was no one else in the Roastery but an anorexic girl Rosie knew from school, who was getting coffee to go, and a drifter you saw around town sometimes who always wore a floppy hat, so she and her mother had nicknamed him Gilligan. He was someone the kids could shoulder-tap if they needed someone to buy for them. He jutted out his jaw in greeting.

They went to the counter and ordered bowls of lentil soup. Rosie was basically a vegetarian now, except for bacon and occasional beef jerky. They sat at a table by the window and stirred their soup while it cooled.

"That girl looks like a skeleton," Elizabeth said. "Like someone from the movie."

"She is. She weighs in the eighties now. Also, she throws up. She's so great at it, she can throw up silently into a Coke can."

Elizabeth drew back. "Jesus. Well, everyone is good at something, right?"

"Why did you make me see that movie? It totally freaked me out."

"Oh, baby, I'm sorry. It's considered one of the great movies of all time."

"Yeah, but maybe a little bit of a downer?"

"It isn't to me. I mean, granted, it's not *Yellow Submarine*." Rosie smiled into her soup, and blew on a spoonful. "Greatness and truth are exhilarating," Elizabeth added.

"Yeah, but the truth in it is like, 'It's all decay, end of the world, shoot me now, dude.'"

"Yeah, that was an awful time. It felt like the end of the world to them. I know what that feels like."

"What do you mean?"

"Well, like when your dad died."

Rosie stirred her soup. After a minute she nodded. Then she turned her head around at the sound of the door opening. In came shaggy sun-streaked hair and tan muscles. She didn't recognize him for a second, because he wasn't wearing his wire-rimmed glasses, but it was Fenn. She looked back at her soup. Would he remember her? And then, impossibly, he came to their table, and said her name. Rosie said hey and looked up, but now he was smiling at Elizabeth.

"I saw you guys at the movie," he said. "Pretty great, yeah?" He smelled so male, like sea salt and leather seats, like gunpowder must smell, like the astronauts said moondust did.

Rosie shook her head with amazement. "Yes," she agreed. "It had . . ." she struggled for the right word. "Truth, and greatness," she said finally. She and her mother exchanged a blank look.

"Hey, how's that soup?" he asked.

"Delicious," said Rosie, and then added boldly, "Want a taste?" He raised his eyebrows with pleased surprise and she handed him her spoon. He reached into her bowl, God, he smelled so delicious, and raised a spoonful to his lips.

"Oh, that is good," he said, and then called out to the girl behind the counter. "Hey, I'd like a large soup to go, and extra bread." He turned back to them.

"How many times have you seen it?" he asked Elizabeth.

"Four, maybe? I first saw it with my father when I was Rosie's age. How about you?"

"Two or three."

"Can you join us for soup?" Elizabeth asked, and Rosie wanted to die. She wanted him to stay, but he said he had to be someplace.

"I just popped my head in the door to say hey, 'cause you were one row in front of me. Then that soup smelled so good. I was surprised to see you there, Rosie."

"Why?" She looked up at him, tilting her head with shy petulance, not knowing whether he had insulted her or not.

"You were the youngest person by far. I couldn't have seen it at sixteen."

"Seventeen."

"Sorry. Still, I was afraid of death at seventeen. I didn't like it—but the fact of death does not have to be the fear of death. I mean, that's the hope in the movie."

"Exactly," Rosie said.

He turned back to Elizabeth. "I'm Fenn."

"Elizabeth. I like what you just said. If your time is up, there's no loophole—no amount of cleverness, prestige, no piety. And this is what we live with. Death in the movie is like the world's greatest teacher, or grandparent—he's very matter-of-fact. No bullshit, kind of tickled by everyone's efforts to avoid him, but also somehow decent. Tired, but tireless. He has his job. He's there, and you come."

Fenn looked stunned. "Wow," he said. "Nice to meet you." He smiled and shook his head. "Are you a teacher or something?"

Rosie swelled with pride. Way to go, Mom. You knocked it out of the ballpark. Then Fenn bowed good-bye. Rosie watched him go, mournful with interest. Come back! His jeans hung off his hip bones.

Elizabeth watched her watch him go. Rosie was not breathing.

"Why are you staring at me, Mom?" You got so sick of having

people stare at you all the time. She crossed her arms against her chest.

"I just love you, Rosie. And you're so pretty." Rosie hated grown-ups' eyes on her. This was why she had so many pictures of eyes on her walls, rock star eyes, animal eyes, the eyes of God or angels, because you got to choose what was looking at you, for once in your life, instead of being stared at by perverty men or your mother. Rosie scowled. Her mother was looking at her like a fawn. But Fenn had been impressed by what she'd said. Like, maybe it would be cool to have a mother more like Jody's mom, Sarah, so self-assured, who could keep a good job and defend her kid against attackers. But this was kind of amazing, too, her mother talking like one of your really great teachers.

"Tell me more about the movie, Mama. I have like fifteen minutes."

"Well, I'm honored, Your Majesty. It's very dark, obviously, but half of life is night. And it is only because he is being pursued by Death that the knight finds and saves the little family, and it reconnects him with innocence, and what is worth fighting or living for: goodness. Once again, after having been nearly destroyed in the Crusade, he starts to experience the triumph of being alive. And besides, Rosie, what are we left with at the end? What does Jof see, after his vision of the *Totentanz*, the dance of death? The baby, the dawn, the birds."

She'd forgotten how different Rosie could be in public, although Rae had been telling her this, how the armor came off and with it the dark energy, the indirect gazes and blankness. Tonight they walked out of the café shoulder to shoulder, like girlfriends. When Rosie was a block away, she turned and waved good-bye to her mother like a child.

The good news was that James was home from the city by the time Elizabeth got back from the movie. The bad news was that he was already at work on a new piece someone at the studio had suggested, and couldn't listen to her story about Rosie and the movie right away. "No, no, don't write," she protested, caressing his head from behind as he sat at his desk. "I have so much to tell you." He grabbed her arms and kissed both hands.

"I missed you!" he said. "But give me half an hour. I have to get these notes down before I forget." He never used to say this when he was working on his novel—he'd always been glad for interruptions then. She missed that time. No one could take from him what he had then, because it was so meager, and no one wanted it, the hard work for so little pay, the domestic peace and pleasures he'd mustered. But now there were several people in his life who could destroy his sense of self with the merest criticism or indifference. "Half an hour, darling," he said, and kissed her good-bye.

James was right: the new job was the biggest thing that had ever happened for him. She wasn't even employable. So she cuddled with Rascal on the bed. A siren blew and in a split second her heart tripped over its own feet and her head filled with a slide show of Rosie in danger, an ambulance, or a stranger's van, the windows steamed up, an evil ugly man inside. She couldn't breathe, and then scenes from the movie dropped into the frenzied hole of a panic attack, and she tried to straighten it all out, to quiet and comfort herself, but she felt anxious and strange.

She burst back into James's office. He looked up from his computer. "I'm sorry to interrupt," she said. "But I'm having an episode. And I'm so lonely." He got up and said it was really okay, and came to stand beside her, and when she told him about the bad van, he made the simple sounds of comfort, no real human words, gentle moans, like during sex, or as to a child who has banged her knee, with lots of ellipses in between. It was like music, his holding her, and the soft moans; certain chords got struck again, and she held on for dear life, and the song she hadn't heard in so long resounded, and standing together hanging their heads by his office window, they could hear the same tune again.

FIVE

Salt

◘

Lank sat beside James on the cushions of the Fergusons' old couch. Their shoulders touched. James's eyes moved from person to person, door to door, through the bay window into their front yard, straining toward every creak and house noise like a bodyguard. Moonlight caught the bare skin of Lank's soft crown. His dark eyes were hooded and his lips pursed, like a man weighing his options. Elizabeth and Rae had pulled up chairs. Rae alone had been crying.

A yearbook from Lank's school sat on the coffee table, opened to the pages of the Journalism Club, of which he was the advisor, where in a photo nine young people looked up from a layout table where they were composing the weekly high school newspaper.

The boy in the photo with the Giants baseball cap, Jack Herman, had died early this morning in a car crash. He had graduated last year and finished two semesters at Cal. Amelia, the Goth girl, had suffered a spinal cord injury. They had left a party in the Valley after police broke it up. Melanie Hertz, who was now in jail, had brought a baggie of Ecstasy to the party. The parents of the kid having the party had paid for a keg, to keep him off the road. The cops allowed the kids to drive home unless they were clearly drunk, in which case parents were called. Jack and Amelia had gone over the back fence, laughing, urging others to join them, but no one had. They had crashed into a tree as they came around White's Hill, a mile from town.

"There's one almost every year," Lank said. "So stupid. He had everything: great parents, a marvelous mind, Amelia. He was the funniest kid I ever taught. Everyone liked him. His father had season tickets to the Niners. And yet partying with friends in the countryside, under the moon, smoking weed that costs what teachers make in a week, something beckoned him, promised more, a little more fun, a little more power, and he followed."

James shook his head, sighed, continued his vigilant scan of the room. Elizabeth poured herself another cup of tea from the pot James had brewed, and stared into it as if to read her future.

"Where are you?" he asked.

"Thinking," she replied. "In the old days, this would have been the perfect excuse for us all to get sloshed. I wish Rosie would check in soon."

The phone rang just then, startling them into small laughs. Elizabeth got up to answer it.

"Hello?" she said softly. "Hi, darling." She could tell Rosie knew about Jack and Amelia. "Oh, baby. Where are you?" She heard Rosie breathe, sniffle, sigh.

"Out at Jody's aunt's house."

"Are you?" Elizabeth bit her tongue, silent for a moment, pissed off but wanting to appear sensitive. "You didn't ask if you could go to the beach tonight."

"Mama, cut me some slack. A kid died. Someone a lot of us knew."

"He was one of Lank's students. He and Rae are here. Did you know him?"

"Not well. But I knew her—she's at the same fashion design institute where Alice wants to go. She'll never walk again, Mama." Silence. "Some kids knew them both. We're all sitting around. Vivian made us grilled cheese sandwiches. We're safe and sound here and need to be together. Do you understand?"

"Of course I do, darling. But you still need to be home by curfew."

"No, no, not tonight, Mom. Let me come home later. Or stay here overnight—Jody and Alice are . . ."

Elizabeth almost caved in, hating to make her daughter unhappy, hating to defy her and risk her wrath. But if she said yes, then she would live in fear of Rosie's being out all night with other traumatized teenagers. "No," she made herself say. "I want you home by one. I need you to be in your own bed."

"Mom, don't be like that."

"Don't tell me not to be like that. Be home at one. Rae needs you at church tomorrow afternoon, for the ceremony."

"I have a lesson with Robert at two."

"That works—Rae and I don't need you until four. I love you, baby."

Long pause, then a sigh, and, "Love you, too, Mom."

* * *

S he did not actually know Jack Herman at all, nor was she with Jody and Alice, at Vivian's house, eating grilled cheese. She was in the phone booth at the gas station. But she was definitely feeling terrible about the boy's death. How could you not? The thing was, you knew your luck would give out if you kept driving too fast when you were drunk, let alone on Ecstasy, too, and the kids who'd known him said he always drove fast with the stereo blasting. So the other thing was, if you were tripping, like on E, but you *had* to drive for some reason, you should go extra slow, and totally focus.

She was with some girls from school whom she had come upon at the Parkade, three blonde girls you always saw together, who had a reputation for being stoners. Jody was with Claude at the Fillmore, Alice was trying to break up with Ryan because there was a new guy she liked. The blonde girls were fairly popular, not Homecoming level, but still bottom of the top tier.

They ended up hanging with some guys in the dark at the top of the trail that meandered through the countryside, the bay and laurel, live oak and manzanita, where people ran and walked their dogs during the day. One girl had brought her dog, Brownie, a beagle, and someone else had brought a pint of vodka, which they were mixing with cranberry juice and lime juice from a plastic lime. The girls had perfect bodies, like Alice, not so tall as Jody or her own horrible freakish self; two of them took AP classes, two had their own cars. They all had it going on, way on, way more than Rosie ever would, but the best thing was that it was fun to talk to them—she made them laugh and they seemed to like her. All the boys smoked, so the girls sat apart from them and talked about books and guys and life, while chewing on the ends of grass, or their hair. The girls listened to Rosie with respect as she spoke, maybe because she was going to be a senior. She felt beautiful in the moonlight. It illuminated the foothills below, which looked like a theater backdrop, each one higher than the one in front, until they stopped at the summit of Mount Tamalpais, bowing before the sleeping lady.

She had to walk the two miles home, tipsy, maybe drunk, and it sobered her up. Things would be fine as long as she didn't get stopped by the cops. There was a town-wide midnight curfew for teenagers, which was a joke, since they never brought anyone in unless they thought the person was holding. Rosie wasn't, except for a roach; actually, a pretty good-sized roach. They had smoked some killer dope, and the moon lit the town like a Christmas diorama. The cops were a joke. They wanted all the kids to like them, so when they busted up a party because the music was too loud and neighbors were complaining, they mostly shooed people out in a mellow and groovy way. Sometimes the parents were at home, sometimes the parents had even bought for their kids, so they wouldn't be getting drunk somewhere else, but the parents always said innocently that they thought the kids were just listening to music, even though everything smelled like a concert at the Fillmore. If the cops did stop Rosie, she could probably talk her way out of it. She had used the arsenal of products she always kept near, Visine, breath mints, and moist towelettes.

▣

A siren roared in the night, waking Elizabeth, and her mind began to spin with scenes of Rosie being killed, by rapists, murderers, burnouts who milled around town all night, sleeping at dawn in the brush, but mostly with a vision of every parent's nightmare: a bloody car crash, Rosie going up in flames when the engine exploded, or even dead but untouched after hitting her head in that one lethal spot, like the father in *A Death in the Family*, with only the small blue mark on his chin. The second siren was the last straw, and Elizabeth ran to the phone to call Rosie at Vivian's house. She was actually gasping for breath as she dialed, digging the fingernails of her free hand into the back of her phone hand as hard as she could to contain herself, when the front door opened. It was almost two.

"Jesus!" Elizabeth shouted, slamming down the phone.

"Hi, Mommy," Rosie said, stepping through the front door, and Elizabeth whipped around at the sound of her voice, so crazy with anxiety and adrenaline that she simultaneously wanted to sob with relief and tear out chunks of her child's hair.

Rosie comforted her the best she could. She talked her mother into going into the bathroom with her, where she peed while Elizabeth leaned against the sink. Rosie believed this would create a sense of intimacy. "Let me brush my teeth, Mama," she said, easing her mother over to the side. She brushed her teeth and tongue, and then washed her face with warm water, and looked up at their reflections in the mirror as she dried her face with the towel Elizabeth handed her. Her mother looked grim, but not majorly so— more like she was pretending to look grim and stern. Rosie studied the pterygium creeping over her iris. "Is this getting bigger?" she asked with false alarm, and Elizabeth's face fell with worry.

◘

James was furious with Elizabeth in the morning for not grounding Rosie, although he had been asleep when she got home.

"She was an hour late," James said. "She missed curfew. It's black-and-white."

"But it was a special case, what with the accident."

"She doesn't get to come home at all hours. Period. We've talked about this," he reminded her. "Teenagers need to feel a corral around them. They're not safe without one."

Elizabeth knew this was true.

"But it was a crazy night for the kids," she said without much conviction. "We need to choose our battles. I was glad she came home. You didn't even wake up."

"Because I wear earplugs. I choose not to let Rosie destroy my sleep."

"Well, I don't have that option—I'm her mom."

"She says one thing and does another. She blows off curfew. She randomly announces she's spending the night at the beach, instead of asking us if she can. And then what, she hitchhikes home? That's your system. Did you ever think that maybe if Rosie keeps pulling the rug out from under you like this, it's partly because you keep getting back on her rug?" Elizabeth nodded, so glad Rosie was safe in bed. But James went on. "Listen: Every time you draw the boundary way outside of what we've agreed on, she has to come back *that* much farther, to even meet us halfway."

◘

Lank had arranged for a substitute so that he could take a mental health day, and he stopped by at nine to pick up James for an all-day hike at the water district lakes. Elizabeth made them cinnamon toast and ersatz mocha, with strong coffee, Rosie's cocoa mix, and whipped cream. "These are all my favorite foods," Lank said. He looked older. Elizabeth reached out to stroke his fair freckled cheek with the back of her hand.

"Is there a service?"

"Yes, on Sunday. At the Catholic church in Larkspur."

"Oh, so the family is Catholic. Maybe that helps a little. Do you think?"

"Rae thinks so. And Rae is right about almost everything, eventually. Nothing can help these people today. But maybe in a year, they will have come through."

They sat nursing their drinks. Lank took off his glasses to wipe his eyes. James called from the bedroom that he was almost ready. "I wish I had faith, Elizabeth," Lank said. "I wish I were a Catholic or a Jew. Or Anabaptist. Or AA, or anything. I wish I believed Jack was still alive somewhere, being silly, cracking jokes. I wish I believed that he did not die in vain." They sat in the comfortable silence of old friends. "I do believe in kitchens, though," he said, looking up. "I believe they are holy ground."

Elizabeth smiled. Lank burst out laughing.

"What?" she asked, somewhat taken aback by the shift in his demeanor. He laughed and laughed, and again had to take off his glasses to wipe his eyes. The soft red hair around his tonsure was sticking straight out on one side like a baby rooster. "You want to hear a joke Jack Herman told me once?" Elizabeth nodded, skeptical, and concerned for Lank's mental state.

"There was a second-grader named Mike who could not do math for the life of him, no matter how many tutors or how much extra help his parents gave him. He was always just barely getting by or falling behind. So for third grade, his parents put him in the local Catholic school. Right away, he starts doing better—coming home right after school, doing his homework, and starting to pull ahead of his classmates. And when the first report card comes, he's actually gotten an A. His mother says, 'Mike, what was it? Was it the nuns? Was it all that structure?' And he says, 'Nah. But on the first day of class, when I saw that guy nailed to the plus sign, I knew these people weren't fooling around.' "

Lank and Elizabeth laughed so hard that he had to take off his glasses yet again to wipe his eyes and nose, and they sat that way, heads hung, until James came in, took a look at them, and not knowing what else to do, got a box of Kleenex, setting them both off again.

Rosie slept so late that at eleven Elizabeth poked her head into the room. Rascal was sitting on the edge of the bed, watching Rosie sleep. Elizabeth sniffed the air, detecting the faintest whiff of alcohol. She came closer, bent in to smell Rosie's breath, which she'd surreptitiously sniffed last night. It had smelled fresh. It smelled dry and musty this morning, and there was definitely the hint of alcohol in the air. Elizabeth realized with a start that it was coming out of Rosie's skin. She reached to shake her awake, sickened by the memories of her parents' own scent as they metabolized vodka from the night before, and in fact, by the memories of her and Andrew on mornings after, which for her had become pretty much all the time after Andrew's death.

"Were you drinking last night?" she asked, shaking Rosie. "Wake up."

Rosie couldn't focus right away. "God!" she snapped. "Get away!"

"Were you? I'll go buy a Breathalyzer if you won't tell me the truth."

She had been urged to buy one, along with some home urine tests, by a counselor who addressed the junior class parents. And she had certainly meant to buy both, and definitely would now, later today. Rosie sat up.

"After we left Jody's aunt's last night, we stopped by the

Roastery, with a girl Alice knew, a girl who went out with Jack freshman year. And the girl had a half-pint of tequila. So we all sat outside for a while, and we all had a couple of sips—that was all there was! A half-pint, for four of us. I had like, two big sips. That's all."

"It shouldn't smell this strong if you only had two sips."

Rosie threw her hands up, exasperated, disgusted. "Fine, don't believe me. Call Vivian."

Elizabeth was glaring at her, huffing.

"Mama, maybe you're just extremely sensitive to it, because you don't drink anymore. Remember how you thought Rae had been drinking that time, and it was just polymers from her wrinkle lotion?"

Elizabeth looked away. Then she sank to the bed. "Could you please do only a little bit of everything, and not get in trouble with it, and live to be eighteen, and not scare me to death? Very often? Please please please?"

"I don't do much of anything, Mommy. Come here." Rosie patted the space next to her on the bed. Elizabeth stretched out beside her. Rascal came to stand on her chest, treading as if she were his mother and he a kitten.

"Love can be so painful," Elizabeth said, grimacing each time he flexed. Rosie watched her out of the corner of her eye. Then she slid a blanket between her mother's chest and the cat's claws. Rascal continued treading, eyes closed, drooling. "Are you teaching tennis today, darling?"

"Yeah. I told you, at two. And then church at four, to help set up."

"I'll see you there. Rae thinks a lot more people may come for the salt ceremony, because of the accident. People need to cry together. She and I are going to cook all afternoon."

* * *

Elizabeth wandered around the house, exhausted in part from having had to get up when Rosie had finally gotten home, and partly because of her antidepressants. Some days they left her feeling logy and too mellow. Yet at the same time, her stomach was often filled with butterflies. She wanted to experiment with taking just half a dose every day. She should tell James or Rae that she was having this thought. Or even her psychiatrist, come to think of it. But they really didn't have the money. An hour with the shrink cost what James made at his radio job every week. So she went to an AA meeting at noon instead.

A young businessman in his mid-thirties was the speaker, with a wild story of alcohol and coke, involving violence, crazed spending, jail for public displays, and two overdoses. It was hard to believe—he looked so Ivy League. When he was finished with his story, he chose service as his topic for discussion, and when no one raised a hand, he volunteered that every morning when he took his psychiatric medication, he knew he'd done his community service for the day.

Elizabeth went up afterward and thanked him profusely for saying that.

◘

Robert was late for their lesson, but Rosie had tucked a copy of *Waiting for Godot* into her racket cover and stretched out to read in the grass beside the tennis courts. She pretended to focus as she turned the pages, chewing on the ragged nail of her baby finger. But she couldn't stop thinking about Amelia, now imprisoned in a frozen body. She had called Robert to see if he wanted to cancel his lesson, and he had all but begged her to meet him at the courts, saying he had never needed a work-out so badly. Her heart wheeled around inside like it was on a tricycle.

Her feelings puzzled her. There was definitely something between them. Alice, who was the best at understanding guys, said that if you thought there was something going on between you and a guy, there was. It wasn't like Jody and Claude; more like when Stuart Little falls in love with the beautiful two-inch Harriet Ames, and buys a souvenir birch-bark canoe in which to take her rowing at twilight: love in an old-fashioned way. She would try to love Robert from afar. He kind of seemed to love her, for her mind—the only A student in her physics class—and for helping him to get so good at tennis; and the looks on his face when they talked about stuff like *The Seventh Seal* and literature made him seem entranced. She thought about him more and more these days, in a deeper way than when you have a crush.

She yelped when he sat down beside her, and felt herself turn red. Raising one hand to her chest, she said, "You startled me!" She gave him a look of mock aggravation, then crossed her arms.

"I'm sorry," he said, sitting down. "I thought you saw me walking here. You were lost in your book."

"It's okay." She was still lying down, using the log as a headrest and pillow. He sat with his back against it. Her long brown legs stretched out before them. She sat up, and they both swiveled so that they faced each other, and he asked her if she knew anything more about Jack and Amelia, and she told him there had been Ecstasy at the party, that Melanie Hertz was in jail.

He shook his head. "Melanie Hertz is a wonderful kid. She's a honeybee. There's a funeral at St. Patrick's on Sunday," he said. "Are you going?"

"I didn't really know him," she said. "We're doing a grief ceremony at Sixth Day Prez this afternoon, if you or anyone wants to come. At five."

After a while he said, "Can we just sit here by the creek?" She nodded. Neither spoke. Time fluttered in the glade where they sat. There was still some water in the creek, making a soothing, clean burbling murmur.

"What are you thinking about?" he asked.

She didn't answer right away. His eyes were as big and almond-shaped as Rae's. She liked how serious he was. She dipped her head shyly and said, "Jack."

The energy, sorrowful and close, was now stretched taut between them like a fishing line. He looked so sad that she almost reached out to touch him, like you would anyone who looked in such distress.

"Tell me about the creek," he said.

"What?" She had no idea what he meant. "I don't know."

Neither of them spoke for a moment. "I guess," she said, "a creek is like the rush of my thoughts." Oh no, it sounded like the first line of a little kid's poem. "But because the brook keeps moving forward—unlike my snaggy, plugged-up thoughts—it smooths me out."

"It washes out the roar of rushing, tumbling thoughts," he said.

"Exactly."

He fished a wadded-up handkerchief out of his pocket and handed it to her. She wiped at her eyes, and held the handkerchief to her nose to inhale all his smells, and the sweet, sticky child smells, too.

"Let's get up and hit for half an hour," he said, and she didn't want to, she wanted to sit with him by the creek, but he gave her shoulders a squeeze, stood, and handed her a twenty-dollar bill.

◘

E lizabeth and Rae made rice, black beans, corn bread, and salad with lettuce from Elizabeth's garden, for a large crowd. People had heard that there was a commemorative ceremony and somehow thought it was in honor of Jack and Amelia, and that was to some extent what it had become, since that was the community's most immediate shared sorrow. Rae had brought ten avocados, but they wouldn't cut them up to add to the salad until the last minute. She and Elizabeth chopped tomatoes and onions and cilantro for the salsa while they talked about the same old things they always talked about, politics, periods, sex, books they were reading, books that they were reminded of by mention of these books. They washed lettuce and talked about Jack, Amelia, their bodies, Rosie, Lank, and James.

"Jack is this year's sacrificial lamb," Elizabeth said. "Half of the kids are drinking and using, driving badly, way too fast, while lighting up or fiddling with the radio. And almost every year, the gods seem to come and collect. Or the devil does. I don't know how these things work. But it feels like a bored evil is hanging around town, waiting for one false move."

"My understanding is not that there's a devil outside, prowling Pali Park or the Parkade. But that there's something inside that's always bored, that beckons us, knowing what it is we each want most desperately. And adolescents have fewer defenses."

"Do you think that we're wired this way? With the devil inside?"

"Yeah, in the same way we're wired for God. But not to the same extent. I think it's tiny, and insidious. Like hairline cracks that let in the water that shatters the rock."

◘

Reverend Anthony and Rosie had filled the sanctuary with candles, flowers, and origami cranes from the origami crane ministry, and every chair the church owned, which was sixty. Anthony asked the fifty or so younger people to please sit on the floor or stand, and he began with a prayer that the fire marshal not show. Even the people who were crying laughed.

Rosie couldn't believe how good her own mother looked. Maybe it was the light, or the solemn occasion. Other girls from her class were there with their mothers, and the mothers seemed sort of frumpy and stressed, even bottle blondes and brunettes. Elizabeth's hair did not seem as gray and mussed as usual, but frosted, casual, confident. Her mother was actually a fine-looking woman, as Jody's soldier, Claude, had said after meeting her. She was wearing black linen pants, a dove-gray blouse, a bamboo-patterned Japanese scarf, and shoes that did not for once make you want to die or join the government witness protection program.

She smelled delicious—that was her best quality—of soap and baking. Rosie felt proud standing beside her, and wished desperately to be a better child. No matter what happened from now on, she was going to stop lying so much.

Anthony wore the clerical dashiki of wine red and green and gold that he wore when he presided over unusually joyful or tragic gatherings. Rae was at the altar holding a small bowl of salt. She winked at Rosie. She always looked so great, in comfortable flowing clothes, cool accessories, an elegantly messy bun.

Rosie's head felt like an anthill. What could Anthony possibly say? Plus where on earth was Robert? She had scanned every inch of the sanctuary, like a jumpy spy, but he was not there. Anthony began, and Rosie turned to listen, although she knew his pitch by heart. He would begin by saying that most of the time in our lives we were taught to silence our sorrows, because they were so hard for others to bear, and so he did. "But today," he continued, "we welcome you to a sacrament of expression, a ceremony of salt, of tears and sorrow. We are drawn here every year by the suffering of the world, of our church members, and now today, for the families and friends of Jack and Amelia."

He looked out at the congregation, took a deep breath, and seemed to choose his words carefully. But Rosie knew exactly what he would say, that he had no easy bumper-sticker explanation for what our losses meant, and that there was no sweet, hopeful, cute saying that made them less of a nightmare. He did say something like that, and then surprised her. "People make decisions that have horrific consequences," he intoned. "Sometimes these are political decisions, and we get to rise up and fight them. Sometimes terrible things happen to the most innocent people, and we come together as one wounded body, as Christ crucified. The psalmist, in Psalm Fifty-six, says, 'You have put my tears in your flask,' and that means that God is paying attention to the pain of God's people. And we may not get what we want, but we will get what is needed. God is struggling in this with us, in all the sadness of our lives, in the car accident, and God is the answer. Our tears are in God's flask, and if what is needed is going to get done, it's going to be through divine love working through us. So we acknowledge as a community that what is going on sucks—if you'll forgive my French." People laughed and said, "Amen."

Rosie's mouth dropped open. Whoa—that was pretty good.

"In closing, we ask ourselves, what is the next right thing we can do? How can we stop the bleeding of those we love? How can we fund-raise to get the money for a burial, or therapy, or medicine, or a walker?" Rosie sighed: The End.

There was a large glass bowl on the communion table, filled with water, and Rae stood beside it with her container of salt. Anthony asked everyone to come forward, take a pinch of salt, and drop it into the common bowl, twice. "A pinch for each sorrow, and one for each joy, to express the bittersweet aspect of our paradoxical faith." Rosie went up with Elizabeth, who said for her sorrow, "Jack and Amelia," and for her joy, "Rosie." Shame for her endless lies nearly made Rosie cry out loud. This, and the fact that Robert hadn't come—she had so gotten her hopes up. She felt crushed, and that made her feel insane. "Jack and Amelia," she said, for sadness, although she was more sad that she didn't have a boyfriend. For joy, she said, "My friends." She should have said her mother; it would have made her happy. Later, Anthony said a prayer for the community, and Rae stirred the water, troubling it the way angels did in the Bible so people could enter and be healed. Then Rae went to join Elizabeth in the fellowship hall, to cut up the avocados for the salad, and serve everyone who had shown up.

◘

Rosie threw herself into bed when she got home, and fretted. James came in and tried to get her to tell him what was wrong, but even she didn't know. Elizabeth had gone to her psychiatrist's after the ceremony, which Rosie found extremely annoying. What kind of crazy person saw a shrink at seven p.m., she wondered. God, her mother was never here anymore when you needed her. James sat at the foot of Rosie's bed, but when he put his hand on the blanket covering her feet, she nudged his hand away. He went and got her a cup of sweet, milky tea, his solution to everything. After a while, she sat up, but she wouldn't meet his eyes.

"Is this about a guy?" After a moment, Rosie shook her head. "You tell me where he lives—I'm going to go over there and knock some sense into him."

Rosie glared at him, and then into her lap. "I said no."

"But your eyes said, *Oui, oui.*" Rosie punched him, smiling, teary. "'Love makes your soul crawl out from its hiding space,' to quote the late, great Zora Neale Hurston. It's not much fun when the love that beckoned you out gets cold feet and leaves you there alone, like a snail in between shells. Very scary."

"That's the thing, I don't love anyone. I hate my life. Why do Alice and Jo have boyfriends and not me? What's wrong with me?"

James didn't say a word, as any other adult would have done, like "You're so pretty" or "It'll pass," which was so meaningless.

"It's even worse than that—I think I like someone who is a hundred percent unavailable. Someone who's totally taken. I'm a total cliché."

"Never, ever, that."

She drank the tea he had brought, and blew her nose. He went back to his office to work. She lay in bed reading a book by Roy Blount, Jr., that Claude had lent her. When James came in later to check on her, they talked about what a genius Blount was. She read him her favorite lines. Then she talked him into lending her the car. It was not hard to disarm him with a subtly vulnerable expression, a nuanced compliment about how sweet he had been, eye contact, using his name: he was putty.

He squinted. "Didn't you lose driving privileges for another couple of days?"

"Yeah, technically." She gave him a pained look, and his face softened. She watched him hem and haw. "Let me go out for a while. I just have to be with my friends. Please, James."

"Okay," he said finally. "It's a special night. I think your mom would let you go. But if you get home past curfew, my ass is grass. And I'll be pissed."

He could be so great, and she swore to him and to herself that she would be home on time.

◘

She put on her sexiest tank top, her tightest, lowest jeans, with a zipper barely three inches long, and makeup so she'd look good for whatever she and Jody and Alice might end up doing—a party at someone's house, or up in the hills, or even under the streetlights of the Parkade. "Fucking *A*," she said out loud in front of the mirror, blending in foundation, what a douche to fall in love with this old teacher, a married teacher with a wife and little kids, who didn't even like her back. Thank God she hadn't made a move all those times; and the best thing was, no one knew. She hadn't told anyone else. She outlined her eyes in kohl, smiling with relief, still a little sad, but talk about close calls. She looked good in the reflection. She practiced looking hard, then tender and dewy, sassy, ecstatic, bored, and above it all.

◘

She picked up Alice, Jody, and Claude. Alice had found out about a party up in the hills way above the Manor School tonight at nine. This was so great, much better than a house party. Everyone was going. It was sort of in honor of Jack and Amelia. It was one of those parties where you had to pay five or ten dollars, depending on if there would be E there or only kegs. People would meet at Safeway, get shuttled by the older guys who were throwing the party. Nobody got to drive themselves down the hill, because most of them would be pretty trashed, and the guys giving the party couldn't risk legal problems.

They stopped at the Parkade, bought a joint for Alice and Rosie, shoulder-tapped Gilligan, in his floppy hat, who bought them a six-pack of lager, and the four of them sat at the park getting high. Rosie and Claude had a lively talk about the Roy Blount book, like one you might have with Robert. Claude was sweet and cool, surprisingly sophisticated when he spoke, even with that drawl. Alice was all about this new guy she was hooking up with later. Rosie felt a little down, but not too bad. She imagined talking with a new guy tonight, too. Her mind retraced the scene today with Robert, how easily they talked and how deeply, and the shape of his eyes, oval, pointed at the sides, so blue but not as blue as her own. It was such a nice memory, heightened, elevated, unspoiled.

"I have a teacher I think you'd love," she told Claude, though she meant it as an introduction of the topic to Jody and Alice. "He's like we are about books. Like the other day we were totally jamming about *Waiting for Godot.*" She knew Jody would care, because she'd done the summer program with ACT her sophomore year, before her troubles with cocaine.

"I love that play so much! Remember, I was Lucky in the junior production."

"I was Dorothy in sixth grade," Alice announced.

"Really, Alice," Jody said, like a mortified schoolteacher. Rosie smiled. Then Jody turned around to face Claude: "Do you know that play? About the two little tramps, waiting for this guy Godot, or maybe it's God, but nothing ever happens, the whole play is about them waiting, waiting, and then this guy comes along finally with his slave, Lucky, who he's dragging along like a dog, to sell at the market. It's like about the meaning of life."

"It sounds like a regular shoot-'em-out night at the theater."

"Samuel Beckett only won the Nobel Prize for it," Jody snapped. "God, you're my only hope," she said to Rosie. "So what were you saying about Tobias?"

"Nothing," Rosie said. "He's just totally cool to talk about books and science with. Plus, he pays me twenty bucks a lesson. I've made a fortune this summer—lucky for you two deadbeats."

Only she and Claude had any money that night, and they paid for the others when a guy with a Hummer and at least two woofers picked them up in the parking lot at Safeway. It was ten dollars tonight.

"Where are the bracelets?" Jody asked.

"You get them at the next station," he said. "Or else too many people find out."

Too many usually meant more than a hundred or so. Bracelets would be issued—either a certain color yarn or a plastic tie like the kind her mother used for tying tomato vines to stakes with, or for ten dollars, maybe even the glow-stick kind. The bracelet got you a plastic cup for beer once you got to the party.

The driver dropped them off at the Old Manor trailhead on the outskirts of town, where others were massing, looking for friends. The four of them immediately started hiking in the dark, a waning moon lighting the trail. It was not steep; more like a bunny slope at Tahoe. Ahead of them, Metallica blared from a boom box. Behind them, the old fire road gleamed, luminous with moon, lighter by far than the night or the trees that lined it. The four of them dropped back to lose the kids ahead of them, who were loud and silly. Then they stood looking up at the sky. The moon was lovely tonight; it was everything good and pure and huge, blessing right down onto them. And yet wafting through Rosie like another form of light was hurt confusion.

"I am going to get so fucked up," she said, and the others laughed. She took in the ambient sounds, dry grasses rustling, crickets. The warmer it was, the more the flowers opened up: the night smelled almost like a lei or corsage.

"You think there are raccoons around?" Claude asked, genuinely worried.

"How you going to be a soldier if you're afraid of raccoons?" Jody asked.

"When I'm in battle, I'm going to have a gun."

"To shoot raccoons with?" Rosie asked, and he shoved her.

"I'm going up ahead and see if I can find Evan Andrews," said Alice. "Wish me luck." She moved off ahead of them, fast but clumsy, stumbling almost at once. Rosie and Jody smiled at each other. They were both so athletic, while Alice had an adorable clumsiness born of impatience, and not tuning in to her body at all unless there was a guy around.

"I have to be home at midnight, don't forget," Rosie called after her. Turning to Claude, she said, "I don't like raccoons, either. They hiss, and they gnash their teeth, and they sneak in through the cat door to steal my cat's food."

The lights of the party campsite grew brighter, and soon they stepped out at the bottom of a hillside that went upward and onward forever. A girl Rosie didn't recognize stopped them, to give them their bracelets and cups. You got to pick out what color bracelet you wanted. Jody and Claude picked magenta, which was light pink until they snapped each other's on and the bracelets began to glow darker. Rosie studied the box of bands, light pink, blue, green, yellow. "The blue one is really pretty," said the girl, "not fluorescent like the others. Blue blue. Tahoe blue," and it was.

The three of them walked up the shaggy dry grass of the corridor to where most people were gathered, where the generator sat. The space was perfect, an endless dark refuge extending the length of a football field up the hill, with lights plugged into the generator that also powered the boom box, and everyone glowed with a bracelet. They could see people leaning against the eucalyptus, bay, and oak, perched on top of boulders and rocks, sitting with their backs against logs, like it was all furniture. The stretch of grass was pretty clear of things to trip over in case you got loaded, no rocks to tumble over or brush to get tangled in. The people giving the party had found a great spot and were going to make a bundle tonight.

They stood around getting their bearings, moving to the music, making small talk. Then a guy Jody knew from rehab passed Rosie a pipe, and held a lighter to its bowl as she inhaled. She held it as long as she could, exhaled, and took a second hit. "Be careful," he warned. Moments later, she was bombed, totally toasted.

Rosie turned away from Claude and Jody because they were shaking their heads and smiling about how wasted she looked. They couldn't smoke at all. She was actually tripping lightly, merging with the crowd, dozens of her peers, all on the same plane. She walked to a group of kids by a cluster of oak trees.

"Hey, who's there?" she asked in the dark, and then their faces materialized, as two people called out hi to her, friends from school. She leaned against a tree, let it hold her up. "I am so wasted," she said, laughing.

One of the three blondes from the night before stepped forward, and they hugged.

"Be careful. Someone here is selling sherms," the girl said—joints laced with angel dust.

"I'm fucked up, but I don't think it was dust." Rosie started laughing with pure joy, at the long stretch of the woods that embraced her, the tree trunk that held her up, the twinkling stars above, the whole fucking beautiful diamond universe, above her, below her, around her, inside her. This was the Truth, the capital-T truth, even when you weren't stoned. It's what Einstein proved—that it was all energy, and it was all One.

She hugged everyone in the group, her new best friends, and then someone else came up to see who they were. First you heard the crunch of leaves, the rustly, scuttly sound of the dry oak leaves. No one could sneak up on you. Every time someone entered the meadow, you heard their shoes crunching on the fire road, and heard them greeted by the girl with the glow-stick bracelets and cups. It was like having a sound map of the new world.

She wandered off to see who else was here. Each time the drill was the same—"Hey, who's there," then faces materializing in the dark, hugs, or introductions, then hugs for the new best friends. Whatever she had smoked had given her bright and dreamy hallucinations, and they took her to a soft, gentle place where she wanted to hold the whole world like Mother Teresa with an AIDS baby, and weep at its beauty.

After several plastic cups of beer, she ended up dancing for a long time, sometimes with boys, sometimes with girls. She should think about starting back. Everyone was getting pretty loaded. Several girls had thrown up in the chaparral, one boy was having a loud sobbing nervous breakdown about what a misfit he was. His friends surrounded and comforted him. The hillside smelled more like eucalyptus than the fire road had, which was closer to the flowers in people's gardens. The bay smelled like your father slapping aftershave onto his cheeks, but you didn't have to have hair in the sink, all the slapping sounds, or the father.

She climbed up the hillside, squinted into a group of ten or so kids. "Who's there?" she asked, and was soon reconnecting with friends from school. They had washed out an empty milk carton and filled it with beer so they wouldn't have to return to the hub so often. It was great, but after another cup, Rosie needed to sit. She plopped down onto the grass, clumsy as Alice, laughing at her efforts. Others sat down with her, and filled her cup. Everyone loved her, she could tell by their faces lit by glow sticks in the moonlight.

And then she heard cars down below, several at once, not like when the shuttle came by from Safeway, and then kids were shouting and screaming. Rosie and her new crowd gaped at each other, as people in nearby crowds leapt to their feet. "It's the cops, it's the cops!" various people shouted in the night, and then there were cops shouting, "Stay where you are! Stay put!" Everyone was swearing, scrambling, streaming down the hillside to breaks in the brush on either side of the trailhead. It sounded like they were having fun, a mob moving as one.

Rosie and her friends scrambled farther up the hill, trying to avoid the police flashlights. There had to be five cops at least, shining their flashlights, grabbing at the nearest kids, but some kids ran past them and out of their grips like greased pigs. The cops caught a couple at a time, and led them off to the fire road where their cars were, and came back for more, but mostly the kids outmatched them and got away. Everyone in Rosie's group hung together, standing behind trees, holding their breath, peering down. Now a lot of kids were falling and rolling down the hill like an avalanche, like logs or little kids, laughing and screaming when they hit against rocks and branches, twenty of them rolling below where Rosie stood, all the way down the hill.

It was a movie, a crazy strobe-lit movie gone bad, and no one in Rosie's group dared to move. The kids below who had gotten hurt stopped where they were and called out for others to help them, but only more cop cars arrived, and police poured into the corridor. "Shit fucking hell, if my parents find out," someone whispered. The boys Rosie was with took off for the higher area, trying to tug the girls, who were rooted in the pandemonium and shouting. They let go and took off when a woman in uniform stepped out from behind a redwood trunk.

"Stay where you are," she said to the girls, cold as the moon, and reached out a black-gloved hand for Rosie's wrist, extinguishing the light of the glowing blue band.

SIX

The Big Fish

▣

Elizabeth lunged for the phone in the dark, but James got to it first. When she tried and failed to grab it from his hands, she clenched her fists at her chest like a child praying.

"Yes?" he said. She turned on her lamp and watched his face. He was digging his fingers into his scalp, and she was relieved to see anger, not grief. "She's fine," he told her.

"What is it, for God's sake?"

James listened on the phone a moment, before turning to her. "The police busted her and a few kids at a party in the hills behind Manor, where there was alcohol. They've got her at the station." Elizabeth climbed out of bed, clutching her chest. "We can go get her, or they will take her up to juvenile detention for the night."

"I can be there in ten minutes."

But James shook his head. She grabbed for the phone. He ducked, dodging her.

"Has she been drinking? . . . Just beer, are you sure?" He nodded to Elizabeth. "And what about drugs? . . . Okay. . . . Yeah, I *bet* she's mad. She'll get over it." He threw his free hand up with general frustration. Elizabeth looked around frantically for her shoes. "Can we leave her there for the night? . . . Why not? . . . I see, I see. Of course." Elizabeth pulled on a shirt. "What's the very longest we could leave her with you at the station before you had to take her to juvie? I seriously do not want to make this easy for her." James listened. "I mean, what if it took us five or six hours to get there?" After a minute, he said, "I cannot begin to thank you. You must be a parent." He looked at his watch. "Fantastic. Six it is."

Elizabeth turned on James the instant he put the phone down. "She'd just been drinking beer, so what—she's seventeen! It was the last of the big summer parties! For Chrissakes!" This is what Elizabeth's mother used to say whenever she was drunk or annoyed. Hearing her own voice repeating these words silenced Elizabeth briefly. Shaken with anxiety, she did not know what to think or feel besides doubt and worry and questioning of her every move as a mother. Then she plunged on. "She's such a good kid— and you're going to leave her in jail?"

"She's not in jail. And we've found rolling papers. Pipes from our friendly neighborhood smoke shop. And you found pills in her pocket after Jody's party."

Elizabeth pinched her arm as hard as she could, and it hurt like hell. But she had to be dreaming. How had they gone from Rosie hoisting tennis trophies above her head at the net to Rosie under arrest, or whatever she was under?

"This is a lucky break for us, Elizabeth. It's so important that we really see what's going on," James said. Elizabeth ground her teeth to keep from slapping him; even though she knew he was right, she hated him for it. He went on, seemingly impressed by his own calm and insights. "A, that when you're dealing with an alcoholic or addict, you're already outnumbered. And B, it's revealing what we're about to dig up in her room. Because the cops aren't supposed to keep her there just so we can teach her a lesson—but they're going to. Come on, baby—we can go through her stuff while they watch her for us. We can find out what's true."

The room was relatively tidy, compared with, say, Jody's, which looked like an explosion at the flea-market jeans hut: twisted jean corpses, incense, used plates and bowls, plastic smoothie bottles. But because Rosie's was not so bad, it took a while to break the code; to discover the resiny smell of dope at the bottom of a box; to find among all her books the two hollowed-out volumes holding papers and a plastic cigar tube of bud; to locate the Cuban cigar box with a false bottom beneath which were flecks of weed, razor blades, three lavender-pink tablets that Elizabeth recognized as Percocet from James's first gum surgery, and eight hundred dollars in cash.

"It's the money that she's made this summer," Elizabeth said defensively.

James nodded nicely and said, "Okay."

"For Chrissakes, James, she's worked nearly every day at Sixth Day Prez, or teaching tennis."

"Hm," said James, "good point."

Elizabeth blew up for the second time. "Don't you dare use that Al-Anon crap against me. 'Uh-huh. Okay. Good point.' I hate it when you do that."

"What do you want me to say, baby? We just found a razor blade in Rosie's shit. Do you remember what you and I used razor blades for?"

"Not very often. That's my point! She's experimenting."

James looked exasperated, furious at her for not seeing things his way. "Experimenting means you try something two or three times. More than that is 'using.'" James found a pint of rum in Rosie's tennis racket carrying case, where the can of balls was supposed to be, and a festive four-pack of vodka lemonade at the bottom of her laundry hamper. "Jesus Christ," Elizabeth said in despair, as the pile of booty mounted on Rosie's neatly made bed: Zig-Zag rolling papers, a roach clip, lighters. "What next? Glue?"

She began to cry. "This is going to be good in the long run," James said. She sat on the floor with her back to the wall by Rosie's door. "There are all sorts of people locally who help kids and families in trouble with drugs. Anthony, for instance."

"Jesus, you make it sound like *Panic in Needle Park*. It's weed." James rolled his eyes. "Okay, weed and pills. And one razor blade." Elizabeth almost managed a smile. "This does not make her a drug addict." James nodded sagely.

She screamed into the air between them, then buried her face in the bedspread and kept bellowing until she felt better. James got to his feet. "I'm going to go make us some mint tea." She sat breathing deeply with her eyes closed when he left. The stuff on the bed was like the display at the museum at San Quentin, of shivs and syringes made out of pens and toothbrushes. Elizabeth laid her head in her hands and rocked.

They managed to sleep for a few hours, then lay in the dark, resting their eyes. The dawn was light gold above the tree line.

By the time they went to pick Rosie up at the station, the golden border was gone.

◘

Rosie sat hunched over a table in a small room behind the front desk, and Elizabeth watched her for a moment through the window in the door. Her long arms were crossed, eyes opaque with disbelief. "Look at her," James whispered. Rosie looked up at them, and then slowly down at her watch with a hint of a smirk—she was not going to show anyone much of anything in this public place. "As if we all work for an airline, and her flight has been delayed," he said. A police officer led them in.

"Rosie," Elizabeth called, but Rosie didn't seem to hear.

"Rosie!" James said sharply, and she looked up slowly.

"I hear you," she said. "The whole town can hear you. Can we just go, please?"

"Listen, you don't get it, do you, baby?" he asked. "You're in a fuck of a lot of trouble." Rosie looked away with contemptuous amusement, as if he were delusional. He seethed. Elizabeth stepped between the two of them.

"We are not bringing charges this time," the officer told James and Elizabeth. He turned to Rosie: "But next time we catch you with dope or alcohol, I will throw you in juvie so fast you won't know what hit you. We'll be watching for you." He shot James a knowing glance.

Rosie considered his words, as if he were a waiter at her table reciting the specials of the day. "Okay," she said slowly, as if he had talked her into the lasagna.

The officer advanced upon her. "Listen, miss," he said quietly. "I will be god*damned* if some snotty-nosed stoner high school kids are going to burn down our beautiful hills. I see you so much as smoking a cigarette in an open space again . . ."

Elizabeth wanted simultaneously to fling herself at his legs and pull him off her daughter, and to choke Rosie with her bare hands. In her corner Rosie seemed to have decided that the service at this joint sucked. She got to her feet and walked out the door, head held high.

□

In the car, she let herself fall apart, crying, spewing out rage and accusation: How on *earth* could they betray her like this, leave her there for hours in that piss hole; what the hell good did they think that would do? Did Elizabeth *ever* think about anyone but herself? Did James even have a clue what it was like to be a real parent? Did it matter to them at all that they had turned her into someone who *had* to lie, just to have the semblance of a life, and not be treated like a baby? It was stupid bad *luck*, for God's sake, that the cop had grabbed her and not the other kids. She hadn't even done anything wrong.

Horrible James didn't say anything, and he looked like he might start humming. He had learned this at his meetings— Rosie realized that she was now the gorilla in the cage he had to stay away from. Her mother cried daintily, like a little old lady. They made her sick. In her core she felt a deep fury and a rage for freedom.

A cold calm descended, all at once, like there was hard glass inside her. She knew she was scary, and that this immobilized them. Rosie smiled.

By the time they got home, the rift was so big that it scared even her. Where could they go from here? No way would they let her out today. "Go to your room," said James, reading her mind. "You're grounded forever."

She lay in the dark on her bed, listening to music. Nothing could capture the feelings inside except Axl Rose and Bob Dylan. She played them as loud as she could without risking a warning—her parents were turning into old neighbors who hassled the young—or a visit. Worst of all would have been a real conversation.

She began to open drawers, her hamper, and handbags, and raged as she discovered they'd taken almost everything; they'd raped and pillaged the room. She sat on the floor and fumed, breathing hard like she'd been running. Everywhere she looked, her stuff had been taken. She whipped open her tennis racket case to find the rum missing. Then she looked in the well of a marble-based pen-and-pencil set, a trophy for winning the state doubles tournament in San Jose, and found a plastic bag that earrings had come in—thank God they had not found her stash of Ecstasy. She and Alice had gotten it at a rave in Oakland, a while ago, before summer began. The memory lifted her spirits. An older woman—maybe in her thirties—had brought her little boy, in his one-piece sleeper, although he must have been at least seven already; it was decorated with rave glow spots, white plastic cut-outs that the black light would catch, the M&M's logo on each one. Maybe the mother thought he would blend in, like a prop or the gigantic peanut M&M's decorations. Rosie had played with the boy for a while in a corner, even though she was stoned out of her mind, had taken two tabs at once because she had been taking it too much and had a little tolerance going. That was why she had quit E.

She dozed. When she woke up, she found that her mother had left a tray of kindergarten food on her bedside table—peanut butter and jelly on wheatberry bread, cranberry juice and carrot sticks,

Oreos and an apple. She didn't want to be in this abyss. The first time she saw her mother come in, as the sun sank beneath her windowsill, she turned to the wall, and said, "I have nothing to say to you."

The second time her mother came by, Rosie was blubbering like a baby, partly out of exhaustion and fear, but also so her mother would comfort her, hold her quietly, promise it would all be okay. She wanted her mother to save them both, so she could get on with what she had been doing, with her wonderful grown-up life—Jody and Alice and the guys they hung with, lying on the sand at the beach, lying on the golden grass in the hills. What, was there a law now, you couldn't smoke outside?

They were all so careful, the kids she knew. They would never start a fire. She missed Robert and Rae and the kids at the church, the little ones, her bucket kids, whom she pulled around on the lawn in the big plastic tub, singing their funny songs and screaming every time they hit a bump.

She was starving to death by dinnertime, but when Elizabeth came in to get her, she claimed not to be hungry. This usually freaked her mother out, but tonight she did not try to change Rosie's mind. Rosie heard her footsteps recede down the hall.

"Wait a sec, what's for dinner?" she called after her, but James answered.

"Bread and water."

⌾

Robert and she had a lesson tomorrow—they had to let her out by then, or she would lose all respect for them both. Jailers!

But the next day at one, Elizabeth drove her to the courts, waved in the friendliest way to Robert, as if from a float, and said she'd pick Rosie up an hour and fifteen minutes later. The fifteen minutes was to prove how serene Elizabeth was.

Elizabeth got a cup of coffee at the KerryDas Café while waiting, and took it to the steps of the Parkade. Townspeople went about their business in every direction you looked, walking in and out of stores before her, getting gas at the station to her left, lining up with little kids for the last big matinee of the summer, heading to their cars in the parking lagoon behind her. Some of the town's delinquents and no-hopers and high school kids milled around the Parkade, Rosie's peers, younger or a few years older. Among them were two who had had nervous breakdowns, one out of nowhere her first month in college, one after massive amphetamine use at Santa Cruz. They milled in groups at the bottom of the stairs, in the bus kiosk, in the steps in front of the theater, making themselves villages of commerce and knowledge and sulk. Otherwise, they would feel small and ridiculous. Please God, even though I don't believe, please, if you are there, don't let Rosie end up here next year, Elizabeth prayed.

She studied the amulets hanging from their necks, the earrings, the wife-beaters, the strange caps that kept them warm and signified how different they were. How did the younger kids get such extensive tattoos, snakes slithering up their necks, dragons fanning out across their chests? It was illegal in California, even with parental authority; they must be the prison tattoos you could make with pens and heated wire guitar strings. Don't let my scrawny muscles confuse you—see how dangerous I am, with my piercings and jail tats.

The coffee was warm and milky, and woke her up. The mountain behind the town shone with woolly green expansiveness like Oz. A man walked up alongside her on the steps and said hello, and it took her a moment to recognize Fenn. He greeted her as if they were friends. God, he was sweet. The young blonde woman he was with had African-pierced ears, with plugs that stretched her lobes to the size of dimes, and as the three of them made small talk, Elizabeth tried not to stare.

Elizabeth tugged at her own earlobe. "Did that hurt?" she asked. The girl shook her head.

"Not at all."

The earrings brought to mind watch batteries, or hearing aids.

"Are you interested?" Fenn asked, smiling. Elizabeth shook her head hurriedly, no no no. "'Cause we can plug you into our connection."

Elizabeth looked shyly into her lap. "I don't really understand the concept of most piercings, I'm afraid, or tattoos."

When she raised her head to meet his eyes, he said, "It's about finding openings."

After Fenn left, she said to an imagined listener: I don't believe in you, but please don't let Rosie get those earrings; or any neck tattoos; or AIDS. Also, help her not fry her mind. Oh, one more tiny thing: Could you please help keep her alive, and not have a spinal cord injury, like Amelia the Goth girl? Thank you: that would be great.

◘

By dinnertime, James had arranged on the table everything they'd found in Rosie's room, like a holiday centerpiece, including a bottle Jody and Claude had asked her to hold for them, that she had maybe had a few hits from, and the Percocet she said she'd stolen from James. Why, why, her mother kept asking, and Rosie wanted to shout at her what Rae always said. That "Why?" was not a useful question.

Rosie did not answer, nor did a hint of her thinking show on her face. She shrugged. "Because it was there. Because it just made me feel like I had a secret. Like I have some parts of me you don't own or get to have an opinion on. Because everyone puts so much pressure on me. And I'm a teenager, and sometimes I want to swipe things. Didn't you ever steal?"

"Bikini underpants from little boutiques," Elizabeth said.

"Is that all?" Rosie demanded.

"My parents let me drink in front of them, and looked away if I lifted a six-pack, so I had no excuse to steal from them. It sucked."

"Mommy! Can't you pay less attention to me? I'm a good kid. But I'm seventeen. Couldn't you let things slide every so often?"

"We have, and now we're worried that we're letting too much slide," said James. "We don't know how much you're using. Maybe you don't even know that anymore. And a razor blade?"

"I just told you like the total truth!" There was the faintest and most terrible smile on James's face, like when they played poker and he'd just been dealt an ace.

"Whatever," he said, and looked over at Elizabeth. She looked back, puzzled. "So you did steal those Percocet from me in the spring?"

"Yeah," Rosie said, and right before their very eyes, she seemed to give up. "I did." She looked back and forth between them. "And I just need a chance to start over, and prove myself to you."

"Okay. You're grounded for four days," he said. "Except for tennis and church." He seemed to relax. "You can catch up on your AP English reading." Rosie started to smirk, but something inside her shifted, and she sighed wearily instead.

"What ev," she said. James looked about to react, but she threw her hands up.

"You win," she said. "I hear you, I get it. I'm sorry. Okay?" James nodded.

Elizabeth poured the rum and pills into the sink, ran water, and tossed everything else into the garbage pail.

She said, "Great! Now can we eat? Start to get this behind us?"

James took a bite of food. "This is so good. What did you stir-fry this with? Cilantro?" She pointed her finger at him: Yes, exactly. And Rosie couldn't believe her ears—they had already switched the topic to food and she was busted for only four days. Boy, this works for me, she thought to herself, and poked at her food winsomely.

"We've gotta stop with the whole meat thing," Rosie announced.

"Why?" asked James.

"Because it's immoral? And disgusting?"

"Rosie darling, we eat almost no meat these days."

"So what do you call this, Mommy?" She held up an incriminating cube of meat, as if she'd fished a cat turd out of the stir-fry.

"Oh," said James, smacking his forehead. "You mean lamb doesn't count as a vegetable?"

◘

We trapped her in a lie," he whispered to Elizabeth behind the closed door of their bedroom. "Fong only prescribed a total of four Percocet. They're synthetic opiates, the same as Oxy-Contin. I took at least two, maybe three. So no way there were three of mine left. She had to have stolen them somewhere else."

Elizabeth, sitting on the bed, let her head fall heavily to her chest. He went to sit by her and started to put his arm around her shoulders, but she pulled back, raised her hands, let them fall into her lap. "Can't we drop it and start over?"

He looked at her for a long time, hard, surprised. "Our daughter got opiates from someone, Elizabeth. It's for acute pain, Elizabeth, and highly addictive. It's called Appalachian heroin."

"I know! I'm not stupid. Maybe I don't write for NPR—you know, most of us don't. But I'm asking you to dial it back for now, while we figure out what to do—both of us, move back to Defcon Two, slightly increased force readiness."

James closed his eyes, the Buddha with a migraine, nodded. "We need to start testing her, now." Elizabeth sighed. "Do you agree?" After a minute, she nodded. He got up, and went into the bathroom to floss.

Lying in bed that night, he whispered that he loved her, and she whispered back that she loved him, too. There was a moment's silence in the dark, and then he asked, "Is there any chance that we could ever get a dog?"

"What?" she asked too loudly, sitting up.

"I really want a dog, Elizabeth, I've wanted one for so long. I thought maybe when Rosie goes off to college, but why not now? It might actually be a good thing for our family."

"We already have a perfectly good cat." Rascal was kneading her stomach. "And when Rascal's gone, I think I'll be done with animals forever."

"Why?"

"Because they are fur-covered heartbreak waiting to happen. Plus, if we got anything, it would be another cat—cats are so much smarter."

James squawked in agreement. "They are. You throw a tennis ball to a cat, they say, 'Fuck you, I'm not your maid.'"

"See, James, I like that in an animal. Dogs are obsequious." When James laughed, she smiled and smoothed Rascal's cheeks.

In the sweet, close quiet, he asked, "Can we get a drug-sniffing dog?" She managed a laugh, too.

Later, he wanted to make love, and she was glad to because her gratitude trumped the new feelings of mild revulsion she had begun to feel toward sex. Besides, it gave her a sex credit. She could look forward to a week off now.

◘

Rae called first thing in the morning to see if Elizabeth wanted to drive to Sacramento with her for a rally in support of teachers and nurses, but Elizabeth begged off.

"I haven't felt at all like myself since Rosie got busted—I totally need a meeting."

"Please, Elizabeth? I'm exhausted, I have bad breath, and my vagina smells."

"That's why I don't want to go."

◘

James was in his office, moaning and groaning about his deadline when Elizabeth stepped in. "I'm going to drop Rosie off at the courts, and then I am running away from home. I need you to pick her up at one, when she's done."

"What do you mean, you're running away from home? Where would you go?"

"I'm going to the noon meeting. Then I'm going to hang out at a bookstore, and maybe the home consignment center. I absolutely will go crazy if I have to stay here all morning."

"Don't buy anything—we honestly cannot afford anything now."

"I may need to. I'm thinking of remodeling."

"Don't be crazy, Elizabeth. Of course we're not going to remodel. Maybe if I get a contract for the new book."

"You don't work on anything anymore except your radio pieces."

"So maybe I can put together a collection of those. Jesus, Elizabeth. I'm working my ass off. Today is really no good. Besides, can't Rosie walk home?"

"No, she's grounded."

"I don't think we're supposed to be giving her consequences that make life more of a pain in the neck for *us*."

"James. Please. Pick her up."

"I am so under the gun!"

"Don't do this to me!" Elizabeth said, much too loudly, and instantly regretted that she'd resorted to one of Rosie's battle cries. She stalked out of James's office and went to shower. She needed a break today. James's life definitely improved when he first got the NPR job—he brought in eight hundred dollars more a month, and people stopped him on the street to say how much they loved his stories of the world, of global warming and suffering, not to mention a teenage daughter, a bad back, a gut, bad teeth, and a difficult cat. But there was so much more pressure now, for both of them. When his producers weren't quite as wild about one week's radio essay, he moped, obsessed. Were he and all those other NPR essayists okay only when their producers jumped up and down? Were they sweating blood the rest of the time, waiting for the next hit, ignoring their families as they tried to get a piece just right, because airtime was Cinderella's ball? Sometimes she felt as if he were having an affair, with someone so exquisite that she couldn't fight back.

* * *

Rosie rolled out of bed at eleven. She had pimples all over her forehead, baby-sized but disgusting. Her shoulders sagged. She knew what her mother would say—you could hardly see them; she had her father's beautiful skin. The sun and fresh air would help them heal! And blah blah blah.

She washed her face, patted it dry, and then carefully, like an expert at Macy's, covered her skin with foundation. She stepped back to check herself in the mirror. She swirled a brush daubed in rose-colored blusher onto her cheeks, outlined her eyes in kohl. She applied a coat of mascara to her thick black lashes, and then another. She imagined Jody studying her, jealous and exposed: she had no real knack for makeup, but wore it anyway—powder, eyeliner, gloss. Alice, on the other hand, had taken an Intro to Cosmetology class at nights, and had taught Rosie everything she knew. "Cosmetology is a feel-good profession," she had insisted more than once. Rosie and Jody had laughed hysterically.

She put on a clean thong, black lace, stolen from Nordstrom accidentally. She had tried it on in the dressing room, tried on jeans over it, paid for the jeans, and not remembered until she was at the cashier's. James had found it stuck to his own laundry by static electricity. He had thought it was a broken shoelace at first.

She pulled on short cut-offs, her favorite pair, not too tight, with the strap of her thong showing in the back by at least an inch. She pulled a sports bra over her head, which flattened her and kept her tits from bouncing so much, but then she took it off and replaced it with a white lacy bra of her mother's, the only one from Victoria's Secret that her mother owned—mostly she got her bras at Macy's, along with the huge underpants. They wore the same size everything, except jeans. She found a clean, cute, tight T-shirt, and her shoes, which were totally worn out. It so sucked living in this family, no one ever had any extra money. If she asked her mom to take her shopping for tennis shoes, she would sigh, like they were going to end up on government cheese.

Elizabeth looked at her clothing strangely but didn't say anything except, "Do you have your racket? James will pick you up at one. Does that give you enough time?" Rosie had managed an SOS call to Jody while her mother was in James's study, to meet her at the courts early. Jody would try to get hold of Alice, who was shopping for school clothes with her mother. Both of them had money; also dads, although Alice rarely saw hers. Rosie had been a little girl with a dead dad, and there was no getting around that or over that. Even a drunk dad, even an asshole, was better than a dead dad, which shouldn't reflect on you but did, and left a cannon hole in your heart.

◘

The meeting hit the spot. Nothing was more important than Elizabeth's staying sober. Everything good that could happen for Rosie depended on Elizabeth's not drinking. Leo, the speaker, had done some time at Napa State Hospital after having taken too many trips on LSD. He'd been released too early the last time, and spent most of his second day studying a large fish in an aquarium at a pet store, convinced that it was trying to speak to him. The fish had opened and closed its lips, mouthing, "Leo is God." When he started talking back to it, sincerely—"No, no, it's just that I'm so big—*all* of us out here are"—the authorities had come for him. He was adorable.

Some women invited her to coffee afterward, and she almost

went. But instead she went to her favorite bookstore. She got an espresso, chocolate-dipped biscotti, and a copy of *The New Yorker*, sat at one of the window tables alone, and read away the day—about as close to heaven as she was going to get, what with this mortal coil. Every so often she imagined the big fish swimming out to center stage in her mind. The first time he mouthed to her, imploring, "Elizabeth is God," the second time, beseeching, "Elizabeth is loved." Then "Elizabeth must be crazy to listen to a big fish."

▣

Both courts were busy when Rosie arrived, and there was no sign of Robert, so she sat and read the book she'd brought in her racket cover. She had to write a paper on it as summer homework for AP English when school started. *The Odyssey: A Modern Sequel*, by Kazantzakis. James had owned a copy. It was one of the greatest books she had ever read, although she was only a few pages in. *O Sun, great Oriental, my proud mind's golden cap, I love to wear you cocked askew.*

She struck a pose, legs outstretched like a 1950s bathing beauty, baby finger hooked over her bottom lip, like a girl in a window seat, and immersed herself in the poetry: *Freedom, my lads, is neither wine nor a sweet maid, not goods stacked in vast cellars, no, nor sons in cradles; it's but a scornful, lonely song the wind has taken. . . .*

Robert sneaked up behind her. She wasn't aware of him until he was ten feet away. Even so, she pretended to be immersed in her book until he reached over her shoulders and grabbed it out of her hands. "Hey!" he exclaimed, like she was his very best friend. "Can I borrow this?"

"Hey, yourself." She looked down into her lap, mock disgruntled, and then up at him. He was only a few feet away. He'd shaved, and the skin there was paler, and God, his lashes were so long and black that his eyes were like caterpillars. He got to his feet and bent down to pull her up. Her heart raced.

"How are you?" he asked. "Getting ready for school?" She groaned. "Oh, senior year's a breeze—junior year is the killer. And I'll help you with your college apps." He took a ball out of the pocket of his khaki shorts, bounced it menacingly on the court. "You ready? I've been practicing my toss at home."

She found herself dipping and ducking with such shyness, wondering whether or not he had heard about the bust. Probably not. "We need to warm up for a while, first," she said, turning around. "Otherwise, an old guy like you might get injured." She was so glad to see him. She felt genuinely happy for the first time since the party—more like herself, but older.

"Ow," he cried. "That's hitting below the belt." But he was smiling. It made her think of what was below his belt. She walked back to the baseline.

When she turned to face him, he was squinting at her like now she was in real trouble, and he whacked a ball that nearly hit her. She hit it back, and they rallied, low, hard shots, until he missed. He had gotten better so fast, and she told him this when they met at the net to gather the balls. She took her sunglasses off and used them to sweep back her hair. "Look at you," she said in the voice of encouragement she used with her kids at church. "You're doing great."

"Thank you," he drawled. He looked into her face for a moment, her eyes, as if searching for something. "Hey—I hope you don't mind my asking, but what is that thing on your eye—that thickening?"

Her heart sank. She'd thought he was going to ask her out, she really had, no matter how crazy that was. "Oh, you never noticed it before?" she said. "It's called a pterygium. It's a sun injury to my eye, from all those years I played on the junior circuit. I can get surgery on it if I ever care enough." He was studying her, like an eye doctor. She was terribly embarrassed.

"Can I ask *you* something?" she countered. He nodded. Her heart knocked in her chest like a woodpecker—what was she doing? She didn't even have a question to ask him. She pulled a ball against her shoe with her racket, and expertly jerked it so it dropped and bounced; with one hit, she caught it on the strings of her racket and froze it, in rapid succession like a top. She panned the court behind him until she knew he was looking at her, and she looked at him, and then smiled like the world's biggest jerk. Quick, think of something!

"Okay—you know that line of Walt Whitman's, 'You are so much sunshine to the square inch'?" He nodded. "Well, in terms of physics, is it true?"

He laughed, and looked off, thinking. "Well. Sunshine is energy, and life is energy, so you are energy, and energy is all linked by what Einstein called 'spooky action at a distance.' Other physicists have called it 'nonlocal connections'—you remember Bell's theorem, of course. So we are all energy, and connected, and will remain so. There's a man named Gary Schwartz at the University of Arizona who calls that energy 'love,' as Tolstoy does, and since there's plenty of sunshine in Tucson, Schwartz ought to know."

God, it was so great, he talked to her like a grown-up, like a colleague. She listened to her heart, to the *thwok thwok* of people playing on the other court, to the squeak of rubber-soled footsteps on the grass beside their court. He dropped his voice, and spoke like a gangster, surreptitiously, out of one side of his mouth. "Your friends just arrived," he said, holding her gaze.

"Okay," she said, looking back at him.

She popped the ball up and down on her strings, then made it freeze, and stuffed it in her pocket.

She looked over at Jody and Alice, who were sitting in the grass, watching. She waved, then looked at her watch, and flashed her hand at them twice—ten minutes. She and Robert rallied until one, the best they'd ever played, smiling secret smiles. But she never once looked into his face. Instead, she looked at her two best friends, who were leaning against each other, Jody's arm tucked into Alice's, lolling together like her mother and she did sometimes, or like lesbians.

When she and Robert were done for the day, they thanked each other formally. She felt like when you were listening to great music and the bass got inside your body.

◘

A lice and Jody both looked as if they were close to tears when she walked over to join them. Four arms reached out to her, desperate as widows for her touch. Jody with her great posture and neat, sharp features looked like a secretary in an old movie, like she might whip out her pad and take shorthand, except for her chipped black nail polish and jaggedly sprouting hair. Alice shone as fair as the moon, all curves and curls, cheeks that looked like some auntie had just pinched them lightly, rose-pink blurs. There was a dusting of powder over the freckles on her nose, but in general she was wearing less makeup now, since she'd fallen in love again.

Rosie plopped down in the small space between them, and they folded themselves around her in a sprawl. "I missed you guys!"

What was it like being at the police department, they wanted to know. Was she in a cell, were there other kids with her, did she get arrested? She shook her head and smiled, trying to reassure them that she was really all right. How long was she grounded for, and when would she get her phone back? This had been such a nightmare! They acted like she'd been in isolation in a Turkish jail. It made her almost cry with self-pity.

"Did your moms find out?" she asked them, and they shook their heads.

She told them how cold it was in the police office, how she wasn't in a cell, how two drunk men were brought in separately. She told them about how tweaked Elizabeth had been, as if Rosie had been busted with a pound of heroin and some syringes instead of just having two puffs of weed and some beer at a party. And what an asshole James was, how mean he was being to Elizabeth the last few days, but how her mother was totally on her side now, and that they were all made up. She was grounded a few more days, which was okay because she had so much work to do for English before school started.

She felt Alice stretch out over her back, and dig that small cleft chin against her shoulder blade. "It will all be back to how it was," Rosie assured them. "No biggie." Then as one, they all shifted to the left, rearranged themselves as if they were trying to get comfortable sharing a berth, instead of lying on a huge green lawn.

Rosie immersed herself in their smells and familiar bodies. Her love for Jody was the reason Rosie was able to keep it together at all these days, it was like a crush where you didn't want to have sex—just kiss maybe—but then Jody asked, "And what on earth was that all about on the court?" in her bad clipped voice. Rosie drew back to look at her, askance.

"What?" she asked, playing dumb, but secretly thrilled.

"Like, hello?" said Jody. "He's totally into you."

"That is all in your head," Rosie insisted.

Alice made her Kewpie-doll face of concern. "I know, I'm going to ask my guy friends if they know anybody good for you."

"Don't you dare. I'll never forgive you. Anyway, all the guys we know from around here are biohazard." This made them all laugh. "I mean, except Claude." The three of them shifted again, and wriggled together in a shimmy, like a bird composing itself on a piling. Rosie had her face burrowed into Alice's warm neck, smelling of Nivea and weed, and Jody, on the far side, smelled salty clean like a girl just out of the sea.

Jody stretched her arm all the way across Rosie to hold on to Alice's arm. Out of her squished left eye Rosie could see the court where not long ago she and Robert had stood. Something had happened, like they'd exchanged a kind of rain check. She let herself be enveloped in the softness and heat of her girls.

That night, she had a pleasant vegetarian dinner with her parents. Rosie read in her room all night with the door closed, James worked on his new story, Elizabeth puttered. Things were better.

◘

Rae called Elizabeth again the next day to see if she wanted to drive to Oakland for a concert at Lake Merritt, with Anthony and young people from church, but again Elizabeth said no. Now she was remodeling the living room.

"You're what?" Rae asked.

"It's like soul feng shui—I'm shoving things around, trying out new arrangements, trying out other rugs that we had in storage."

"And you're doing that because?"

Elizabeth plopped down into her father's old leather easy chair.

"I don't know. I'm stuck in manic doldrums. Do you want to come help me?"

"No, I want to hear the concert—people from the Oakland Philharmonic, Bach and Schubert. Please come. You never go anywhere anymore."

"Next time, I promise, okay? Next time, no matter where or for what."

"I already know what the next field trip is. And it will be very bad for you. Yet you have sworn to come along. You're going to kick yourself." Elizabeth smiled. "*Very* bad."

"I'll take my chances."

It was wonderful to be pushing the couches and tables from place to place. It gave Elizabeth hope, shifting everything around and cleaning out drawers to get better function, new perspective. Look at me, she thought, pleased: she was not stuck in her old ways, where the shoes went here and her afternoons were spent there. This was a way of starting over. The big fish would be pleased.

When she stopped to pee, she noticed that the medicine chest was jammed to bursting, too—so how could you possibly notice things missing? She filled a Hefty bag with outdated medicines and bottles of glop, and threw it in the trash.

Then she sank down in a chair. Glancing at her watch, she saw that it was noon. Rosie was still asleep. This made her afraid, panicky even. James was in the city. She should have gone with Rae, but she needed to stay home to keep an eye on Rosie, make sure she didn't sneak out. The spatial contours and sounds of her living room were once removed, as if she hadn't come quite all the way back after space travel, or as if a thin invisible film separated her from where she was.

She felt funny, like she was on an island, floating away. It was too quiet. Bad thoughts flowed through her mind like a stream, and she tried to clear her head of the mental flotsam—James in a car crash, Rosie in a coma. Rae with breast cancer, Lank teaching at Columbine, Elizabeth in the bin, in a silent scream. But right here and now, weren't things just fine?

Watery fear filled her. She had to distract herself, get herself to look away, like when you shook your keys at an otter at the zoo to get it to look up. Columbine was also a flower, growing in her garden, blue blossoms in the flower beds outside Rosie's window. She should go look at them, or drive with Rosie out to the creek beside the redwood where lavender and golden columbine grew.

What was going on? She was having some sort of episode. She couldn't call her shrink, he didn't go into the office today. She tried to anchor herself, focus on the island instead of the flat gray water, the limitless depth of the ocean. What did we have on the island? Our bodies, our fear, coconuts and mango, our books, modest entertainments, goats if you were lucky.

There was always Rascal, asleep on the kitchen counter, and Rosie, come to think of it, still in bed. Lots of connections you could make, if you just got up off your butt. She could see both Rosie and the columbine in one trip. She stood and walked across the invisible bridge to Rosie's room, but when she threw open the door to let in the day, the bed was empty, the window open wide.

SEVEN

Speck of Light

◘

The three girls tramped up the walkway to Rosie's front door. Rosie and Alice supported Jody between them like a wounded soldier. What could you tell your mother to lessen the consequences of having snuck out in the night while grounded in the aftermath of having been busted? Certainly not the truth, that Jody and Alice had tossed pebbles at her window until she woke and let them in, at two in the morning. Jody had broken down because Claude was going to be transferred. Alice said she'd threatened to kill herself, which was why they had both needed meth to get through the night, which would show up in Jody's drug tests, unless she gave her parents no reason to test her until the drugs were out of her system, which was why Jody needed to call from Rosie's and say she'd been there all night.

Rosie was clean and thinking clearly: She had been the

designated driver of Alice's car. She would tell a bit of truth in the interest of credibility, explain about Claude's leaving. She intended to deny having snuck out in the middle of the night. She would say instead that the girls had come for her at dawn, one of them in more pain than could be borne, and stood beneath her window, in the midst of columbine and impatiens, in the airy floral first light of the day.

Rosie neared the door of her own house, relieved to be sober and in the self-important role of a nurse. How often she, Alice, and Jo were up at dawn, on something or coming down, no ground beneath them, wired or fried or tripping, the sky not necessarily overhead. But this time she was only tired. She rehearsed her speech to raise as few suspicions as possible. You had to feel sorry for Elizabeth, she thought—getting tricked like that all the time, like a child.

As Rosie helped hold Jody up, forging the path to the door, pride stirred inside her. She had seen herself in hero moments like this her whole life, in waking dreams: badly burned in the movie where she had saved a family from a fiery death, straggling home into her mother's arms with one useless leg wrapped in charred rags, or holding her bloody side where a bullet had entered, in the movie where the madman shot her as she pulled the beaker of anthrax out of his hands. But this time was especially sweet, because Alice and Jo were real, her comrades, and they needed her. She felt calm and warm; peers with her peers, all she had ever wanted.

◘

Her mother opened the door, and stood pale, mute, and stunned, taking in the sight of the three girls as if they were polar bears. She reached for the collar of Rosie's jacket, to yank her inside, but Rosie shrugged her off.

"Stop, Mama!" Elizabeth grabbed for her again. "Stop it, I said!" Elizabeth drew back, as if winding up to strike Rosie, or about to be struck. Rosie stepped forward and reached for her mother's wrists, and Elizabeth did not shake her off. They stared into each other's eyes.

"You two need to go home," Elizabeth said, finally peering over Rosie's shoulders at Jody and Alice. But Rosie shook her head no. Elizabeth exhaled with contempt. "God damn it," she spluttered. "I am so mad at you guys I could spit." Another hated expression of her mother's. She gritted her teeth, made fists, fumed. "Get the fuck in here and start explaining."

Rosie sized her up, then eased her into the lead, pushing her toward the living room. Elizabeth shook her off and stormed forward. Rosie stepped into the house and the other girls followed close behind, like a line of ducklings.

As Rosie launched into her story, of the pebbles on the window at dawn, Elizabeth listened in silence on the couch, between Rosie and Jody. Alice had pulled up the easy chair and from time to time raked her fingers through Jody's short hair.

Elizabeth glowered at Rosie. "I was sound asleep, Mom—and I know I was already in trouble, but I snuck out to hang with Jody until she could get in touch with her shrink, because it seemed like an emergency." Jody fiddled with the tips of her fingers. Alice pulled her sweatshirt sleeve down, and moved on to inspecting her palm, tracing the life line, reading her future. Rosie began to pick at her cuticles. When Elizabeth let her eyes go out of focus, she could see four-year-old girls rubbing the silk edge of their blankets, four-week-olds with tiny fingers knitting.

Jody's eyes were downcast, like those of the Madonna, unprotected and innocent, all the eyeliner and cool fallen away, grief eyes. Elizabeth reached for her hand. Now, as she sat between such tall girls, as tall as she was, five-ten, Jody taller, they looked like lost giraffes instead of ducklings.

Jody cried. After a while, Elizabeth began to ask her questions, harsh yet concerned. Why was Claude leaving, and when? Soon. Why hadn't Jo told her own mother, and why hadn't they just called, for Chrissakes, with Rosie already in so much trouble?

" 'Why?' is not a useful question," Rosie said. "Like Rae always says."

"I'll call my mom now," Jody said, standing, but Elizabeth pulled her down. "Alice, go get Jody the phone," Elizabeth commanded. "It's in the kitchen." They turned their three giraffe heads as one to watch her go.

"Please, Mom, please don't tell James I snuck out—just this one time. I promise I won't ever do anything like that again."

"I have to tell him, he's my husband. And besides, I'm so angry at you, I could see red." Her mother again: so angry she could spit or see red, but instead she always had a nice drink, and two hundred cigarettes.

"But I'm your child. And I need a break so badly now." Rosie managed to be both piteous and commanding.

"I don't know," Elizabeth said. "You're so grounded." This was ludicrous, as Rosie was already grounded. "Just let it go at that for now." She did not want to ease Rosie's misery—any willingness on Rosie's part to pull herself together would come only from pain, from finally wanting to come in from the cold. Alice returned and thrust the phone at Jody. Jody keyed in her number and had hardly begun explaining before they could hear her mother start shouting. "I know, but Claude is moving!"

Elizabeth and the two girls listened. "I was headed home, when

Claude broke the news. I lost it! I sat in Alice's car all night, crying. Then we came to get Rosie. And we're still here." This was technically true. "You can talk to her—I swear, she's sitting right next to me."

Elizabeth reached for the phone, but Jody shook her head. "So call her if you want. I'm out the door. Home in ten." A siren bawled in the distance, and Elizabeth felt a flush of fear in her stomach, even though her daughter was sitting beside her. She got up to go to the bathroom, and so did not see the girls look around at one another, sad and also amused, their faces as flat and wide-eyed as those of china dolls.

▣

Elizabeth went out later that afternoon and bought some over-the-counter urine tests for marijuana and cocaine, and hid them away in her bathroom. Dinner was pleasant enough, and Elizabeth hated to risk stirring things back up, but after Rosie had cleared and washed the dishes, Elizabeth sent her into the bathroom with a plastic cup for pee. Rosie went without protest. It tested positive for weed, but not for cocaine. Rosie assured her, "Don't forget, it could take a couple of weeks to be clean. THC stays in your system so long." Elizabeth was relieved about the cocaine, but two weeks seemed a long time to wait for a sense of progress. Not telling James her secret was eating at her, too, and in the morning, she called Rae, meaning to share it with her.

But instead, she blurted out, "Rae, I'm having such a hard time with Rosie, or maybe I'm having a hard time with me—but it's like there's no difference anymore. I get so afraid that something bad is about to happen, and I tried to talk myself out of that, and I go to a meeting, and I'm better for a while, but when I come home, I have to shut down because the vibe at this house is so intense—and then all the repressed meanness underneath me wants to burst out. Mommy as ultimate mean girl. Some days I could explode from all the warring states in me, the whole convo under the convo." She stopped then, to listen to what she'd said: "convo under the convo" was their private slang for the deeper conversation under the audible conversation, the world beneath the words.

"Then tell me, Elizabeth, honey—what is not being said that is causing the screaming inside you?"

Elizabeth stared off into the middle distance and shook her head. "So many things."

"Oh baby, I'm going to meet Lank at the Target in Novato, he just got paid. Want to come with us?"

Elizabeth stifled a mewing sense of disappointment. "No. I only needed to hear your voice. I'm okay."

"I'll talk to you tomorrow. Give Anthony a call at the church, and make an appointment. He's great with adolescents, and drugs, pretty good on marriage, and free." Elizabeth filed away the recommendation about Anthony: the mood at the house had perhaps been better in the last three days. Rosie acted resigned to her fate, sleeping late but then pouring herself into books and assignments, James hard at work in his office. Elizabeth stuffed down her unease.

James insisted that Rosie cancel her tennis lessons. When she called to tell Robert she was grounded, for missing curfew, he made sounds both accusatory and sympathetic, and said it was actually fine, as he was buried in things to do before the start of school. He asked her how the paper on Kazantzakis was coming along, and she read to him from the epilogue of the book but hoped he thought she had memorized it: "*O sun, great Eastern*

Prince, your eyes have brimmed with tears, for all the world has darkened, all life swirls and spins, and now you've plunged down to your mother's watery cellars."

He said, *"Jeez,* Rosie, you're only grounded a week!" and they laughed like friends.

In fact, she had read only thirty of the seven hundred seventy-four pages between the epilogue and the prologue, but that was because she had a gnarly project on Reconstruction due for AP history, in which she had to argue for the South, for its rightful rage and resistance to the North's military occupation; and a paper in French on Simone de Beauvoir, of whom she did not approve because of her submission to the awful Jean-Paul Sartre.

"You're a Soviet hard-liner, Ro," James commented at dinner. "No margin of error for the weaknesses of two people who changed life for the good, forever?"

"Don't hector the children," Elizabeth said to James.

"And I'm not a child," Rosie said crossly to her mother. But then everyone smiled.

▣

Three dinners in a row were lovely, something that could not have been said any other time recently. But keeping the secret from James pained Elizabeth off and on. She had been cooking special dinners to compensate, and two nights ago they had made love. She was a bad person. Tonight she had made garlic eggplant, dragon prawns, brown rice, and as usual, salad from the garden. Also, she had bought everyone a cheap present at Landsdale's variety store: socks for James, lip gloss for Rosie, a catnip Spiro Agnew for Rascal. It was like old times, Rosie jacking avocado off James's plate, James responding with a droning air attack on Rosie's last prawn.

* * *

When Lank called later in the week, Elizabeth answered the phone. It turned out he was calling to talk to her, and a ray of gladness shone through and surprised her.

"Are you doing okay, Elizabeth? Rae told me you were struggling after the bust."

"Maximumly." She heard a quiet sniffle of laughter and a moment's silence, the way Lank held space for you in case you wanted to continue, without crowding the words that might need a minute to form. She found herself desperate to ask him about the secret, but did not want to talk behind James's back. "But we've had a few nice days in a row, and I'm trying to go with that."

"I'd say go with the flow," he replied, "except James says that the people who tell you that are usually the angriest people on earth. Who'd stab you if they had a fork."

"Yeah, I've heard that riff." She laughed. "I am grateful things are better, and at the same time, what comes most naturally to me is pretending everything is okay whenever I can, and that ends up making me nuts—my mom used to pretend I was okay when I was getting wasted as a teenager, and then she'd smoke three packs a day. So it's a fine line."

"I hear you. It's about paying attention. When people ask me how I am these days, I say, 'Better than I think,' because it's good to notice that my life is pretty great, even if my mind isn't."

"Exactly," she said. "I think my inner groundskeeper drinks or does crack cocaine, probably both. But at least I'm starting to realize that this stuff with Rosie is something to get through, and not figure out. There is no figure. The only figuring I can do is work on my own equilibrium. So most days, or part of most days, I'm doing okay."

"That's good to hear, but at the same time, I'm worried for you, Elizabeth. I remember that phrase you used after you had your little breakdown, to describe your feeling of cluttered numbness. I remember because it was so beautiful, perfectly descriptive of most of us most of the time, but for you, it was overwhelming, and it knocked your equilibrium out from under you."

Elizabeth caught her breath in the silence that followed. Then she smiled. "I love you, Lank," she said. "I love that you reminded me of that. That's exactly right." She began to form the first words of the sentence she was so desperate to share—*I've been keeping a secret from James*—but Lank said he had papers to grade. Sigh: everyone else was so busy, James with his deadlines, Rae with her good deeds, Lank with papers to grade, Rosie with her lessons, her homework, her bucket kids, her all-consuming drive for independence.

But then he asked her, "Hey—you wouldn't by any chance be willing to help a bunch of us clean up dog poop on the Sunnyside fire road, would you? We're in danger of losing it as an off-leash trail."

She paused. "Wait, what?" she then said. "You want me to help you pick up *dog* shit? What kind of crazy invitation is that? I don't even have a dog."

"I know, but I do, and this is the last place in Novato our dogs can run off leash. Look, I know it's a long shot."

"No, no," she said, "I'll do it."

◉

Rae was perplexed. "You say no to my offer of a free noontime concert at Lake Merritt? To Schubert and Bach? But yes to this?"

"I haven't told James, and it's making me nuts."

"So tell him when we get off the phone. Jeez. Did you call Anthony?"

"No. I didn't want to rock the temporarily sweet boat. I have to betray either James, by keeping the secret, or Rosie, by telling, when I promised."

"You are betraying you, is whom you are betraying."

"It sounded therapeutic, to hang with Lank. And I'm on the side of the dogs."

"Jeez, Elizabeth, you are not getting out enough."

"Well, then, here's my chance."

◉

It was definitely counterintuitive, to choose dog shit over a quiet talk with Anthony in that bright and aromatic office. But at any rate, she met up with Lank and six other middle-aged people a few days later. The weather had cooled down. Lank looked five years younger in the Giants cap that covered his bald spot; he had begun referring to what was left as his hair spot. He gave her the greatest hug, and she looked over his shoulders to the dry golden foothill, covered with oak and laurel, spreading out below them like a hoop-skirt, all the way to the glistening bay.

It was heaven up here, sky unscrolling baby blue all the way to Berkeley and San Francisco, socked in with billows of gray fog to the west, on the way to the beaches. He handed her a wad of plastic bags, blue ones that had once held *The New York Times*, clear ones from the *Chronicle*.

They worked together, commenting on the more prodigious piles, comparing notes with others. An hour in, just as she was about to ask his advice, Lank pantomimed throwing a knotted sack at her, like a discus. They'd stopped to laugh, and it took another half-hour for her to say the words, "Lank? I need to tell you something."

He sat her down on a log and took a seat beside her. She sighed, and began. She told him the secret she'd been keeping from James, of Rosie's sneaking out while grounded, the lengthening list of Rosie's lies and mistakes this summer, what a good father James was, but how unyielding he could be. And by the same token, how easily he caved when Rosie's attitude improved; his wretched need for things to not trouble Elizabeth, for Rosie to be nice to them both. And how maybe, with James out of the loop and this incident behind them, there was a chance for the family to start afresh.

He took off his glasses and rubbed his eyes, took off his hat and rubbed his head, looked old and squinty again. "Honey," he said finally, "listen. I love Rosie almost like she's my own. She's everything cool in a person—she's sharp, sensitive, funny, articulate. She's got it all." Elizabeth nodded, smiling, pleased. "But she's also a lying suck."

Elizabeth did a double take. "Jeez," she said. "That's a little harsh. And besides, she's *my* lying suck."

"I work with them every day, and even the good kids break your heart. They can be so wonderful, then just diabolical. They'll all lie, even when the truth would work. And how much more evidence do you need that Rosie can't be trusted? She's trying to break free, to individuate. Like you are, from James, by keeping the secret. I know you feel too dependent on him. Rosie hates how dependent she is on you. Rosie feels cornered, and she thinks you and James are her problem. And she'll do anything to win, to get away with more and more. But James—oh my God. Has there ever been a more loyal friend?" She shook her head slowly. "He's a mensch, and he'll stand by you through thick and thin. He's your guy, hon, your beloved. Don't let Rosie win this round. I say, or rather Rae says, Tell the truth and shame the devil."

□

The next night, Elizabeth asked James to take a walk with her after dinner. They went out in T-shirts and rolled-up jeans. A glowing moon, still more than three-quarters of its disc illuminated, was ringed in a fuzzy corona. They held hands, walking under the branches of their neighbor's persimmon tree.

"Rosie's in such a good place tonight," said Elizabeth. She was working up to the half-sentence blurt that there was something she needed to tell him, and she knew by now that she did. After leaving Lank yesterday and heading home for dinner, she had tried to convince herself that she was keeping the secret so as not to endanger her relationship with Rosie. It was draped in virtue: I'm doing it for others. But she admitted the truth to herself as she'd drifted to sleep in James's arms. Keeping the secret was a kind of protection from her daughter's wrath.

She took James's hand under the moonlight and said again, "She's in a good place."

James was silent for a while. "Tick, tock, tick, tock." This pissed her off, and she reconsidered telling him, but the imps inside were pushing out and through. He had noticed her preoccupation at dinner. "You seem far away," he'd said, but she had shrugged it off. She hated to admit that it gave her the power of double-dealing, playing Rosie off James. Now, walking around with him, she tried to say the first words. "James?" she managed. So far so good. She almost said, "I've been keeping something from you," but now he seemed distant, and at the same time, it was so lovely to be alone, holding hands, and she knew what he would say: "How could you!"—the mantra of the betrayed. Then, "We're supposed to live in trust, Elizabeth, and you've dumped all over that."

Then he began to talk. "Even though I get so angry with Rosie, I know things could be a whole lot worse—look at what other parents are going through. Some of these kids are total lushes already. I don't actually think Rosie is. We need broader-spectrum tests than the ones you got—her eyes are clear most of the time, and she doesn't smell boozy." They both sighed loudly at the same time, and this made them laugh. "Hey, want to walk to the Parkade?" he asked. "At least we can see how much worse her scary little friends are doing. That'll cheer us up." Elizabeth poked him, and he laughed enthusiastically at his own awfulness.

They walked along for another five minutes, and came up the steps from the movie theater. At nine p.m., the Parkade was crawling with teenagers, some huddled in groups, plopped on various stairs, furtively peering out from the bus kiosk. There was a random milling quality, and yet a sense of cohesion and sanctuary. "I want to write a piece about this place," James whispered. "Don't tell Rosie."

They knew many of the players tonight. Some of them had been friends of Rosie's since kindergarten, in the school district she was in before they moved to Landsdale. Alexander, a friend of hers from kindergarten who'd moved to town a few years ago, stood leaning against a tree near the liquor store, a beautiful blond hippie boy now, the former Eagle Scout who was doing smack. The senior class lushes who had overdosed on alcohol and ended up in the emergency room.

Antonio Brooks, who was leaning against a car near the kiosk, and who had accepted a full basketball scholarship to Marquette, was said to be dealing hash oil. You baked it into brownies, or somehow smoked it using the tube of a Bic pen. It was hopeless: you could close every smoke shop in the county and the kids would still find a way to get high.

"What would the angle be, James?"

"Let's sit here on the curb." They lowered themselves, groaning. "I would go into the medieval-modern aspects of their lives, how they try to come off as nomads, from olden times, even though they're rich kids with homes to go to, even when they're wrapped in blankets for a few days. Maybe they stay out nights, and sleep in cars, but their homes are up the street. Some of them go too far, like Alexander, and become primitive, and dirty. The parents keep bailing them out. Setting new and lower standards."

"How do you know all this?"

"The Al-Anon mothers tell me. The ones who are trying not to let their kids live at home when they're using."

"How on earth could you turn your child away, if he or she were suffering?"

"What if trying to save them was helping the kids stay sick? What if your help is not helpful?"

"Oh, stop, James. That's dereliction."

"Some of the older ones really are street people," James said, ignoring her, pointing to an older boy who was obviously on a long-term brute course, a preppy caveman in a button-down shirt, with dreadlocks and a slack mouth. "I know they are lost cases, and I feel for them and their families. But they buy beer for the kids—for *Rosie*."

This was true. She recognized Fenn coming up the Roastery steps, stopping to talk to the young street guy with the floppy

hat whom she and Rosie called Gilligan. "That's a sweet guy—
Fenn. We say hi to each other," she said. He looked his usual sun-
streaked self, shaggy but composed, in a button-down shirt, dark
glasses tonight instead of the wire rims. He fished a pack of cigarettes out of his pocket, handed it to Gilligan, then reached into
his back pocket and took some cash out of his wallet.

"Oh my God, is this a drug deal?" James asked. But Fenn gave
Gilligan a bill, gripped his shoulder like a politician, smiling, and
took off down the steps.

"You've gone crazy, James. He's helping out a street person."

James continued to glare in Fenn's general direction. Without answering, he pulled out his notebook and scribbled into it.
She read what he had written: "Clusters of arrogant young people
filled with self-loathing, sharing beliefs in a circular cage of parked
cars, holding beliefs that make them feel safe, connected, guarded.
Surfer Samaritan, or dealer?"

Elizabeth remembered herself at ten, still lonely and always
worried, about how crazy her parents and the friends of theirs were
scaring her half to death with their moist affection, their fights and
crying, and the drunken end of their night dancing. She remembered how much time she'd spent alone in the backyard, setting
up horse jumps with broom handles, being the jumper, being the
horse. Blink, and she was twelve again, and she had huge breasts
and boys ogled her, and men did, too, and shouted things to her
from cars and construction sites; blink again and she would sleep
with a teacher in high school, who would give her all the great books
in the American canon, and with whom she would start drinking,
and who she would feel had finally thrown on the lights for her.

After a while they got up and walked home, without Elizabeth's
telling him the secret.

*   *   *

James started a draft for his Parkade piece that night. Rosie was on her bed with Rascal, reading Robertson Davies. She came in later to say good night to Elizabeth. Rosie smelled clean and delicious, and lay down beside her mother, burrowing. She had brought Rascal with her, and flicked lightly at his ears to pester him, and when he batted at them, Rosie and Elizabeth laughed; it was silvery and warm, heaven. "You didn't tell James, did you, Mama?" Elizabeth shook her head. "Thanks. That's great." Rosie sighed. "Hey, let's get James a dog for Christmas."

"I'll get you a drug-sniffing dog, is what I'll get you," Elizabeth said in a menacing voice. Having a secret gave you a hit of power, a kind of self-esteem, and love was unleashed in her; love that had been dormant during the recent bad weeks flowed. It was like a magical opening: she and Rosie were learning to love and trust each other in a new way. Maybe it was an illusion, she thought, but hell, she would take it.

◘

Elizabeth was asleep when James finally came to bed, and when she woke up in the morning, he was already back at work. He'd left her a first draft on the kitchen table. It wasn't good yet—there were too many details, and no ending in place. She did not like it when he needed her to read new material before he'd nailed it; so when she finished reading the draft, she only said it was going to be great.

"You hate it," he said, which he always said.

"I love the material," she responded, "but it's just not there yet." She liked the stuff about the wealthy kids dressed alike in rags, how afraid they were underneath it all that they might lose their individuality. She liked where he'd said that even with their piercings and tattoos, with all that was so alive in their souls— their wildness, spontaneity, silliness, spirit—they were consumed with thoughts of death, their own, and that their parents lived in a kind of death, gray and hassled, multitasking, microwaving organic food, plopped in front of the TV, because these things were all they had energy for. So yeah, they loved coke and speed and Ecstasy, driving too fast, dangerous sex with people who had had dangerous sex with multiple partners. But what, she asked James, was the *story*?

She had been too brusque, had hurt his feelings. He went into his office and slammed the door. She sat down at the kitchen table and stared miserably into a cup of black coffee: This was not about his work. It was about the distance between them now because of the secret. Having it had been like nectar initially, even last night, lying with Rosie in bed. Then it was like nectar that has gone off. Now she held on to her stomach because the secret was indigestible, sitting there in her solar plexus, where indigestible emotions lodged.

She went into his office to apologize, and started to try to tell him the secret, but he had already moved from having his feelings hurt to gratitude for her great job editing him, and it seemed a shame to muck with his love and reliance on her. "You saved me from looking like a jerk," he said, and kissed the back of her hand.

"Oh, I thought you were mad at me for being so abrupt with my suggestions."

"I'm sorry I was such a baby. You nailed the problem—too many details and ideas. Not enough structure or story. It's like Gertrude Stein said, that she could always write good sentences, but she never quite understood paragraphs. That's me, in this piece."

Deeply relieved, she left him to his rewrite, her secret still untold.

◘

Rosie woke up the next day and wondered what it might be like to take acid or Ecstasy with Robert. They could candy-flip—take a little of both—although maybe not their first time together. Maybe he'd go to a rave with her in Oakland. She doubted he had ever done E. The fantasy enthralled her; time turned soft and druggy.

She kept trying to reach him at the office the next day, but he never picked up. She left a chipper message on his machine, and waited for him to call back.

Alice called twice, Jody once, speeding on Alice's Adderall, saying she was going to run away from home to be with Claude in San Diego, she knew a girl there from rehab she could stay with, but Rosie thought it was just the speed talking. A couple of hours later, Rae called to discuss the schedule for next week, after which, with school starting, the summer program at Sixth Day Prez would be over. Alice called to say Jody had phoned her from the Greyhound bus station in Salinas—she really had run away from home to be with Claude. They both cried out in worry and loss and amazement, and Rosie's stomach wrenched with jealousy, that Jody loved someone this much that she would throw away everything to see him again—God, she was going to be in massive trouble when she returned. Rosie couldn't stop thinking about Robert, how close she felt when they sat on the grass side by side, how she could feel the tuning fork between them.

The grass had just been cut the last time they played before she was grounded, and it had stained her shorts and smelled as strong as lacquer. It turned her on even to remember it. This feeling, of love, was so much greater than the few times she'd had sex, when you felt like you and the guy were meat machines with various levers. All that slapping flesh and spit and grotesque rearrangements; plus things going numb. But she and Robert were like a beautiful movie, or like the part after you're done in bed, when you get to lie in that bubble wrap of closeness. It was your souls touching.

◘

The next morning, Elizabeth was on her knees weeding in the flower bed near Rosie's window, impatiens and columbine. Rosie discovered this when she threw her window open, her room already hot and bright with sunshine. She said hello to her mother, and her mother answered, "Hello, darling. What are your plans for today?"

Jeez, Rosie thought, it was like living with a secret agent. She shrugged.

They were only five or six feet apart, separated by an open window, so Elizabeth heard the phone ring, and saw Rosie race for it. "Hey, cuz, wha' up?" Rosie said, without enthusiasm. "No. I'm fine."

She must have a crush on someone, Elizabeth realized, and went back to weeding. Then she heard the beeps of Rosie's dialing, and then a moment later heard her hang up. Rosie dialed again, and hung up again. Ten minutes later Elizabeth saw her near the window, on the phone, heard her leaving someone a message in her smallest voice, high in her throat, trying to sound casual as she asked the person to please call her back.

Elizabeth fluffed the soil around a flower, straining to hear. A few minutes later, she listened to Rosie dialing again, heard a soothing male voice. She pretended to be fully engaged when Rosie opened the window wider.

"God," Rosie screamed through the opening. "Are you *spying* on me?"

Elizabeth rolled her eyes with disdain and went back to weeding. But later in the day, when Rosie was in the shower, Elizabeth hit the redial button, waited for the connection, and frowned when she heard the distinct voice of Robert Tobias on his answering machine.

◙

Rae picked Elizabeth up early the next morning, as the sun was coming up, for the field trip Elizabeth had agreed to show up for, come hell or high water. They drove along Highway 1 listening to the classical station and eating pumpkin scones, and it was sweet. Not until they passed Bodega Bay and entered Sonoma County did Rae reveal their destination: she had signed them up for a women's sweat lodge.

Elizabeth felt sure Rae was joking. Signing her up for a sweat lodge was like signing Richard Nixon up for Sufi dancing. She laughed at the very idea, even as far as Jenner. They discussed real things, like why it was taking Elizabeth so long to tell James the secret—she even promised Rae she would tell him tonight. But when Elizabeth wanted to stop at the Kruse rhododendron reserve, and Rae shook her head, and said they were in a hurry, Elizabeth's heart sank. "I wasn't kidding, hon," Rae said. Elizabeth passed rapidly through the first four stages of grief—denial, as this could not be happening; anger and swearing, the way she had reacted when Rae took her on that backpacking trip years ago, during which they met James and Lank; bargaining, I will give you anything, plus two chits for alternate field trips, if we turn around; and depression, eyes staring, wide, dead.

She did not ever get to acceptance. They drove to the banks of the Gualala River, on the border of Mendocino.

There were six women waiting for them. Two were beauties, one blonde and tall, the other tiny and dark with voluptuous lips. One woman was plain, in early middle age, with the light brown skin of a child. One was at least seventy, with fluffy, feathery white hair and a huge black mole on her cheek that looked like a licorice gumdrop. One was black, average size and Elizabeth's age, with a friendly face. Her partner was black, homely, quiet, fierce. She looked as if she had been dragged along, like Elizabeth.

"What brought you here?" the friendly black woman asked Rae.

"Our church may start offering members sweat lodge as a spiritual tool—so we'll have more to offer than talking and worship. I wanted to see what it was like. But mainly, it's a chance to spend the whole day with Elizabeth." Rae turned to beam at her. "She's the angel God sent to me when I was at my lowest."

Elizabeth shook her head. "I'm not even speaking to you, Rae."

"I came because I'm sluggish and toxic," said the elderly woman. "My mother was big on Adele Davis and taught me that when the skin excretes toxins, it's like the soul excretes all this shit, too."

They were standing near a round hut about ten feet in diameter, four feet tall, covered with blue plastic tarps and army blankets, that looked like a Volkswagen Bug–sized wigwam. The leader, Bonnie, a tall, solid woman with braids, in a shift, attended to the nearby fire, on which small rocks heated.

Bonnie told them briefly about the sweat lodge tradition among
Native American tribes, and then had them strip to their under-
wear, which they did shyly, not looking at one another's bodies. She
then held the tarps open so each woman could bend low to crawl
inside the lodge. They seated themselves clockwise, as instructed,
east to west like the sun. Rae was the plumpest, but her fat was
firm, with only a few dimples. Flattened cardboard boxes served
as seats. Inside, the unsightly hut was a hemisphere created by
bending willow branches into a dome, connecting them, and covering them with more sticks. In the center was a hole, into which
Bonnie soon placed the hot rocks.

It was like a sauna in a cave made of trees. Elizabeth was glad
she did not have to sit next to Rae, who was on the other side
of the hole. Bonnie handed a bucket of water to the woman nearest
the opening, and came inside, pulling the tarps down, and sat.

Elizabeth felt for a few moments that her mind might snap.
This reminded her of the bamboo cages in *The Deer Hunter*, like
rats might swim by. But then curiosity settled into her, and she
started taking notes for James in her head, only partly to stay
calm. It was pitch black. In the darkness, you felt like one organism, she told him, enclosed in the membrane of willow.

"It's going to get very hot," Bonnie said. "We'll do four rounds.
I think you will be pretty uncomfortable, and want to bolt. You
can do that if you need to, or you can tough it out. If you breathe
in the heat and steam, they will center you."

Someone nickered in the dark, like a pony. Elizabeth did not
think she had made the sound.

Bonnie spoke. "First, try to release the lies the world has told
you about yourself, okay? See if you can connect with the person
you were, before the lies."

The rocks in the center sizzled and hissed when Bonnie poured a cup of water over them. Terror flushed through Elizabeth. It was shocking, so hot and elemental. But she breathed, and remembered being croupy as a little girl, how her mother created a steam room in the bathroom with scalding water from the shower pouring against the porcelain tub, and held Elizabeth on her lap as the steam burned its way through Elizabeth's nose, throat, and chest, and how after a while mucus jiggled loose from her lungs and she stopped barking like a seal.

Elizabeth felt like she was in the bottom of the earth; guck jiggled free from her lungs. That was satisfying. She savored it, then moved into a tumbled oceanic nonbreathing panic, and then into neutral spacelessness. In and out of the feeling of being faceless, nameless, unconnected. When the hiss of the steam subsided, she whispered across the rocks, "Rae, are you there?"

"I'm right here, darling. Right across from you."

In the darkness, and closeness, she imagined telling James that she had felt like a marine mammal voluntarily on a rotisserie. Stuff continued to loosen from her lungs. Bonnie called out prayers to the east, prayers to the west, and Elizabeth felt her soft, ploppy body pour off sweat. At the second round, though, when Bonnie poured more water on the rocks, the blast of heat was unbelievable, and Elizabeth felt like she was trapped in the trunk of a car next to a fire; the smoke and the mist stupefied her like a huge fish. It was hell. She hugged her knees to her sweaty, rubbery chest, and somehow the twig that was jammed into her ass helped her breathe, like Andrew gripping her hand too hard through a contraction. She heard someone get to her feet, and then a voice in the dark saying, "That's it for me, I have to get out."

"Okay," said Bonnie. The tarp opened as one of the black

women left, and flapped shut. The women gasped for the cool air that came in. Bonnie crooned, "We are *here*, to heal the damage, for the next generation. We are here, on the earth, in darkness, to heal the damage, in ourselves, for the next generation."

Elizabeth heard Rae say, "I can't breathe, I have to get some air," and Elizabeth called across to her, "It's okay, you can do it," and Rae said, "No, I need to get outside for a second. I'm claustrophobic." Elizabeth almost got up, too; anyone would have understood. She heard the rustles and shuffle and slap of Rae getting up and heading out. Elizabeth couldn't see anything except the burning rocks, and the rocks weren't giving off light. The flap opened. She saw Rae briefly as she wiggled out on her stomach, her heavy thighs illuminated by the sunlight now flooding into the hut along with cool, clean air.

She was surprised to find that she was okay with Rae gone— free, and strangely less alone. Beings of some sort seemed to hover nearby, banging a teakettle softly, saying, Pay attention to us.

She took long breaths, still holding her knees to her chest, breathing in the steam, and it was the only thing she had felt since Rosie's birth that might qualify as dilation. Through this, something in her slipped lower, or deeper, or something, to a place where she did not feel the burden of her wrinkled, aching bones. She felt as if nesting dolls surrounded her, Andrew, her parents, lovely and much older than when they had died, aunts and uncles, old friends. She felt more contained and larger inside the willow dome than she had ever felt in her life, except for the times she had taken acid or mushrooms, so many years ago. The heat was terrible. She felt miserable and ecstatic, listening to invisible voices in the silence, and for once she could hear them above her own human whir, anxiety, manners, biography, armor, distractions; she shed these all like a

virus, and found a speck of light inside that was not her at all, a
fleck of gold in the sandy streambed soil within.

◘

L ater, having survived a fourth round of steam, Elizabeth and
the other two survivors—the oldest woman, plus Bonnie—
stepped out into the sunlight. They cheered themselves. "This
is probably the single greatest achievement of my life," Elizabeth
said, and when the other two women laughed, she said, "You don't
understand. I'm not kidding." They toasted themselves with cold
water, and stretched. Later she found Rae in the river, sitting in the
shoals, deep in conversation with two other women. Rae turned to
Elizabeth and said, "My warrior." Elizabeth managed a small smile
as she stepped into the river and splashed around. The water was
freezing; it forced her to snuggle with Rae.

"I'm sorry I tricked you into coming," Rae said in front of
everyone, and even though Elizabeth was now glad she had come,
she stayed silent. "And I'm sorry I had to get out so early. I felt
like an armadillo on a grill."

It was a lovely afternoon in the sun, eating beans and corn tor-
tillas Bonnie had brought, talking about the experience, laughing,
shaking their heads, swearing they'd stay in touch.

On the way home, Elizabeth slept all the way south to Sea Ranch.

When she woke up, she looked over at Rae in the driver's seat for
a long time. "What," Rae said finally.

"I felt something today. A speck of something, way deep down
inside me, at the bottom of the well. It wasn't God. I don't believe in
God. But it was not me."

Rae drove along, considering this. "'Not Me' is a good name
for God."

"Thank you. As long as you understand that it's lowercase."

"Some people call God Howard, as in 'Howard be thy name.' Or Andy, as in 'And he walks with me, and he talks to me.' Was it anything you could ever turn to in prayer?"

"You're suggesting I turn to an entity called 'not me,' lowercase, for answers, and comfort?"

"What does it matter? If prayer works, does it even matter if there's a god or not?"

"What if I prayed for knowledge, and it turned out Rosie's using a shitload of drugs?"

"Then you'll know one thing that's true. But to find that out, all you need to do is buy fancier drug tests and test her more often, no matter if she has tantrums."

Elizabeth mulled this over. "That's what James says. So maybe I'll do it."

When they approached the mall off 101 in Novato, Elizabeth told Rae to pull onto the exit. More accurate urine tests would make James happy. And as long as she was going to tell him how she had betrayed him, she might as well do something to please him, too. Rae pulled into the parking lot outside Target.

Inside, they searched the aisles until Rae finally found the drug tests in the back.

Elizabeth reached for three boxes. They were expensive. Turning toward the checkout lines at the front of the store, she grabbed Rae by the shoulder. "Rosie is going to go ballistic."

"Better furious than dead or brain-damaged. It's not your problem. Your problem is to find out what is true and to do the right thing."

As they walked past the endless shelves of shit for sale, the smell of disinfectant stuck to Elizabeth's nostrils. "I'm sweating like a pig, Rae. I wish we'd had this discussion at the river, on sacred ground."

Rae pulled her to a stop. She mopped Elizabeth's forehead with her sleeve. "There's only sacred ground. The only holy place is where we are." Elizabeth stared up at the store's fluorescent lights. All she knew after what they'd been through today was that she was going to tell James the truth, tonight, and test Rosie for all kinds of drugs, in the morning.

She put her fingers to her throat to feel her weak, rapid pulse, and put her boxes on the counter. Her shoulders sagged. Behind her, Rae pushed her nose into the space between Elizabeth's shoulder blades, like a big dog. Usually under the stark fluorescent lights of stores, Elizabeth felt like a rump roast on display at Safeway, but she was not thinking about that now. She was thinking of how Rosie used to be, before whatever it was had gotten her: the siege, the possession, whatever you wanted to call it. She listened to the buzz that the lights above her were making, to let people know that the bulb was about to go out, a soft, not unpleasant buzz, tissue paper on a comb.

EIGHT

Twoest

□

Rosie rarely used cocaine, because she hated to spend so much of her money at once—sixty bucks or so in one night—when it took so long to earn. When you got blow free, there was nothing better. It didn't show up in your urine for long, which was good since her mother was now on a testing jag, giving Rosie OTC piss tests every few days. She had been in Elizabeth's bathroom one day recently, using the tub for a bubble bath, when she'd seen all the new urine tests under the sink. The new batch of kits tested for THC, opiates, methamphetamines, E. She hated that Elizabeth had become so distrustful. That was no way to live. What her mother did not appreciate was how much stuff Rosie had weaned herself off by the end of her sophomore year, like cocaine, which she had been doing many weekends. When she first got close to Jody and Alice, they were doing blow all the time. But it had been easy to stop in the spring, and the only reason she had gotten into it the other night was that Jody had run off to be with Claude in San Diego, and she and Alice had felt genuinely heartbroken.

Jody was really gone; it hadn't just been the speed talking, after all. She had called two days ago, to say she was staying with a girl from rehab in San Diego, near the base where Claude was stationed. The girl had stayed clean, and Jody had to if she wanted to crash there for a while. She got to see Claude briefly every day, and go out with him on weekends. They went to motels for their dates. There was nothing her parents could do about it, either, because she was eighteen: she was free.

Rosie was still dozing at noon, the last Saturday before school started. She lay in her messy bed with Rascal asleep beside her and daydreamed of school and of Robert. Every so often James poked his head in and called her a sleepyhead, told her to get up, make her bed, seize the day. She was seizing the day her way—a made bed meant you were in *their* world. All kids wanted to dive into bed and be lying down safely, especially until about noon. When you were standing up, you were so vulnerable. Lying there, floating on the surface of the bed, like a cushioned pond, you didn't know where it would float you, but surrounded by a hundred images and scribbles, you knew it would be somewhere lovely, a portal to take you someplace more real than the jail of your parents' home and school.

She rolled over and fished a miniature Snickers bar out of a plastic Halloween sack from her night table. The OTC tests didn't scare her: she had it all worked out. She could test positive for weed for a while without it being a problem, since it lingered in your system for a month or more, even if you had stopped using, which Rosie insisted she had on the day after she'd gotten busted.

Then, in two weeks, she could use bleach to mask the THC. Her mother had tested her before she did the cocaine, and it would be out of her system before she got tested again. She didn't ever use opiates or meth, so that wasn't an issue. She hadn't done Ecstasy in weeks. There'd been so much speed in the E lately, but someone said it wasn't meth or dexedrine, so she didn't have to worry about her mother knowing about it from the urine tests.

Whatever it was, Rosie hadn't liked the jangly nervousness it produced. She turned on her side. Rascal complained. That speed was the kind that made you want hard-core rave music in the party house, unlike pure E, which made you want trance music and was so lovely. The bad speed could make you think too much. Then you had to make sure Alice was right there to be with you. Then it would be like, "I'm so happy right now with Alice," passing a pacifier back and forth till it was in shreds. You'd laugh, but then ten minutes later, you'd be like, "Now I don't want to share this feeling with people," so you'd wander off to be by yourself in some quieter space. Then in ten minutes, the speed would make you go, "I'm superlonely right now, no one is talking to me," and you'd wander off to another room to look for people. But even with a bunch of people, a certain song could play and you'd turn around and see all these happy people, dancing and taking care of each other, and you'd think, "Aren't *I* supposed to be happy?" Then maybe a few minutes later, you would be happier than you'd ever been before.

She was going to chill, take a break from the E till some good stuff came through town. Where everyone wanted to give to each other, do PLUR—peace, love, unity, respect—share ChapStick and gum, pacifiers, massages. Sometimes when she was peaking, she would feel her eyes roll back in her head and she'd get afraid that something bad might happen—but then people would steady her, and she'd be dancing again. She'd get a mix of butterflies and wanting to puke, but this was just all part of what they called coming up, part of the E coming on, the elevator going too fast; and then she'd get really cold and know she was getting high, about to be in bliss.

Rosie got up and went into her parents' bathroom. She found a bottle of eardrops on the bottom shelf of the medicine cabinet, rinsed out the bottle and dropper a few times, then went to the laundry room and filled the bottle with bleach. She heard James talking to himself as she passed his study. He must be on the final draft of a story. He always read late drafts out loud. No one in her family had gotten an earache in ages, plus this was past its expiration date. Her parents should try to stay on top of stuff like that. Like, what if she really had an earache, and there was only this expired shit? It was typical. She screwed the dropper in tightly, and returned the bottle to the shelves. This time when she passed the study, she went in.

James looked over his shoulder at her. When he smiled, the terrible crow's-feet around his eyes grew deeper. He looked so much older lately. He should take better care of himself. "Hey, Buckerina," he said. "Want to read my story?" She shook her head, wandering over to the far wall. His work embarrassed her, but she loved it in here. It was like an older-guy version of her room, words and images all over the walls, like decoupage without the varnish. Bits of paper with things jotted on them, stuff he was working on, quotations, photos, art.

"Whatcha workin' on?" she asked, to be polite.

Something about the Parkade, he said, but not to worry, she wasn't in it. There was a beautiful line of Rilke's on the wall that she'd read before: "Love consists in this, that two solitudes protect and touch and greet each other."

"Where's Mama?"

"At a meeting, then a hike and a rally with Rae. Sure you don't want to read my piece?"

"Later," she said, although his asking was supposed to be an honor; he usually asked just her mother. His pieces were direct and ordinary, like journals, which she liked about them; they were dry and wistful like Salinger, but maybe not with that same genius. He could be snarky and judgmental about everything and everyone, like she and Alice and Jody often were, but his stories always stopped on a dime, ended all wrapped up too neatly, like packages, which was not at all like real life. He was trying to get on her good side by letting her seem to be of service to him. She knew all of his moves. It smelled of paper and books and pencils in here, like you'd expect of a writer's study. But also honey candles from France that he splurged on—how could you not love a guy who burned lightly scented candles, who loved and offered up the fragrance of honey and beeswax? And she did love him, she always had, in all the years since he'd become a part of her family. He went back to the pages he held in his hand, and she ran across the other quotations on the wall until she got to the scrap of paper in Thelonious Monk's own reproduced handwriting, "Make the drummer sound good." She was going to do just that, make both her parents sound good by doing well. She'd stick to beer and a little weed for a few months, until her first-semester grades were in and she was home free. Maybe an occasional hit of Alice's Adderall. She studied the back of James's head, how gray he was getting, the widening bald spot, the turkey-skin neck. When he dropped his head onto his chest to think, the baggy skin on the back of his neck looked less wrinkled, more like it used to. He peered at her over his shoulders, his reading glasses at the end of his nose. "Go make yourself some breakfast." She hated how strict he had gotten, and how he always thought he was right, but he was great, too, if you thought about it: hip, hardworking, and steady. She and her mom were lucky to have him. He was their drummer.

◘

Elizabeth was sitting in a noon meeting, drinking bad coffee and eating an Oreo. She had deliberately plopped down next to a grumpy old man from San Francisco, because she didn't want the happy alkies to foist themselves on her. It was good to be here, away from James and Rosie for a while, out of the fray. She was glad that Jody was gone. She hoped she would find her way, but Jody and Alice were such a part of Rosie's recent frightening behavior; maybe now there would be less temptation.

She found herself thinking about Robert Tobias. Was it even possible that Rosie had something going on with him? Why else would she have been calling him like that and hanging up, then speaking in such a nervous baby-doll voice? Elizabeth remembered the wired, obsessed hell of being the girl who called the boy a dozen times and hung up. She saw Rosie in those tiny tight clothes she wore for tennis all summer, those breasts barely contained in sports bras and halter tops. It came back to her now, how Rosie showed off for Robert on the court, sitting so close in the grass afterward. Trying to pay attention to the meeting's speaker, who was really funny, she imagined Rosie flirting with Robert, and him looking at her with hard eyes. Even the grumpy guy was laughing about how when the lady speaking had a few drinks she went from being dark and runty to feeling tall and Swedish. But

Elizabeth's mind kept jumping to Robert. Surely he would not risk losing it all—his wife, his children, his job, his benefits, his future—to take advantage of Rosie's schoolgirl interest in him.

But then again, it was the oldest story told. A lovely girl had always been the prize.

The speaker said something that James would have liked, and Elizabeth wrote it on the back of her checkbook. Its acronym was LOVE: letting others *voluntarily* evolve. Very kicky. But what about when the person was your child, making bad choices? How could you trust life with your own kid, when you knew how unforgiving and capricious life could be? What was so wrong about wanting your gifted kid to ace her classes, get a good scholarship, go on to do great things in the world? Let alone survive adolescence, without brain damage, or paraplegia, or AIDS?

◘

Rae's knees were bothering her, so she and Elizabeth walked only a couple of miles on the old fire road behind the baseball field by White's Hill.

Scattered like confetti in the tall golden grass were tiny salmon-colored stars, almost like taffeta ruffs for circus dogs, surrounding magenta petals, with bright yellow centers—"So much crammed into one teeny flower," Elizabeth said, laughing. The air was dotted with butterflies, white and yellow and cheap knockoff monarchs; butterflies were wind energy made visible. And sticky monkey flowers were everywhere this time of year, even growing out of the craggiest rocks near the road, where all the renegade flowers and succulents hung out.

The rally they were going to was to support Marin's low-cost housing, minimal as it was, and even that threatened by developers who wanted to run out the poor and retired, and install nice malls and apartments. Not many people turned out, maybe a hundred or so, mostly from the low-cost housing at the retired Air Force base in Novato. But two county supervisors showed up and spoke, rousing the crowd, and Maria Muldaur led the crowd in a shimmying rendition of "We Shall Not Be Moved." Most wonderful of all were four men from Darfur, who'd gotten the dates mixed up— their big rally here was next week, and many people who stood near them promised to attend, including Rae. The men looked tired and displaced, wearing ceremonial clothes—fur loincloths tied across their blue jeans, over their rumps; metal headdresses, adorned with hawk or eagle feathers, that looked like a cross between Julius Caesar and football helmets—but they stayed to lend their support, doing a Darfur dance to the old civil rights song.

◘

The morning school began, Jody called to let Rosie know she was thinking of her and to say she wasn't necessarily coming back right away. She could not bear to be away from Claude, she said. If her parents came after her, with no legal right to do so, she and Claude would go hide out in Mexico, one mile away.

"What about your life here?" Rosie wailed. "What about school? What about us?"

"I'll see you whenever I can," Jody cried. "Please try to understand." She planned to get her GED at the local junior college. She might split her time in two places, San Diego and Landsdale. She might get married. They wanted children.

"Oh, Jo, you're so young. This is going to take you down."

"I was going down again anyway, not getting anywhere, just treading water up there. At least now I have company."

"But what about me? Alice and I were your twoest—I mean, your two truest pals."

"I love you forever, but you know what I mean. Claude is my beloved."

Getting ready for school, which meant choosing just the right torn jeans, a light blue camisole over a lavender tank top, and a red bra whose straps showed, Rosie spiraled down into mad jealousy. Jody was someone in a movie, she was someone's comfort. The man she loved might end up broken, but he'd always have a beautiful girl's love to protect him. The thought of a child living on was a kind of immortality. It was like going from pimply, clueless, trivial, to being a Rilke poem: "I know that there is room in me for a huge and timeless life." Rilke must not have been in high school when he wrote this.

She told Jody she'd send money if she got stuck, and hung up. She put on makeup, a light coat of foundation, kohl under her eyes, sugar-pink gloss.

She couldn't eat breakfast. Her parents were at the table with coffee, reading the paper. James was shaking Red Rooster hot sauce onto his scrambled eggs, and her mother asked if she had everything she needed, like she was a child. "Come give me a kiss," she said, like Rosie was about to go off to kindergarten. Rosie bent in, and kissed her mother behind an ear.

"Pew," Elizabeth said. "Your hair smells like smoke!"

"Thanks. I was with people last night who were smoking. Sometimes I'm in places where people are smoking dope, but I'm definitely trying to stay off it now. I'll be able to give you clean urine soon."

"Honey, look," said Elizabeth, "if you can avoid smoking dope and cigarettes, and don't start sneaking out all the time, we can do this on our own, as a family, without having to get out the big guns, like therapists, or outpatient rehab."

James looked over the top of his paper, over those old-man reading glasses.

"I know! God, Mommy! How many times do you have to tell me?" Rosie frowned at James as if he had been eavesdropping, slammed out the door, and stormed off to school on foot.

◘

Senior year meant you were royalty in the muscly shuffle of the corridors, amid the voices; the clanging, banging, reverberating locker doors; the announcements to which no one, not even the teachers, listened; and the odor—Stephen King ghost smells of old meals from the lunchroom, ancient sour milk, and chalk, and over the B.O. the boys' body wash that made them smell like clean wet dogs, and the girls' delicious fruity shampoo, and the toxic locker odors of food death that the janitors could not eradicate over the summer.

She met up with Alice near the glass trophy cases. Alice wore a long, skinny knit skirt with a baby-sized camisole of saffron silk. Her hair was gathered in four braids secured with shells and bows. She was bohemian beautiful, but not like the popular girls who were all thin and gorgeous, like models in expensive almost identical clothes. Rosie told her about Jody's call that morning, and Alice covered her face with her hands and said she was going to cry, although she didn't. They had ten minutes till their first class, French 4, and Alice had to run to the bathroom. "Come with me, baby girl," she begged, but Rosie said no, that she'd forgotten something.

"Meetcha back in five." They hugged and kissed as if it could be months until they met again, clutching at each other and smoothing out each other's perfect makeup. Rosie walked as fast as she could through the throng, herding herself through the multilegged beast of the student body to Robert's science lab. She had meant to make herself wait until third period, when inorganic chemistry met. But it would be fun to poke her head into his classroom and see his reaction. She opened the door a few inches and peeked in partially like she'd seen women do in movies, as if they were behind a veil instead of a door. He was at his desk, talking to students: clean-shaven, hair trimmed, killer handsome in a white button-down dress shirt open at the neck. She smiled in at him, but he did not seem to see her at first. Only she knew how gorgeous his legs were, tan and soft with golden hair; only she knew what he smelled like close up, over the scent of the grass on which they sat so close, so often. Yet still he didn't look up.

And when he did, he seemed puzzled, friendly but puzzled, like why was she there? He had almost no expression, then smiled distractedly and went back to talking to a pale pimply boy. She was stunned for a second, but then she got it, as the first bell rang, the five-minute prison yard warning. Oh, duh. She got it: He was trying to act natural, like she was any old student. She raced down the hall.

◘

Adelle Marchaux's French classroom was like an elegant garden compared with the smelly chaos of the hallways. Rosie took a seat beside Alice in the front row, to show honor and affection for her odd and petite teacher. Adelle had the same young-boy hairdo as always, poorly cut, the elf liquid eyeliner, poorly applied, pointy ears, tiny arms, loose and flowing clothes. *Bonjour bonjour bonjour* flew, all of the kids were seniors, all almost fluent. Adelle talked to each student, charming as could be, asking them about their summers, their health, their parents, in French. She spoke and clutched at herself and grabbed at the air, then pouted. It was such a part of being or speaking French, that pout. Alice had put it exactly right last year, explaining to Elizabeth why they loved this odd woman so—"She's psycho, in a good way, like us. She's a true person."

Rosie gazed off; the beautiful French sounded faraway and romantic, like Robert on the beach that first night, on the court, the grass, shoulders skimming. "Rosie," Alice hissed, and Rosie tried to snap back to reality.

God, let it be that Robert was playing it cool, only feigning the casual stance toward her. Let him love her. They wouldn't even ever need to touch—simply love each other, that would be enough. *"Mademoiselle!"* Adelle was calling. *"Concentre!"* Rosie heard Alice hiss again.

She looked up slowly at Adelle, in time to see the pout. She tried to clear her mind, smiled to indicate her embarrassed return; but Adelle was staring at her. *"Où es-tu aujourd'hui? Nous te perdons. Reviens, reviens."* Where are you today? We are losing you. Come back, come back.

Second period was boring, civics with an androgynous troll who'd been teaching here since the year Kennedy was elected president, so the class was mostly on the greatness of JFK. And inorganic chemistry was a nightmare.

She might as well have been invisible, or anyone. She did not cry during Robert's class. She went up to his desk, once the other fifteen mostly nerdy kids had filed out, but he got up and passed her by and did not stop until he got to the door. Turning back, he asked quizzically, "Is everything okay?" She cocked her head at him, and he said, "I need to be somewhere."

And that was it. He was gone. She pushed past kids in the hall-way and burst into the girls' bathroom, into the hornets' nest of primping girls. The buzzing stopped and she locked the door of her stall closed, and when the buzzing resumed, she started crying.

◘

A re you stoned?" Alice asked her when they met up for lunch. "Your eyes are so red. What happened? Here—here—have my Ding Dongs. Here's a napkin." Rosie reached for the napkin, and tried to dry her eyes without smearing her mascara and kohl. Alice enveloped her in a hug. Rosie said she was getting her period, was PMS'ing like crazy, that was why she'd been crying, why she couldn't concentrate.

"Oh! Do you want an Adderall?" Alice clucked with concern.

Rosie shook her head. All she wanted was dope. She felt for the pouch in her pocket, full of eye drops, mints, and towelettes. Sighing, she scanned the crowded blacktop until she saw a cute guy who always had good dope, who waved when he saw her, and beckoned her over. The three of them walked around to the back parking lot and got high.

The rest of the day she walked around feeling like a bird that had flown into a plate-glass window. The weed didn't help at all, and in fact she was glad when it wore off. She didn't eat all day, and couldn't eat that night, either, and she kept starting to cry, and of course her parents tried to pry it out of her, and Alice called and tried to pry it out of her, too. She kept saying she was having really bad PMS and was going crazy.

She retreated to her bedroom and tried unsuccessfully to study. How could she even go back to school? She couldn't believe she was still stuck there. It was literally a nightmare, a Kafka novel.

God! She couldn't believe she had to see him every day for the rest of the year. She was so miserable in her own skin, an ugly unwanted fraud. This was the story of her whole life. She was a too-tall, dead-father girl. She leaned forward and lowered her head all the way to her desk, and hid in her own arms.

◘

E lizabeth had kept Rosie's secret from James for so long that the substance no longer held much meaning—it must have passed the statute of limitations—but it had inserted a slight reserve between her and James, and they had let this distance slide. She found herself picking at everyone—picking at James for gobbling his food, picking at Rosie for picking at her face.

Finally, when they were doing dishes one night, when Rosie was locked in her room doing homework, Elizabeth managed to say, "There's something I wish I'd told you a few weeks ago."

James dried the salad bowl with a flourish and put it on the counter. "Shoot."

"Oh, I don't know, it sounds silly now."

He turned to look at her, worried. "What?"

She turned off the water and shook her head, and told him a brief version of what had happened: How Claude was leaving, how Jody had been distraught, how she and Alice had sneaked over to their house that night, how Rosie had sneaked out. She had hoped against hope that James would wave it away, but he tilted his head, his face contracted and dark. "What?" he said. "How could you? We're supposed to be in this together."

"I'm sorry," she said, genuinely, and tried to take his hands, but he pulled away.

"God, what else haven't you told me?"

"I'm trying to find a balance between you being my whole life and Rosie being my whole life, too. Trying to celebrate times when we all get along—and screwing everything up."

He looked at her with hostile disbelief, put down the dish towel, and trudged out of the kitchen.

"Stop," she called out when he stepped through the doorway. She stood facing him, penitent and bristly and teary. He stared back at her. Tears ran down her face. She hoped they might soften his heart. Her tears had on occasion washed the motes out of both their eyes, obstructions from the stream. But not this time, or at any rate, not right away.

" 'We are each our own devil,' Elizabeth. 'And we make this world our hell.' " He vanished down the hall.

She heard his office door close. She went and stood outside but didn't knock. "Can't you forgive me this one time?" Silence. She did not know where to start. Rebuilding trust was the hardest work, hopeless at first. You felt like Humpty-Dumpty. She stood at James's door until Rosie's opened.

"What are you doing out there, Mommy?"

"Can I come into your room?" Elizabeth asked miserably. Rosie sighed, and held the door open so her mother could come in. They sat at the foot of the bed.

"Your dad's mad at me for keeping the secret about you sneaking out."

"A, he's not my dad. B, that was days ago—like, get a life, James. C, he's always mad about something, because he's short, and now he's losing his hair."

"You can't really believe that," Elizabeth said defensively. "That's such bullshit. Don't you think it may have to do with you sneaking out—or me lying?"

"I don't know. It's not my problem, Mama! Can't you see how unhappy I've been? I can't study. I'm not eating. I'm picking at my face. Look at my skin!" There was a scattering of pimples at her hairline, red and sore.

"Darling, why? Tell me what's going on."

"Hello? Jody is not coming back? She's my best friend. And I hate school this year, it's like prison. I can't believe I'm stuck there with all those outcasts and snots and infants. And Robert's class sucks this year—he's changed. He's an asshole now."

"Just since school started, honey?" Rosie nodded. "Can I ask you something? Without you getting mad?" Rosie nodded again, touching her forehead until Elizabeth drew her hand away. "Was something going on between you two this summer?"

"How stupid are you? You're a joke. Why would you even think that?"

Elizabeth studied Rosie's face, full of scorn and fury, and knew in a flash she was lying. "I don't know. You seem to have this great rapport. And closeness."

"Stop spying on me! You're the one going crazy—call your shrink." And it was the disgusted sneer more than the words that made Elizabeth erupt.

"How dare you! I'm not a liar, or cruel! You're a spoiled little shit!" She got to her feet, hating herself and her child. How could they say such hateful things?

She locked herself in the bathroom and cried silently until she was raw. Desperate, she tried to pray, until she remembered she didn't believe in god—but she had felt that shard of something deep inside that she could only call not me, so she cried out in silence to the speck of light, *Help me! I'm begging.* She felt the wet pounding of her heart in her stuffed-up head. She hit the bathroom rug so hard that her fist hurt, and she cradled it like an injured bird.

Eventually, James came knocking.

"Honey?" he asked. "What are you doing?"

After a while, she said, "I'm praying."

There was a long silence. Then, astonished, "You are?"

"Go away. I hate everyone. Rosie made me promise not to tell you, so I didn't, and then when I did, you blow up, and she hates me. Everyone is horrible to me, and I hate me."

She heard his footsteps going away, down the hall. She wiped her nose on the top of her T-shirt, waiting. After a while, she heard him return.

"Do you even hate Rascal?" he asked.

"James? Why do you make me choose between you and my child? I can't."

He poked something into the lock, and after a minute it popped open. The door opened a few inches, and Rascal dropped to the floor inside. "Leave me the fuck alone!" she shouted. Rascal lumbered to Elizabeth's side, tasted her blurry wet face, and butted his huge orange head against her until she took him into her lap.

◙

She finally came out, and went to James's office and sat on the carpet by his desk. He got out of his chair and sat facing her. Then they both sat on the rug, like children at a tea party on the floor of a pool. She felt disgusting, red and unstable.

"That was so hitting below the belt," she said. "To bring Rascal into it."

"To begin with, you need to tell me all of your unsaids, Elizabeth.

They're killing us. You've been using your sincereness in counterfeit ways."

"I'm so sorry," she said, sick to her stomach. She did not point out that the word was "sincerity." Her mouth tasted like matches. She looked away, at the darkening night through his window, the branches of the kumquat tree. She wondered whether there was such a word as "sincereness." They sat unspeaking until her tears and misery wore him down.

"Tears give you such an unfair advantage." He shook his head. "I've always hated to see women come undone." He hit the carpet with his fist, hard, and it startled her. "Okay," he said after a moment, coming to a decision. "We start over." He scooched closer to her, and they held each other on the bottom of the pool.

◘

They clung to each other in bed that night, and he rubbed her neck in sympathy. "She's an awful child," he whispered. "We must be saints, the both of us." She smiled in the dark, against his skin. "Let's get rid of her," he whispered. "Let's kill her."

"We could drop her off in a basket at the convent," Elizabeth whispered back.

He was spooning her when she woke, still patting her with sympathy, and the pats turned to love.

◘

Elizabeth woke Rosie for school, and Rosie was tense, not knowing where they stood.

"That's so scary when you do that, Mama," she pleaded. "When you flip out."

"I won't have you speak to me like you did last night, Rosie. I'm not going crazy. I don't believe you when you say you and Robert had nothing going on. You were lying to us all summer, repeatedly. But I am trying to avoid having to pay for you to see a shrink or go to rehab. But you need to talk to *someone*. Your counselor. Or Reverend Anthony."

Rosie considered this. "How about Rae, instead? She's my safest person."

Elizabeth talked this over at breakfast with James, and they both agreed to Rae.

◙

A few days later, after school, Rosie went to see Rae at church. Rae's office was no bigger than a walk-in closet, which is what it had been before she'd brought in a narrow desk, a white rattan bookcase, and a worn easy chair. There was a framed photo of Lank, and a framed shadowy book cover, from *The Luminous Darkness* by Howard Thurman. Rae looked soft and pink in the low light of the lamp, the pupils of her large eyes full. Rosie held her knees to her chest, her head hunched over, her long limbs tucked beneath her.

"Everything is going so badly! Mama and I fight all the time. And I hate school."

Rae was silent for a moment. Then she said her churchiest thing: "How can I serve you?"

Rosie let her hair fall over her face, tried to hide behind it like it was a duck blind.

"You know Jody's gone, right? Maybe forever."

"Yes, your mother told me. Is she safe? Do you know where she is?"

"Not really. Somewhere near Claude's base. And Alice has a

boyfriend. My two dearest friends! School's screwed up, too, and I hate all the dweeby little boys."

"And tell me what else is going on. Are you getting stoned a lot? Drinking?"

"No!" Rosie said vehemently. "I mean, God! Did my mother put you up to this?"

"Look, I was sitting here innocently reading Mary Oliver when you called."

"Well, of course I was smoking a little dope, like everyone, until a while ago. And I've been trying not to smoke since then."

"Trying not to? Or not smoking, since then?"

"Jesus, give me some slack."

Rae sneered in the nicest possible way. Rosie growled.

The smell of lemons wafted in from somewhere, or oranges, or grapefruit. "It seems like there's something else, way deep down, that's troubling you."

Time was stopped and fluid at the same time, like resin, and Rae's face was a blur of chestnut hair and big eyes and a child's cheeks.

"I would never trust you again if you told my mother."

Rae considered this for quite some time. "All right," she said finally.

Rosie studied her. "I sort of, I don't know. Fell in love with a married man."

Rae's mouth opened. "Wow."

"I am so totally fucked! I feel like I'm in a whirlpool, going down."

Rae nodded in sarcastic agreement—like, Yeah, no shit.

Rosie looked at her. "Thanks a lot."

"What do you want me to say? You *are* fucked. Not morally.

But I've been there, honey bear. It's the worst I've ever felt in my life. Worse than when my folks died."

"Well, we're not sleeping together yet."

"Seriously? Thank God. I mean, that would make it so much worse."

"It would?" Rosie asked. Rae nodded, visibly relieved.

"Then why do I think about it all the time? And why do I want it so badly?"

"Because you're a little lonely. But sex with him is the fail-safe line, Ro. Who is he?" Rosie looked away. "Is he a teacher?"

"God, no! And I thought we loved each other. But now I don't know. He has a family." Rosie expected Rae to roll her eyes, but she only tilted her head slightly, as if Rosie were a painting or a view. "Nothing's turning out right. Senior year was supposed to be so great. It's all broken and fucked up. My best friend has run away, and my other best friend is in love, and I'm so lonely and stressed. I'm *already* behind in school. Plus I'm going to have to see this guy every single day—"

"So he is a teacher, right, darling?" Rosie shook her head, pleading. "It doesn't matter. What does matter is that you haven't started sleeping together. That is so huge, hon. Once you go there, I can promise you'll eventually come to know what hell truly means."

Rosie pulled back to look Rae in the eyes. "Swear you're not going to tell my mom?"

◘

Rae called Elizabeth two minutes after Rosie took off.

"She's madly in love with a teacher, who she thought was in love with her, although she says they haven't slept together, and she says it's over."

"Oh, shit. It's Robert Tobias. That jerk! What an asshole. What do I do?"

"I guess we hope, if she's telling the truth, that she really is done."

"You mean, you think she may be lying? She may be—she lies about everything."

"Or that it's mostly in her mind. That he gave her mixed messages, and she ran with it."

"Yeah, but Rosie didn't make this up out of thin air. I don't want her to drop out of inorganic chemistry. She needs it on her transcript if she's going to get a scholarship to a good college."

"Elizabeth! What she needs is tough love. Allegiance, and a chance to start over. She doesn't necessarily need to go to some Ivy League school."

"She'll still need to get a scholarship—and that means she needs one last great semester."

"You say those are the things she needs, hon—but those are all things you need for her. And your parents probably said those exact things to you. They were a lie then, and they are now, too. I mean, I don't even know what inorganic chemistry *means*. Do you? What is it, dead compounds with their little feet sticking up in the air?" Elizabeth managed a laugh. "Wait, that would be AP inanimate chemistry."

She felt less sure of everything when she hung up. It was a nightmare. All she could think to do were the most ordinary of things: plant the flowering pear that was still in its pot from the nursery, labor over a vegetable stew, clean out the bottom drawer in the kitchen where the whole world ended up.

When she went in to say good night later that evening, Rosie was in bed, wearing a lacy white camisole, almost Victorian really, her thick hair spread out on the pillow like a peacock's tail.

Elizabeth sat on the bed with her for a few minutes. "I'm so tired tonight. Are you?"

"Exhausted," said Rosie. She rolled over to face her mother, and let Elizabeth massage her neck and shoulders. Her mother smelled like an old lady in a thoughtful mood.

"How are things going in chemistry, darling?"

"Fine," Rosie answered, "same old same old," although they weren't. Chemistry was much harder for her than physics had been, and more competitive because all of them were preparing for the AP test in May. It was so painful to have to see Robert pretend that she was any old student; she'd been used to being his physics star. He was kind and funny with all of the students, they were the cream of the crop, and he loved their debates, even when they were just trying to show how smart they were, but there was no way anyone would know by watching him with her that they had had something special between them. Now it was just him asking for her take on acid-base reactions or how to determine what pH you'd end up with when you used different combinations of chemicals, or what ev, like she was some random nerdy nerd. Instead of how they used to talk about love, and rivers.

She thought about Robert all the time now, even more than she used to, all day every day, and waited for him to approach her with an explanation for why he had cut her off. *I love you,* he would say, *but my wife was catching on.* Or, *One of my children is sick; and I have to play it cool for now.* But as the days passed and he didn't come forth, she began to give up. He made her sick. The only thing, she thought, was that she had the goods on him, if he even thought about giving her less than an A.

* * *

Jody didn't call the next week, and Alice got grounded for taking a twenty out of her mother's wallet—her mother was suddenly worse than Rosie's, after hardly ever having been home before. Now she kept tabs on the amount of cash she carried, like the Treasury Department. Elizabeth wasn't that bad yet. One Monday somebody told Rosie that Fenn and his roommates were having a party that coming Friday, and Rosie went into overdrive: she was easygoing and hardworking all week, and did not have one fight with her parents. Thursday night she passed a drug test, thanks to a few drops of bleach from the bottle of eardrops. Her mother gave her the high five—such a cornball—and Friday morning Rosie asked if she could go to a party at her chemistry lab partner's house, if she was home by midnight. In her most persuasive voice, thick and creamy with lots of eye contact, she said the lab partner's parents would be home—she could have them call Elizabeth once Rosie arrived, since she didn't have the number on her. Elizabeth allowed that they didn't need to go *that* far. James said they did. Her parents argued while Rosie put on her makeup. Her mother said, "Don't make me be the lone vigilante mom tonight," and James backed down.

Rosie was going to walk to Fenn's, as her parents had gone to a meeting and movie. "Wild times, huh?" James had said. Rosie put on her sexiest tank top and more makeup, and set out down the trail to the main street in town. It was a mile away. There was not much light on the trail, only a crescent moon and distant streetlights, and this made her very afraid, which made her hate herself. What a loser, to be almost eighteen, and still scared that creatures might pop out at her in the dark.

She walked as fast as she could past the bushes that lined the trail, and told the story of her walk to herself in her head, as if she were telling Alice, and she made it funny because this made her less afraid. There was rustling in the bushes, she said into her imaginary phone, a rusty kind of rustling, which could have meant a mountain lion, or a bum. Her heart pounded like bongo drums. What if a raccoon with rabies jumped out and clawed me, or possums, which were so disgusting, with those penisy hairless white tails.

She got a side ache from walking so fast, but did not stop until she saw the lights of the Parkade.

Rosie found some people congregated under the streetlights like night church, had a few sips of beer, and then walked to the apartment that Fenn and a few other older boys rented, a block and a half away. There were two guys from her class hanging out by the door, two kids hardly anyone at school ever talked to, although she tried to be kind whenever she saw them, who hung with the other nerds in the distant fourth corridor of the school grounds, along with the special-ed kids. She hung out with them now for a few minutes while working up the courage to go inside. One of them shared his beer with her.

There were two Valley kids sitting in the stairway, slow-paced long-haired organic types who lived in the counterculture town just over White's Hill, and at the top of the stairs, two Landsdale kids who had grown up here and would never leave. A girl from her French class was inside, along with a few other popular girls, who were there with their boyfriends, looking through the racks of CDs above the stereo, from which reggae rap blasted. She waved to them from the stairs, where she'd stopped to get her bearings, and then someone handed her a pipe and a sip of screwdriver.

Alexander was here. Everyone said he was only smoking heroin, not shooting it. He'd told her once in the Parkade that he was often at the apartment where Fenn lived, he was friends with the roommates, and sometimes they let him spend the night on the couch when his parents had kicked him out. She went over and stood with him, and when he handed her his cigarette, she took a puff, and then another. "You can keep it," he said. He'd told her once that he'd been a fourth-corridor kid freshman year, and then he got into smoking dope, and then dealing a little, and then suddenly he looked like one of the older Parkade dirt children. A lot of kids had tried to save him for a while: he was smart, but goofy on purpose, to make people laugh. She really liked him, and loved the cigarette.

"There's beer, and Fenn's squeezing fresh orange juice," he said. Rosie shrugged. The living room was cozy and pleasantly lit, with so many candles that the light was golden, as if there were a fire in the fireplace, and it smelled of all sorts of delicious fragrances—flowers, grasses, citrus, oranges, weed. A few girls from the sophomore class were sitting with a guy on one of the couches, each holding a beer. Rosie said hey to everyone and stubbed out her cigarette. The girls on the couch were pretty, with thick eyeliner and long, poufy hair. They said hey back, and one of the guys she didn't know pointed her to the kitchen, where a machine whirred.

Her heart raced and the side ache returned.

Fenn was at the counter, bent over a whirring juice machine, and did not hear her when she said hello. His curly light brown hair, clean and thick and sun-bleached, was pulled back into a short ponytail. She reached forward and tugged on his T-shirt to get his attention. He turned around, holding an empty orange half. "Hey, what a nice surprise!" He had such a handsome face, long wide slanty blue eyes, a straight nose, and high cheekbones. "Where'd you come from?"

"My house. What're you making?"

"Fresh screwdrivers. Make ya one? Will you take these to Cassie and Andrew?" He handed her two glasses. When she returned from the living room, he handed her juice in a marmalade jar. She stood behind him while he squeezed orange juice for himself. He was not as tall as she was, but had long legs, poking from his worn khaki cargo shorts; he had a faded, perfectly frayed black T-shirt. When he turned around, he handed her a half-pint of vodka. She poured some into her juice but couldn't even taste it, so she poured in more.

He whispered, "Let's sneak outside and sit on the steps. People can squeeze their own damn juice if they want refills. There's the prettiest little moon."

They never even got around to a second drink. Out on the steps, he handed her a pipe, which turned out to hold the most amazing mellow dope, and she paused only a few seconds before taking it, flushing away the thought of her shocked and betrayed mother, and they sipped their drinks in the warm evening, with the moon lighting up the backyard at the foot of the steps. He smelled like oranges and the sea, and it made her faint and giddy and mute. He lit a cigarette and handed it to her, and lit one for himself. Pretty soon their shoulders were touching. He had muscles in his arms because he worked construction with his uncle Joe.

"I thought you were a drug dealer," she said smiling. "That's what people say."

"Sorry to disappoint you," he said. "Have you also heard of the fourteen-year-old girls who hang out here all the time, that me and my roommates have sex with? And that I got Alexander onto smack?" He shook his head. They talked about the house he was helping build in the Valley, solar-powered, and about how their parents' generation had destroyed the earth. He was five years older than she was.

Sometime later, when the fog came in, cold and damp like heavy smoke made of snow, they went inside. He got a zippered hoodie for each of them from his bedroom. She peeked in: there were a girl and a guy on his bed, about her age, sleeping. The room emitted a sweaty smell.

He and Rosie sat on one of the couches and listened to Nine Inch Nails with everyone else for a while, then stepped outside a couple of times to smoke.

They moved on to plain fresh-squeezed orange juice, and then he got them a wool blanket and they sat outside on the steps and ate an entire quart of Jamoca Almond Fudge, passing it back and forth. She thought of turning sideways to kiss him with a mouth full of coffee ice cream, but didn't. She felt too shy. They talked about movies, they loved all the same ones. He said that *The Seventh Seal* had changed him—because it turned out that Death hadn't won, even though the knight was going to die. What Fenn said took her breath away, and made her love the movie, too. They shared at least three cigarettes, Camel filters. And then it was nearly midnight. He let her use his toothbrush so her breath would be fine if she got caught sneaking back indoors at home, and offered to drive her, but now she wanted to run up the trail because she was full to bursting. Her new life, her true life, had finally begun.

◘

She was on the phone all morning with Alice, telling her about the party, the joyful news of her and Fenn's connection. "God, he's so hot," Alice said, and Rosie said yeah, but that wasn't even the thing; the thing was his mind and how cool he was, and Alice kept saying, "Oh my God," that it was totally awesome, dude. Rosie studied hard most of the afternoon. She felt so happy that she helped a little around the house, did her own laundry, and even ate dinner with her parents without making it an international incident. After dinner, by prearrangement, Alice called and Rosie listened for a minute and then said, "Oh, I don't know. Let me ask." She turned to her parents with the phone tucked. "You know that guy Fenn?" she asked her mother, as she helped clear the table. "Who we saw at *The Seventh Seal*? And then at the Roastery?"

"Yeah, I know who he is. The surfer."

"He's having a party tonight, and he's really good friends with Alice's boyfriend—they work on the same construction crew sometimes, for Fenn's uncle Joe, and Alice wants me to go with her, in case things get a little wild, because she's being piss-tested, too." The Uncle Joe part was so innocent, and convincing, but her parents still had to have a secret conference in James's office, like it was Yalta instead of some stupid party. "I passed the piss test yesterday, remember?" she shouted through the closed door.

So she got to go to Fenn's apartment that night with her parents' permission and the promise to be home by midnight again.

◘

His roommates were still in the living room, like they'd never left, and different girls were drinking beer and there were more teenage boys, all of them juniors or seniors. Another woozy couple was passed out on Fenn's bed. Alice was at her boyfriend's house; his parents were out of town. Rosie knew hardly anyone here.

Fenn kissed her in the kitchen, slowly, deeply, and she stepped back, smiling. They made fresh-squeezed orange juice for themselves again, and poured in vodka from a fresh half-pint, and went out on the back stairs, again, to look at the crescent moon, again, and they talked about the music they loved, slow rap, and the Beatles, and the trouble Fenn had gotten into when he was still drinking too much, and the time she got busted at the party on the hill, which he'd heard about.

As they cuddled, she told him about Jody running away with her army man, and he said, "Well, if he gets sent off somewhere scary, she'll be tucked in his heart as he goes into battle. She'll mean so much to someone."

"That is incredible for you to say, because she doesn't mean much to herself, because her parents basically destroyed her when they sent her off to wilderness. And none of the adults can see that." He touched her thigh as she spoke, as if smoothing out a crease. They were both in worn khaki shorts, and his legs were as long as hers, which no one's but Jody's and maybe Elizabeth's were.

It was like talking to Robert or Rae. Their legs touched on the steps, his warm, soft, furry smoothness on hers, and she felt her soul amplified, like at the end of a party at someone's house with perfect people there, and Led Zeppelin on the stereo, or up on the mountain with Jody and Alice, 'shrooming late at night under the stars. She didn't feel small and cringy like when her parents were all over her with their suspicions and Gestapo commands. She was someone real and meaningful, with Fenn on the back steps, legs touching, about to go to bed together, tomorrow, maybe. She could literally fall into his sloping blue eyes. Love was like that, when it was no longer just your own soul howling in its own dingy wilderness. You got to feel draped with something noble instead of something sloppy and always falling short, like you felt secretly on the inside half the time.

Right before she had to leave, he said, "Can I ask you something?" She nodded, thinking he would ask her about her first time, or if she was on birth control. But instead, he pointed to a drop of water hanging from a geranium beside him, in moonlight. "In the morning, if the sun was up and that drop was still there, would it contain limitless rainbows?"

"Not necessarily," she explained. "Maybe it would. But my understanding is that it would contain limitless water."

He thought about this in silence. Then they kissed again. When she looked at her watch, it was eleven forty-five—she'd be in huge trouble if she was late. She brushed her teeth with his toothbrush again, and ran home as fast as she could, like a deer, like a colt, like the girl she used to be.

NINE

Lagoon

◻

They made love the next afternoon in his room like young adults in a movie, so loving and slow and yet hot, sexy and romantic and great beyond all imagining, and it hurt only when he first entered her, but it hurt good, and she loved most when it was over and they lay together in a tangle and stroked each other's faces and hip bones and tummies. They used a rubber, the first time, and then they ate hash brownies he had made, and were so amazingly stoned that she couldn't deal with the whole condom thing, only his skin in her, soft, hard, furry, smooth, slow-motion eternity.

After that she thought about him every minute, every hour all day every day. In chemistry she thought about the soft yellow streaks in his hair, the downy blond fuzz right below his belly button, his large hand on her hip bone. Thoughts floated like fish through her mind as she tried to concentrate on what Robert was saying. Now she thought of Robert only when she was in class, even when he bent over her to look at her calculations. Fenn had saved her. The smell of Robert's aftershave now made her sick, the smell of someone in decay. She and Fenn were the beauty of youth being adults together. He smelled like the ocean, like a carpenter, like nails and wood, like the field of hot grasses where they lay after school. She knew the smell of his warm brown thighs. He kept his room clean, scented with candles, he always had bud, enough to lay some routinely on Alice. Couples weren't allowed to crash in his room at parties anymore; it was reserved only for the two of them these days—the one of them.

He understood how afraid her parents were now that she was growing away from them, and he kept on baking her brownies with hash oil so she wouldn't smell of weed. They laughed about how it was almost an act of charity. He also had a source for pure Ecstasy, with no meth at all in it, nothing to fuck up her mind or drug tests, and it reminded her of what it had been like her first few times and why they called it Ecstasy. He made her come over and over with his mouth. Alice thought she was exaggerating, but if anything, she downplayed it because Alice's Evan didn't love oral like Fenn did. Anyway, that wasn't even the great part. The great part was after in his arms, under the covers, in his room, in their hippie town, near San Francisco Bay, on the great big wide quilted earth.

He was polite and shyly conversational with her parents when he came to pick her up for meetings.

That's what he and she called it when he came to get her during the week. They had concocted a story about attending the young people's meetings nearby that they'd found listed on Elizabeth's AA directory, and they went to one meeting a week so they

could regale James and Elizabeth with stories. They pretended
to be at meetings twice a week on school nights, so at least they
could be together briefly. The druggie kids at the young people's
meeting were old friends from the Parkade, way cooler than the
general prison population at Rosie's high school. On weekends,
she and Fenn hiked, read out loud in his bed, drank, made love
and vegan meals. She admitted to her mother and James that they
were sexually active, which was the phrase you used with parents.
Her mother hugged herself and hung her head like an old Latvian
widow, and James went off to his study to kill himself, he said. She
promised her mother that they were using condoms, even though
they weren't, and not too much more was made of this. What were
they supposed to do, say, "You cannot sleep with him, Rosie?"
Right.

The parental units had imposed a twenty-eight-day trial period
to see if Rosie could stay clean for a month, go without weed or
anything else they were able to test for with their little Captain
Midnight decoder-ring urine tests. They'd felt powerful and in
charge when they'd changed the curfew to eleven for those twenty-
eight days. Rosie had gone ballistic initially, but it was actually
working out fine. She was getting her homework done, mostly,
stabilizing the parents, and living the life she had dreamed of and
despaired of never having. She was happier than a person had
any right to be. And the funny thing was, her parents really liked
Fenn. They naturally thought he was too old for her, but Elizabeth
understood why she loved him, and James just threw his hands up
and said it was all hopeless, and they'd never think anyone was
good enough for her and blah blah blah. He seemed resigned to
Fenn, and even sort of liked that Fenn had read the same books he
and Elizabeth had, and that he had a full-time job with his uncle

Joe. Fenn even came up with a thought for James—that life at the Parkade was not unlike life at the Bolinas lagoon, in the ebb and flow and symbiosis and beautiful strangeness of its inhabitants, if only you had eyes to see beyond the asphalt and cars.

James and Elizabeth had been so inspired by this that one morning in October, they had gotten up early and driven to West Marin to sit on the banks of the lagoon with rain boots, a notepad, binoculars, and no agenda. You had to do things early in the day now, as Indian summer had descended a week ago, with all the tumult of heat and bugs, lurid sunsets, red as when you've been lying in the sun and it has begun to burn your lids.

Elizabeth always found Indian summer to be a stolen and peculiar time, nature compressed. It was confusing after a couple of weeks of milder days, with hints at the edge of coldness, but not enough mild comfort to rest into. Fall was her favorite season, a season for grown-ups, the wild, bright colors of flame, and when your insides tightened in the cold, you felt more present and on guard than in the balmy softening days of summer. The fall said, Get cracking. Indian summer said, Oh, stay with me just a little bit longer.

The beauty of early morning at low tide in the mucky tidal flats, crisscrossed with ribbons of channels like arteries and veins, made them both whisper in awe.

The last time they had been here, the tide had been high, and the water looked like an ocean that humans could splash in alongside the ruddy ducks and mallards, a big soup bowl filled with cattails, weeds, flotsam. "Duck soup," she said. "Yum yum."

"Oh my God, I am so going to tell Rosie you said that!" They laughed, because Fenn was a vegetarian and so now Rosie was entirely vegetarian, too. When they forced her to sit at the table for dinner, she stared at the roast chicken as if they'd served up one of her bucket children on a platter, piled high with potatoes and carrots on the side. Elizabeth made her brown rice and beans, and she ate the big salads they had every night from Elizabeth's garden, but Rosie must have lost close to ten pounds in the last six weeks. Five nights a week Elizabeth and James ate vegetarian, too—pasta, tofu, beans, cheese—but one night she and James happened to be eating a whole poached halibut with a spicy Thai ginger sauce. Rosie eyed it in despair.

"What is with you tonight, Rosie?" James asked.

"Nothing, just that I'm sitting here staring at what was once a living, sentient being. Like Rascal."

"A halibut?" James shouted. "You're comparing Rascal to a *halibut?*"

She leapt up from her seat. "I'm losing weight because I can't stand to sit at this table watching you pick at dead beings!" She stomped off toward her room, turning just before she disappeared. "It's so disgusting to me. It's evil! I can't live here anymore! I want to be emancipated."

James reached for Elizabeth's hand. "It's a delicious dead being, darling."

He took her hand here at the lagoon today, too, placing it back on her knee only to jot down notes. Low tide had revealed meals for every appetite, crabs, clams, mussels, fish, algae, seaweed, poultry, frogs, slime. Sometimes there were seals, hauled out in the mud, resting. This was their nursery, their bedroom. No one could swim all the time.

"She's doing better since she's been with Fenn," Elizabeth said out of nowhere. Birds hovered, swooped for food, flew in mysterious patterns; who knew what led birds where they went? James nodded.

But within days of Elizabeth's saying this, Rosie appeared to have taken up smoking.

At first the smell was just in her hair and clothes, which she explained by saying she had been in a room with smokers, including Fenn and kids at the young people's AA. Then Elizabeth caught a whiff on her breath, not that she and Rosie were often within breathing distance of each other, and when she asked, Rosie said, "God! I had like two puffs off Fenn's cigarette. I've given up everything! So leave me alone."

There were already so many things on the table that Elizabeth let it go, and did not even mention it to James. He was so busy all the time. But a few days later she found some of Rosie's socks mixed in with her own clean laundry, and when she took them to Rosie's room, she found her window open and the air heavy with lemony freshener spray over a hint of cigarettes.

She asked James what they should do—bribes, threats, graphics, tough love, more groundings?

"What a great idea. I'm sure that will really make her want to quit."

"Shouldn't we at least punish her? Or offer an incentive not to smoke?"

"Elizabeth. Did your parents' threats or bribes get you to not smoke when you were a teen?"

She shook her head. "Are you kidding? They were always bumming them from me. But the thought of Rosie smoking freaks me out. The black lungs, wrinkly mouth—plus it makes people's breath smell like cat boxes."

"Be sure to tell her that."

"Should we ask Rae to intervene? Or ask her to have the Sixth Day elders pray for Rosie? It couldn't hurt, right?"

"The only connection with a higher power that can help Rosie is Rosie's own. She's madly in love for the first time, and her boyfriend smokes. But he seems to be helping her stay clean—they're going to meetings, right? That is a total lowercase miracle. Let's back off the cigarettes for now."

That night Elizabeth began keeping a new secret from James.

After dinner, Fenn had come to pick Rosie up for the young people's meeting. He shook James's and Elizabeth's hands, and pretended to strangle Rascal on the sideboard. Elizabeth walked them out, on the pretext of heading to a women's meeting in Ross. She followed them in her car from way behind, through town to his apartment. She sat in the car awhile but they didn't come out. She noticed the binoculars from the trip to the lagoon, and would have used them to spy on Rosie and Fenn, if it hadn't made her look crazy, especially to herself. The big fish would have had a field day with her: "Elizabeth is whacked." She left a few minutes later.

Elizabeth cruised slowly past the Parkade on her way to her meeting. There were only a few parked cars. Several older kids were near enough so she could see their piercings and tattoos, but not close enough for her to tell what the designs were, each unique, of course, to say that there was something different about each of them, something beautiful. In ragged jeans, ethnic shirts, frayed knit caps, and even one cape, they might have been the children of gypsies, from communal families who slept and wept and danced and sang together, instead of from nice suburban homes. Where else could they express all those inchoate feelings about their gypsy yearnings and the embedded sadness of life but here at the Parkade? They were smoking cigarettes, she could smell them through her partly opened window. She drove on. A block away, across from the movie theater, another group of kids had gathered, to smoke and yearn and sneer, mostly young women in scarves, coral and turquoise jewelry, torn lingerie. Elizabeth drove to her meeting, partly for cover, partly because her mind buckled with anxiety.

The speaker at the meeting, a blonde woman in a fine tailored suit, shared how alcoholism had stolen her own childhood, and had now come back for her kid. She had tried everything she could think of to save him—giving him endless freedom, but mostly giving him endless consequences and no freedom, but neither had worked, and now he lived in his car. So she went to meetings, did not drink, swept her own side of the street, and released him to his higher power. He was a child of God, too. She said, "God does not have grandchildren."

Elizabeth smote her own forehead—she'd forgotten again that she was not Rosie's higher power. The speaker noticed, and they exchanged smiles. Elizabeth went up afterward and thanked the woman for that line.

She called Lank later. He was her expert in mutant teenage behavior. More than anyone she knew, Lank had seen the result of parents' not setting clear boundaries—gifted teenagers going down the tubes, parents' lives and hearts destroyed.

"What do I do?" she asked. "Do I give her freedom and a long leash, wait for her to blow it in a big enough way for me to use heavy artillery? Pray that she survive? Or do I try to rein her in and hope she finally stops?"

As usual, he did not answer right away, but she felt him draw close. She shut her eyes and leaned over as if their shoulders could touch. Finally he said, "You're doing the right thing, Elizabeth, asking people with experience to help you find your way. Rae swears by Anthony's counseling, for the kid and the parents. My experience with kids who are into drugs and alcohol is that they will get high, until the consequences become intolerable. So the parent can create consequences, by taking everything away—freedom, computers, and so on—but then you have to endure the kid's hatred of you. And besides, kids will find a way to score anyway. They're like trapped rats."

"I know you mean that nicely," Elizabeth said. They laughed quietly and returned to shared silence. She listened to his light breath, pictured his monk's strawberry tonsure, the rainforest-mammal brown eyes. "When I was a teenager," she said, "and I went out to drink with my friends, it was like we were slot cars on predetermined courses. We'd walk in the same old ruts and grooves every time, like it was preset, and they always led us to the same messes. But did it stop us? No way."

"It's like a board game," he replied, "the teenage doper equivalent of Chutes and Ladders, or Candy Land. Only they land on Whirly Head, or Grutty Bedroom, or Pool of Puke."

She laughed. "That's great, Lank. Can I give it to James?"

"Of course."

She sighed, and ran her hand through her hair. "But some kids land in the morgue or jail. And Rosie's not going to fold up her board—she loves the game. She lives for it. And even when she puts a week or so together of clean time, that whole milieu, the Parkade, it's like Velcro."

"But if she doesn't pull out on her own, you may have to fold up the board for her."

"You mean by sending her away? I don't think James and I could do that."

Lank was silent again, and this time she could not hear his

breath. Then he said, "James could." She knew Lank was right, and it angered her, and it was her one ace in the hole.

◉

At bedtime, she set a trap for Rosie. "Sweetheart," she asked, undercover again, this time as a masseuse, "how was the meeting?"

"We didn't go. We went last night, but tonight we changed our minds at the last minute, made a fire at Fenn's and read—I read a book of his while he paid bills. Berryman's *Dream Songs*—he had it, can you believe it? James has the same book in his study." She held up a tattered copy as proof. Elizabeth had loved those poems so much. She and Andrew had read them out loud to each other in bed exactly one lifetime ago. He would have adored this daughter of theirs.

The next morning Rosie was so churlish at breakfast that Elizabeth wanted to scream.

"I can't believe you think it's okay to eat like that," Rosie said to James, sneering, as she walked past the table where he sat wolfing down his cereal.

"I always eat this way, Rosie. Way too fast, like a rat, okay?"

"It makes me sick," she replied, pouring herself a cup of coffee. Elizabeth had wrapped an English muffin with peanut butter and jam in a paper towel for Rosie to eat on the way to school, and she stuffed this into her jacket pocket. "My mother hates it, too," she sniped at James from the door, as if suddenly possessed. "It reminds her of her mother, eating bacon. She told me that once, when you first started going out."

"Jesus, Rosie," said Elizabeth, looking contritely at James. It was true, it used to drive her crazy, and still could, but he waved it away.

"That's amazing you remember that from ten years ago, missy, since you can't seem to remember to flush various products out of sight."

"That's disgusting, James."

"It's true. You're almost eighteen and you didn't flush last night."

"How do you know it wasn't Mom?"

"Because Mom flushes," he replied. "Everything that has ever been inside her, except pee."

"You're a pig, James." She turned in fury to the counter, picked up a vegetarian sausage Elizabeth had made for breakfast, and flung it at James. "You hate life."

In a split second, James, with an oily bullet hole on his T-shirt, leapt up and grabbed her by the wrists, but she was bigger than he was, and just as strong, and she twisted away.

"Eat your animal flesh, James. Go ahead. You're like the trappers in San Francisco Bay, who picked off all the otters last century."

"I didn't kill any otters," Elizabeth offered weakly.

"Yes you did, darling, remember?" James said. "That one time. Remember?"

"Don't mock me!" Rosie thundered. "Your whole selfish generation has helped kill off this planet!" She stormed out the door.

"Come home after school, you're grounded," James shouted, but the door had already slammed. It was doubtful she'd heard. Then the door opened again, and she shouted, "It was easy to kill otters, because they trusted humans! How does that make you feel?" Then the door slammed again.

He came to sit beside his wife at the table. "God almighty, Bertha," he said.

"Jesus. She's gone nuts again. Just like that." She snapped her fingers.

"We need help," he said.

She sat with her chin on her chest, eyes closed. James sighed, shook his head, and lifted her chin with one finger. "It's good that we're getting the otter thing out in the open, baby. If you don't get it out, you can't let it go."

They sat holding hands at the table. Rascal came in, yowling for food. James got up to feed him. "Look at poor innocent me," he told the cat. "I was eating muesli!"

▣

Several days later, Elizabeth and Lank drove out to the lagoon. They sat on the bank where she and James had hiked a week before, not far from Lank's favorite barbecued-oyster joint. James was going to meet them here and treat them to lunch, in exchange for letting him steal their observations. Lank and Rae were on a new diet, mostly seafood, vegetables, and fruit. His face, shaded by a Giants cap, was wider than when she'd last seen him, fat, fair, and open as the man in the moon's.

"Lank?" Elizabeth said. "Do you believe in evil?"

The tide was high today. A thousand birds flew overhead squalling, gulls and terns tracing the shape of the sky, the dome, the globe, swooping for food, frogs and crustaceans and worms.

"You mean outside of our addictions, puritan guilt, projections, domination, and generally despicable behavior? You mean like a force? The Big Bad? You mean like Henry Kissinger?"

"Yeah. Like a grim force loose in the world."

Lank thought this over. "You mean besides the depravity of human will?" Elizabeth nodded. "Some sort of dark intelligence that's pitted against God, and goodness?" She nodded again. Lank handed her the binoculars. "You mean like—" Elizabeth laughed and jabbed him with an elbow. "Nah. Not really. If I say Rae does, will you think she's a wingnut, like Oral Roberts, and get a new best friend?" Elizabeth nodded.

"I know she thinks the drug trade is evil," he said. "But we haven't lost her entirely. She's not about sulfur and rats, or Al Pacino as Satan. Yet."

"But you don't believe."

"No. I believe in extremely sick people. I believe in extreme childhood abuse that leads to sociopathic adults. I believe in loose screws."

"I feel that dark forces are around the kids now, in this town and in their minds, and in the world. Lank, did you know Rosie smokes?"

"God, I hope you haven't said anything to her about it," Lank said.

"Why?"

"Look, I'm a high school teacher. And rule one is, Any idea which comes from the parents must be resisted."

"I keep forgetting that."

"Oh, sure. My parents used to send me helpful things from *Reader's Digest* like 'I Am Joe's Lung.' That alone added seven years to my smoking."

The lagoon smelled so much sweeter at high tide, less gucky and fecund, less like frogs. It smelled of fresh nutrients, a salad bar for crustaceans.

Later James scribbled down everything they said on his paper placemat at the Oyster Corral. Lank said, "The fish travel in clumps, the birds fly overhead in clumps—as above, so below."

Elizabeth gazed at Lank's peaceful face as James scrawled away. Lank had taken off his cap, and the sun poured through the window above the beach directly onto his head. His thin red hair caught the light, like saffron threads in glass, just as it must have when he was a baby.

They had all been heavy smokers once, and all considered quitting to be the hardest thing they'd ever done. James and Lank agreed that the more parents tried to get their kids to quit, the longer the kids would smoke. Elizabeth thought about all the ways she could try to persuade Rosie to quit, and started to offer her ideas, but James interrupted. "No, darling, Lank is around teenagers all the time. Listen to what he says."

"I think I'm right about this, Elizabeth. Helpful parents get in the way almost all the time, even when they're right—especially when they are right."

"I wonder what Rae would say." Elizabeth sounded mournful.

"I already know the answer," Lank said. "I actually asked her once what Jesus would do about my students who smoke, because at one of the reunions at my school, there was a woman who had early-stage emphysema. Rae said he would have held his tongue. That Mary had one very stressful encounter with him when he was an adolescent. It's when he gets lost one day, for a long time, and she and Joseph finally find him in the temple. They do not beat him senseless. Mary just gives him the stink-eye, and asks, quietly, 'What the *fuck?*'"

"Rae didn't say that!"

"She did!" Lank replied. "Then Mary gets him back home asap." James wrote this on his placemat. "Seriously. She doesn't order him to never return to the temple, or he would have snuck back the first chance he got."

"Let's enforce the drug laws at our house, Elizabeth. And release her to her own higher power when it comes to smoking, grades, and so on."

"But if someone had stopped that high school girl from smoking, she wouldn't have emphysema now." Still, she wondered whether the men were right.

Lunch was lovely—calm, fun, delicious, the best she had felt in a while. But half an hour after she got home, she left a message for Robert Tobias on his answering machine.

◘

He called back after dinner, and Elizabeth heard Rosie pick up the extension. "Rosie, hang up," Elizabeth told her. "Hi, Robert." She heard a click, and then silence. "Thanks for returning my call." And then Rosie burst in on the phone.

"My mother called *you?*" she shouted. "You traitor, Mom. Mata Hari."

"Hang up, God damn it." Rosie hung up loudly. Elizabeth shook her head: he must think they were crazy. "Sorry, Robert."

"That's okay," he said, but he sounded skeptical, as if expecting gunfire to ring out.

"I called because I'm a bit worried about Rosie, and wanted to make sure she's doing okay in chemistry."

"To tell you the truth, she isn't the pistol she was last semester. Her work is definitely off. How much detail do you want? She does fine with the warm-up problems most days, but doesn't join in the review of the content we've been studying in the textbook, or the current event in science we're discussing. Her lab partner is carrying more than his share of the work. She seems distracted, and vaguely annoyed."

"That's what I was afraid of."

"She's a brilliant girl, but she's been late a few times with her homework."

Elizabeth hesitated before asking, "Can she still get an A, though?"

"She can get a B-plus for the quarter if and only if she aces the big test next week."

"God. What a difference a summer makes."

"It's probably senioritis. Tell her to get her butt in gear. A B-plus shouldn't hurt her on her college apps."

"Okay."

"Is there anything else?"

She *almost* told him about Rosie's crush, but she had already done enough damage. Rosie would be livid. "No," Elizabeth said. "That's all." After she hung up, she knocked on her own forehead. Then she went down the hall and knocked on Rosie's door. Silence. Then a long-drawn-out "God," followed by a sharp "What?" Elizabeth gingerly let herself in.

"Darling, I'm sorry I did that behind your back. I was worried. I'm your mom and I'm paid to be anxious. I was afraid you weren't even getting an A-minus or B-plus, but he said you will if you do well on next week's test."

"I already knew that, Mommy, and it's humiliating that you called." Rosie stared at her from bed. "I'm happier than I've ever been. I'm doing fine in school. I gave you a clean urine test. I'm going to meetings with Fenn. Will you please be a little happy for me?" Elizabeth picked at her cuticles and nodded. "I'm a good kid, Mom." Elizabeth so wanted to believe her. Rosie was her outside heart.

Elizabeth followed them to a meeting again two days later,

and after they went inside, she raised her fist in victory. But the next afternoon, when she picked up Rosie for a dentist's appointment, she swore she could smell a hint of marijuana when Rosie slid inside the car. And Rosie went nuts when she mentioned it: "Sniffer dog! Let's go straight home so you can test me."

Elizabeth talked her down, and Rosie got her teeth cleaned, and when Elizabeth sent her into the bathroom with a piss test that night, it came out clean.

Two days later, it happened again: Elizabeth could have sworn she detected the smell of burnt grass in Rosie's bedroom. Rosie was on the bed, cramming for her chem test, clear-eyed and minty, and watched Elizabeth with pity as she stopped to sniff the air like a squirrel dog. And again, clean urine.

This time in the bathroom, holding a cup with her daughter's no-longer-warm pee, the dipstick negative for everything, Elizabeth thought she smelled disinfectant, and felt a pang of fear. She sniffed around for the source. She went to get James, who was stretched out on the couch with his *New Yorker*. "Please don't make me get up," he begged. "It's not unusual to smell disinfectant in a bathroom. Even in ours." She let it go, although she checked out the medicine cabinet, and under the sink—for what, she did not know. Nothing was out of place. She wondered again if she was going mad.

If she wasn't, it meant Rosie was lying. Elizabeth's mind was better than it had been in the past, still troubled and obsessed but not desperately so. It may have had to do with her going to extra meetings, now that she went at least once more a week after spying on Rosie. It might be that she was finally on the right medications. But for perhaps the first time in her life, she now had the conviction that when she thought something was going on, it was.

The next time, before letting Rosie go inside the bathroom with her plastic cup, she frisked her daughter's pockets. Rosie sneered at her. "You're getting worse, Mama. Next you'll want to do a cavity search, and you'll still find nothing. Poor Mommy."

◘

When Rosie brought home a B on the chemistry test, Elizabeth tried to be reasonable about the end of a straight-A transcript, surely not the end of the world. But when she searched for and found Rosie's journal and discovered the sporadic entries were in French, her first reaction was panic. Then she felt a stab of embarrassment and hurt feelings, which turned into slightly amused admiration. Rosie had trumped her. So one day Elizabeth called Adelle Marchaux, who said Rosie was getting an A, and behaving well, except when she and Alice were too silly. *"Elles se comportent commes des enfants,"* Adelle trilled with mock annoyance: they behaved like children. Then Elizabeth rechecked the shelves, the bathroom drawers, Rosie's room. Nothing but her birth control pills and matches—no papers, pipes, prescription drugs. Then she called Anthony at Sixth Day Prez. He made time for her to come in.

◘

He had gained weight but was still what Lank had once dubbed homely-lovely. His coffee-colored skin had a few more wrinkles, his smooth white hair was thinning, and his eyes were tired behind horn-rimmed glasses. He hugged Elizabeth so fervently in a bear hug that she was afraid he would lift her off the ground and hurt his back, or hers.

"You've created a marvelous, magical child," he enthused,

sweeping his arm around the cluttered kumbaya office, full of art, candles, poems, batik. "Half of the art on these walls was made by our children under her guidance this summer." A flock of origami doves flew at various levels from his ceiling, clumsy ceramic crosses hung from the walls, along with a banner of finger-painted palm prints.

"Tell me what brings you here," he said finally, looking at Elizabeth, and although she had confided in him before, she let everything pour out this time—the pills they had found in the summer, and the papers and pipes and the alcohol, and the Visine, the smell of weed, and the times they'd found out she had gone to a rave with Alice, the endless layers of lies and half-truths, footprints in the flower bed beneath her bedroom window, her getting busted at the party on the hill, the recently imposed twenty-eight-day test period, and the clean urine tests.

Anthony steepled his fingers, nodding until she was done. She was going to confess that she had trailed Fenn and Rosie to some meetings, but really, this made her look irrational. As Anthony began to speak, Elizabeth interrupted: "I do smell dope, Anthony. She says she's clean and going to meetings, but I tell you—I get whiffs of it."

He smiled, sad and kind. "I believe you." She felt a flush of relief. "Let me ask you a question. Who would you say is running the show?"

The question caught her off guard, and she laughed ruefully. "James would say she is. She's almost never grounded these days. She's mouthy, and we just let it go."

"And who would *you* say?"

"I'm not sure. It depends. Maybe we're too concerned with her happiness. We walk around on eggshells. If she's sweet and calm, then we can be, too."

"Ching ching," Anthony rang out. "Like Reagan trickle-down, right?"

"Right. Just like it was in my family."

"Ching ching," he said again. She tried not to laugh. It reminded her of the adding machine her father had used with such misery at tax time, the mechanical sounds punching through the silence, the crunch when the handle was pulled, the bell to announce a sum total. But what was the sum total here?

"Ching ching, what?" she asked.

One of Anthony's front teeth was perpendicular to the others, as if someone had turned it ninety degrees before the pink clay of his gums had set.

"This is a very common pattern, where, if a certain person in the family seems to be okay, the entire family can function. Look," he added, "it's hard, the hardest thing you will ever do, to live with a druggy teenager. I've been through it."

"She gets a four-point-two average, because she gets A's in AP classes, or did until this semester. . . ."

"Oh, so she's not druggy? Then I'm not clear on why you are here."

"Okay. She has been druggy. Definitely." Elizabeth clasped one hand to her chest. "Oh my God!" Her eyes filled with tears. "I don't think I've ever said that out loud. But you made her sound like Janis Joplin. And the thing is, she's going to meetings, and seems to be staying clean."

"Seems to be. But you still smell dope, right? Let me ask you something else: Is she sexually active?" Elizabeth nodded, and told him about what the other girls did at parties last year, and how she wasn't a virgin, and now was madly crazy in love with Fenn.

"And they're using condoms?"

"Yeah, she's got boxes. She could open a 7-Eleven. Plus, she's on the pill, and she swears they use condoms."

"But you've caught her lying how many times?"

Elizabeth nodded slowly. "That's a good point."

"So let's assume she is having unprotected sex, and therefore she's exposed to whomever he's had sex with in the last six months. And can we assume that he is monogamous now?" Elizabeth nodded.

"Oh, yeah—they are both totally in love with each other."

"And all the women he's slept with in the last six months were clean of AIDS, STDs, and hep C. What about the ones he slept with in the days before Rosie, who wouldn't have shown up yet? And another thing—we know that he's never used needles?"

Elizabeth's mind was a fever dream of all the dirty girls Fenn had slept with, girls he would slip out the back door when Rosie was climbing his steps. Then she switched to thinking about Rosie in a coma in a hospital, waiting for a new liver.

"So this is already a huge breakthrough day for you, Elizabeth, having this discussion. Facing these things head-on, these considerations." She was glad to hear that, because she felt frantic despair. Anthony peered at her from underneath his brows, as if looking at a crying child. "Now, let me ask you. Under your care, she's done booze, Ecstasy, Valium, Percocet, smoked joints laced with angel dust, and now is having unsafe sex and smoking cigarettes. My question is, When does she turn eighteen?"

"Not for a few months."

Someone knocked on Anthony's door. "Five minutes," he called. "I'm very proud of you, Elizabeth. This has taken a lot of courage. Now let me tell you a few true things. It is your house, and you are the queen of that house, and you get to make the rules.

She is a minor, and you get to demand that she not use any drugs at all, including nicotine. You are responsible for keeping her alive. Rosie needs to play by your rules, and if she simply can't, you need to consider sending her away." Elizabeth gasped involuntarily—how had the conversation escalated to this?

"Nicotine is lethal, and one of the most addictive drugs. Is it still okay for you that she uses it? I ask this of all parents who come: Are you willing to *see* what you are seeing, and to *know* what you know? Are you willing to impose strict consequences and stick to them? If you think she is faking urine tests, do you still let her drive? And if so, who is the crazy person here?"

There was silence in the room while this registered. Elizabeth stood to leave.

"One more question," he said, raising a finger theatrically in the air.

"No, no, please, I can't take it," she said.

"Can you forgive yourself for the mistakes you've made so far—all the times you dishonored yourself by not trusting your own gut and instincts?"

Elizabeth thought for a minute. "Can I get back to you on that?" They exchanged sad smiles. "Can I come back next week? I need this."

"You can come in later today if you need to. But I have to go now."

◉

Afterward she sat in the sun on the front steps of the church, staring into her lap, beginning in her head sentences she intended to say to James that she didn't finish. She scribbled down as much of the conversation as she could remember, tearing up as she wrote Anthony's words about needing to consider sending Rosie away. Then she waved away the very idea, like smoke. Never. She hugged her knees to her chest, wiped her nose on the sleeve of her blouse. She couldn't sort things out. Anthony said no smoking at all, and this made sense, while Lank said children had to run for their lives when you laid down the law, and that also rang true to her own experience. She got up and trudged to her car.

◘

Rosie arrived home that night before dinnertime, clear-eyed and friendly, as if nothing had happened at breakfast. Elizabeth was caramelizing onions to pour over wild rice, and when Rosie came to watch, they ran through the litany—how was school, fine; where've you been, studying at Alice's house; are you and Fenn going to a meeting tonight, probably; how many clean days do you have now, eighteen.

"Wow!" Elizabeth exclaimed. "Fantastic." Rosie shuffled, at once pleased with herself and cool. Then Elizabeth smelled something alien and awful on Rosie's breath, like sauerkraut. She said, "Pew!" and stepped back. "What have you been drinking?"

Rosie burst out laughing, relieved. "Rejuvelac! At Alice's. Do you even know what that is? It's this nasty fermented shit that Alice and her mother swear by—for digestion and energy. I'm going to go brush my teeth."

"Is it alcoholic, though?" Elizabeth tried to appear unperturbed.

"Of course not. It's just a nasty hippie raw-food fluid."

Elizabeth smiled and stirred the onions. They smelled of butter and burnt sugar, but the smell of Rosie's breath lingered in her nostrils after Rosie left the room. It was the smell of rot. The word "ergot" came into her head, and later, at the dinner table, she asked James about it.

"What was it again?"

"Some sort of grain fungus," he told her. "I associate it with the Middle Ages, for some reason, or the Salem witch trials. It grew on rye that had gotten damp, and hungry humans consumed it, despite the taste, and everyone went crazy, and then died."

Rosie studied him, impressed. "You're like a zoo key, James."

He doffed an invisible hat, and everyone laughed and devoured dinner. But peace did not last the night. Before bed, Elizabeth went into Rosie's room with a plastic cup and asked her to go with her to the bathroom.

Rosie protested the timing, but got up, releasing sighs and clicks of annoyance, and pushed past Elizabeth in the doorway. She headed down the hall to her parents' bathroom.

Elizabeth stopped. "Let's use yours tonight, mix things up."

Rosie stopped but did not look back at her. "I'm already practically there."

Elizabeth felt a flicker of alarm but let it go. "What *ev*," she said, mimicking Alice to lighten the mood, but Rosie pressed on, and almost had the door closed before Elizabeth stuck her foot in.

Rosie whirled around. "What the hell? I'm not going to pee into a cup with you here, sitting on the side of the tub like a cop." When she feinted left, as if about to leave, Elizabeth stepped in front of her and took her by the wrists. The air sparked. Silence, as before a storm, or after a slammed door.

"Now," said Elizabeth, staring her down but afraid. Rosie flung the cup into the tub. Elizabeth retrieved it, handed it back. Her daughter's eyes were filled with anger and fear and tears of betrayal. Then she sneered with derision. She put the cup beside the toilet, wriggled out of her cut-offs, glared at her mother.

"I hope you know what you're doing," she said, and the ugliness of the tone sent a chill through Elizabeth. Rosie pulled down her thong as she lowered herself to the toilet seat. Elizabeth saw a flash of dark hair and saw Rosie reach for the cup, but there was only silence. "I can't go," she said, scornfully. "I peed about five minutes ago." She started to stand.

"Uh-uh," said Elizabeth. After what seemed like a long time, Rosie sat back down. Then she hung her head and looked over, solicitous.

"Mommy," she said. "Please just let me pee in peace." They looked at each other a moment, and Elizabeth tried to channel Anthony. She felt she should not leave, but after a moment she did, and waited outside the door like a butler.

When Rosie came out a few minutes later, she handed her a scant cup of urine. The green test strip on the outside of the plastic cup tested ninety-eight degrees. It was fresh and warm, and Elizabeth sat down on the toilet, tipped the cup so it covered the base of the stick, and waited five minutes. The five tiny windows each showed a single pink line, which meant negative. But Rosie definitely had been trying to hide something: Elizabeth squinted at the faint pink lines again, mulling it over. She felt efficient and suspicious at first, like a crime scene detective, then confused, deep in her animal being.

◘

Rosie asked if she could spend Friday night at Fenn's.

"Of course not," said James.

"You force us to sneak around like common criminals."

"Oh, Rosie," he said. "That's the nature of teenage love. Deal with it. You've got it good. As long as you keep producing clean urine, we'll let you use the car, and we'll keep the midnight week-end curfew in place."

"You're so harshing me," Rosie bellowed, bursting into tears. "What's my reward for trying so hard to do well these days?" She smashed her fist against the wall. Elizabeth trembled.

"What a jerk," James said, utterly without sympathy. "Let's go bathe in the moonlight while she stews in her own juices. That would make Anthony happy."

Rosie didn't speak to them again that day, but she was friendly by dinner the next night. She worked on her homework until late. She spent Friday evening with Fenn and was home by curfew, then spent the day and evening with him on Saturday and got home only five minutes late. Elizabeth heard her get up twice in the night, once to pee, once to bang around in the kitchen. On Sunday both of them slept in. James brought Elizabeth café au lait in bed, along with *The New York Times*, and crawled in beside her to read. "Thank you, love," she said.

"I have ulterior motives," he said. "I need you to read my piece later."

She raised the cracked blue bowl of hot pearly-white coffee to her lips, drinking deeply.

◘

Early that afternoon, Elizabeth went out to read on the front steps, under a bright cheerful flag of blue sky. She could see from where she sat that there were no footsteps in the dirt outside Rosie's window, no flowers crushed in the dark, and she wondered as she often did how Jody was doing. She was glad that Jody had left town, even as she hoped that she was okay. She reached for the pencil tucked behind her ear and began James's story, "The Wild

Lagoon," looking for things she and Lank had said that wonderful afternoon. The best thing of all was pure James: "Like Arthur Murray dance steps in the muck at low tide, you see a squirt from a clam when you put down your left foot, and when you lower your right, a crab raises itself and brandishes its pincer at you, menacing, absurd, and magnificent." She corrected typos, made a few penciled suggestions. She was proud of this story.

Before going back inside, she peered in the closed window at her long-sleeping daughter, her ropy curls fanned out over Raggedy Ann pillowcases. She still had the broad shoulders of an athlete, but her waist was as small as a child's, dipping down like a valley between the hills of her breasts and her flanks. She was definitely thinner than usual, but this could be from falling in love, and with a vegetarian smoker, who had gotten her hooked on cigarettes, too.

But when Rosie stirred, and the sheet at her neck fell down, her clavicle showed, white and skeletal. Elizabeth could only stare. She wanted to pound the glass, hard, with her fists against the window, crying out Rosie's name, and then force-feed her milk shakes. She prayed to the speck of something she'd seen at the sweat lodge that wasn't her, and then in desperation to Mount Tam, as the Miwok had, "Do something. Help, please." But she was faking belief. She felt nothing. She tapped the glass, and her groggy daughter opened her eyes, saw her mother, turned to look at the clock, looked back, small smile, and they waved small barely perceptible waves, like spies.

◘

Rosie lay in bed awhile and felt like she was dying. She and Fenn had taken ketamine the night before, and then a few sips of cough syrup to come down. She lay as still as she could, like when she was little, after her father had died, when she used to lie in bed and pretend she was dying, wearing a white Victorian nightie. She and Fenn knew all the drugs that either didn't show up in over-the-counter drug tests, or were easily masked, the way the bleach in the eardrops bottle kept masking the THC in her system. There were other great products out there that totally flushed toxins out of your urine, but only for five hours, and she hadn't quite figured out her mother's test schedule. Definitely one weekend morning, but then maybe once midweek, although her mom hated to send her off to school in a bad state. "Keeps a girl on her toes," she had said to Fenn.

Her parents would be very down on ketamine, Special K, because all the literature said it was a horse tranquilizer, but it was really a perfectly safe drug. It was lovely, or at least the stuff Fenn's connection in San Francisco gave them was fine. Fenn's guy had a nurse he bought from, so it was the good stuff, pharmaceutically pure. It was both deeply relaxing and beautifully hallucinatory, like good mushrooms, like a waking dream. Also, twice they took LSD in the low golden hills, sitting in hippie Buddhist poses, lying together gazing into each other's eyes, feeding each other sections of orange; the afternoon in bed, naked but not having sex, warm and close as she'd ever been with another human being; and then at sunset, on the steps where it had all begun for them, under the crescent of moon.

Rosie was genuinely glad to see that her mother was in less pain since she had started testing negative for everything. She loved her mother and hated that she suffered so. Everyone was more relaxed. Dinners were calmer now, always based on food from Elizabeth's field trips with Rae to the farmers' market. Then she often got to go to a meeting with Fenn, or she would pretend to, and would stay up a little later doing homework. She and James and Elizabeth talked about regular old things at the dinner table. James asked her stuff that he needed for his stories, and this made him grateful, and she loved doing this for him. Like the other night he had demanded to know in his agitated, joking James way how it could be true that a feather and a coin dropped from the Transamerica pyramid would land at the same time. She felt like he was treating her like they were equals.

"Here's my best shot and simplest answer," she began, and tried to explain that gravity acts the same on everything no matter what its mass.

"Theoretically," James qualified. Rosie shook her head: Sorry, Charlie.

James put down his fork and reached for his notebook. You're not going to like this, she warned him, but as far as she knew, it was something that was just accepted, based on lots of experiments and observations. The reason a feather and a penny fell at different rates was wind resistance. The feather was not allowed to accelerate to its full potential of approximately ten meters per second per second, which was the acceleration of *any* falling mass in a vacuum—that is, a place where there was no air resistance. "Slow down," James cried out, and her mother smiled. Rosie had to repeat it. When he finally caught up, she continued. The lighter an object was, and the wider its mass was distributed, the more it was affected by air resistance.

James stared at her with amazement when she paused.

"I'm sorry my explanation is so shallow, but I guess I don't really get it, either," she added, which made them all laugh.

"It was the opposite of shallow," her mother said.

Rosie was on a roll. "It does all seem very counterintuitive, though, right?" Her parents both nodded, and James even had to write that phrase down, too. It was sort of pathetic. Her parents' memories were going, tearing like fishing nets. She wanted them to feel better about themselves, so they could leave her alone. "It's frustrating," she added compassionately, "how much must just be accepted for the explanation to make sense."

◘

All day Sunday she felt so poorly that she didn't even want to get together with Fenn; they talked on the phone twice. He didn't feel great, either, but he was still going out to Stinson to surf. "Want to go with?" he asked, and she almost said yes; just to watch him from the shore was heaven. Yet she sensed that he was only being nice by inviting her, and in the end she said no, she needed to catch up on homework.

Elizabeth babied her with trays of healthy food, but Rosie's mind felt whipped, jangly. Though she wished she could make her mother happy, she wanted to be happy, too, happy and free—was that so crazy a desire? She wanted to be with Fenn every minute she could, wanted to be out in the world, mostly wanted to be done with high school. She took a nap with Rascal and then such a long shower that she used up all the hot water and made James be pissy and have an episode.

She felt like she was always trying to keep six plates spinning in the air, trying to keep her stories straight, trying to keep everyone happy. No wonder she was tired all the time. Monday morning she felt somewhat better. Then her mother had to go and give her a piss test.

"I took one a few days ago," she said, "and it's a Monday. We never do this on Mondays, so I can start the week out on a positive note." But her mother held firm, and marched her into Rosie's own bathroom, as if to trip her up.

Thank God she had finally remembered to put a cosmetic bottle with bleach in it among her makeup and lotions. She closed the door wearily and went to the toilet. You sort of had to laugh about the whole thing—how dogged and determined her mother was, like a little child trying to make letters. She peed into the cup, reached for the Clinique toner bottle, and poured a few drops into the urine.

"You almost done in there?"

Rosie yawned and wiped herself, put the bottle back, washed her hands.

"Here you go, Mama," she said, handing her the plastic cup. She watched Elizabeth check the temperature strip, and was heading back to her bedroom to get ready for school when something stopped her in her tracks: her mother was sniffing loudly, like a cartoon character, only not funny.

Rosie turned around to find her mother's nose deep in the plastic cup.

Elizabeth looked up, wild-eyed, terrified. "Do I smell *bleach?*" she asked, and smelled it again. "Rosie! Is there bleach in this pee?"

TEN

The Fall

◻

Rosie faced her mother, eyes narrowed with disdain even as she felt the ground beneath her turn to sand. Her heart pounded the way it did after the cheapest cocaine, going so fast that she felt like she might be having a stroke, and yet still she sneered with disbelief at such bald-faced foolishness, at her stupid, stupid mother who stood there in the bathroom holding out the cup of pee like it was plutonium. Rosie's mind churned and she desperately tried to figure out the angles. If she went ballistic, she could beat her mother down, deflate the story into something more manageable, and continue her life as it had been. And then there was a second person inside her, composing excuses and words of contrition. She wondered if she should try to calm this crazy idiot by throwing her mother the bone about having smoked one hit with Alice. That would get her to do what Rosie wanted: dial back the drama, love

Rosie again, be grateful for her honesty, and relieved—it could be *so* much worse than Elizabeth imagined. But a third person inside Rosie calmly pointed out that it really was so much worse than Elizabeth imagined, way worse, all the raves and Ecstasy, all the unsafe sex she'd had before Fenn, the times she'd gone down on some guy, all that fucking oral, because he was holding cocaine. It was so disgusting, so shattering to recall, that it stopped her in her mental tracks—maybe she had been out of control for a while—and right when she looked up, her mother got this crazy look on her face where frozen disbelief met rage and weirdness the way it had that day on the trampoline three years ago, and that pierced Rosie, knowing what her mother looked like when she went crazy. All in a swirl like when drugs were coming on too hard, she needed to calm her mother down, needed to sneak out of this mess with her freedom intact; she needed her mother to be strong, she needed a mommy.

Then her mother started to shake, Rosie could see this from six feet away in the carpeted hall, and the first voice inside her came back and she saw that she could win now by going cold, and derisive, although lying might do real damage to her mother, who was tilting her head and looking at Rosie as if she were a speck on the horizon, way far away, and she heard herself saying out loud that she had lied, she had had a hit with Alice at school on Friday—one hit after all these weeks—but then she felt like you do when you see an outlying breaker on the ocean coming right at you and you're thrilled because you think you can catch it and ride it all the way into the shore. It's getting bigger too quickly as it approaches, but you'll still be able to ride it, even though it rises above you, now such a gigantic wave, with so much more water than you could have possibly seen, that it's going to wipe you out, it's going to hurt.

And she glanced at her mother, who was looking into the small cup of pee as if now she were about to raise it to her lips, and the wave came crashing down.

◘

Truth poured forth as Rosie wept from a makeshift mourner's bench on the rim of the bathtub, where she cried over her sins, or at least the sins of the last month. All the grisly details spilled out, the secrets, the lies, the truth, that she had smoked dope a number of times during the last few weeks; that every time she had had a pee test during the last few weeks, she had added some drops of bleach to mask the THC. She'd taken acid, too, once, and 'shrooms, too, with Fenn. Also, she and Alice had sniffed her boyfriend Evan's plastic cement, on his dare. She buried her face in her hands and wondered out loud what was wrong with her.

James, running from the living room, confronted a locked bathroom door. Muffled sounds of Rosie choking for breath followed, interrupted by a tinkle of water. When Elizabeth unlocked the door, he stepped in, taking in the scene as if at a car accident: Elizabeth slumped against the wall, her face pure white, her neck flushed red, her chest heaving. A cup of pee with a stick in it sat by the sink. Rosie clawed her fingers through her hair, trying to pull it out. She insisted that she loved the meetings, the kids there, the whole scene, and was finally done, really fucking done with getting high. She hated herself for what she had put them through, but it took what it took, right?

She repeated this until James robotically told her to shut her up. "Why are you letting her talk, darling?" he asked Elizabeth. She looked at him as if she hadn't noticed that he was there, then bobbed her head around like a wooden toy bird, pecking. Rosie got to her feet, sizing up the situation: James sniffing at the bottle of eardrops that Elizabeth held to his nose, as if it were wine; the cup of pee with two Advent windows turning blue.

"You can test me every day, and I'll go to outpatient rehab—I'll even help pay," Rosie cried at the door. "Believe me, I'm done."

"Honey, that's wonderful," said Elizabeth, and Rosie seemed to think she meant it. Her face was watchful yet safe, like a gopher that has nearly made it to his hole. She slunk away. The unbleached urine was positive for THC and methamphetamines.

"Jesus," said James. "The hits just keep on coming." He stroked the stubble on his chin. "What bothers me is that she admitted to mushrooms and acid, yet those didn't show up."

"This panel doesn't test for those," Elizabeth explained. "How can I be so stunned and numb at the same time?" He shrugged. She dug her nails into her brow, making indentations in the skin, then into the back of one hand, making red half-moons.

"Stop that," he said. "What do you want to do?"

"Maybe outpatient treatment. We can afford it, it's not very expensive. But it didn't work for Jody, they eventually needed to send her away. There's Allison Reid's Adolescent Recovery, which costs a fortune. But one of Allison's big success stories OD'ed her first semester in college. We cash in your SEP-IRA, pray for our own early deaths. I'll call Jody's mother later, see what she knows—she won't know about low-cost programs, because they have money. Alexander's family went through the county program and thought it was great—he graduated early, and got a scholarship to Santa Cruz, but of course, now he's smoking heroin."

"So there's that." He reached out and touched each fingernail of her right hand.

She limped toward their bedroom but stopped at Rosie's door

to listen to the silence. When she opened the door and saw Rosie sitting on her bed incuriously glancing at a textbook as if it were any other school morning, Elizabeth felt a twig snap inside. She slammed Rosie's door so hard she thought it might come off its hinges. She bellowed, opened the door, and slammed it full-force again and then again and again. But still it did not break or splinter. She felt sick and dizzy from the seesaw of trusting Rosie and then being betrayed; from caving, saying yes, when she was more afraid of defying Rosie than of Rosie's safety; felt exhausted from trying to find enough resolve within to say no and then being pilloried by Rosie, from the overwhelming fear of saying either yes *or* no. She opened the door and slammed it closed again, sick of being afraid, of holding her breath, sick of feeling numb, and then feeling the rage. She opened the door and slammed it.

James came into the hall but did not stop her. When she was done, she collapsed on the carpet in the hallway. She heaved for breath. Still James did not come to comfort her, because there was no comfort, and Rosie had been right—it took what it took.

◙

The next day's sky was lower and rich, silver gilt like vermeil. Fall's first snap called for sweaters, and Elizabeth usually loved this, when the sky was washed-out blue and cool until you noticed the low sun on your skin, the fresh briskness of the air. This time, as in the autumn when Andrew died, she wished it behind her, wished to be already months past these miserable heartache days.

She called Anthony, who insisted she call Allison Reid. She did, and was stunned by the cost. She asked if there was a sliding scale for payment. There wasn't. She called the county's biggest outpatient rehab next. Though it was much more affordable, there were no spaces. "But they come up all the time. I'll call you the minute we have an opening. Just hang tight," the receptionist told her, sounding tired.

James wanted to issue a fatwa against Fenn and Alice, or at least a no-contact clause. Elizabeth fought for strictly monitored visits, largely because she felt that this would help maintain whatever peace they could manage and would give Rosie less to rebel against—and something they could take away from her if she fucked up—but also because it would please her. Elizabeth was so hungry for this, and so defenseless against Rosie's verbal freeze, the thin, stilted monosyllabic tone. Elizabeth felt James's impatience with this plan, but to her surprise, he said it was her call.

So it was nighttime young people's meetings for Rosie. Elizabeth and James drove her there together. They planned to stay at each meeting with her the whole time, but she adamantly refused: they would be the only parents. So they agreed to meet her on the porch outside when she was done. Fenn was usually waiting with Rosie when they came to pick her up. Where there had been seven-o'clock curfews for dinner on school nights, now one of them picked Rosie up right after school three days a week, and Alice dropped her off the other two. She had to walk through the door by three-thirty, or she would lose her computer, too. Weekends had been canceled entirely until further notice. If she could put together two weeks of meetings and sobriety, she could meet Fenn for a movie. They would drop her off ten minutes early, pick her up at the theater ten minutes after the movie ended.

Rosie was okay with this at first, relieved if slightly impatient with the new structure. The first few days, she swept through the kitchen like a bear in a campsite, grabbing food. She talked on the phone with Fenn and Alice and did homework. She looked better right away: her skin grew clear, and she began to put on weight. It could have been so much worse. She wasn't allowed to smoke at all, anywhere, and that was sort of a drag. But she bore down on the long-term homework assignments, and took the Valium that Alice had brought her from her mother's stash. Some mornings at school she mixed Adderall and Valium. Nothing else, as she was pretty much on the wagon. She'd thought James and her mother would totally prohibit her from seeing Alice and Fenn, so any time at all with either of them was a victory.

There was even a part of her that liked these quiet days, a chance to settle down and regroup, prove to herself she was fine. Being a senior was actually kind of cool, because you ruled the roost, and people looked up to you. She made sure to get her homework done after school and still had time to check in with Alice on the phone. She had boring but mostly friendly dinners with her parents, and frequent AA meetings with Fenn and the chill kids from town. Sometimes the speakers were so hip and hilarious and wise that it almost made you want to be an AA person. Other times meetings gave you funny stuff to talk about later, like this blonde babe named Cassidy who shared that the pain of betraying her parents had been crippilizing—a word that Rosie, Fenn, and Alice now used all the time. Or at the very least, the hour passed quickly and got the parents off her back. She made it a point to share in a pleasant voice with her parents what was going on: Alice had applied for early admission to the Fashion Institute and RISD; Jody's boyfriend had shipped out to Dubai, and Jody might be coming back from San Diego; Fenn was on a new construction site, in Point Reyes, and he wanted them all to drive out to the coast to see it some weekend. Sometimes, though, it hurt so much to have lost Fenn and her freedom that she felt cold and dead. She tried to stay up about it—this was only temporary. Some days she came home and crashed until dinner. You were exhausted all the time when you were a teenager, stooped with the weight of early mornings, pressure, and backpacks.

"Maybe the worst is over," Elizabeth said to James one day.

"Oh God, don't *ever* say that again. It's the worst possible bad ju-ju. Go get a chicken bone, wave it over the both of us." They continued to wait for the outpatient rehab people to call.

◘

On the second Saturday of Rosie's confinement, her mother dropped her off at the theater to see a movie with Fenn, who stood there like a young Amish man in a white dress shirt. They waved good-bye and turned toward the door. Elizabeth drove away. One of Fenn's roommates had seen the movie, and he told Rosie the high points while they sipped cold canned piña coladas in Fenn's living room on the way to bed.

The movie the following Friday was two and a half hours long, plus trailers, so they took a light dose of mushrooms and sat in his backyard. House finches, goldfinches, song sparrows, wrens; the weather was bright and warm and sweet and cold all at once. He brought out a sleeping bag and they lay on it and looked at the stars, and then they climbed inside to hold each other.

He wanted to make love but she felt shy and cold, and the mushrooms had kicked in hard. It was like the K-hole you hit with ketamine, when you peaked and felt yourself a few feet away from your body, and your body got paralyzed, in a good way. They talked about how he wanted to live in Humboldt County, grow great weed to get ahead, and then convert the soil to organic farming and maybe grow apricots or something. She could go to

Humboldt State, infinitely mellower than the colleges her mother was trying to coerce her into applying to. Rural, coastal, close enough to visit her parents.

They tripped without speaking for an hour or so, listening to the birds in the redwood. Fortunately, they began to come down; she had only an hour until she would be picked up at the theater. He made them fresh-squeezed orange juice, with a bit of vodka to soften the edges. It was funny that her parents hadn't figured that they needed a Breathalyzer.

Over drinks, Fenn looked deep into her eyes, and said, "I want us both to live by different codes than our parents did. This is my only dream. I'm reading a book called *Songlines*, about Aborigines, and I think it may be what I'm looking for. They had a system to communicate throughout the vast lands, which was so alive to them. Like birds do, right? There were invisible paths the Aborigines traveled by, that crisscrossed Australia because the Ancestors taught them that geography had a song—it's alive and singing, and you are never lost or alone, because you can hear it telling you where you are."

"Hey, we're having Ancestors' Day soon at Sixth Day Prez if you want to go," she said. God, how stupid that sounded after what a brilliant thing he had just described. He did not respond for a while, but stroked her shoulders. "Don't you totally love Aborigines?" he asked finally. She guessed she did. They came down gently as clouds.

⊡

J ames," Elizabeth whispered in the dark one night, "Rosie really is doing better." They held each other tightly in bed, and she was about to drop off. She had begun to recognize her life again but still lived for bedtime. The dark was warmer than the light of day had been, skin to skin: it was nice not to see each other's worn faces and flaws. He yawned loud as a dog. She knew every single personal noise James made—grunts when he got up, light snores when he went to sleep, medium snores throughout the night, groans from repositioning, occasional farts, all part of the marital soup. They hadn't made love in so long. She had the sex drive of a haggis, but when he slid his leg between her legs that night, she smiled and climbed on top of him. It was a temporary but very sweet fix. He knew the moves, the combinations, and it was lovely once they started. Then she was able to fall asleep, all thoughts chased from her head.

◙

Elizabeth spent the next few days killing time as pleasantly as possible while waiting for the county rehab to call. One Thursday, she went to an early AA meeting after dropping Rosie at school, and took the ferry to San Francisco afterward with Rae to see a new exhibit at the Asian. Rae looked like a buttercup in the drizzle, wearing a soft yellow parka and a knit cap. Elizabeth enjoyed the boat ride, although the whole time they were on the water she thought about jumping overboard. Her psychiatric meds dulled this desire but did not take it away—she had always wanted to jump out of any window, fall overboard and be done.

Rae's cheeks grew red on the windy deck, and after a while they went inside. Elizabeth bought two cocoas with whipped cream from the bar, and as they sat nursing them below deck something leapt onto Elizabeth's pant leg. It scared her out of her mind. But it was just a grasshopper. She pointed it out to Rae. It looked like a husk, desiccated and vigorous at the same time, a seedpod that could spring way high.

The grasshopper quivered a moment on her knee. "Wow," said Rae, bending down low to peer at it. "It's so pretty, isn't it, like dry grass or foxtails." It leapt off Elizabeth's leg to the floor and then into the shadows. Elizabeth clutched her heart as if she felt faint.

"Oh my God," Rae exclaimed. "Do you even understand what a great omen that is? It's almost as auspicious as encountering a cow."

Wary but game, Elizabeth said, "Okay, I'll bite. What does it mean? Money, I hope."

"Someone helpful and distinguished is about to enter your house. True!"

Nothing happened the first night, or the second. But on the third, while heating up soup, Elizabeth heard someone at the door. It was probably Witnesses, or maybe Rae was right and the grasshopper person was here. Maybe it was Ed McMahon. She smoothed her hair behind her ears, and went to open the door.

She found a tall person of nonspecific gender standing or rather jouncing on the stoop, beaming, chubby and beautiful, and it took Elizabeth a moment to recognize Jody in the punk shirt and pegged black jeans, long straggly blond Kurt Cobain tresses and kohl.

Jody cried and threw herself into Elizabeth's arms. Elizabeth half lifted her in a hug. "My grasshopper girl." Jody stepped back and peeked, puzzled, through unkempt bangs. Elizabeth yelled for Rosie: "Rosie, Jody's home!"

Rosie came barreling down the hallway toward them, shouting, "Jody!"

"Ro-Ro." They hugged as if someone had told each of them that the other was dead, and Elizabeth joined them in a group hug, so there were six long arms, women's arms, everywhere, cries and chirps of disbelief. Jody said not to look at her, because she was obese; she looked healthy and soft and sturdy.

"I quit smoking," she announced. "Oh my God, and look!" She pulled up the T-shirt, and Elizabeth thought she was displaying the baby fat on her stomach, but something dangled from her belt, a chain of colored plastic key tags, strung together like soda-can pop tops, whites hooked onto white, then orange, then green. "I have sixty days clean in NA."

Elizabeth gaped. Each key chain was stamped "NA" in black; the white ones said "Just for Today," the orange one "30 Days," the green one "60 Days."

Rosie claimed her. "Come into my room! Mommy, can she stay for dinner?"

"Of course. And call Alice. Rosie's clean, too, Jo!" Elizabeth hugged Jody again and let her go. "Can I ask you something? Are you still with your soldier?"

Jody shook her head. "He shipped out. A month ago, but it's okay."

"Can you believe you fell in love with a soldier?" Rosie asked.

"You love who you love, Rosie. Like you should even talk."

"I know, but I mean, Claude wasn't even a Democrat."

"One more question," Elizabeth said. "Why so many white key chains?"

"I kept slipping. I'd get a week, then Claude would get paid, and we'd buy blow. But we got a month clean together, and now I have sixty days."

"Sixty days!" James shouted when he arrived. "You don't get shit at my Al-Anon meetings. You get wrinkles, tear tracks, and a knuckle sandwich." Elizabeth was serving up black bean soup with dollops of sour cream, a garnish of cilantro.

"Are you going to finish up high school?" Elizabeth asked.

"I told you, Mom. She's getting her GED. Which is exactly what I want."

"Do you go to AA, or just NA?" Elizabeth asked.

"NA. Alcohol counts as a drug, so I'm sober, too."

Elizabeth reached forward to stroke her cheeks. "Oh, Jody. Will you go to College of Marin in the spring—or get a job?"

"Both."

Rosie gave Elizabeth the evil eye. "Mom, what do you think this is, Special Ops?"

Elizabeth ignored her. "Well, want me to ask Rae if they can use help at church? Maybe they need to fill Rosie's old job."

Rae called while Elizabeth and James did the dishes—it was that sort of grasshopping day. Elizabeth caught her up on Jody's surprise arrival, and asked if there might be part-time work. Rae said Jody should call her. Elizabeth headed to Rosie's room, where Alice had joined the other two girls. They were in bear-cub mode, sprawled all over one another on the bed, that thick glossy hair a blur of dirty blond, reddish, and black. Alice was saying, "Are you like a lesbian now?" and Jody said she didn't even know at this point. Maybe, maybe bi. Or celibate. But single.

"I mean, who cares, what *ev*," said Alice. "I *love* that you cut bangs. It's *so* hot."

Elizabeth brought them sundaes to eat in Rosie's room, then threw Alice and Jody out at nine so Rosie could finish her homework.

◘

Within a week, Rosie's coloring and Elizabeth's confidence were restored. Rosie put on five more pounds in Jody's company. They ate cookies at the young people's meetings, doughnuts at NA. Elizabeth went along some nights, and watched with pride and profound relief as Rosie inhaled cheap cookies. Elizabeth lived by the adage that expectations were disappointments under construction, and savored the family's progress from frequent angry chaos all the time, to mostly peace and quiet.

But then, in November, everything came crashing down. Elizabeth fell hard in the middle of the night. She had gone to the bathroom to pee, so tired that she didn't bother with the lights, stepped into the bathroom, and tripped, falling against the rim of the bathtub. She smashed her shoulder on the faucet, her head against the tiled wall, and dropped through pitch-black outer space until she finally landed on the floor.

She heard James cry out in the distance, and some old woman mewing like a hungry cat. James turned on the lights and helped her sit up. Her head, shoulder, and arm were radiant with pain, but after ten minutes, she felt normal again. Her head and shoulder hurt, though not enough to go to the hospital. James wanted her to go, but she refused. They compromised and stayed awake for an hour, icing the worst of her injuries, waiting up in case she got a headache. In the morning, she looked like the Elephant Man, and her shoulder was badly bruised.

Rosie fawned over her at breakfast, calling her hon as she held an ice pack to her shoulder. James had to leave at ten to record his latest piece at the studio in the city, but first he called Rae and asked her to stop by. Rae finally arrived, with a homeopathic ointment for deep bruising, lemon mousse, and the *National Enquirer*. She stayed until noon, then had to leave, as the yearly ancestors' ceremony was scheduled for this Sunday. Jody was gathering sticks for the service as they spoke. Rae helped Elizabeth get dressed in her prettiest blouse, like someone's auntie in an old folks' home. And the next few days Elizabeth felt more scared than ever. She could not shake her conviction that something was up with Rosie, or going on below, in a subterranean realm, although it was nothing she could put her finger on. Yet she could tell, just as she would know if James ever had an affair: it was as if Rosie were impersonating herself, but with only a crescent of her showing, a whole side of her in the dark. Elizabeth wrote on a card in her tiniest script, "Now I am afraid all the time," and tucked it into a book by her bed. The lump on her head receded and the bruises turned to gold, but her shoulder still ached and she felt old and in the way. Worries felt like fishhooks sticking out of her solar plexus, connected by almost invisible lines to Rosie, and she couldn't jiggle them loose.

James said you had to let people sink or swim, but he hadn't let Elizabeth sink. And how could you ask a mother to let her child sink?

Even if things were looking better, all the months of cumulative failure were pulling Elizabeth under. Release might mean that you didn't drown, but what if your child did? She knew that fishhooks connected people only to one another's disease. But that was better than nothing.

Rae said, "Let's see her rising up, okay?" Elizabeth tried; some days went better than others. James said, "We need a united front. Next time she blows it, we put her in rehab—no negotiations, no enabling, and no matter her excuses, promises, hysteria."

◘

On Sunday, James and Elizabeth hiked up the hill to Sixth Day Prez. Below them, fog was burning off, rising in a thick mist through the trees of orange and yellow and red.

But the wild field behind the cottage of worship was almost warm with a low autumn sun; two dozen people in sweaters and jackets milled around a circle of branches in the center of the meadow, while children played at the periphery. Rae waved from a table covered with ribbons and strips of cloth, where the church grandmothers sat.

Not knowing anyone there except Rae, James and Elizabeth walked over to where children were playing Frisbee basketball with yogurt lids and the bucket-kid buckets. Jody was to be in charge of them today, with Rosie as backup, but Rosie was not there. She had borrowed Jody's car to pick up Fenn, Jody explained, and had said she'd be right back. Elizabeth's heart opened and closed like gills. She fiddled with Jody's hair as they talked, and Jody fiddled with the ends of Elizabeth's. Still, no Rosie. Jody's small face pulled closed, like a purse. She stared off at the children, sad, thoughtful, but then her face softened, opened with relief. "Look, there's Rosie," Jody said, pointing.

Rosie had stepped into the field alone, and was standing by a hollowed log in all her towering glory, looking around through the crowd for them. She might have been arriving at a beach party, in dark glasses and a dress with spaghetti straps over a tank top. Most of the grown-ups turned to watch her approach. She had this effect on people. There was just so much of her. She moved so big. Elizabeth smiled and waved, happy and relieved.

Her daughter had an earthy gloss you might find in a garden; everyone else seemed tidy and dry by comparison. Elizabeth had seen dignified men start talking like crickets when they spoke to her, too fast and high.

Rosie waved to her parents and Jody, and came over to embrace them. She handed Jody the keys and said that Fenn had to work all day. Jody headed back to the kids. Elizabeth reached forward to take off Rosie's sunglasses, but she flicked her head to the side. "Hands off," she said. "Don't be touching the princess."

"Aren't you freezing?" Elizabeth asked. Rosie shook her head no.

"I brought one of Rae's shawls if I get cold," she said, and as proof, she tugged at the top of her satchel, and a loosely woven band of lavender rose like tissue.

"Please, baby girl, put it on, I'm so cold!"

"Mommy! Leave me alone. Work your program. Call your sponsor."

Anthony, in a gold and black cap, stepped out from a door in the back of the cottage, and the ceremony began. People made a half-circle around him. He looked at Elizabeth right then, and winked. "We are here to celebrate the ancestors, to thank them for their company and guidance, and to give of ourselves, to be not of the world we see, but of the whole world before us and behind us and around us and above."

Elizabeth looked at her daughter beside her, who watched, enrapt, amused. Elizabeth turned back to Anthony. " 'Out beyond ideas of wrongdoing and rightdoing there is a field. I'll meet you there,' " he quoted Rumi. Then he showed everyone how to carve sticks, scraping off bark with penknives. When his stick was smooth, he wrapped it with threads, ribbons, and strips of cloth. The only sounds were from the children, and from meadow grasses blowing in the breeze. He took bits of paper and announced the names of his ancestors: "Jonathan, loving father, I forgive you. Eva, my mother, singer of songs, rocker of chairs. Louis, beloved grandfather, who taught me to whittle at the lake."

His deep, beautiful voice soothed Elizabeth. He stuck his stick into the ground amid weeds and grasses, some golden, some green. "To rot," he said, like a toast. "To the rot that lets the earth take our loved ones back home." This sort of situation was so Rae and her women at the sweat lodge, like soul arts and crafts, but it was a real stretch for Elizabeth. Side by side with her daughter and husband, she tried to do as Anthony had instructed, as well as she could. Rae was the teacher's aide, going from person to person, standing with each awhile, hearing the names and memories. Over in the children's corner, Jody helped the kids sand sticks until they were smooth and pale.

Anthony said to concentrate on something important—who you are, what you so desperately need—going way back, going forward, in paths, in mist, in darkness, in light. Human, alive, you couldn't understand much of this mysterious world, but maybe our ancestors hungered for us like we hungered for them today.

Elizabeth said Andrew's name out loud. James said his parents' names, Mitch and Dottie, and then couldn't go on. Rosie said, "To Andrew, my daddy." Tears sprang in her eyes, and she wiped them with her hand, trying not to smear the kohl. She left her parents' side. She needed to be with Jody. Also, she suddenly felt funny, woozy, nauseated. She walked toward the children's corner of the field. Ten of the dozen children broke away from Jody and threw themselves at Rosie, like sticky little groupies. She got down in the grass with them and wrestled, tickled and flung, hugged, luxuriating in that precious warm skin.

She remembered all of their names—how bad off could she be? Ava, Lew, Tiana, Sophia, D'ron . . . She swung some of them for a few minutes, but this made her feel more nauseated, so she plopped down in the earth and made a lap for them. Jody called the other children over and they all sorted themselves out, some on top of Rosie's neck or legs or head, some on Jody's, some rassling with one another.

The cough syrup she and Fenn had drunk was hitting her hard.

It was over-the-counter, not even something anyone could test for, except that sometimes the DXM made your urine test positive for PCP. What a stupid fucking idea that had been. She couldn't believe she had drunk it with him; she'd done it only because he couldn't come today and it made them feel close. She was seriously mad at herself. She hadn't meant to have any, she'd meant to say no. Her hands were trembling. She wanted to lie against Jody, but there was no space to do it with all those kids, like Jody was the old woman who lived in the shoe. She and Jody held hands, and she knew Jody could see the tremor, but she didn't say anything judgmental. Rosie had to keep swallowing back vomit.

◘

"We are here for all generations." Anthony's voice broke through Elizabeth's memories. "Our babies, children, youth, adult, and aged, all the way through to the wise ancestors who are always around for us. We feed them by saying, 'I remember you, love you, need you.'"

Elizabeth went to find Rosie, needing to hold her, ecstatic that her girl was here, on sacred ground. She could not find her in the crowd. Finally she saw her, sitting on a bench in the children's area, Jody squatting in the dirt beside her. Elizabeth headed over. Rosie's black hair spilled down over her back, halfway down the lavender shawl she had wrapped around her shoulders. Jody must have said something to her, because she looked up slowly. Jody wiped something from the side of Rosie's mouth, pushed away strands of hair, put her dark glasses back into place.

Elizabeth knelt on one knee and peered into Rosie's face, as if she had complained about having something in her eye. Leaning in, Elizabeth gently removed the dark glasses. Rosie closed her eyes as tightly as she could, and Elizabeth waited. Rosie didn't breathe. At last she sighed, and her lids fluttered open, and she looked calmly back at her mother. Her pupils were full: the pterygium crept from the bloodshot whites to a fine rim of Siamese blue surrounding a total black eclipse of the sun.

How quickly the urge not to make a commotion took over. Instant composure kicked in, masking Elizabeth's dread, even as word went out that something was terribly wrong with Rosie.

Rae came rushing over. "We need the keys to your car," Elizabeth whispered. Rae fished them out of her pocket and handed them to Elizabeth. Rae, James, and Elizabeth led Rosie away in slow motion through the crowd, as if showing her to a seat for afternoon tea. Elizabeth decided on the spot that she would not take her home. People looked toward them and spoke softly with concern. Rosie started protesting, but Elizabeth whispered, "Shh," and they went around to the side of the church toward the parking lot. As they approached the parked cars, Rosie tried to break free, and James gripped her arm. Then he all but shoved her toward Rae's car.

"She's stoned," Elizabeth told Rae. "Her pupils are dilated. What should I do?"

"Take her to the emergency room. Check her into an inpatient rehab." Rae took hold of Elizabeth's shoulders. "Just don't do nothing today. Today, do something big."

◘

It was perfectly quiet in the car. Rosie thought about jumping out at every traffic light, and again when they were on the freeway. She saw herself standing on a mountain, screaming for Fenn. She looked down at her nails, bitten to the quick. So much adrenaline was pumping through her that she had to persuade James to pull over so she could throw up. When he did, she was too weak to bolt into the woods.

◉

The fresh paper under Rosie's body on the examination table crackled as she turned away from the wall. She stared at the ceiling. There was a water stain. That was a little tacky. The attending psychiatrist did not show up for at least two hours.

James and Elizabeth stayed in the waiting room while Dr. Reynolds examined Rosie. James paced. Elizabeth studied her nails and tried to hold back tears. She did not feel like talking. Talking led to thinking, and thinking led back to talking, and for the time being she was done.

She watched movies in her head, of Rosie's peers in failed rehabs. Jody had gone off for three months at a cost of $30,000, and found it very easy to score while in treatment. Then she had used again almost the whole time she'd been back, until fairly recently. A senior named Jane had successfully completed county outpatient, before needing a shot of Narcan during fifth-period art class. Alexander the sweet heroin boy was high his third night home from a sixty-day program. Several of the girls in Rosie's class had been sent from the ER at Marin General, after overdosing on alcohol, to recovery places out of state—one to Montana, two to Utah—and you saw them all the time at the Parkade, buzzed out of their minds. It seemed that most addicts, especially the young ones, needed to try and fail a couple of times. After a full year at Allison Reid, one girl had gone on to Stanford, a total success story, but she overdosed on OxyContin her first semester there and died.

Elizabeth and James did not have the $10,000 to send Rosie off for a month of rehab, let alone three, unless they dipped into her college fund. Also, the odds were good that as soon as Rosie got back to town she would keep trying to figure out how to get high without being busted. There seemed to be no way to stop her. Elizabeth stared fretfully off into space, seeing Rosie on the blacktop of the Parkade, surrounded by burnouts and friends, getting a shot of Narcan in her shoulder or heart. "It's like she keeps climbing into a dryer," Elizabeth said to James. "And her head keeps hitting the sides, hard. So I get in there with her, to try and protect her, to keep her brain from getting too banged up. But isn't that just crazy?"

◘

Rosie lay on top of the crackly paper with her eyes closed. Her parents had come back in, but she did not look over at them. She kept repeating a line from her French test, a mock cooking class on crêpes, using invisible ingredients and bowls: *Utilisez votre main droite pour tourner ce groupe de deux bulles sur elle même!*

"Did you say something, darling?" her mother asked. Rosie shook her head. In the French test, you had to describe cooking something: Use your right hand to fold this grouping of two bubbles over onto itself. What did that even mean, this grouping of two bubbles, *ce groupe de deux bulles*? And she'd gotten an A on it.

Rosie sat up on the exam table, looking like her old self, slightly embarrassed, wary.

"Have a seat," Dr. Reynolds said to Elizabeth and James, indicating two folding chairs against the wall. Elizabeth swiveled around to study her daughter for another minute. Rosie had her best face on; you might momentarily believe that she understood her place in the order of things: a minor, in a psych emergency room, with the head of the department and her parents watching.

"Things are in some ways worse than you may have thought," Dr. Reynolds began. "We've sent off a urine specimen, and Rosie has prepared us to find a medley of illegal substances—mushrooms, cough syrup, alcohol, inhalants, plus prescription Adderall that she buys from a boy at school."

"Inhalants?" James sounded aghast. "In*hal*ants?"

"As a result, she is close to a diagnosis of borderline psychosis, along with deep exhaustion from the use of OTC stimulants and cough syrup." Elizabeth gritted her teeth to hold back the bile. "Obviously, this isn't good, although it is almost surely temporary." James took his wife's hand. "But we've reached an understanding, Rosie and I. Right?" the doctor continued. Rosie nodded. "Why don't we check her in on a fifty-one fifty, a seventy-two-hour hold, while she detoxes. We can help her build her health back up, help her get some sleep. In a couple of days, we'll sit down together and figure out our next move."

"Yes," said James. "We agree. Seventy-two hours. And only the two of us can visit, plus Rae."

Later, Rosie didn't really remember their good-byes, although she didn't think anyone had cried. Her mother had hugged her and said they'd see her in the morning, but the video in her mind of everything else had been erased. They'd been here and then they were gone. She had to share a room with a fat woman with acne who had a clear plastic tube up her nose, and a dust mask on her face. Rosie used the pay phone to call Fenn and tell him where she was, left a message on his machine that everyone was watching her like the Gestapo, so she couldn't call often and he couldn't visit. But she would be out in a day or two, and if he called Alice, Alice could call

Jody. What a joke, she added, that all this had come down because of over-the-counter cough syrup.

She ate the crappy food, and read a copy of *A Passage to India* that her mother had found in the lending library. It was amazing. She stayed in bed. The room was too white and smelled like cleanser. They gave her some syrup to help her sleep. She slept deeply, but as usual, she did not dream. It had been months; none of them was dreaming anymore.

◘

The rain turned to slashing storm around the time that James and Elizabeth crawled into bed. She'd been crying off and on since they had said good-bye to Rosie at the hospital. The whole world was in a deluge. James had phoned a local twenty-eight-day rehab called Serenity Knolls, to see if it would take Rosie for a month—it was close, built on a low hill by a creek, surrounded by redwoods—but he learned you had to be eighteen years old to get in.

"Can you tell us the name of another place?" James pleaded. "If this were your child, where might you consider?"

"I'm not supposed to make recommendations," the employee at Serenity Knolls told him. James took a deep breath. "So I'll just mention that there's a wilderness program in Utah called Second Chance, that's different from the rest."

"We're not looking for a wilderness program—I read that a kid died in one back East last week. But tell me this," James said. "How do you know about Second Chance?"

"I got sent there by my parents when I was seventeen. It's probably why I'm still alive."

Elizabeth stood behind James at his desk and watched him try to log on to his computer, but the phone line was acting up in the storm, and he gave up. He got the phone number from Salt Lake City information, then called and left a message.

"How can we have gotten to this place?" he asked Elizabeth. "She could probably get into almost any college she applies to. But we may need to send her away instead." She nodded. "We'd have to use her college fund. And cash in the IRA that Andrew left for her."

Outside, the rain crashed against the house and the wind howled. Elizabeth read until three, listening to the downpour; it sounded like the surf. Rosie in wilderness? Elizabeth went and stretched out on the couch, then pulled into the fetal position and tried not to throw up. Help us, she cried, feeling insane and numb, a silent roar inside. Help us help us fucking HELP US.

The wind shrieked like oil pouring up out of the ground.

When she was little and it rained, she and her father would walk the dogs down to Harrington Park. He would take a matchbook from his pocket, tear two matches out of it, bend the end of one, and leave the other straight, to distinguish whose was whose. Then they would lay them in the gutter on Appleby Street, which would be rushing with water, and race their matches.

❏

She woke to discover that they had not in fact blown away in the storm, but the cost was spiky fatigue. She had been holding the house down all night with bungee cords. Green redwood branches whipped in the mist like sails, where the day before the juncos had played. Rascal snored beside her. "The storm has been waiting, patiently, grimly," James said, handing her his mug of coffee.

"The storm? Waiting for what?"

"Release. Muttering, creaking around behind something in the closet, till now."

The phone was working again, and he logged on to his computer. She stood behind him and read over his shoulder about Second Chance, and The Camp in Santa Cruz.

"These are places kids run away from. And I bet they hate their parents forever," Elizabeth said.

"I know," said James. "Now leave. Go visit your spawn. I'll find out everything I can."

◘

Rosie slept until seven, and woke up feeling better than she had in weeks—sort of stoned in a mild way. It was storming outside, crazy, maritime, and she loved it. She daydreamed about Fenn, and how she would be out that night, after a shower. Her mother would be here by nine, and if Rosie was clean, smelling like shampoo, totally contrite and like her old self, her mother would help get her out of here. It was ridiculous she was here in the hospital at all, but she could see that it was time to pull her act together. She was freaking her mother out.

She got up, put on her robe. There were ten people sitting around, mostly looking completely ordinary, except that they were in pajamas. She was the youngest person. She had breakfast with a group of four, and they talked about the storm. They all had interesting, poetic ways of talking. One guy about thirty said he'd stayed up all night listening to the fitful wind nag and fret. One aging lady said she thought she'd heard the howl of wolves. The most intense man said Rosie had the best vibe, like she must be great with children. Rosie said yes, she was, that was such an intuitive thing to say, and she told them all about her bucket kids.

Then an older psych nurse came along and broke the peaceful spell by horning her way into the conversation, like she was one of them. Her name tag said "Angie," and had a happy-face sticker next to her name, but she was not happy. She looked like a mixture of Gertrude Stein and Mrs. Danvers from *Rebecca* or like the bad fairy who, at the end of the lovely christening, after all the good fairies had said lovely things and given various talents and blessings, came along and cursed Beauty.

"I seriously need my mother," Rosie told Angie, confidentially, worried.

"You're okay. Visiting hours start at ten. Let's getcha going."

She felt sort of normal again on her feet. All she had to do was kill a couple of hours reading until her mother could come and get her out. Whatever bad spell it was had passed. She glanced at Angie, at those eyes staring right at her, and did not look away, just tried to look composed and bemused as Angie lumbered off. But she had to look down at her bare feet in slippers just to check that there was still a Rosie body there and not a pile of smoldering ashes.

◉

R osie was in the lounge, lost in her book, when Elizabeth arrived at ten. She got up and raced toward her with outstretched arms. They both held on for dear life.

"God, Mommy. I'm so sorry." She shook her head. "Did you bring clean clothes?" Elizabeth nodded. "Did you smuggle Rascal in?" Elizabeth smiled. "I'm so much better. I feel like I've come back from a thousand miles away. And I feel okay today—rested, like me again. Did you bring me a brush? Will you brush my hair?" She turned her head so that her black hair cascaded down her back. Elizabeth fished out Rosie's toothbrush, toothpaste, and lotion, and put them on the table. Then she took the hairbrush, and gently drew it through Rosie's hair, pausing for extra attention to the ends. Rosie reached back for her mother's hand, to stop her for a moment. "I can't believe what I've put you through. I am so starting over—I just got off the phone with Fenn. He understands completely, that we have to start over. Hey," she called to a middle-aged woman, "this is my mom!" The woman, a pretty housewife of forty or so, started pointing with burlesque enthusiasm at Elizabeth like she was the *bomb*, and Elizabeth smiled and waved, the shy celebrity. "So Mama, will you ask Reynolds if I can go home now?" Elizabeth continued brushing. "Say something. I'll go to a meeting with you tonight."

"Rosie," Elizabeth managed to say, her throat closing up, "I offered to look away from it all, if you would stay on campus at lunch. But you wouldn't even give me that much. Another night here won't kill you."

"I changed my mind, I will totally obey you. I swear to God." She whirled around to face her mother.

"You need to stop smoking weed, and taking anything else, till you're eighteen. Period."

"God, this is such an overreaction. It's crazy. I don't want to be like the one Mormon in my senior class."

Elizabeth turned her palms upward. "It's very simple, Rosie. You've been doing weed, Ecstasy, cocaine, getting drunk, taking cough syrup, acid, mushrooms, sniffing glue."

"Glue *once*. Jeez, I can't believe this. You've gone crazy." Rosie stopped reacting then and nodded, as if the second person inside were whispering in her ear, telling her to fake understanding and agreement. She heard her mother say her name.

◘

R osie did not speak during the short morning group meeting, although she found that her face was wet. She would say later, when Elizabeth came back with James, that she was okay with not drinking, that she would quit everything. Study, be with Fenn and her friends, get through senior year. She would say what her parents wanted to hear. There were good prescription drugs at school now, plus Alice still had Adderall. She could make it work. She would stage a moment of clarity later today. Some people from a local AA or NA group were bringing a meeting to the inmates, like little temperance union missionaries. She could win her parents' trust back, do a great job on her college apps, score a scholarship somewhere, maybe San Diego, eventually get to spend weekends with Fenn again. Angie, standing in front of the meeting group in her satanic fashion, delivered a passionate speech on recovery, and how they might make the most of this opportunity. It was just ludicrous, a howler, as Alice would say.

◘

T he storm had begun to subside. Elizabeth and James sat huddled at the kitchen table with papers strewn around them, computer printouts of rehabs and wilderness programs, price lists, photographs of natural beauty and healthy teenage hikers.

"She'll go berserk when we tell her," James said. "She's just going to lose her mind." Elizabeth nodded. "How will we get her to Utah? No way we can afford a transport service. Those cost a fortune, thousands of dollars. This is going to break us as it is."

"I think you and Lank need to fly her there. You'll have to lie, and say it's some kind of weekend program for at-risk adolescents, strong-arm her if she resists."

"You and Rae make more sense, because you're women. But she'd have an easier time escaping from the car than she would if she flew with me and Lank, wouldn't she? So yeah, I'm in."

Elizabeth covered her ears with her hands as if she had sudden earaches. "Are we serious about this? About wilderness? A month in the snow? It's freezing in Utah this time of year."

James looked at her, faking deep concern, tugging at his chin. "Wow," he said. "Bummer."

Elizabeth almost shouted at him with shock and hurt—how could he be so glib, so callous? But she surprised them both when she laughed quietly, and the thin shell that surrounded her heart creaked like fault lines breaking open; her laughable armor of resistance, denial, delusion tremulously cracked like a coat of ice on a muddy puddle, and in the silence that followed, she gazed into her husband's wide green eyes for the answer she already knew.

ELEVEN

Snow

It was snowing and it was going to snow. That was a line from a
poem Rosie had been assigned sophomore year, but she couldn't
think of the name of the guy who wrote it. She could not think
straight or remember simple things, she could only sit in the dark
mutter of her mind, in full hatred and devastation of her parents
and life.

James and Lank had kidnapped her. She was going to be away
for ninety days. It had taken thirteen hours to get to Utah in a car
that Lank had rented because it had snow tires and a children's
safety lock to turn the backseat into a holding cell from which
Rosie could not escape.

They had gone east at Sacramento, cut across Nevada, and
taken her to a renovated cabin in a small town somewhere north

of Salt Lake City. She had slept or kept her eyes closed most of the time, but not when she was upset. They had arrived in a blizzard at night; there were four other silent, furious kids who'd arrived before her, and their parents and duffel bags, and bearded men with clipboards hovering around. A lady found Rosie's name on a computer. Lank had stayed in the car. Rosie had turned her back on James when he tried to say good-bye and how much they loved her. "Fuck off," she said.

She was not allowed to speak to the other kids. They were offered lots of camping snacks, but no one accepted any. Then they were each given a ridiculous pack that weighed fifty pounds, according to the three male instructors, with a sleeping bag and a pad all wrapped up in a tarp that would also be their tent. A cooking tin, baggies of bulk food, a few pairs of dry socks, a journal, a pencil, zip-lock bags of sanitary pads and baby wipes for the girls, toothbrush and toothpaste were tied up into the tarp with what the instructors called p-cords. Rosie had gotten her birth control pills—you couldn't just suddenly stop taking them, or your skin would break out, and the boy named Joel got his Zoloft. An instructor with a goatee escorted them outside and they started walking, just like that. There were three boys and one other girl. The p-cords cut into your shoulders and back. The other girl was screaming that she hated her parents, would never forgive them, and they'd never see her again when she got out. They hiked to a clearing where there was more dirt on the ground than snow, half an hour away, and then set up camp. One of the three instructors made a fire, and the other two helped the kids make tents with their tarps and low branches, thirty feet apart from one another.

She woke in the wilds before dawn, stunned beyond stunned, enraged beyond all words, a frozen deserted ghetto of one.

◘

I t was not snowing right now but there was snow everywhere, and pine trees, hundreds of feet tall. She was sitting against a ponderosa pine that smelled faintly of vanilla, and she was hungrier than she had ever been. There was only so much food in her pack, and it had to last seven days. The younger pines had tops that looked like pyramids. She decided to run off that night as far as she could and bury herself alive in the snow.

There were five silent kids in her tribe. That's what the instructors called it, a tribe, like they were Scouts, two Girl Scouts, three Boy Scouts. Maybe they'd make potato prints later. The girl was like having someone on your chain gang who screeched and sobbed and flung herself to the ground, tripping up and dragging down everyone else. Rosie imagined killing her before they headed out tonight.

The three outdoor instructors were all huge woolly mountain men, and they followed you everywhere.

◘

T his first full day Rosie held snow in her gloved hand until it turned to ice balls, and then threw them at one instructor like a pitcher. He looked back at her with kind and infinite calm. "The gift of patience," he said, "is patience." All of the kids acted out all day, but the instructors had a way of getting you pretty calm pretty quickly. The handsome boy, Tyler, punched the smallest instructor, Mike D., who was only six feet or so, and he just said, "If you hurt me, I still love you. Tyler? I still love you." Tyler wrestled Mike D.

to his knees, and tried to kick him with his boot in his face, but Mike D. caught his foot and pushed him off balance. "However, we *will* tackle you if you go nuts," he said.

Joel cried a lot in the beginning, like Rosie and the other girl, Kath, did, like when they were frozen solid or unable to learn the lessons the instructors taught, like how to set the traps made out of sticks. Joel was a meth-head junior from Chicago, small and ratty with bad skin. All the kids had exchanged whispered shreds of information and then gotten called on it because they were not allowed to talk to one another yet. This phase was called isolation, and the instructors said the idea was to throw you back on yourself.

Tyler was black-haired and arrogant. Joel never looked anyone in the eye, but he was good with his hands and could make the traps. Jack was kind of a goofy Arlo Guthrie knock-off, who didn't talk much but made funny googly-eyed faces.

Kath was skinny and slutty-pretty with scraggly dyed black hair. There was no way she had done well in school. She flung herself onto her back like a turtle every fifty feet when they hiked, and they had to wait for her to get up, while they froze to death. She definitely needed to be here.

They hiked for hours, lugging the hefty packs through the cold, heavy snow like prisoners of war, and Rosie laughed bitterly to herself, about her mother's conviction that parenting was so hard, oh, oh, it was *so* arduous, like Bataan. Yeah, right. After a couple of hours, they made camp. All of them had to set up their own tents, using their tarps and trees, quite far away from one another. Even though she felt nothing for the people here, she hated the isolation of sleeping so far away from others. At the Parkade, you felt inclusion, you were locked into your people, but here the instructors were doing divide-and-conquer or something, so you got that when you're so solitary, you're also absurd.

She was too tired to run away and kill herself the night of the first full day.

By the second morning her skin had broken out and there was no mirror, so she picked at the zits and they bled. There were no combs or brushes, so you had to use your fingers or else your hair would start to dread. She should let that happen, plus let her nails grow long and black so that when they found her body, she would look insane from what they had done to her, like Howard Hughes at the end. Being here skanked you out. You could only take a billy bath, using a sock to wash yourself with water drawn from the river in billy cans. She was lonely as a loon, with an unfamiliar inside crazy laugh bubbling up from within. At the Parkade, your voices united together in a song, called We. Out here each person's voice was thin and reedy and waiting to blow away.

□

Elizabeth cried hardest at three every day, when school let out, even after James pointed out that Rosie came home in the afternoon only when she was grounded, and how rude or distant she'd be. Elizabeth threw up the first time she remembered that Rosie would not be home for Christmas, even after James reminded her how awful Rosie had been last year, withdrawn, spoiled, needing to be told two and three times to set the table, to ice the cinnamon buns and recycle the wrapping paper from her glut of presents.

James tried to make Elizabeth stop crying, until he called his sponsor, who told him to get off her back. It was what she needed to do, and besides, something beautiful was being revealed. James told him, "I am never going to call you again," but then called him that same night and asked him what was so goddamn beautiful about his wife's broken heart. "Truth," James reported to Elizabeth. He looked years older in three days, blackish-red half-moons under his eyes. With his reading glasses on, he resembled a little old man. Elizabeth lay on the couch petting Rascal like a post-lobotomy patient. James slid underneath her feet, and placed them in his lap, and pretended to chew on the big toe of her left foot through the sock until she laughed for several seconds. But a few moments later she was crying as if the sorrow came in on the same wave as the laughter.

He made them both ginger tea. A moan of comfort escaped her. "I am temporarily semi-okay," she said. They sat in silence, sipping their tea. "I used to drink this when I was pregnant with Rosie. I had the worst morning sickness." She inhaled the scent. "Andrew was much happier than I was about having a child. I was afraid of how doomed you would be as a parent. And I was right." Her reading glasses fogged up with steam, and she took them off and put them on the coffee table and screamed.

◻

The girls combed their hair with their fingers and braided it. This was one of the few things that calmed Rosie's rabbity freaked-out mind, besides the sheer physical exhaustion. Every morning they broke camp, hiked, set up their tarp tents in a new site, gathered wood, and failed at fire instruction. The instructors said, "You'll get it, we promise," and the kids' hands bled.

Rosie obsessed about how long ago the first night seemed, the line of demarcation between all she had ever known and this new, alien existence. Time was all swirled up into a tangle, but she could still see the raggedy-ass cabin where this had all begun, the so-called

SAR base, where she had been discarded by James and Lank. The cabin was used by search-and-rescue teams that operated in the mountains here. It was like a motel in the movies where all the promiscuous teenagers get killed. There was a box of shitty food for dinner, pita bread, peanut butter and jelly, granola bars, yogurt tubes. The instructors said, "Trust us. Eat the yogurt. You're going to wish you had." But all of them refused to eat, like six-year-olds.

Hiking out that first night, Rosie had thought they would at least sleep cuddled together like freaked-out puppies, but instead they slept apart and she was scared to death all night. That night they got all their food for a week, which they were living on now—bulk hippie shit in plastic bags with twists, not even ziplocks except for the Kotex: oat flakes, powdered milk, raisins, dried fruit, sunflower seeds, bouillon, rice and lentils, and that was it. There was also this carcinogenic powdered-cheese product the instructors called "cheesy," and a tin cup with a handle, sort of a tin bowl you could put over a flame.

The second night the instructors made a big fire for all of them, but threatened that this might be the last time they did. They would need to start making their own, or live on dried fruit and cheesy. "So let us begin," said the instructor named Tom. He looked like a basketball player who had gained fifty pounds and joined a militia. He told them to dig holes in the ground with sticks, and then gave them each an Altoids box with a hole in it, and a small square of red cotton. They put the cotton in the tin, and their tins on top of the fire.

After a while, you could see a little flame poking out of the holes, and Rosie got two sticks, like the two instructors were doing, lifted her tin out like someone eating Chinese who didn't know how to use chopsticks, dropped the tin into the hole she had dug, and then buried it. When she dug it out, the red cloth inside was black, and fragile, burnt but not ashen. It was called char cloth, Tom said, and he gave them waterproof plastic containers, smaller than film canisters, to carry them in. The instructors also passed out quartz rocks that the kids had found themselves at that day's site, as well as steel handles, and showed them how to make a fire. Rosie did not pay attention to how you used the char cloth and tinder, the steel and quartz, because to do so would have indicated a willingness to participate in this charade. She was desolate, enraged, hating her parents, psycho-homesick, all these things at once. It was the worst she had ever felt, except for one time on acid when she had believed she was buried underground.

She daydreamed endlessly of Fenn and her friends on the steps of the Parkade at night, definitely some of them looking druggy and vacant, like they had washed up on the concrete shore, but the others so happy and plugged in to one another and to the sense of ongoing transactions, and not just drugs, but stuff that filled and defined them: their music, most important; woven bracelets they tied to each others' wrists; maybe a pipe; sometimes little things they had stolen, like turquoise jewelry, harmonicas. Under the sun and stars, just like here, but free and safe as carrier pigeons at their home lofts.

Tyler got his fire going the fourth night, and the instructors showed them how to make rice and lentils in their tin camp cups, letting them use Tyler's fire, and it tasted so great, though she hated to say so, especially with a bunch of cheesy on it, and sunflower seeds; she was starving. She loved it. She must be losing her mind. You stirred your food with a twig, and one of the instructors told them not to let the food stick to the cup, to wash the cup right away after eating, because they had to use it again in the morning for oatmeal, and anything you didn't wash off was going to haunt you then.

She lay sleepless in her sleeping bag, under the tarp she had tied to a tree, and she thought about dying in the cold, but mostly she thought about Fenn, his body so warm and tawny, his lips so soft and insistent, the feeling of sleeping in his arms. She wondered what it would be like to make love with Tyler, or get high with him, even on something legal, like salvia. She and Fenn had done salvia a few times because it didn't show up on the urine tests. You could buy it right in town, over the counter at any head shop in the county. It was a legal herb, in various concentrations, on the shelves in the store right across the street from the bus kiosk on the north side of the Parkade.

She got so depressed thinking of her old life, way back in history, like last week. Her heart was like a little dead animal. What had she done that was so terrible that her parents had to ship her to this place? Later she calmed herself, because she had to stay strong; she had to put on her game face tomorrow, try to start a fire, try to get released as soon as possible. She replayed great Ecstasy nights in her mind to hypnotize herself, replayed entire tennis matches, tennis lessons with Robert, sitting together talking in the grass by the side of the courts, acid trips, French finals, making love with Fenn, movies, meals. Salvia was sort of ridiculous if you thought about it. She and Fenn and Alice had taken it together. Jo had never done it—it hadn't really been around when she was using. Plus now she was so into collecting her NA plastic key rings. You smoked salvia in a bong. You used a butane jet lighter so you could suck in the maximum smoke possible. It was totally legal. If you took five times extract, 5X, you went cartooning, but it left you on earth, which was totally a blast. With 10X you were still on the planet, but the planet had changed a little, for the better, a yellow brick road and a gingerbread house, really fun. And with 40X, you were ripped out of the world for a minute. It was so great. God, what if someone could get hold of something here? She and Tyler could get high together, under the white stars that broke through the black sky like the flames in their Altoid boxes.

For some reason the first twenty-four hours of her being here were never far from her mind. In the morning, the instructors had cooked oatmeal with raisins over a fire Tom had made, and pow-dered milk, which was basically foggy water, and then they broke camp. Rosie had memorized every detail of the hike from the SAR base to the first campsite, committed every detail to memory, because she was going to run away. A girl Rosie knew had snuck out of wilderness in Montana and hitchhiked home. Her parents hadn't made her go back.

Rosie and the others had to write in their journals for an hour every day. She marked off days on the back page like a prisoner. Up at dawn, breakfast, filtering water in the Nalgene bottles, break-ing up the old camp, learning wilderness skills and lore from the instructors, trying not to die of the cold, hiking to the next site, setting up the new camp, listening to the wilderness instructors, waiting for Bob to arrive.

Bob was pretty cool, actually. He was a therapist who came around lunchtime every day, occasionally with baked treats from women who worked in the office back in town, and the kids got to talk to him for an hour. He looked to be in his thirties, maybe forty, not as tall as Rosie, with gray hedgehog hair and wide, thoughtful brown eyes and wire-rimmed glasses. She ranted about Fenn with him, about what a rip-off this was, about her perfect grade-point average, and how she missed her life, how much she hated her mother and was going completely crazy, how her mother and James had taken acid when they were first together, how she'd found her mother drunk on the bathroom floor a few years ago, how she could feel the hair under her arms growing in like a wolf's.

She told him how afraid she was of going crazy, and asked when could she call Fenn and Alice and Jo, which turned out to be never, although they could write, and she could respond the second month, when they were inside the hogan by the river. She'd see her mother and James in three weeks.

She told Bob she had been sort of in love with her teacher Robert, had taught him tennis all summer and fantasized about going to bed with him, and how Fenn had come along and saved her from that. Robert had a wife and all these little children—it would have been a complete disaster for everyone.

"But weren't you able to see on your own what a terrible idea it was—and so, not do it?"

"We'll never know now. I think he wanted it, too."

"It's common for high school girls to fall in love with young teachers. It doesn't make you a bad person. But it also doesn't mean Fenn saved you—except he actually helped you fail more quickly."

"What if I kill myself with a sharp stick?"

"You wouldn't be able to, at least not for another couple of weeks when we give you knives. We care that you want to damage yourself. We know how it is to have such feelings. We want you to learn to live with those feelings without having to hurt yourself."

"Fuck you. I'm going to smoke dope as soon as I get out."

"We're not drug bounty hunters. This is a place where we try to leave you off better than we found you. That's all we can do. And no matter what, we love you."

* * *

Elizabeth was in severe physical withdrawal, feeling as strung out and tweaked as when she had stopped drinking. Her hands trembled off and on during the day. Jungle drums beat out their message of needing a fix, needing time with Rosie. She could not get songs and jingles to stop playing in her mind, "Didn't She Ramble" for a whole afternoon, and the jingle from Mr. Clean. She would get to speak to the therapist, Bob, on the eighth day, and he would read her a letter Rosie had written. But not knowing whether Rosie hated her forever, whether she was near death from starvation or cold, plagued her every thought. She felt scooped out, eviscerated, wispy, and dazed.

It was rather amazing that after everything they had been through, the different kinds of drugs, the lies, the sneaking off in the night, all she wanted was Rosie. Elizabeth was any junkie coming down; craving had entered her brain and was not going away. It was a sharp, pointed, immovable force, just like not getting the substance your body and mind were crying out for— nicotine, booze, sex, coffee. The voice of craving was extended, high-pitched, but muffled. She felt helpless as a bug.

"This is a bottom for you," James told her. "And that means there is a chance things can rise. We could have lost her. She had become insane." He held Elizabeth in bed until she fell asleep, which was after one, even though she had taken a pill.

⊡

On the fifth night, Rosie made fire. She spent that afternoon slogging through the snow searching for sticks. It was getting colder. She called out her name every single minute, like the instructors had told them to. She was seriously numb but ended up with an armful of sticks and twigs.

The sun was going down. Tyler's fire flickered thirty feet away. She tried to find her own ingenuity and bedrock, as Bob had talked about; he told them that if they did not give up, they would find it. He had promised. Kath keened and pounded the ground in between her efforts to start a fire. The instructors had shown them how to do it a few times, and they could all make embers of their char cloth. But Rosie could not make fire.

The sunset was orange in the white sky between the pines. Her stomach cramped with the thought of warm rice and lentils going down, with cheesy. She squinched her toes to try to get some feeling back.

She made a fire nest. First she wrapped a thick hank of grass around her thumb and twisted it the way she twisted her hair into a messy bun after combing it with her fingers. She laid it on the ground, shredded tinder—dry leaves and pine needles and twigs—and tamped these down into the nest.

Her knuckles were scabbed from all the times she had tried to get fire going before. You had to take your gloves off so you could feel the quartz strike the steel handle just right, and your hands froze, but it was good to have frozen hands in case the quartz sliced into your skin. Her nails and skin were nearly black. Jo and Alice would die if they saw her hands now. Alice got her nails done every two weeks, short and French-tipped. Rosie took the steel in her right hand, and the quartz in her left. Then she put the bit of char cloth on top of the finest shredded grass in the nest.

She struck downward as hard as she could. When nothing happened, she struck downward again, and again, smashing the steel in her right hand against the quartz, over and over, listening to the click amid the pine trees, until she was out of breath and her knuckles were bleeding. Finally two sparks flew off the steel and onto the char cloth on her tinder bundle and a wisp of smoke appeared, but died. She kept going. Her body warmed, and then she was sweating like a pig, and it was dripping onto her nest, so she moved her head so she wouldn't put out the sparks, and one landed on the char cloth and there was another wisp of smoke, like a tiny bird's snowy breath, but it went out, too, and her own breath dissolved into the freezing-cold air, and she kept striking the quartz and rivulets of blood trickled out of her knuckles.

She shook the sweat off her brow, stretched her aching neck, and prepared for one final strike. She smashed the steel down against the rock, and a spark began to glow on the char cloth, nestled in the nest on the ground. She dropped everything and bent down to fold her nest in half, like an open-faced sandwich of spark and smoke and grass. She continued to blow on it, barely exhaling at first, then breathing softly like a mother blowing on her child's poison oak, and she did not stop until the spark and smoke and tinder bundle turned into flames.

◘

On the sixth morning, Elizabeth first noticed that it was sort of lovely with Rosie gone.

There was no tension, no metallic vibe, no mean glances, no wet towels on the floor. She read the paper over a cup of coffee by herself in the thin sunlight pouring through the kitchen window.

She went outside in her bathrobe, stood still in her garden until the air, moist and cold, slapped her—Wake up, wake up—like after a hangover. Almost everything had died in the cold except the California stuff that was always there, purple flowers, myrtle maybe, funereal lilies, weedy daisies, muck, mush, and grass. The grass was fresh green with old dead stuff underneath.

There were two tiny roses, one alive and one dead. In the middle of the live one, a deep peachy pink throbbed, the petals lighter and lighter as they gradually scalloped out. The dead one was ivory and sapped, like a used tissue, but still beautiful because it held its shape. Ah, note to self, Elizabeth thought, sitting down in the dirt: Hold your shape. The earth was damp but she sat still anyway. A red-tailed hawk hovered in the sky not far away. Really red, she thought to herself. That's a dye job.

After a while she went inside to get ready to go to a protest rally with Rae at San Quentin, where there was to be an execution that night. Joan Baez was going to sing by candlelight sometime in the hours before midnight, but Elizabeth would miss that part: James had an essay due, and she had promised to edit it after dinner.

◘

"So whatcha got for me today?" Bob asked.

Rosie was dreaming again. They all were. She told this to Bob. "I forgot what it's like to dream. It's like being Alice in Wonderland."

"With THC in your system, you don't dream. And you need to. Otherwise it is like losing one of your senses. Dreams are part of your wholeness."

"Why?"

"Because when you're dreaming, you're not the one calling the shots. So it's a reprieve." The instructors made them keep track of their dreams in their journals. Tom, the tall, heavy one, said, "There is a lot of power in your dreams—hopes, fears, truths." Hank, the instructor with the goatee, told them that the dream world had rules in it. You couldn't read a clock in your dreams. It would not give you the time. If the lights were on in a room, you could not turn them off in a dream.

She woke up from food dreams, double cheeseburgers. Some of the grease had dripped and she woke up licking her forearm. It was so real. She wanted that taste of salty grease so badly.

Bob told her that in indigenous tribes all over the world, the dream world was like church.

She used to dream: she could remember bolting from nightmares and gasping them away, desperate to get back to her normal crazy daily routine.

Every day Bob was willing to hear whatever dirt any of the kids had going on anyone else, mostly Kath, whom they all had a hard time understanding, and besides, she was a whiny pain in the ass and brought them all down. You could admit to that, if you tried to respect her anyway, for doing everything they did, even the steepest hikes and dressing on the coldest mornings, eventually. "Let me hear what you got," Bob would say.

"I hate it here so much I can't even say it in words. I'm so furious I could die."

"Rosie, look. You're mad because you made a choice to be stoned all the time, to hang with an older guy with a drug problem, and to fail. You and he agreed to lie and cheat and steal to stay stoned, even though your parents said they would send you away. Your choice to do that is what is making you mad."

The only way to warm up during the day was to move around, but you didn't want to when it was so cold. The cold was like daggers, even in the heavy all-weather Search and Rescue gear. Kath kept flinging herself onto her back like Yertle the Turtle and screaming that she wouldn't walk one more step. The wilderness instructors would say nicely, "I hope we can get to our site before dark." The other kid would start to shout at her: You pussy! We're just trying to get to where we're going. Get up. Start hiking.

"I'm going to run away while you're sleeping, you brown-nose losers," she would reply.

No one had ever made it a mile, the instructors explained to Kath. She'd be lost instantly, she'd just go around and around in circles, and they would find her. Plus, the program was the second-largest employer in Davis, so if somehow she got to the road—which was unlikely—anybody who picked her up would either work for the program or have a relative who did. This made Rosie smile unexpectedly and think of Rae, who saw the world that way: Everyone was on God's payroll, whether they knew it or not. Everyone was part of God's scheme, having been assigned to either help you or drive you crazy enough so you'd give up on your own bad plans and surrender to God's loving Love Bug ways.

She was plagued by thoughts of her future, ruined now by her parents' behavior: What decent college would take a girl who had missed her senior year? Was she supposed to go to some ordinary college now? Be any old person? No, that couldn't happen—it would mean they had won.

Early on the sixth night, at dusk, the instructors had them go gather wood for a communal fire, and then select a staff-shaped piece. This would be the truth stick. Bob came out that night, and they had their first truth circle, only Kath went to hide in her tent and brood.

They took turns burning symbols on the truth stick with a heated nail—moon, flames, a primitive eagle, their names. Bob taught them about how to do an emotional rescue, when you went to help another person by showing up and handing them the truth stick, so they all went over to Kath's tarp and handed her the stick. She was sitting with Hank and crying like a baby, but she took the stick, and then joined them at the fire; she burned her name into the stick. They all said why they thought their parents had put them here, drugs and alcohol, and in Kath's case, a boyfriend with hep C with whom she had shared a needle.

"But only one time!"

The boys tore into her about being an idiot, and Rosie thought she was lying, that she had used a needle with the sick boyfriend more times than she could count. If it had been Rosie, it would have been way more than one time; crazy but true, not that she had used needles, or ever would, probably. They tried to get Kath to tell the truth, but she was in total denial. Bob was right, Rosie thought, remembering something from the other day: Trying to reason with an addict was like trying to blow out a lightbulb.

▣

Elizabeth still felt skewered by cravings for Rosie, but things were ever so slightly better. Rae was getting her out. They had gone shopping at the local garden store, which was having a sale on bark nuggets and mini bark nuggets, with which she would need to blanket the garden when the weather turned really cold, but she could not decide which to buy, bark or mini bark, and they left rattled and empty-handed. Then, in Rae's car, she could not remember how to roll the window down. The button was on the panel between the bucket seats, but it took her a few minutes to remember this. She and Rae drove by the Parkade, hoping that the kids would look as insane and vacant as usual, and some of them did, and this helped, but a few looked lively and young and free. Bark or mini bark, she kept thinking, bark or mini bark?

Elizabeth chewed and sucked on the knuckle of her thumb, as if to extract marrow. It hurt. Rae did not say anything. Elizabeth suspected a conspiracy between James and Rae, to let her feel like shit for as long as it took, instead of trying to fix the unfixable. But Rae usually cracked under the strain of holding back comforting words and advice, as she did now: "You get to talk to Bob, soon! And you get a letter from Rosie. In the meantime, we know where Rosie is, and that she's safe." Relief flooded Elizabeth's nerves, and the anxiety on Rae's face subsided.

"You know one thing I may be getting used to, Rae? You know one thing I sort of like about not having Rosie underfoot?"

"What's that, baby?"

"Call me crazy, but I love not having someone endlessly challenging me, and making me feel like a crazy shit all the time." Elizabeth looked around in the car with wonder. "I'm pretty sold on that."

▣

Every morning at dawn someone shook them awake in the dark, time to get up, and some mornings the instructors handed out pepperoni or cheese sticks that had mysteriously appeared in the night. Every morning her heart sank when she woke and found that she was still in the woods. She obsessed about Fenn and knew he had left her. Maybe ninety days from now, when she was back home, he would leave the new girlfriend for her, if he had one. Or she could wait in a lovely way for him to cycle through, and arrive back at where they had left off. Not knowing was making her lose her mind, so she made herself think about what her friends were doing right that minute, and how great it would be to smoke a joint, and about her bucket kids, the littlest ones playing in the tall grass.

She wondered whether the parents of her Sixth Day kids knew she'd been sent away, and whether they were upset that such a bad person had been in charge of their children. She wondered whether she could ever work there again, with this on her record, although what sort of record would this be on? The county Bad Persons ledger? And how about the parents of the other high school seniors— were they horrified to find out she'd had to be sent away? Or were they jealous, that her parents had done what they couldn't?

There was no ease in the snow, just plodding and clomping ahead. It found the imperceptible cracks in her Search and Rescue gear, and managed to splat in there. It was squeaky on the soles of her boots, and thudded when it fell from the branches. She felt like a speck of protoplasm on a stick under the sky.

You always needed to squint, and this made your eyes hurt. Sometimes the snow was fluffy and light like feathers—how could anything so pretty make you feel so bad? Other times it was heavy and wet. The gloves were supposed to be good enough for the Arctic, but you were so cold you felt your hands were made of skeletal corpse-bones because none of your fingers could work together. But it was better than not feeling them, which meant you were in trouble. Trying to warm them up was agony, rubbing your big paws together, but it helped. The tips of their noses froze, and they rubbed them with the back of their frozen gloves like lepers.

◘

On the seventh day, Bob did an incredible thing. He showed up with candy, peach gummy rings. You tied a piece of floss to the ring, and then the other end to your middle finger, and held the ring about six inches from your mouth. You had to focus on the ring and how badly you wanted it, and make it come to your mouth without moving your finger. "There are tiny muscles in your finger-tips that you've never noticed you had, because you never needed to," Bob said. "Your mind *is* in contact with that which will help you move the floss in a circle, until the ring passes by your mouth and you can eat it."

It was true, like a Ouija board, how without your fingers' even seeming to move, you could get the muscles to flicker, tremble, stir, and bring you the ring.

Bob said: "There is so much you have all been ignoring inside you, that you let die in yourselves, deep psychic muscles. You used your skills to get high, to get by, to maintain whatever illusions you needed to keep using." He let them each try the rings five times, and they could all do it, could get the string moving in a circle, and each got five candy rings. Their moods were expansive as they laughed and chewed and marveled.

"What other flavors do you like?" he asked when he left that day. It was ridiculous—gummy rings as some sort of payout for their neglect and misery. Oh, well, what *ev*: "Watermelon and lime," she called out one second before he disappeared.

"You got it. See you tomorrow, then."

They all got to their feet and waddled on, like toddlers, or old people worrying about breaking their hips. There were so many ways to get hurt—fall on the treacherous surface and twist your ankle, or plunge through the ice that crunched underfoot and drown.

◘

Whatcha got for me today?" Bob asked.

She didn't want to say. Last night she had felt psy-chotic in her sleeping bag, although she had not made a sound, just thrashed and moaned. He coaxed it out with his patience and his kind face.

"I'm going crazy here. My mind is like a horrible yammering, so noisy and miserable. Being here is destroying me. I'm afraid the cold will freeze me, but it will be so seductive that I won't fight back. That I'll die alone. Or go crazy and hurt someone. I'm afraid my mother will die while I'm gone. That if I let up, I'll go nuts."

"We're all afraid of the same stuff. Mostly we're afraid that we're secretly not okay, that we're disgusting, or frauds, or about to be diagnosed with cancer. Really, nearly everyone is, deep down. We want to teach you how to quiet the yammer without drugs, and TV, danger, et cetera. We're going to teach you how you can create comfort, inside and outside, how you can get warm, how you can feed yourself. And even learn to get through silence."

"There is no quiet place in me to rest, especially in all this snow."

"There is, though. There is wilderness inside you, and a banquet. Both."

◘

Elizabeth sneaked off to the library to use the computer there. She rarely felt the need to go online. She could use a computer in a limited way, and James had just taught her how to Google, but today she didn't want him to find out what she was looking up.

Logging on, she felt like a pedophile looking over her own shoulder, heart pounding. She Googled "deaths at wilderness facilities, from exposure, suicide, violence." She found a few mentions of death by neglect at army-style boot camps in the United States, and endless diatribes against wilderness programs in general. But she also found testimonial essays by kids who said they would have died without intervention, or ended up in jail or as runaways. Then she Googled "teenage traffic fatalities": six thousand kids had died nationwide the previous year. She would have thought more. Then she looked up Greyhound schedules from San Francisco to Salt Lake City. Then she Googled James, and withheld breath read responses to his radio essays, most of them complimentary, a few effusive, and a few fully demonic. She Googled the people who had written the most wrathful letters, but didn't find anything actionable. She Googled Rae: her website, random praise for her weavings, and displays of her public successes. Then she Googled herself: nothing. That pretty much said it. What had she been expecting? Elizabeth Ferguson, stay-at-home mother and wife, recovering alcoholic with a history of psychiatric problems and a teenage child recently institutionalized for drugs, spends her days reading, ruminating, and playing with the cat.

"Where were you?" James asked when she returned home.

"Oh, just hanging out at the library."

After dinner the phone rang. When Elizabeth picked up, a woman with a sultry voice asked to talk with James, and Elizabeth's mind flared with panic. He *was* having an affair. She'd been right all along—it wasn't that KQED was his mistress: he'd been seeing someone young from the production department. Or who waitressed next door to the station. "Can I help you?" Elizabeth asked with enormous hostility. It was a woman from the valley, with a dog. Someone had come by who could take him, but she had promised James he could have first dibs. "Really," Elizabeth said. "First dibs." She felt busted—here she'd leapt to the conclusion he was having an affair, when he'd just been out *dog* hunting. God, maybe she'd been wrong about the extent of Rosie's dark and secret life, too; maybe she and James had overreacted, and they could go pick her up. Then she smiled kindly to herself, and remembered the Post-it: Tomorrow.

She handed him the phone. "It's a lady with a dog," she said.

He grimaced with guilt, took the phone and listened. "Oh, dear," he said. He looked over at Elizabeth. She kept her expression neutral, although she was seething—he'd gone to check out a dog behind her back. Their family was in deep shit, they were broke and overwhelmed, but he was saying to the woman, "Boy, Ichabod is a great dog. I fell in love with him. But I had no business pursuing this, and I have to say no. Thank you for checking, but we've got way too much going on."

Elizabeth looked away, looked back at James in his guilt, and grabbed the phone.

She clenched her teeth. "Wait," she said into the receiver. "Let us at least come by in the morning. Is nine too early? Let me find a pen." Then she turned to James and mouthed, "Ichabod?" He nodded with deep contrition.

◉

Rosie was raw all the time but she plodded on. Her nose ran and froze, and she tried to rub it away and that rubbed her skin raw. You sniveled all the time here. The snow turned you into something pathetic. It made your horrible leaky self visible.

On the seventh night they all got to write to their parents. Bob was going to call the parents tomorrow, and read the letters over the phone. They could use one whole side of a page of binder paper. And the parents could fax them a letter the day after.

Rosie thought for a long time before she began to write. It was so weird, how friendly she felt all of a sudden. Mama, who gave

me life, she wrote. I am okay. I hated you for the first few days.
I know you think you sent me here to save me. Although I think
this is pretty extreme and I am still very mad. I miss you, though,
and Rascal and James (sort of) and Lank and Rae. I want to come
home. I would be so good, you could test me every morning. I
know it is too late but I feel very desperate. Please find out from
Jo or Alice about Fenn, even if it is bad news for me. I didn't
use NEARLY as much as the other kids here. Never meth. Well,
once or twice. They say I get to see you and James at the end of
the month. Please smuggle Rascal in your biggest purse. It is so
cold here you won't believe it. And at night it is so quiet that it is
like hearing music among the planets (if there are owls in outer
space). The snow is beautiful and a nightmare, and I will never
voluntarily go into snow again. It looks like clouds and smoke and
fog, and it burns the inside of your nose and lungs. It has incredible shadows in it and is also full of light. Every so often we see
jackrabbits frozen in motion behind the trees. They look like they
are judging us. (Tell James he cannot use this stuff!) Love you,
miss you. Give Rascal a treat for me or a smack on the butt. Rosie.

□

The first thing Bob said to Elizabeth was, "Rosie is healthy—
doing fine."

"Fine? What does fine mean?" At her AA meetings, FINE
was a common acronym for fucked up, insecure, neurotic, edgy.

"It means she's eating, she's learned to make fire. She's doing
her chores."

"Does she hate me? Does she hate us?"

"No, no, not at all. Listen to this letter. I'll stick it in the mail
later so you'll have the original. You can each fax one letter a week,

as can any adult in her life. Except Fenn. Here it goes: 'Mama, who gave me life.'" Elizabeth clenched her fists in sudden joy.

When Bob finished, neither of them spoke for a minute, until he broke the silence to say he would fax her and James a copy later.

After they got off the phone, she went and curled up on the couch, beneath where Rascal lay. He stared down at her like a vulture in a tree. James came over and took her feet in his lap and rubbed them with her socks still on. Ichabod lumbered over and planted a huge, heavy, hairy leg across her chest so that she couldn't have gotten up supposing she'd wanted to. It was hard to say or even guess what kind of dog he was, but he was mellow and large, maybe eighty pounds, with short brown fur, orange eyebrows like a rottweiler, and hanging folds of skin around his jaw, like a shar-pei.

Pearly mist covered the garden when she went out the next morning, and her baby rose was already dead, and no new ones had bloomed. The willow tree branches, without leaves, were sticky, witchy fingers. There was broad green grass, and grass like sparse old-lady hair. The yard was not hospitable now, but lovely in its way, full of green gray brown. It was not neat and efficient, though. It was taking its time. Ichabod sat near her, a solemn blur of dark. He watched her have her morning cry. Then they got up together and went inside.

◘

On day eight, the beginning of the second week, the day Bob was going to read Rosie's letter to Elizabeth, the fax machine at the office broke down, so he couldn't fax it to Elizabeth, too, so she could read it to James later. Rosie spent all afternoon trying to hold back tears, feeling she would freak out entirely, like Kath, with whom she had bonded in the last few days. The kids muttered with paranoid thoughts about how the instructors were fucking with them—what were the odds the fax was broken today, when they were supposed to get letters from home tomorrow? As they murmured angrily together, Rosie felt strangely close to the other kids. Tyler, who was not only handsome but smart; small Joel, whose skin was about eighty percent better; goofy Jack, the quiet, googly Arlo kid; and Kath—they had each other's back. If one of them got called out for slacking off or doing something stupid and potentially dangerous, they all exchanged glances of commiseration and of what general dicks adults could be.

Bob said that if the machine wasn't fixed tomorrow, he would drive into town to retrieve their parents' letters at Kinko's. Then he told them he had a surprise for them later, after dinner.

Rosie was fire-maker for the whole tribe that night. She got a roaring fire started. Kath still hadn't made one, but now was at least trying. Rosie and Kath had helped each other finger-comb their hair that day, and plotted how to steal some duct tape from the instructors so they could wax each other's eyebrows. They pooled their rice and lentils with the boys and cooked the food in one battered pot that Hank gave them. They sat in a circle with their instructors, gobbling it down under the thinnest slice of moon that could ever be.

◘

At the business store in Landsdale, a young man tried to help Elizabeth fax Rosie her letter, full of details about the new dog and how much they missed her, and how much she'd scared them, and how proud of her they were. But something was wrong with the recipient's fax, and the young man promised to keep trying until it went through. Elizabeth went to visit Rae. She pounded on Rae's door over the sound of the loom and then, without hearing Rae's voice, stepped inside the cottage. It smelled of lanolin, fiber, and wet wool. Rae looked up from the loom in the middle of the small living room. It seemed as big as a grand piano. Elizabeth came up behind Rae to kiss and nuzzle her soft, sweet-smelling neck. Then she sat in the window seat to watch, and dreamily imagined Rosie reading her letter again and again.

Rae, shoving the comb downward through the warp, looked somewhere between harp-playing and rowing, as she dragged the woolen thread down.

"Can we drive up to Utah when you're done, and get my Rosie back?"

"Sure," said Rae, running the threaded shuttle through the warp. Then she smote her forehead with the palm of her hand. "Wait—shoot. Never mind. This tapestry is due tomorrow morning. Besides, bringing her back might kill her."

Elizabeth thought this over. "Finish up already. I'm bored to fucking death." Rae held up five fingers: five minutes. Elizabeth let her shoulders slump and sighed loudly, and went back to daydreaming about Rosie.

"Did you get your letter off? And how's the dog?"

"The fax machine in Davis was down. The entire town has probably been wiped out in an avalanche. And the dog is sweet. Ugly-adorable. Except for the penis."

"That red lipsticky thing? Or the whole furry outside situation?"

"James says that the furry outside thing isn't the penis—it's a codpiece. It's just his little underpants."

Rae rolled her eyes. "Thanks for sharing, James. I'll have Lank Google it."

Elizabeth stared. "Really, Rae? You can Google that?" Rae shrugged, nodded. "Isn't it wild, how you can find out so much, yet know so little?"

◙

Rosie whipped her head around to the sound of voices in the woods. "Listen," she said. The kids looked at one another with fear. What was it? They gaped toward the sound of crunching boot steps on the ground, on ice and branches, but then heard other kids' voices, and the instructors could not keep straight faces. Maybe it was *over*, Rosie thought, her heart hurdling over itself. They had learned their lesson—God almighty, had they learned their lesson— and now they were going home.

Six teenagers in orange Search and Rescue gear stepped out of the woods, followed by two huge male instructors and a woman. The new kids, three girls, three boys, were all smiling, and reached for Rosie and the others, who had clustered around. After a while these new kids shepherded Rosie's tribe over to the fire.

They'd brought them brownies from someone in the office and a chub of pepperoni. "We are your emotional rescue," one of the boys announced. "The isolation phase is over, and from now on, we're going to check on you every week, no matter where we are in our own process."

Rosie's whole body flushed. "You mean, we're not going back with you?"

"Of course not. You have three more weeks out here, then two more months to go. We have one more week, and then we move to the hogan and the longhouse, and then Academics. We'll come visit you from there. And in another week, you're going to visit a new tribe who will be on their eighth day, as their emotional rescue, because you'll be old-timers by then. We'll be your mentors, and the newer ones will be your mentees."

"We brought food and ourselves," one of the girls added. "Plus, the truth. That we've been in your shoes, we uniquely know how bad this week was, and we swear it gets better."

What a bunch of mental cases, Rosie thought. I wonder what the instructors are paying you—thirty peach rings? They'd obviously drunk the Kool-Aid. She wouldn't let that happen to her.

She looked around until her eyes landed on the woman instructor, who was brown-haired and homely in the firelight, talking quietly with Kath, who was laughing, and Rosie's heart broke with longing for her mother, but she refused to cry. She froze herself out, cauterized the place where she wanted to sob, and drew in the dirt with a stick for a few minutes. And then the woman came over and sat beside her.

She was prettier up close, with a cute smile and dark eyelashes, but she had a big nose.

"Hey," said the woman. "You're Rosie. I'm Taj. I'm with the kids who are two weeks ahead of you." Rosie looked at her and nodded but couldn't think of anything to say. She had a nice smell, with a hint of something womanly, like lotion. Rosie hadn't smelled a clean female in more than a week. "I wanted to tell both you girls, we're sorry about the Kotex, but you can let Bob know when you have your period and we'll help you get rid of the used napkins at the end of every day. I know it can be kind of gnarly."

"Then why didn't they just give us Tampax, that we could bury, and have some privacy?"

Taj sighed, shook her head. "About two years ago, a girl here hated it so much that she left one in for days, to induce toxic shock—so she'd either get to go to the infirmary or die."

Rosie stared at Taj, and let her mouth drop open. "Death by tampon?" Taj nodded enthusiastically. "Now I have heard everything," said Rosie. Taj laughed and put one arm around Rosie's shoulder, and Rosie let her draw her in, and she buried her nose in Taj's neck and smelled it as long and deeply and quietly as she could, holding on to the smell like a life preserver and trying to hold back tears.

"You're going to end up being glad for this experience," said a boy with red curls poking out from under a navy blue watch cap. "I know it's hard to believe." That was a good one. Rosie grew hard and imperious. Then the aroma of chocolate wafted over. It smelled so much like her mother's kitchen that her mouth began filling with desire.

"It starts getting more interesting for you tomorrow," said the curly-haired boy. "Now that you know how to survive, you get to be a family, a community. In another week, you start learning Search and Rescue. We've got our first real assignment tomorrow at dawn, joining forces with the local SAR squad and firefighters."

Rosie took off one of her gloves and reached for a brownie. She could see the cracks in its surface by firelight, like dried desert. The inside was wet, moist, exquisite. Search and Rescue, that was another good one. As if adults would trust a bunch of loser kids to rescue something precious out here in the middle of nowhere.

TWELVE

Ox Eye

◻

Elizabeth took a picture for Rosie of Ichabod in the garden near a dead rosebush. Rain would come soon enough and bring watercolor skies and riotous green to town, but in the meantime, everything was dry, bristly, sticklike, as if the garden itched. Ichabod was a good dog and a mellow companion, and Elizabeth liked talking to him, as he looked Hasidic and thoughtful. She told him to smile before she took his photo; someone should smile around here. James had found two cheap plane tickets to Utah for a family weekend, and they would fly there Friday afternoon. There was a lodge near the wilderness facilities in Davis, thirty miles from Salt Lake City, where the parents would stay and the group sessions would be held. Things could go well, or horribly, or be a mixed grill of progress and discouragement, whereas she and James needed something major to have happened to Rosie; they'd spent their last dime, and run out of options. After dinner the first night, the parents would meet the instructors and therapists in the big upstairs room at the lodge. The adults would have orientation, and then the kids would come in, do a presentation of their wilderness skills, and spend an hour with their parents. Saturday was breakfast together, all-day family therapy with all five kids and all ten parents. Sunday was breakfast, half a day's family therapy, and then the kids would go to the next leg of their journey, called the Village, a month indoors at the longhouse and the hogan by the river.

Elizabeth spent some time in the garden, where she usually found solace, but not today, not with Rosie gone. Today it was dry like someone who had cried too much. She moved through her plants slowly: since Rosie had left, four weeks ago, she and James had both slowed down. Maybe they now got to act their age, instead of trying to act more energetic around Rosie so she would not think they were decrepit.

They both had much to do before leaving. They had to pack for the snow—it was only twelve degrees in Davis. James had a story to record, and an appointment with the dean at the College of Marin, where he would begin teaching English comp half-time after the first of the year. It was a real break: they needed the money, and it might be great material for his radio pieces. He was only medium bitter about having to take a real job. Elizabeth had to drive Ichabod up to Lank's house for the weekend, and arrange for a neighbor to feed Rascal. She was to have one last talk with Bob on Thursday afternoon. That night she and James were going to a rally at the Parkade that Rae had helped organize with the people of Sixth Day Prez, to consecrate this piece of land on which so many of the town's children had gotten so lost. It had been planned since Jack Herman's death. And she had a date for tea with Jody and Alice on Friday morning.

She reached Bob at his office at four.

"How are you?" he asked gently.

She thought about this for a moment. "I'm okay in a number of ways. Scared, worried, excited, desperate, flat. If that makes any sense at all."

"It makes perfect sense," he said. He walked her through a few details of the weekend: "We'll all meet upstairs. There will be a fire, and snacks. We will catch you up on your children and the program, and prepare you to see them. They are not the children you left with us a month ago. Then they'll do a demonstration of what they have been learning. And then you get them to yourselves for an hour. Each family will stake out an area of the room. There will be lots of crying and laughing and blame, the kids will be angry and ecstatic, and they will binge on the snacks and get stomachaches. There will be anger and there will be extraordinary healing. There's no way around it being one of the toughest things you'll ever do. This is parenthood on steroids."

"What are the kids doing right now?"

"Finishing up their truth letters to you parents. Have you written yours to Rosie?"

◘

Rosie sat on a log beside the rare afternoon campfire, bent over her journal, gripping her pencil; there was so much to say, but they could use only the front and back of one sheet of binder paper. She looked around at the boughs of the nearest trees, heavy with snow. Boy, were her mother and James in for a bad surprise—it was not cute Tahoe cold here, but cold cold, Outer Mongolia cold. She turned back to her paper and began.

Dear Mama and James, I am still sick with anger that you sent me here. You stole something from me that I can never get back, my senior year in high school. I worked so hard and so long for this year, and there were other ways you could have reined me in when you got so freaked out by my behavior, which believe me was very typical of all the kids I know. At the same time, I know you honestly believed that sending me here was the only way you could save me. So I am trying to look forward. James, I want to say you made things really horrible for me this year, you were always on my case and riding my ass. I love you a lot, mostly, and overall you have been a great blessing to this family, but you spend way too much time on your work, to the neglect of my mother and myself. When you look back over your life, I think your memories of us will matter much more than your success as a writer. And mama, it really hurts me that you did not make more of your life. I know you are shy and have had mental trials, but just being a mother and wife is not enough. This has not set a good example. I think your work with Rae as activists is very important and that you should stop using your fake fragile condition as an excuse to lie on the couch and read, or putter around in the garden. I love you so much, you could never in a million years imagine loving someone as much as I love you.

◘

That night, dozens of people came to be a part of Rae's candlelight procession in the Parkade, mostly from Sixth Day Prez—old folks in their Sherpa caps, the youth group, parents, even the parents of one kid who had died. Lank and James had built a primitive wooden stage with a row of steps for the candle ceremony.

It was cold and windy. People pressed in close to the stage, and some of the teenagers who had been huddling under the bus kiosk wandered over to listen. Everyone received a candle inside a paper cup. Rae's co-organizer opened the event by saying simply, "Tonight we bring fresh air, light, and hope to the Parkade." A guitarist played "Lost Children Street" by Malvina Reynolds. The newly formed church choir sang "Ain't Gonna Let Nobody Turn Me Around," and then "Blowin' in the Wind," completely off-key until the crowd joined in and straightened things out.

Parents and relatives and friends who wanted to light a candle for a specific young person gathered to the right of the stage. Rae gave them red plastic party cups with candles inside. From where Elizabeth stood, they looked like a bread line, or people waiting for soup. It was a modest ceremony. The red plastic cups were supposed to guard the votives inside, but the wind was strong and the flames fizzled out, and had to be lit over and over. One person got his candle lit, walked to the center of the stage, said a girl's name loudly, and placed the candle on one of the steps. Then he went to rejoin the line at the end, while people near the front of the line tried to light their candles. People from the crowd came over to whisper names to the people with red plastic cups, as if making requests, and more and more names were lifted up. The person at the front of the line would step forth like a bridesmaid after the person ahead placed a candle on the step. James took someone's red party cup and went to the step to lift up Rosie's name. Elizabeth had had a vision of the heat and light of flames moving the message of the rally into the world, a baby conflagration to stir the cold and unseeing parts of oneself, the cold and unseeing parts of the world, but the candlelit step looked like a beggar man's war memorial.

Rae also lit a candle for Rosie, and made a very short speech
when all the parents were done. "Tonight, we lit something inside
ourselves to be spread, lit a tiny flame to consecrate toxic ground,
to consecrate our caring, our attention to this matter, our wish that
there would be help for the parents of the dead. My belief is that
their children did not die in vain and their children did not die
alone. Tonight was about our huge desire to help, a few of us poor
schlubs trying to light a little flame that almost no one was here
to see, in red plastic cups." She laughed at how impoverished an
image this was, and continued, looking right at Elizabeth: "Each
candle is so temporary, but it says that there is light and there are
people who can help: it says the time is now."

◘

Alice and Jody came at nine on Friday morning. Before answering the door, Elizabeth stopped at the mirror in the hall, saw
a tired, graying woman with curved and questioning shoulders.
She straightened them up, sucked in her stomach, ran her fingers
through her hair, practiced an upbeat smile, and checked once
again in the mirror to see if she looked any more like her old self.
She thought that she did, that it was pretty convincing.

She made them both cocoa with white chocolate shavings, and
said that James would be out to say hello as soon as he finished
something he was working on. The girls sat on the rug in the living
room and played with Ichabod like huge young children. For Rosie
they had brought a picture of themselves dressed to the nines in
vintage clothes for a party; a lavender, rose, and light blue cap
that Alice had crocheted; and a bronze butterfly recovery medal-
lion that Jody's sponsor had given her. Jody looked dykier than
before, with spiky maroon hair, and heavier, yet still with those

long fingers and bony wrists. Alice was almost gamine now, with a short stylish pixie cut, fitted black capri pants, a silk scarf, a heart locket from a new boyfriend. But they were so much the same, their fingers always busy, constantly tracing on their palms and pulling on their ears, rubbing their knuckles, inspecting their cuticles. They had something terrible to tell Elizabeth—or at least Rosie would think it was terrible—which was that Fenn was going out *seriously* with two different girls, and Elizabeth cried out, "Thank you, Jesus," so loudly that James came running from his office.

"Are you going to tell her?" Alice asked.

Elizabeth didn't know. Her skin itched, her brain itched. She shrugged. "I don't want to be cruel, but I want Rosie to know that Fenn isn't back at home waiting for her like in the movies."

"You will intuitively know what to do," said Jody, and Elizabeth smiled, because it was something you heard at every AA and NA meeting, the Ninth Step promises. Then she shook her finger menacingly at Jody.

"You and your little NA friends better be right, or your ass is grass."

It was painful and sweet to be with the girls, Alice so stylin' now, as Rosie would have said, so confident after having gotten early acceptance to three design schools, and Jody fingering the strand of plastic key tags that hung from her belt loops like a rosary, both of them peering at Elizabeth with concerned affection. "I'm so proud of you both," she said, and she was—Alice was going to be a star, Jody was going to work at the KerryDas Café every morning, before heading to her daily meeting—but guilt squeezed her heart like fingers. Had she done the right thing, sending Rosie away? And would it even work?

Alice broke off a corner of a chocolate chip cookie and nibbled at it thoughtfully. "I want to tell you one more terrible thing." James and Elizabeth turned toward her. "I gave Rosie a lot of Adderall over the last year—I mean, I just shared my stash with her. You know, I take it for ADD." Elizabeth felt something verging on hate. Then Alice dipped her head. "I actually take it 'cause I love speed, and I'm so sorry that it makes me sick." She looked up tearfully and smacked herself hard on the head a few times. Elizabeth grabbed her wrist to make her stop, and held on as they collected themselves, Alice's fingers clenching with the desire to keep hitting herself.

"You're not Rosie's problem," Elizabeth said. "Rosie is Rosie's problem."

"Jesus, Alice," James exclaimed. "Didn't you ever hear that speed kills?"

Alice rolled her eyes angrily, and muttered about what a jerk she used to be.

"Stop, James," said Elizabeth. "You girls are totally amazing. You're Rosie's two best friends, and you get to start writing to her pretty soon." Then she narrowed her eyes at Alice. "It goes without saying that if you ever give Rosie drugs again, I will so rat you out. I will call every college that has taken you, and say you are a pusher—and I will hurt Ichabod," she said, and both girls screamed in protest. "I mean it," she said. "This is not an idle threat."

At the door, Jody took Elizabeth by the hands. "You did the right thing," she told the older woman sternly. "You made the same messy decision my parents did, when I made such a mess of my life. They know now that they did the right thing, and I do, too, for sure. And Rosie will too, someday." A shard of

Elizabeth believed her. Most of her was filled with worry, fear, and self-loathing. They all hugged, and the girls did the secret gang handshake with James, the roe-sham-beau and gibberish sign language. Elizabeth watched them walk away, Alice so fine and thin, Jody with a few inches of fleshy back showing, a sparrow in flight tattooed above her leather belt, orange, dark blue, rose, outlined in black.

◘

James did all the talking at the airport ticket counter, while Elizabeth stood beside him trying to calm herself. Her shoulders had rolled forward again. She felt like a mental patient being transferred by a federal marshal, or a drunken boater on the Seine, one foot in the rowboat, one foot onshore, her arms holding oars unsteadily above the water.

Everything in her ached like the visible part of the garden, dry from crying, twiggy, scratchy, holding its breath until the rains came. You had to remind yourself of all that the soil held, or you'd lose all hope. She found a seat near the ticket counter, took three aspirin, held her hands over her roiling stomach like a pregnant woman, and got out her letter to Rosie.

"Darling," it began in her best penmanship on stationery. "This will be an inadequate attempt to tell you how devastating your drug use was to your family, your future, and especially to your health—mental, psychiatric, psychic, physical." She looked up at James, still at the counter, tucking their boarding passes into the inside pocket of his ratty old jacket. His letter was so concise—you scared us to death, you treated your mother and me like shit, you were throwing away everything most precious to you, and to us—but hers meandered from mentions of Rosie's lies and betrayal, to proclamations of love and respect and hope. James had helped her edit out the guilt-mongering, but insisted she not minimize the destruction they had lived through. How honest were you supposed to be with your kid, how honest was healthy for them to hear? Certainly not a cathartic spew. But in the jumble of terror, hatred, resentment, hope, rage, guilt, shame, and overwhelming love, what were the salient points? She'd written a heartbroken, lonely list of treachery and deceit—the drugs and alcohol, the money missing from Elizabeth's purse, Rosie's lies about where she was going, whom she would be with, the Adderall Alice confessed to, the raves Jody told Elizabeth about, a week after they sent Rosie away, the Ecstasy, the cough syrup, the bust on the hill, the sneaking out at night, driving stoned and drunk—good God almighty. As she read her list in the airport, it finally struck Elizabeth full-on in her gut—her kid had been totally out of control.

She shared this with James when he came over from the counter. Leaning over, she rustled her letter at him and whispered in his ear, "It's starting to occur to me that our child *may* have had a little problem."

He drew back to study her, incredulous, until they both smiled. "Ya think?" he said. He read the letter again. "You hit all the right notes." She folded it and tucked it into her purse. He got up to get them some water—she had not seen him sit still once today—while she closed her eyes and pretended the snug plastic armrests were a straitjacket. She clung to what Jody had said, and to the candles lit the night before, for the kids who had died. All she could think to do was turn the whole shebang over, without knowing to whom or what she was turning it over. She imagined sliding it into the in-box of some lowercase god. She held one palm

close to her face, and said in silence, as a supplicant, *I'll be respon-*
sible for everything on this side of my palm. You be in charge of
the outcome of everything else. Today I turn over the waves. I turn
over the shore, and the oars, and will sit in the boat quietly with my
hands in my lap, as we prepare for whatever is to come. Nothing
I do, think, say, insist upon, or withhold will affect the course of
events this weekend, only the course of me. That was so depressing
to think about, although James would probably say, Maybe not.

◘

Four hours later, at the lodge in Utah, they got food to go from
the restaurant downstairs and took it up to their plain, cozy
room. There was a down quilt, worn Oriental rugs, an antique chest
of drawers, and a round ox-eye window near the ceiling. There had
been one just like it in her grandmother's house, no bigger than a
porthole, with a vertical molding bisecting a horizontal one so it
looked like the sniper sight on a giant's rifle. Thin moonlight showed
from the other side. She didn't know how James could eat so much of
his spaghetti: he had a lot at stake, too. He must have assumed that
she would partly blame him if it didn't work out, and maybe she
would at first. He had been strict with Rosie all year, so hard on her
sometimes. Elizabeth picked at a salad and fries.

At quarter of seven, he went into the bathroom and brushed his
teeth. "It's time to get going," he said, pulling her to her feet. "I just
brushed my one remaining tooth. Your turn."

◘

A dozen adults were sitting in a circle of chairs in the center
of the conference room when Elizabeth and James stepped
inside. People introduced themselves, and the parents announced

which child was theirs. Rosie had described Bob to a tee in one of her letters—the hedgehog hair, the wide brown eyes, his quiet voice.

Rick was the therapy leader, a fireplug of dark hair and eyes, maybe Italian-American, who bristled with gregarious authority. Bob and the instructors would be there only the first night. Rick took the parents through the story of the past weeks, telling how far the kids had come from the first grim days, describing the willfulness and insolence the instructors still encountered, the anger the kids still felt toward their parents, their deep desire to come home, their impressive wilderness skills, their Search and Rescue techniques, and then outlined what this night would be like. Finally he looked up and smiled. "I know you are not desperate for me to keep talking. Let me get your kids."

Elizabeth felt James holding his breath, too, as Rick signaled for the big instructor Hank to open the door. The shuffle of boots on the ground broke the silence, and one by one teenagers in bright orange outdoor gear came in, not making eye contact, and trudged over to an alcove at the far end of the room, which held some gear, drums, a pile of twigs and sticks. Rosie, second in line, was the tallest of the five, and Elizabeth stared at the apparition: Rosie, broad in the shoulders, especially in foul-weather gear, her face thin and focused, pale as a soul, black tendrils spilling from her cap.

Hank closed the door.

The kids stood side by side like soldiers, holding branches in their hands, like ancient twig configurations, or rune sticks, and after a moment Elizabeth saw that the letters formed the gnarled word "trust." Rosie, second from the right, had a letter S, twigs bent, curved, and held together with thin green vines.

"Trust," the lead male said loudly at the far left. "T. Trust in ourselves, trust in our teachers, trust in the land. T."

"R. Respect that you and our teachers had for us once, that we had for ourselves, that we lost, that we threw away getting high," said the girl holding the R. "R." Rosie had written about Kath's tantrums and episodes, but not about how pretty she was, black-haired, fair-skinned, with gigantic round brown eyes.

"U," said the boy with the goofy expression. He looked sort of stoned. "You being here for us, you having the courage to be here. And us—the courage we have tonight, to face the past, to face the future. You, and us. U."

"S. Sacred trust," said Rosie, looking straight at Elizabeth, solemn, tired, older, but younger, too, without makeup, lost here, in the weirdness of the drill, but also found in a dark, deep confidence, and in her tribe. Their shoulders helped hold her up, as hers held them. "The sacred trust between parent and child, to try and do the best we can, to grow. The sacred trust of our instructors, to teach us the ways of survival, to teach us the ways of the elders. And sacred trust in ourselves, finally. S."

"T. Trust!" intoned the black-haired boy on the end, the handsomest male, and the kids shouted together, "Trust!"

Then they broke into smiles. All the mothers wept and began to rise, but the instructors shook their heads and gestured for them to sit down. The kids put down their branches, then picked up various packs that were leaning against the wall, and one at a time brought them out. Kath announced, "This is the pack we each carry on our shoulders every day," and took apart the tight bundle, held together with what she called a p-cord: a tarp on the outside, a thin pad inside, a sleeping bag, a change of clothes, cooking gear. Once it was all laid out, one of the boys said, "Go," and in minutes, she assembled it all into a tight, lumpy burrito, which she slipped onto her back.

The parents cheered. Scowling, Kath stepped back. The mothers and James wiped at their eyes. The U boy demonstrated the water filtration system for the tribe, a banged-up steel water filter device with a red pump lever and plastic tubes, the ultimate symbol of sacred trust, because if you didn't clean the filter perfectly when it was your turn, everyone ended up sick.

Rosie gathered dried leaves and grasses from a pile on the floor, and shaped them into some sort of nest, which she set down on a granite square that one of the boys had placed at her feet. She got an Altoids box from another pile of gear, and extracted a bit of black flug. She laid it on the leaves, and from her pocket pulled a rock and a metal handle of some sort. Then she smashed the metal handle against the quartz, over and over, until a thin plume of smoke rose from deep inside the nest, which Rosie blew into a low flame.

Finally the demonstration ended, and the kids looked over at Rick, who nodded. The room dissolved into pandemonium as the kids raced for their parents. Rosie plowed into her mother's arms and then into James's, tears pouring down her face. She pulled them into one corner of the alcove, then pushed them to the floor so they could all huddle together, cuddle and weep and exclaim over one another. "I know I only have you for an hour," she implored. "I never thought I could forgive you, and I haven't quite, but now I cannot stand that we can't stay up all night together—I will go crazy between now and eight o'clock tomorrow." She pawed Elizabeth's weepy face with her sooty hand, and barreled up against James's chest, handing him a horribly grimy olive-green kerchief on which to wipe himself up. Her face was bleary and scrunched with emotions, everything at once, all three of their faces showed ecstasy and pain, and they rolled into a mass, like bears, shoulders and chests, arms and legs. Rosie pulled off her foul-weather jacket. She was wearing the gray sweater she had worn when Lank and James had kidnapped her, over a black turtleneck. The hem of a pale blue undershirt peeked out below, and reaching to tuck it in, Elizabeth felt the bones of Rosie's waist.

◘

Rosie's heart burst with joy and anger and pain and homesickness, and she couldn't possibly gather together all the thoughts and speeches she had rehearsed, her charges and excuses and her hopes. She wanted to tell them how angry she still was that they'd sent her here, but she got only as far as how desperately she missed them. She'd forgotten how beautiful her mother was, those high cheekbones and the perfect nose and the eyes as smart and soulful as a dog's; there was more gray in her hair. Rosie had been waiting to see what the other kids' parents looked like, and she'd caught glances of them during the demonstrations—Tyler's parents looked rich and proper, with black hair like his and good bones, and Kath's mother was a bleached-blonde anorexic and her father was fat—but Rosie really didn't care now. Her mother had such great thick short hair.

Behind them were cries and exultations and even fists pounding on the carpet—that was probably Kath having one of her episodes—and Rosie turned back to her parents. God, her mother had gotten more wrinkly and James was so pale and exhausted, with dark circles under those beautiful green green eyes, and his hairline had receded since she'd last seen him, and she cried again that she would see them only for another forty minutes tonight, it was cruel and inhumane, but her mother was saying they had all weekend. She loved these two people so much, they were by far the greatest-looking parents, and at the same time she was still mad and hated it here and hated that they'd done this to her. But clean, combed hair helped her spirits immensely, as did having her own clothes, and warm dry socks.

Rosie told them everything she could in the forty minutes remaining—about wilderness life; about the emotional-rescue kids, who had lent them this batch of drums, which they had made, and Rosie and her tribe would make some, too, but they could already play these tonight, a welcome rhythm, duh, how dorky was that, since everyone would be saying good-bye. But they hadn't learned the good-bye song yet. James was dispatched to bring a bowl of trail mix over, and Rosie ate two fistfuls without stopping. She dropped her voice to nearly a whisper as she pointed with her chin to the other families, and told them who each child was. Elizabeth caught Rosie up on Rae and Lank, Ichabod, Jody, and Alice, and told her she had all this stuff from the girls to give her—a cap Alice had made, and Jody's butterfly recovery medal, and a card they'd made with photos. Jody had a foot-long strand of NA key tags now. Alice had a new boyfriend and a short pixie haircut. And Jody said that Fenn was seeing other girls.

Rosie cried out an unintelligible sound. "Did he call to see where I was? And when I was coming home?"

"No, but Alice and Jo told him." Her mother held her, and James stared mournfully at his wooden bowl of trail mix and picked out M&M's to offer as communion after Rosie was able to stop crying.

In her last letter, Rosie had said that her nails were pitch-black and she smelled like monkey island at the zoo, but she and the others had gotten to take hot showers at the SAR base camp, and wash their hair. Elizabeth burrowed now into the warm, delicious

long curls. The parents were permitted to give their kids brushes
and combs in the morning—they'd all had to share one last night
at the base camp. Rosie pulled up her foul-weather pants to show
them that the hair on her legs was almost as thick and black as
James's, but there would be no shaving allowed until the Academics phase at the old house in town, in another month.

And it seemed like only minutes had passed, but Rick was
standing and telling everyone it was time to go. The three of
them clung together, and then all the kids returned to the alcove,
and each took one of the drums against the wall, and a folding
chair, and they sat in the same order in which they had spelled out
"TRUST" and began to play their song.

The drums drew the kids together into the beat of itself, into
its rhythmic tribal heart, steady and firm. They looked up at one
another as they played, or down at their hands and drum skins.
Their playing was like a community pacemaker, and when they
stopped, the silence was profound.

Then the parents burst into wild applause and whistles. The
kids looked sheepish, vaguely contemptuous, and totally at home.

◘

Rosie glanced over her shoulder on the way out the door, one
last look for the road. God, her parents were so cute, like little
rabbits, staring back at her, waving like she was getting on a school
bus. She had presents to give them tomorrow, rings she had made
from bark fibers of a tulip poplar. All the kids had made rings
for their parents. It had been a whole day's work, which left their
hands sliced with paper cuts. She had fashioned thin cord and it had
taken forever to break it down between her palms, twist and plait
two almost invisible strands. One of the boys had started twisting

dogbane into cord until Bob had discovered this and told him it could be deadly, at least to dogs, and could cause heart problems in humans. There were actually more ways for kids to die out in the woods than there'd ever been at home. Her parents were crazy. But she had come through. She had shown everyone that she could survive in the snow with almost nothing, make cord from the skinniest fibers, play an ancient rhythm on a drum. And she could make fire.

◘

James and Elizabeth milled around their room in the lodge like dogs at the pound. Only one bedside lamp was lit. Elizabeth looked mournfully at the cold smelly French fries she had barely touched.

"All of a sudden I'm starving to death," she said. "I feel faint."

"Do you want me to see if the kitchen is still open? I could get us some of that pie."

"In a minute. Will you come sit on the floor with me?" He came over and sat down beside her on the worn rug, against the wall. They both sighed.

"How did she look to you?" he asked finally.

"Beautiful. Full of breath. I love it here. I love Bob, Rick, I love them all."

"Something with big healthy teeth has broken through her polluted cocoon. Broken had to happen. Otherwise, there would have always been another inch of wiggle room, and Rosie had become a wiggle artist."

The air in their room smelled faintly of mold, dust, and evergreen trees.

"What about that drumming, James! Was that wild, or what?"

"Wild," he agreed. "It overwhelmed me at first. But it seems to take all the inner jangle and work it through their bodies, so it came out as power. It turned it into one loud heartbeat for a few minutes."

They sat in the near dark, shoulder to shoulder. She looked up at the thin moonlight through the porthole, divided into quarters, and felt another hunger pang. Her stomach growled, but over the rumble she heard the sound of footsteps crunching against the snowy gravel below. "Listen." The kids were talking in the night. She strained to hear but could not distinguish Rosie's voice from the others'. A car door opened, and then another, probably belonging to the van that would take them to the hogan and the longhouse for their first night inside. Life would be easier there. The fire in the hogan was always lit, and they could prepare all kinds of hot food. There was candlelight to read by. They'd make their own drums the first days there, then do drum circles daily, practice community living, continue with therapy. Still, not senior year in Landsdale. The doors slammed one by one, and the engine started up, but Elizabeth and James did not see the lights of the van up here, only the dim reading lamp by the bedside and the thin quartered light of the moon through the ox-eye window, and they listened to the van pull away in the night.

ACKNOWLEDGMENTS

Jake Morrissey is a great editor. Plus, we have so much fun. I have found a wonderful home at Riverhead Books—thank you, Geoff Kloske, Susan Petersen Kennedy, Mih-Ho Cha, Craig Burke, and Sarah Bowlin. Anna Jardine is such a tough and profound copy editor: thank God no civilians get to see my material until she has had a chance to help me get it right.

Sarah Chalfant and Edward Orloff of the Wylie Agency are just great. I love you, Sarah.

Tom Weston, I can't believe I get to be so close to someone with such a brilliant, beautiful, and deeply disturbed mind. I'd be lost without you.

Many people contributed so much to this book, and I can't ever thank them enough: Sam Lamott, Amy Tobias, Veronica Erick, Rachel Sullivan, Brooke, Nicole Guerrera, Steven Barclay, Karen Carlson and her marvelous children James and Eliza, Ellen Blakely, Mary Carabell, the profound Alldredge community, and my beloved uncle, Millard Morgen.

ANNE LAMOTT is the author of the *New York Times* bestsellers *Grace (Eventually)*, *Plan B*, *Traveling Mercies*, and *Operating Instructions*, as well as several novels, including *Rosie* and *Crooked Little Heart*. A past recipient of a Guggenheim Fellowship, she lives in northern California.